# DEFENDING SAME-SEX MARRIAGE

# DEFENDING SAME-SEX MARRIAGE

## Volume 3

## THE FREEDOM-TO-MARRY MOVEMENT

### Education, Advocacy, Culture, and the Media

*Edited by Martin Dupuis and William A. Thompson*

*Mark Strasser, General Editor*
Praeger Perspectives

Westport, Connecticut
London

**Library of Congress Cataloging-in-Publication Data**

Defending same-sex marriage / edited by Mark Strasser, et al.
   p. cm.
   Includes bibliographical references and index.
   ISBN 0-275-98772-8 (set : alk. paper)—ISBN 0-275-98773-6 (v. 1 : alk. paper)—ISBN 0-275-98808-2 (v. 2 : alk. paper)—ISBN 0-275-98894-5 (v. 3 : alk. paper) 1. Same-sex marriage—United States. 2. Same-sex marraige—Law and legislation—United States. 3. Gay rights—United States. I. Strasser, Mark Philip, 1955– II. West, Traci C., 1959– III. Dupuis, Martin, 1961– IV. Thompson, William A.
   HQ1034.U5D44 2007
   306.84'80973—dc22      2006031058

British Library Cataloguing in Publication Data is available.

Library of Congress Catalog Card Number: 2006031058
ISBN:    0-275-98772-8 (set)
         0-275-98773-6 (vol. 1)
         0-275-98808-2 (vol. 2)
         0-275-98894-5 (vol. 3)

First published in 2007

Praeger Publishers, 88 Post Road West, Westport, CT 06881
An imprint of Greenwood Publishing Group, Inc.
www.praeger.com

Printed in the United States of America

The paper used in this book complies with the
Permanent Paper Standard issued by the National
Information Standards Organization (Z39.48-1984).

10 9 8 7 6 5 4 3 2 1

To
Tom and Ginny Helm
Friends and Mentors

# CONTENTS

———————— • ————————

# GENERAL EDITOR'S FOREWORD

Lesbian, gay, bisexual, transgender, and intersexual (LGBTI) people, like their heterosexual counterparts, form families; they have children to raise and elderly parents to take care of. LGBTI people wish to marry for many of the same symbolic and practical reasons that most people do. These include love, religious beliefs, security, the ability to make important decisions about education and medical care for family members, and a variety of financial benefits. The latter range from insurance or employment benefits to tax benefits to the ability to make sure that one's estate will go to one's loved ones.

The state benefits when LGBTI individuals marry in the same ways that it does when their heterosexual counterparts marry: the individuals themselves are happier and more productive, children are given an environment in which they can flourish, and the individuals themselves provide services for each other that the state might otherwise have to provide. For example, when an individual is legally recognized as belonging to and being a part of a family, he or she may then have the financial and emotional security to invest time, energy, and effort in taking care of a spouse, a child, or a parent who might otherwise have relied on the state for such services. Further, the state benefits when marriage is viewed as a desirable institution worthy of respect rather than as a political football or as a tool by which undeserved burdens can be imposed on disfavored groups.

Notwithstanding the benefits that would accrue to the individuals themselves and to the state and society as a whole were marriage laws more inclusive, many oppose same-sex unions generally and same-sex marriages in particular. Sometimes such unions are opposed for religious reasons, although there are many misconceptions about the relationship between same-sex unions and religious dictates. For example, some mistakenly believe that no religion permits same-sex marriages to be celebrated, while others mistakenly believe that were the state to recognize same-sex marriages, religious institutions would be forced to perform religious ceremonies for same-sex couples even if such unions were not permitted by that particular denomination.

Other individuals oppose same-sex unions for nonreligious reasons. For instance, they have a mistaken belief about what LGBTI individuals are like, or, perhaps, they worry about what would happen to the institution of marriage were same-sex unions recognized. Still others oppose such unions out of animus toward those with a same-sex orientation. That such marriages are opposed by a substantial portion of the population is made clear by the number of states that have passed constitutional amendments precluding the recognition of same-sex marriages; even more states are expected to do so in the future.

Each volume in this three-volume set addresses the recognition of same-sex unions from a different perspective. The first volume examines some of the legal issues associated with the recognition and nonrecognition of same-sex unions. Examples include the following:

- Whether or not such unions must be recognized in a state where they have been prohibited if they have been validly celebrated elsewhere
- The degree to which federal law has afforded states more flexibility than they might otherwise have had under the United States Constitution
- The similarities and differences between same-sex unions on the one hand and civil unions and domestic partnerships on the other
- The kinds of benefits that are sometimes offered by private employers
- The political effects (and noneffects) of the same-sex marriage debate
- The devastating effects on children that result from a refusal to afford legal recognition to families headed by two individuals of the same sex

The second volume contains chapters that explain why and how same-sex marriage can be understood to be compatible with a variety of religious traditions, including Judaism, Islam, Buddhism, Hinduism, Catholicism, and several Protestant sects. The authors wrote as adherents within their respective faith traditions and were thus better able to address the arguments of opponents of same-sex marriage from the same faith.

The third volume discusses three different areas related to same-sex marriage: advocacy and activism, education and the media, and cultural perspectives. The advocacy and activism chapters were written by individuals who seek to inform the public about these issues through open meetings, public demonstrations, or postings and discussions on the Internet. The chapters on education and the media chapters discuss the ways that same-sex marriage is analyzed by its opponents in college textbooks in particular or in the media more generally. Chapters addressing cultural perspectives convey how same-sex marriage bans affect or are viewed by various minorities. For instance, one chapter addresses same-sex marriage and Native

American traditions, while other chapters reveal attitudes within the African American and Hispanic communities toward same-sex marriage. These latter chapters help clear up misconceptions about who wishes to marry a same-sex partner, explaining that there is a much higher percentage of African American and Hispanic same-sex couples than might be thought and that those families are especially adversely affected by current marriage policies.

The kind of recognition that should be afforded to same-sex couples and their families is likely to be hotly debated for a long time to come, whether the focus of discussion involves recognition by the state, society, or a particular religion. The chapters in this three-volume set provide practical advice to those seeking to convince family, friends, and neighbors about the wisdom of affording recognition to such unions. They also help clarify and correct some of the misconceptions regarding individuals who want to marry a same-sex partner (e.g., what those people are like) and what legal, religious, and social ramifications would occur were such unions recognized and do occur precisely because of the refusal to recognize such unions.

Public attitudes toward recognizing the families of LGBTI individuals are changing, albeit slowly and gradually. There is a growing understanding and acceptance that LGBTI individuals deserve to have their families afforded recognition, not to be subjected to invidious discrimination. The chapters in these volumes are designed to help increase that understanding so that, one day, LGBTI individuals and their families will be able to focus on the kinds of challenges that all families must face. When that happens, the individuals themselves, the state, and society as a whole will be better off.

Mark Strasser

# ACKNOWLEDGMENTS

———————————— • ————————————

The editors wish to acknowledge all the people who are working for equal marriage rights at home and abroad. We contacted literally hundreds of groups and individuals to assemble this volume. While not every perspective could be included, we were overwhelmed by the dedication and commitment to this cause. We appreciate the support of friends and family as we undertook this project. Finally, we are most grateful for the professionals at Praeger Publishers for all their assistance.

# INTRODUCTION

———————————— • ————————————

*Martin Dupuis and William A. Thompson*

———————————

The institution of marriage encompasses over a thousand responsibilities and bene-fits. A great deal of the work to secure these rights has taken place in courthouses and state legislatures across the country. Religious institutions and people of every faith have been called on to consider when spiritual blessings should be given to families. Others advocate separating the religious and civil recognition of families and promoting civil unions for same-sex relationships. Complementing this politi-cal activity and religious discussion have been grassroots organizing, educational outreach, and efforts to speak to the cultural perceptions of same-sex families. This volume complements the multifaceted debates around same-sex marriage by addressing the issues of education, advocacy, culture, and media.

In less than two short decades, the question of same-sex marriage moved from the far (and farfetched) margins of political and social activity into the 2006 State of the Union address, in which President George W. Bush spoke of "activist courts that try to redefine marriage." Evan Wolfson, the executive director of Freedom to Marry, observes that the nation is in a "patchwork" period in which some states rec-ognize gay and lesbian families and some states resist such recognition. Even where there is opposition, people are forced to reevaluate their beliefs. Evan Wolfson explains the rapid ascension of this struggle for same-sex marriage rights, "Nothing is more transformative, nothing moves the middle more, than making it real, mak-ing it personal." He suggests in his chapter that same-sex marriage as an abstract concept seems impossible and frightening to many persons, but that the marriage of the lesbian couple across the street seems eminently reasonable—especially when it is announced in the *New York Times* or *Chicago Tribune*. The lesbian couple across the street are the sort of people one invites to dinner and not the sort of people to whom one denies a basic legal right. When the gay couple moves down the hall, they become neighbors. When they look after a neighbor's dog when they are away, send care packages to a neighbor's son or daughter in Iraq, and organize the local Festival of Trees, they are claiming responsibility for the community. If people take responsibility, if they do the work, they get the privileges. This is an American compact, one as old as Jamestown.

Achieving this recognition was not an overnight process. Randolph Baxter's chapter on the contested meaning of slave marriage and the transition from slave marriages to legitimate marriages provides a startling and clarifying point of comparison to the struggle to legitimize gay marriages. He reminds us that the control of marriage—and through marriage the control of families—is one of the most powerful means of oppressing people. It was a matter of debate then as to whether slaves were civilized enough to *really* marry or whether promiscuity was their natural state. Many marriages between slaves were seen as nothing but a parody of civilized marriages and therefore degrading to real marriages. Nonetheless slaves were determined to marry and did so by improvising their own rituals. Yet slave marriages were private affairs not legally recognized by the state and wholly subject to a master's whims. In a similar way for same-sex couples, legally recognized family members can deny gay or lesbian spouses custody of their children, visitation rights in hospitals, and even revoke a partner's inheritance. Yet Baxter's look at the past points the way to the future. African Americans achieved their civil rights through a determined, vigilant, and very public civil rights struggle, and gays and lesbians are doing the same.

Mark Vezzola's chapter examines another past, that of Native Americans, which points toward a tolerant and sophisticated future for marriage. Vezzola highlights evidence that many Native American cultures recognized the biological fact of two sexes but also recognized a multiplicity of genders—in some cultures as many as five. People could legitimately accept a variety of gender roles, and marriage occurred between persons of different genders, not necessarily between persons of different sexes. While male/female pairings were the usual practice, it was not uncommon for a male to take another male as a second wife. Nor was it unknown for females to become warriors and take wives. Vezzola reminds us that our way of marriage is not the only way or even the best among many ways. Rather, there are many kinds of successful life partnerships and many sorts of love, not all of which fit into such strict categories as gay and straight, male and female.

Intriguingly, Laura Pople remarks in her chapter that in its first iteration New Jersey's domestic partnership law picked up this thread by defining domestic partnership not as a romantic institution but as a committed relationship between two adults; that is, a domestic partnership might define a relationship between two roommates or siblings who are financially dependent on each other, or an aged aunt and her caregiver. She documents the grassroots efforts to achieve recognition of domestic partnerships while simultaneously educating the public and pursuing litigation for full marriage rights. Pople chronicles her growth from citizen to activist as she recounts her experiences from the front lines.

The recognition of same-sex relationships required the existence of a viable gay and lesbian subculture: a reef of bars, bathhouses, discothèques, and urban gay ghettoes that stretched across the country and supported music festivals, gay pride parades, circuit parties, and cultural productions of every sort, including magazines, plays, newspapers, pornography, music, publishing houses, and record labels. Many in the larger community found the gay and lesbian subculture offensive and even frightening. Yet this subculture allowed for the creation of social spaces in which people not only learned they were not alone but also that they were joined together with many others. Gays and lesbians began to act politically and began to raise money for candidates, to vote, and to successfully challenge and change laws.

Susan Murray and Beth Robinson's contribution tells the story of the gay and lesbian community in Vermont's grassroots campaign around what was then thought to be an exotic issue—gay marriage. Murray and Robinson detail the process by which political naïfs became canny and successful activists. Key to this process was relying on the power of the stories of individual couples relating what it means to live out their love for one another outside the law—exactly the kind of activism that Evan Wolfson describes. Under Murray and Robinson's legal and political leadership, Vermont became the first state to recognize same-sex couples through civil unions. Laura Pople's chapter relates a story similar to Murray and Robinson's, albeit in a very different setting, New Jersey. Murray, Robinson, and Pople reveal how numerous groups were mobilized and the differing strategies that gay and lesbian activists simultaneously pursued in the courthouse, the statehouse, and in communities. They also describe the sometimes difficult compromises that had to be made to get laws favorable to gay and lesbian couples passed. They emphasize the importance of gay and lesbian people telling their stories in public and *to* the public.

The notion of who or what constitutes "the public"—that is to say "publicity" in all its senses—is one of the recurrent themes of this volume. *Publicity* originally meant "the state of being public or commonly known or observed." Marriage is a public statement *par excellence* about a couple's commitment to each other and to their relationship with the public. Legal marriage is the reclassifying of gay love from something prohibited and therefore necessarily private and even secret, to something allowed and therefore necessarily public and even promoted. In a real sense, gay marriage is the end point of the coming-out process for the gay and lesbian community as a community; the point at which gays and lesbians move from the shadowed margins of society into its public center; the point at which gays and lesbians are reclassified as citizens and declassified as deviants and criminals. It is no surprise then that coming out, the public affirmation of one's sexuality, is featured as an important part of couples' experience in Murray and Robinson's chapter as well as in Pople's.

Evan Wolfson's call to make gay relationships and gay marriage "real" and "personal" is a call to reframe these experiences in gay people's own terms. In sociological terms, a frame is the method that controls the way stories are told, images are edited, and behaviors interpreted. A frame is like a lens through which people see and interpret the world. When gay people come out, they reframe their homosexual experience from something private, secret, and shameful to something public, common, and acceptable—and they challenge others to do likewise. To the degree that other people agree to use this new frame, they too see homosexuality as acceptable and part of the ordinary course of things. Gay people are not, however, the only ones engaged in framing—and reframing—stories about gay life.

Seth Goldman and Paul Brewer's chapter makes the case that the ways in which the broadcast media frame the question of gay marriage powerfully shape how viewers respond *to* gay marriage. They point out that gay activists typically frame marriage rights in terms of equality: "Gays simply want the same rights as anyone else." Surveys have shown that a majority of people are receptive to this approach. If the question is framed in moral terms, however, as in the statement, "Heterosexual marriage is the best one for raising children," the majority of people are unreceptive to gay marriage. Goldman and Brewer discuss the subtle ways that antigay messages are conceived. For example, the preceding message about heterosexual marriage does not mention gays at all, although it implicitly devalues gay marriage. Goldman and Brewer discuss ways that gay activists can frame the debate in moral terms for their own benefit.

Renée Rotkopf and Anthony Brown describe another contest in the battle for the public's attention and understanding. Rotkopf and Brown, both media professionals, decided to use the media to publicize the fact of gay and lesbian love and introduce the question of same-sex marriage into American homes. To do this Rotkopf and Brown organized a series of mass gay weddings as part of an ongoing project they call The Wedding Party. These events use the media's love of celebrities—Susan Sarandon and Mary Louise Parker have attended the events—and spectacle to provide a counterbalancing frame to the distorted images of gay life distributed by the right-wing media. Images meant to induce fear and loathing are replaced with images of joy and love.

While television remains the most powerful means of engaging the public around the world, the Internet has profoundly altered the shape and size of the public square in ways that television cannot. Despite its global reach, television remains a localized phenomenon. What people see is controlled by the networks, the cable companies, or the satellite providers. Moreover, television transmission is just a one-way street. Television viewers cannot talk back to the producers, directors, writers, and stars—let alone talk with one another through the television. The Internet has changed all that. People can interactively share information with one another and can do so in a variety of ways, including making home videos. The bar for wide transmission of information is far lower now, making it much easier for like-minded others to meet and share information—and disinformation. The Internet came of age in the early 1990s, the same time that the same-sex marriage debate was heating up. It is no surprise then that gay marriage has been a topic of recurring interest on the Internet.

Michael Stevenson and Markie Oliver examine and explode the rhetorical strategies that conservative groups use on the Web to shape their constituencies' response to same-sex marriage. Robin Tyler and Andy Thayer take on not only conservative critiques of same-sex marriage, but also fervently chastise Democratic politicians and leaders of the LGBT social movements for not fully embracing the marriage rights movement. Eric Rofes, a longtime gay activist, recounts the complex and iterative process through which PerfectUnion.net, a Web site for activists organizing around same-sex marriage, was developed. One of the interesting ironies of Rofes's chapter is the way in which the development of a site meant to deliver information to distant others strengthened relationships among a group of local activists as they came together to work on the site.

One of the most powerful ways people obtain information about events and make up their minds about them is the educational system. Charles Gosset and Elizabeth

Bergman's contribution examines the ways in which same-sex marriage is presented in college-level textbooks about American government. Interestingly, most of these textbooks frame gay marriage as a civil rights issue, which Goldman and Brewer suggest may be less effective in changing people's views of the issue.

Finally, insights into how same-sex marriage issues affect the African American and Hispanic communities are examined. Samiya Bashir, H. Alexander Robinson, and Lisa Powell present their own perspectives on the similarities of equal rights struggles, the use of the church to preach both love and hate, and the impact of marriage discrimination, especially on black lesbians. Jason Cianciotto continues this type of inquiry and provides a detailed study of data from the 2000 Census as it relates to Latino and Latina same-sex households. He uses in-depth statistical analysis to demonstrate the many ways in which Hispanic gay and lesbian families experience disadvantages from not being able to marry legally.

# Part I

## ADVOCACY AND ACTIVISM

# 1

## MARRIAGE EQUALITY AND SOME LESSONS FOR THE SCARY WORK OF WINNING

*Evan Wolfson*

AMERICA IN A CIVIL RIGHTS MOMENT

One of the good things about my job is that I have plenty of time for reading on planes and trains. Right now I am reading the Library of America's anthology *Reporting Civil Rights*. They have collected the journalism of the 1940s, 1950s, 1960s, and 1970s in two volumes, describing the blow-by-blow, day-to-day experience of what the struggles of those years felt and looked like before those living through that moment knew how it was going to turn out. It's exhilarating, empowering, appalling, and scary. That's what a civil rights moment feels like when you are living through it—when the outcome is uncertain and not yet wrapped in mythology or triumphant inevitablism.

Recently our nation celebrated the fiftieth anniversary of *Brown v. Board of Education*. While the *Brown* decision was sincerely embraced by supporters, it was disingenuously acknowledged by opponents. In the words of the time, legislators in a swath of states declared "massive resistance." There were billboards saying "Impeach Earl Warren," the former Chief Justice who wrote the decision, and there were members of Congress signing resolutions denouncing "activist judges" (sound familiar?). And, of course, there were the marches, Freedom Rides, organizing summers, engagement, hard work, violence, later legislation, transformations. Pretty much everything that we in the early 2000s think of as the civil rights movement all took place after *Brown*.

America is again in a civil rights moment, as same-sex couples, their loved ones, and nongay allies struggle to end discrimination in marriage. A robust debate and numberless conversations are helping our nation, in Lincoln's words, "think anew" about how people are treating a group of families and fellow citizens among us. Today it is gay people, same-sex couples, LGBT individuals and their loved ones, and nongay allies who are contesting second-class citizenship, fighting for loved ones and the country, seeking inclusion and equality. It is scary as well as thrilling to see the changes and feel the movement. How can gay people get through this moment of peril and secure the promise of equality?

There are lessons everyone can learn from those who went before, for gay people are not the first to have to fight for equality and inclusion. In fact, they are not the first to have to challenge discrimination even in marriage.

## MARRIAGE AS A HUMAN RIGHTS BATTLEFIELD

Marriage has always been a human rights battleground on which the nation has grappled with larger questions about what kind of country it is going to be: questions about the proper boundary between the individual and the government; questions about the equality of men and women; questions about the separation of church and state; questions about who gets to make important personal choices of life, liberty, and the pursuit of happiness. As a nation, we have made changes in the institution of marriage and fought over these questions of whether America is committed to both equality and freedom in at least four major struggles in the past few decades. The people of the United States ended the rules whereby the government, not couples, decided whether they should remain together when their marriages had failed or become abusive. Divorce transformed the so-called traditional definition of marriage from a union based on compulsion to what most of us think of as marriage today—a union based on love, commitment, and the choice to be together and care for each other. The people of the United States ended race restrictions on who could marry whom based on the traditional definition of marriage, defended as part of God's plan, seemingly an intractable part of the social order. The people ended the interference of the government in such important personal decisions as whether to procreate, whether to have sex without risking pregnancy, or whether to use contraceptives even within marriage. And the people ended the legal subordination of women in marriage, thereby transforming the institution of marriage from a union based on domination and dynastic arrangement to what most of us think of it as today, a committed partnership of equals. Yes, our nation has struggled with important questions on the human rights battlefield of marriage, and we are met on that battlefield once again.

## PATCHWORK

As in any period of civil rights struggle, transformation will not come overnight. Rather, the classic American pattern of civil rights history is that our nation goes through a period of what I call in my book, *Why Marriage Matters*, "patchwork." During such patchwork periods, some states move toward equality faster while others resist and even regress, stampeded by pressure groups and pandering politicians into adding additional layers of discrimination before eventual buyer's remorse sets in and a national resolution is reached. So here we are in this civil rights patchwork. On the one hand, as the recent powerful and articulate rulings by courts in the states of Washington and New York demonstrated, several states are advancing toward marriage equality, soon to join Massachusetts in ending discrimination and showing nongay Americans the reality of families helped and no one hurt. Meanwhile, on the other hand, as many as a dozen states, targeted by opponents of equality as part of their own ideological campaign and for their political purposes, may enact further discriminatory measures in 2006, compounding the second-class citizenship gay Americans already endure. These opponents—anti–marriage equality, yes, but also antigay, anti–women's equality, anti–civil rights, antichoice, and anti–separation of church and state—are throwing everything they have into this attack because they know that if fair-minded people have a chance to hear the stories of real families and think them through, they would move toward fairness, as young people already have in their overwhelming support for marriage equality. Most importantly, as Americans see the faces and hear the voices of couples in San Francisco and they witness the families that have been helped, hearts and minds are opening. People, gay and nongay, are engaging in conversations in every state discussing gay families. When they see that no one has been hurt in Massachusetts and they digest the reassuring way in which marriage equality is already finding acceptance there after just a few months, people are getting ready to accept, if not necessarily fully support, an end to discrimination in marriage.

## THE UNION: A HOUSE DIVIDED

In past chapters of civil rights history that unfolded on the battlefield of marriage, this conversation and patchwork of legal and political struggles would have proceeded in the first instance, and over quite some time in the states, without federal interference or immediate national resolution. That is because historically, domestic relations, including legal marriage, have been understood as principally (and almost entirely) the domain of the states under the American system of federalism.[1] The states worked out their disagreements over who could marry whom under the general legal principles of comity, reflecting the value of national unity. The common-sense reality that it makes more sense to honor marriages than to destabilize them was embodied in the relevant specific legal principle generally followed in all states—that a marriage considered valid where it is celebrated will be respected elsewhere, even in places that would not themselves have allowed that marriage to be performed. The states arrived at this logical result not primarily through legal compulsion but through common sense and by addressing the needs of the families and institutions (banks, businesses, employers, schools, and others) before them. Eventually a national resolution was reached, grounded again in common sense, actual lived experience, and the nation's commitment to equality, constitutional guarantees, and expanding the circle of those included in the American dream.

But when it comes to such constitutional principles as equal protection—and, it now appears, even such basic American safeguards as checks and balances, the courts, and federalism—antigay forces believe there should be a gay exception to the constitutions, to fairness, and to respect for families. Inserting the federal government into marriage for the first time in United States history, our opponents federalized the question of marriage, prompting the passage of the so-called Defense of Marriage Act (DOMA) in 1996. This federal antimarriage law creates an un-American caste system of first- and second-class marriages. If the federal government likes someone's spouse, the partners get a vast array of legal and economic protections and recognition, ranging from Social Security, access to health care, veterans' benefits, immigration rights to taxation, inheritance rights, and a myriad of other benefits. In a 2004 report the General Accounting Office (GAO) identified 1,138 ways in which marriage implicates federal law.[2] Under the so-called DOMA, if the federal government doesn't like a person's spouse, the usually automatic federal recognition and protections are withdrawn in all circumstances, no matter what the need. The federal antimarriage law also purported to authorize states not to honor lawful marriages from other states (provided those marriages were of same-sex couples)—in defiance of more than two hundred years of history in which the states had largely worked out discrepancies in marriage laws among themselves, under the principles of comity and common sense as well as the constitutional commitment to full faith and credit.

When this radical law was first proposed, some gay people spoke up immediately, saying that it was unconstitutional—a violation of equal protection, the fundamental right to marry, such federalist guarantees as the Full Faith and Credit Clause, and limits on congressional power. Ignoring these objections, the opponents of gay rights pressed forward with their election-year attack. Now they concede the unconstitutionality of the law they stampeded through just eight years ago and are seeking an even more radical means of assuring gay people's second-class citizenship—this time through an assault on the United States Constitution itself, as well as on the constitutions of the states.[3] Because they do not trust the next generation, because they know they have no good arguments, no good reason for the harsh exclusion of same-sex couples from marriage, these opponents are desperate to tie the hands of all future generations and as many states as possible now. This patchwork period will be difficult, painful, even ugly, and gay people will take hits. Indeed, they stand to take several hits in the states where their opponents have thrown antigay measures at them in their effort to deprive fellow citizens of the information, the stories of gay couples to dispel stereotypes and refute right-wing lies, and the lived experience of the reality of marriage equality. While it is especially outrageous that the opponents of equality are using constitutions as the vehicles for this wave of attacks on American families, in the longer run their discrimination will not stand.

Here are a few basic lessons gay people and their allies can cling to in the difficult moments ahead, to help them keep their eyes on the prize—the freedom to marry and full equality nationwide, a prize that shimmers within reach. Lesson number one: Wins trump losses. While gay people stand to lose several battles this year, they must remember that wins trump losses. Wins trump losses because each state that ends marriage discrimination gives fair-minded Americans opportunities to see and absorb the reality of families helped and no one hurt when the exclusion of same-sex couples from marriage ends. Nothing is more transformative, nothing moves the middle more, than making it real, making it personal. Seeing other states join Canada and Massachusetts will be the engine of victory.

Lesson number two: Losing forward. Even when gay people cannot win a given battle, they can still engage and fight so as to at least lose forward, putting them in a better place for the inevitable next battle. Now let me say a little more about this idea of losing forward. After all, as someone most famous for the cases I lost, I have built an entire career on it. Losing forward is a way that everyone can be part of this national campaign, no matter what state. Even the more challenged states, the states with the greater uphill climb, the states where gay people are most outgunned and under attack, even those in the so-called red states still have a pivotal part in this national movement and can make a vital contribution. In every state—even those where gay people cannot win the present battle, but fight so as to lose forward—they have the opportunity to enlist more support, build more coalitions, and make it possible for more candidates and nongay opinion leaders to move toward fairness. All this contributes to the creation of a national climate of receptivity in which some states may cross the finish line before others, but everyone can be better positioned to catch the wave that will come back to every state in this national campaign. Work on the ground in Georgia, for example, can get a Bob Barr speaking out against the constitutional amendment, or make districts safe for African American leaders or "surprising" voices to speak out in support of marriage equality. Work in Michigan—while perhaps not enough to win this round— can still help enlist prominent labor or corporate leaders to the cause. Working together, this national chorus will indeed swell, with some states further along and all participating until all are free. As long as gay people and their supporters repel a federal constitutional amendment and continue to see some states move toward equality, beating back as many attacks as possible and enlisting more diverse voices in this conversation, they will win.

Lesson number three: Tell the truth about our families. Now the principal reason gay people are going to take hits this year and lose many, if not all, of the state attacks in November is because our opponents are cherry-picking their best targets and depriving the reachable middle of the chance to be reached. They have a head start, more money, and more infrastructure through their megachurches and right-wing partners. Fear-mongering at a time of anxiety is easy to do. Of course, historically it is difficult to win civil rights votes in the early stages of a struggle. But to be honest, there is another reason, too, that gay people will not do well in most of these votes this year. Quite simply, their engagement, their campaigns in almost all of these states, came too little, too late. Gay leaders are starting too late to have enough time to sway people to fairness, and giving them too little to think about. They have to avoid that error in the next wave of political battles. This means that from California to Minnesota, from Wisconsin to Maine, they should start not too late but now, and by saying the word truly on people's minds, do it "right."

Put another way, the country right now is divided roughly into thirds. One-third supports equality for gay people, including the freedom to marry. Another third is not just adamantly against marriage for same-sex couples, but indeed opposes gay people and homosexuality, period. This group is against any measure of protection or recognition for lesbians and gay men, whether it be marriage or anything else. And then there is the middle third—the reachable-but-not-yet-reached middle. These Americans are genuinely wrestling with this civil rights question and have divided impulses and feelings to sort through. How they frame the question for themselves brings them to different outcomes. Their thinking is evolving as they grapple with the need for change to end discrimination in America.

## WHAT MOVES THE MIDDLE?

To appeal to the better angels of their nature, we owe it to these friends, neighbors, and fellow citizens to help them understand the question of marriage equality through two truths. The first truth is that ending marriage discrimination is first and foremost about couples in love who have made a personal commitment to each other, who are doing the hard work of marriage in their lives, caring for one another and their children, if any. Think of couples like Del Martin and Phyllis Lyon, who have been together more than fifty years. Now these people, having in truth made a personal commitment to each other, want and deserve a legal commitment.

Once the discussion has a human story, face, and voice, fair-minded people are ready to see through a second frame. The second truth is that the exclusion of same-sex couples from marriage is discrimination. It is wrong and it is unfair to deny these couples (and families) marriage and its important tangible and intangible protections and responsibilities. America has had to make changes before to end discrimination and unfair treatment, and the government should not be denying any American equality under the law.

When gay people see lopsided margins in these votes, it means that under the gun in the first wave of electoral attacks, they have not as yet reached this middle. They cannot be surprised not to win when in so many campaigns, and over so many opportunities to date (electoral campaigns and just month-to-month conversations), they have failed to give this middle third what is needed to come out right. When, in the name of practicality or advice from pollsters or political operatives, gay leaders fail to put forward compelling stories and explain the realities of what marriage equality does and does not mean, it costs them the one chance they have to do the heavy lifting that moves people. Not only are gay people and their allies not winning, they wind up not even losing forward.

By contrast, consider how gay people lost forward in California. In 2000 they took a hit when the right wing pushed the so-called Knight Initiative and forced an early vote on marriage. Gay marriage advocates lost the vote, but because there had been some, though not enough, education about gay families as well as the wrongfulness and costs of discrimination, polls showed that support for marriage equality actually rose after the election. And the very next year, activists pressed the legislature to enact a partnership law far broader than had been on the table in California before then. The advocates' engagement over marriage continued, and within a few years, legislators voted again, this time in support of an "all but marriage" bill, which took effect in 2005. And California organizations and the national legal groups continue to struggle for what gay people fully deserve—pursuing litigation in the California courts and legislation that would end marriage discrimination. If the work is done right, making room for luck, gay people may see marriage in California, our largest state, as soon as 2006. To go from a defeat in 2000 to partnership and all-but-marriage in 2004 with the possibility of marriage itself in 2005—that is called winning.

Lesson number four: Generational momentum. Remember, we have a secret weapon: death. Or to put it more positively, those on the side of justice have generational momentum. Younger people overwhelmingly support ending this discrimination. Americans are seeing more and more families like Dick Cheney's and realizing with increasing comfort that gay people are part of the American family. The power of the marriage debate moves the center toward gay marriage advocates, and as young people come into ascendancy, even the voting will change. This is the opponents' last-ditch chance to pile up as many barricades as possible, but again, as long as gay people and their supporters build that critical mass for equality and move the middle, they will win.


## THE STAKES

Why is it so important that advocates for gay marriage should redouble their outreach, voices, and conversations in the vocabulary of marriage equality? In part because victory is within reach. In part because they can and must move that middle now to make room for that generational momentum and rise to fairness. In part because America is listening and allies are increasing. In part because this is their moment of greatest peril. And in part because the stakes are so great. What is at stake in this civil rights and human rights moment? If this struggle for same-sex couples' freedom to marry were "just" about gay people, it would be important, for gay men and lesbians, like bisexuals, transgendered people, and our nongay brothers and sisters, are human beings who share the aspirations for love, companionship, participation, equality, mutual caring and responsibility, protections for loved ones, and choice. Yes, if this struggle were "just" about gay people, it would be important, but it is not "just" about gay people.

If this struggle were "just" about marriage, it would be important, for marriage is the gateway to a vast and otherwise largely inaccessible array of tangible and intangible protections and responsibilities, the vocabulary in which nongay people talk about love, clarity, security, respect, family, intimacy, dedication, self-sacrifice, and equality. And the debate over marriage is the engine of other advances and the inescapable context in which Americans will be addressing all LGBT needs, the inescapable context in which gay people will be claiming their birthright of equality and enlarging possibilities for themselves and others. Yes, if this struggle were "just" about marriage, it would be important, but it is not "just" about marriage.

What is at stake in this struggle is what kind of country we are going to be. Is America indeed to be a nation in which all people, minorities as well as majorities, popular as well as unpopular, get to make important choices in their lives or a land of liberty and justice only for some? Is America indeed to be a nation that respects the separation of church and state, in which the government does not take sides on religious differences but rather respects religious freedom while assuring equality under the law, or is it to be a land governed by one religious ideology imposed on all? Is America to be a nation in which two women who build a life together—maybe raise kids or tend to elderly parents, pay taxes, contribute to the community, care for one another, and even fight over who takes out the garbage—are free and equal, or is it a land in which they can be told by their government that they are somehow lesser or incomplete or not whole because they do not have a man in their lives? All of us, gay and nongay, who share the vision of America as a nation that believes that all people have the right to be both different and equal, and that without real and sufficient justification, the government may not compel people to give up their difference in order to be treated equally—all of us committed to holding America to that promise have a stake in this civil rights and human rights struggle for the freedom to marry. And if every state, every methodology, every battle, every victory, and even every defeat are seen as part of a campaign, and if gay people continue to enlist nongay allies and voices in this campaign, transforming it into a truly organic movement for equality in the grand American tradition, they will move the middle, they will lose forward where necessary, they will empower the supportive, and they will win. They are winning. There is no marriage without engagement. Let gay people and their allies vote in November, get others to vote in November, and move forward in their work to win, working together, doing it right.

## NOTES

Evan Wolfson, "Marriage Equality and Some Lessons for the Scary Work of Winning," originally published in *Tulane Journal of Law and Sexuality*, 14, 135–147 (2005). Reprinted with the permission of the *Tulane Journal of Law and Sexuality*, which holds the copyright.

1. *Hisquierdo v. Hisquierdo*, 439 U.S. 572, 581 (1979) ("[i]nsofar as marriage is within temporal control, the States lay on the guiding hand"). As the Supreme Court explained in *De Sylva v. Ballentine*, 351 U.S. 570, 580 (1956): The scope of a federal right is, of course, a federal question, but that does not means its content is not to be determined by state, rather than federal law.... This is especially true when a statute deals with a familial relationship; there is no federal law of domestic relations, which is primarily a matter of state concern.

2. U.S. General Accounting Office, *Defense of Marriage Act*, Pub. No. GAO-04-353R, Washington, DC, 2004.

3. The first constitutional amendment to allow Congress to have authority over domestic relations was proposed (and rejected) in 1884. *Scherrer v. Scherrer*, 334 U.S. 343 (1948) (Frankfurter, J., dissenting). Through 1948, seventy similar amendments were proposed, prompted by a national debate analogous to the contemporary debate, over whether to allow civil divorce. All such proposals failed, and the states were properly given an opportunity to work out questions of marriage and interstate respect among themselves while the federal government honored lawful marriages and divorces. See for example Edward Stein, "Past and Present Proposed Amendments to the United States Constitution Regarding Marriage," *Issues in Legal Scholarship*, no. 5 (2004). After a period of conversation and experience, and generational shifts as the institution of marriage evolved, the United States Supreme Court clarified that lawful determinations as to marital status through divorce must be respected throughout the country, as in *Cook v. Cook*, 342 U.S. 126 (1951).

# 2

# THE GAY MARRIAGE STRUGGLE: WHAT'S AT STAKE AND HOW CAN WE WIN?

•

*Robin Tyler and Andy Thayer*

Decades before "gay marriage" made national headlines and just eleven months after the Stonewall Rebellion sparking the modern gay movement, "Jack Baker and Mike McConnell applied for a marriage license on May 18, 1970, in Minneapolis. That is the first known gay marriage license application. The clerk of the District Court for Hennepin County summarily refused to issue them a license. Subsequently, Baker and McConnell went to Blue Earth County in southwestern Minnesota and got a license on August 16, 1971, from a different clerk. They were married on September 3 using that license. The Rev. Roger Lynn, a United Methodist minister, performed the ceremony."[1]

In a debate reminiscent of those heard in other, older movements, some in the lesbian, gay, bisexual and transgendered (LGBT) movement have argued that the time isn't ripe for them to be taking on the issue of fighting for equal marriage rights for the community. A prominent historian, John D'Emilio, argued at a major plenary of the 2005 Creating Change conference that "a handful of marriage activists have hijacked the gay movement" by asserting their equal marriage rights, and thus have played into the hands of the Religious Right and set back the entire LGBT movement. To hear such "blame the victim" rhetoric from this speaker was astounding. The authors of this chapter were not the only ones in the audience with the words of Martin Luther King, Jr.'s *Why We Can't Wait* ringing in our minds. King stated, "The shape of the world will not permit us the luxury of gradualism and procrastination. Not only is it immoral, it will not work."[2] Dozens of marriage equality activists were in the audience, including some from Massachusetts, where same-sex marriage is legal; all were stunned.

The address was not only a stinging critique of the American activists but also ignored the fact that several other countries, including Spain, the Netherlands, and

Canada, have legalized marriage between same-sex couples without producing the dire results that critics said were the fault of these countries. Could a worldwide movement of activists be so wrong?

What the opponents of same-sex marriage activism ignored was that when confronted with injustice, at least a minority of people will always assert their right to be treated as equal human beings regardless of the counsel of experts and movement leaders. Jack Baker and Mike McConnell were simply doing what so many unsung heroes have done in freedom movements before and since.[3] Rosa Parks was far from the first to insist on sitting in the front of the bus. Going back to the dawn of public transportation in this country during the earliest years of the abolitionist movement, African Americans broke segregation laws by sitting where they chose in the nation's new railroad cars. And they continued to do so in each of the many decades following, even during the worst years of segregationist violence.

No experts or self-proclaimed movement strategists will keep heretofore anonymous LGBT people from asserting their equal right to marriage or anything else. Like it or not, the marriage battle is joined, and in the legendary phrase of the labor movement, the real question is, "Which side are you on?" That many still stumble over this basic question is a sad statement about the level of backwardness and in some cases self-loathing in the LGBT community.

## OPPOSITION TO MARRIAGE RIGHTS ACTIVISM
## WITHIN THE LGBT COMMUNITY

Within the LGBT movement, opposition to activism for equal marriage rights generally comes from two sources—one that styles itself as antiassimilationist and another that includes pragmatic go-slow activists, many of whom look to the Democratic Party as the main vehicle for progressive change. Both are united on at least one point: despite the now-wholesale assault by the Religious Right, now is not the time for equal marriage rights activism.

Antiassimilationists, who typically identify themselves as "queer," say that the marriage issue should be shunned because it expresses a conservative yearning to join a woefully sexist and otherwise oppressive institution. People of all sexual orientations, however, want to get married for a wide variety of reasons ranging from the spiritual to the pragmatic. Some see marriage as intertwined with their notion of romantic love, while others want to get married so as to partake of the 1,138 legal benefits that straight married couples take for granted.[4] Some antiassimilationists see marriage in traditional hierarchical terms, and as uncomfortable as that may make those of us with a feminist consciousness, it is nonetheless their choice. It is extremely condescending, not to mention hierarchical, for any group of people—progressives included—to presume to dictate how consenting adults should live their lives.

What is at issue is the question of *choice* in joining an institution in American society, not an *obligation* to join it and be "assimilated." Queer antiassimilationist activists have to decide whether they will acquiesce to the Religious Right's demand that LGBT people be legally proscribed or segregated from the institution of marriage, however loathsome they may consider that institution to be. They should take a cue from the history of other struggles to join other less-than-perfect institutions.

Central to any understanding of progressive history in the United States is the history of radical labor activism and the demands of various minority groups for equal employment rights. Yet the American workplace is a socially stratified institution, with mind-boggling disparities in compensation and power between frontline workers and upper-level managers. On top of this, the workplace festers with statistically proven racial and gender disparities that should require little comment. Yet few people who profess belief in civil rights would say that LGBT people should shun equal access to *that* demonstrably oppressive institution!

One does not need to pretend that the family is an oppression-free institution in order to understand that many working-class LGBT people seek to join it as they join the workforce, as a survival mechanism for access to health care, adoption rights, and other benefits. Indeed, the objective information indicates that equal access to marriage rights is far more vital to the material lives of working-class LGBT people of color than it is to stereotypical upper-middle-class white male couples.

Two recent National Gay and Lesbian Task Force (NGLTF) studies of African American LGBT people, "Black Same-Sex Households in the United States: A Report from the 2000 Census" (2004) and "Say It Loud: I'm Black and I'm Proud" (2002), give the lie to marriage stereotypes within the gay community. Breaking stereotypes about modern LGBT families, these studies found that African American same-sex couples living together are raising children at *far higher* rates than white same-sex couples:

> Black male same-sex couples in the United States are *almost twice as likely* to be living with a biological child as white male same-sex couples. Black female same-sex couples in the United States are *just as likely* to be living with an adopted or foster child as black married opposite-sex couples in the United States.[5]

Many of these African American same-sex couples, not unlike their straight counterparts with children, want to be able to marry so that they can provide a more secure future for their offspring.

Indeed, the 2000 survey of black LGBT people, which was published well *before* the marriage issue dominated mainstream press coverage of the LGBT community, directly contradicts the stereotype that only wealthy white gay males want marriage rights. When asked what are the most important issues facing black LGBT people, respondents to the survey listed "marriage/domestic partnership" as their number three priority.[6]

Given the enduring racism and sexism, not to mention homophobia, that disproportionately shunt such African American LGBT couples into working-class occupations, it is fair to say that the above figures on child rearing reflect not only racial realities but also class distinctions. In other words, marriage and the family are much more important to the material security of working-class people than they are to wealthier people, who are usually better able to afford attorneys to construct the intricate web of legal documents needed to imperfectly mimic the contractual features of heterosexual marriage.

Queer antiassimilationists often portray themselves as being more sensitive to the needs of people of color or poor and working-class people than marriage activists. The evidence on the marriage issue, however, shows that it is *they* who are woefully out of touch. Indeed, the NGLTF survey of African American LGBT people notes that they overwhelmingly *reject* the "queer" label itself!

When respondents were asked which one label out of a very extensive list…comes closest to how you describe your sexual orientation, 42 percent of the sample self-identified as gay, 24 percent chose the label lesbian, 11 percent checked the category bisexual, and 1 percent marked transgender…. In contrast to the high levels of agreement on the labels gay and lesbian, Black GLBT people do not readily, or even remotely, identify as "queer." "Queer" was one of the least popular options, receiving few responses (1 percent).[7]

The antiassimilationists charge that all the material benefits that marriage activists hope to obtain—such as access to a spouse's medical coverage, Social Security survivor's benefits, and naturalization of foreign same-sex spouses—would be better achieved by winning such objectives as free universal health care, large increases in Social Security pay outs, freeing all borders of immigration restraints, and the like. Many advocates for marriage equality have long favored these reforms; however, given the current economic and political context, in which most progressive struggles find themselves on the defensive (especially in regard to working people's pocketbook issues), only the most Pollyannaish believe that they are going to gain any of these objectives within the next few years.

In the meantime, many working people urgently need the benefits of marriage *right now*, to keep custody of their children, to secure health care, and to get their Social Security benefits. Many older LGBTs cannot afford the tremendous burden of being considered single when one partner dies. Most of these seniors are on fixed incomes, and many risk losing not only their life partners but also their homes. They are left standing at the casket with no rights, while straight family members who may not have spoken to their gay relative in decades, swoop in to make the funeral arrangements and divide the spoils. Who can blame these older LGBTs if they are unwilling to wait years or decades for the profound reversal in the national political climate that is implied in demands like universal health care?

To summarize, the queer antiassimilationist approach to winning urgently needed reforms recalls another observation of Dr. King's: "The conservatives who say, 'Let us not move so fast,' and the extremists who say, 'Let's go out and whip the world,' would tell you that they are as far apart as the poles. But there is a striking parallel: They accomplish nothing; for they do not reach the people who have a crying need to be free."[8]

While the antiassimilationists love to denounce religious fundamentalists for their Neanderthal rigidities, many of *them* adopt a fundamentalist creed by insisting that everyone follow them in *not* marrying. True freedom does not consist in rejecting one rigid fundamentalism just to take up another one. In contrast to the fundamentalists on the political right and left, the equal marriage movement is about making the *choice* of marriage available to all. Whether consenting adults then avail themselves of that choice is no one's business but their own.

## THE "GO SLOW" APPROACH

Some within the LGBT community want to move away from marriage activism because they allegedly cannot win on the issue. It seems to escape them that after only a few years' experience, a majority of Massachusetts voters now *favor* equal marriage rights. These gay people issue the scathing charge that fighting the marriage battle diverts resources away from such life-and-death issues as AIDS.

But how is getting increased funding for AIDS any more realistic a battle than marriage, in this era of ballooning federal budget deficits, extinction of private pensions, and the increased funding demands caused by the Iraq war and hurricane relief? And how is marriage not a life-and-death issue for many in our community who can't get health insurance from their spouse's employer; who worry about losing their children; and who wonder if their houses and other assets will be stolen from their spouses when they die?[9]

The reality is that in an era of faith-based science and social services, whatever issues LGBT activists choose to work on, they will face an uphill fight. It accomplishes nothing to pit the equal marriage fight against the AIDS struggle or any other progressive issue. Instead, thoughtful progressive activists should make it their business to show the linkages between ostensibly separate issues, showing how work on different struggles can be mutually supportive. Showing the linkages also helps demonstrate the urgent need for deeper, more radical changes in society, rather than winning just this or that isolated reform.

In recent years much of AIDS activism has largely descended into a torpor brought about by private organizations focused on AIDS research and funding. In contrast, the equal marriage struggle has enriched the LGBT community by producing a fresh crop of grassroots activists. Many of these new activists will invigorate the community as they broaden their activities to include other issues. Just under two decades ago, many older LGBT activists made the mistake of disregarding the angry and eager young crop of activists who shook up the community's myopia with their AIDS Coalition to Unleash Power (ACT UP) "zaps," disruptive, surprise protest tactics like picketing, mass emailing, heckling, and sit-ins. History has shown that these new activists were the main trailblazers of not just the AIDS movement but the overall LGBT movement of their time. It's a sad statement of how little we have learned, that some of today's older generation are repeating this same mistake of insulting today's new activists, rather than giving them encouragement and access to resources.

## THE MARRIAGE ISSUE AND THE DEMOCRATIC PARTY

> We want marriage. That's the front of the bus. The Democratic Party wants civil unions. That's the back of the bus. The Republican Party wants to give us nothing. That's off the bus. And the radical Religious Right wants us under the bus.
> —Robin Tyler, quoted in the *Washington Blade*, March 4, 2004

The opposition of some moderates to equal marriage activism has more malevolent roots. Put bluntly, they put the electoral ambitions of the Democratic Party ahead of civil rights progress for the LGBT community. They scapegoat vocal advocacy for our issues as the reason why Kerry lost the 2004 election.

Not only is the charge factually wrong, its aura of victim-blaming is morally repugnant, akin to blaming the 1960s civil rights movement for losing the Democratic Party's electoral dominance in the previously solid South. Detailed electoral and polling data show that moral values issues were *not* the pivotal factor in

Kerry's loss of key swing states.[10] LGBT people voted overwhelmingly for Kerry, but apparently, like children—or the mute LGBT delegates at the Democratic Convention in Boston—they are supposed to be seen but not heard. They are allowed to silently deliver money and votes to the Democratic Party; however, they are also scolded to keep quiet about the needs of the LGBT community. But metaphorically if not literally, on the issue of marriage equality or any other issue, silence equals death.[11] Only vocal advocacy gives the community a chance of winning.

This is not the first time that such silence has scuttled the community's civil rights progress. While feisty anti-AIDS activism forced a hostile Bush administration to concede reforms like the Ryan White AIDS Care Act, the Americans with Disabilities Act, and streamlined Food and Drug Administration (FDA) approval procedures, LGBT activists were largely silent during the Clinton years, as many accepted the administration's "leave it to us, we'll take care of you" line.[12] With no pressure coming from the left, all the pressure on the Clinton administration came from the right, which in turn galloped rightward over the ensuing eight years, dragging much of the country with it. And so an administration which began with Democratic majorities in both houses of Congress, promising a radical restructuring of health care and equal employment in the military, closed its term by refusing to enact any of its own AIDS Commission's recommendations, signing the Defense of Marriage Act, and generally rolling over for an energized Republican-dominated Congress.

As Tim Campbell amply demonstrates in his path-breaking article, "Gay Marriage—the Early Years,"[13] leading Democrats, both gay and nongay, have always avoided the marriage issue and have played prominent roles in scuttling its inclusion in standard gay rights legislation:

> Minneapolis and Saint Paul (MN) also beat the rest of the country to the idea of separating the right to marry from the rest of gay civil rights.... The antimarriage contingent included, among others, Alan Spear, a gay history professor who represented the University of Minnesota neighborhood as a State Senator.

Campbell notes that Spear and Steve Endean, who went on to work at the National Gay Task Force and later went on to found the Human Rights Campaign Fund, prevented same-sex marriage from being on the legislative agenda. Campbell explains:

> Gay marriage...was never included in Minnesota's gay rights legislation. Sadly, the Spear-Coleman-Howell laws were carefully crafted to exclude the 'crazies.' That meant drag queens and radicals like Baker and McConnell who wanted gay marriage. The laws also left the University of Minnesota exempt from all these pieces of legislation [McConnell worked at the University]....
>
> [Endean] eventually died from AIDS, but the groups he influenced have been resisting gay marriage ever since the '70s. They consider their compromise wise like Solomon. Democrats around the country have adopted the same 'pragmatic' approach.
>
> For example, Barney Frank, the openly gay Democrat from Massachusetts, who sits in the U.S. House of Representatives, is currently notorious for his criticism of the gay marriages now occurring in San Francisco.[14]

Whether the Democrats like it or not, until we win, the equal marriage issue will continue to be a prominent part of the LGBT and mainstream political landscapes. Democratic Party LGBT activists can either get on board with the majority of the community who value this right, and start loudly assailing their party leaders who fail to openly embrace and advocate full legal equality for our community, or they can continue making excuses for their party leaders, behaving like some of the Log Cabin Republicans they so love to piously denounce.

It is not as if Democratic Party LGBT activists are totally bereft of party leaders whom they could wholeheartedly embrace. The Democratic-controlled California Legislature passed a marriage equality bill that was later vetoed by the Republican Governor, Arnold Schwarzenegger.[15] And the mayor of San Francisco, Gavin Newsom, not only courageously advocated marriage equality but also put his money where his mouth is by actually implementing it, marrying thousands of same-sex couples, and thus giving a strong impetus to pro-equality street activism around the country.[16] If at least a handful of Democratic leaders had shown half as much courage as Newsom, the momentum started by the Supreme Court's *Lawrence v. Texas* decision a few years earlier might have carried through to the gay community's continuing to play offense on this and other issues rather than defense.

It may sound heretical to say this, but the LGBT community's dysfunctional attitude toward the Democratic Party represents as much of an obstacle to progress as the belligerently antigay Republican leadership. Rather than embracing heroes like Newsom, most LGBT leaders keep their distance from him, preferring to heap praise and awards on other Democratic leaders who bluntly refuse to endorse, let alone do anything about, implementing legal equality. What other civil rights movement worthy of the name would fête politicians who failed, at a minimum, to at least endorse their community's legal equality?[17] Can anyone picture the National Association for the Advancement of Colored People (NAACP) or the National Organization of Women (NOW) giving awards to politicians who *opposed* legal equality for African Americans or women? Are members of the gay community still so self-hating that they embrace such politicians, blushing at the mere thought of standing next to important people who deign to publicly associate with them?

Rather than serving as yes-men and -women to antigay party leaders, LGBT people in both parties would do better to emulate the examples of Dr. Martin Luther King, Jr. and the great antislavery activist Frederick Douglass. Whenever President Lincoln and others in the Republican Party gave him cause to do so, Douglass was scathing and very public in his criticisms of their missteps and hesitations, going so far as to repeatedly castigate the president himself amidst a *civil war*! And as we'll see a little later, Dr. King also didn't allow himself to be exploited by John F. Kennedy—a good thing, too, given that Kennedy's Attorney General, his brother Robert, had King's telephone wiretapped.

## MESSAGING FOR EQUAL MARRIAGE RIGHTS

A corollary to the "silence equals death" observation about advocacy is the gay community's need to be bluntly truthful to its audience. With the range of wealth, government forces, and megachurches arrayed against it, truth is one of a handful of advantages that it has. Gay people have the task of telling nongays what their community is and why they need and deserve the same rights that nongays take for granted.

At the 2005 Creating Change conference, some activists complained that after losing the battle to stop anti–same-sex marriage constitutional amendments, people seemed to be running away from the gay marriage issue. Some of these initiatives also precluded recognition of civil unions and domestic partnerships. Many nongay couples will be hurt by many of these amendments, and the LGBT community hopes they will join it in this battle. But everyone knew that the constitutional amendment battles were first and foremost a referendum on the gay community. There is no avoiding that. If LGBT people appear to be avoiding the gay issue, they come off as deceitful and lose. The community does itself a disservice by not trying to educate opponents to accept LGBT people. The point of winning equal rights legislation is not to have the ability to repeatedly file lawsuits just in order to secure rights, but instead to win societal acceptance of LGBT people so that such lawsuits are rarely needed.

Our opponents are operating under a tremendous factual burden, if gay people take advantage of it. For however confused many Americans are about LGBT people, harboring covert or overt bias and stereotypes, most Americans do not like to view themselves as bigots or have others view them that way. A key feature in the demise of Anita Bryant's and Laura Schlessinger's careers was the successful identification of them as bigots in the public mind, with the resultant distancing of many of their former supporters. Against the contemporary anti–equal marriage movement, it is fairly easy to make the argument that anyone who opposes equal legal rights for whole groups of people is indeed a bigot. While leaders of the antiequality movement have in recent years assiduously courted conservative African American ministers in order to give a civil rights gloss to their antiequality battle,[18] a closer look at some of the leading personnel and institutions of their movement shows their deep affinity to bigotry.

Many of the older generation like Pat Buchanan and Jerry Falwell first cut their teeth in politics by using the Bible to preach against the 1960s civil rights movement. Jerry Falwell and Pat Robertson have repeatedly made anti-Semitic remarks over the years.[19] In October 2005, Fisher DeBerry, the football coach at the Air Force Academy in Colorado Springs and one of the heroes of the Religious Right for leading the Christianizing of the Academy, put his foot firmly in his mouth with baldly racist comments about African Americans. Bob Jones University, one of the brightest stars in the constellation of Far-Right Christian institutions, just a few years ago finally dropped its prohibition against interracial dating—yet the university administration claims they are not bigots! The Religious Right provides plenty of material with which the gay community can win the public relations war for marriage equality, but only if gay people are not afraid to clearly say that this struggle is about standing up for equal rights and fighting against the bigots of our generation.


## PUTTING TOGETHER A STRATEGY FOR WINNING EQUAL MARRIAGE RIGHTS...AND MORE

The central theme of this concluding section is simple: If gay people are in need of civil rights, isn't it about time that they returned to acting like a civil rights *movement*? As the example of Jack Baker, Mike McConnell, and the history of Minnesota gay rights legislation has showed, it is ordinary LGBT people like Baker and McConnell who most often have been the *true* leaders of the movement and not the national organizations that like to portray themselves as doing such. Civil rights progress has always been a bottom-up process; that is, regular people making their own history rather than elites having pity on "the masses" and granting them reforms out of the goodness of their hearts. In this regard, the LGBT rights movement has been no different from other civil rights movements.

Against the modern-day myths created about the African American civil rights movement, a key element of its true history is the pivotal role played by an obscure preacher from Montgomery, Alabama, barely known in his own town, and how he had to battle the steadfast resistance of the leaders of the national organizations of his time in order to make progress. It was not only the heads of the NAACP and the Urban League who battled against each of Martin Luther King, Jr.'s major civil rights initiatives; King also had to fight the leadership of his own religious denomination, the National Baptist Convention.[20] Adam Clayton Powell, the Democratic Congressman from New York, was so intent on undermining King's crowning achievement, the 1963 March on Washington, that he tried to sabotage the effort by using the homosexuality of its main organizer, Bayard Rustin, in order to have him purged from the organizing effort.[21] If the history of the greatest civil rights movement this nation has ever seen demonstrates that progress is made mainly through the initiatives of grassroots activists, should we be so surprised that this history has repeated itself in the gay marriage movement?

The question then is that if the gay community must build a movement from the ground up, how should it begin? Any strategy for winning has to begin with a sober analysis of where gay people are as a community and a movement. While the community has made striking gains since the early 1970s and built an array of institutions that boggles the mind of anyone who was alive three decades ago, the movement has also developed many weak spots over the years.

While apolitical pride parades draw tens and hundreds of thousands, overtly political rallies and pickets for LGBT rights are few and far between. Over-reliance on legal and electoral strategies has left in its wake a passive community for whom activism at best means writing an occasional check to their favorite LGBT nongovernmental organization and then letting "the professionals" see the issue through. In recent years, this approach has resulted in abysmal setbacks, not just for the LGBT movement but for other progressive movements as well

On the other side, the Religious Right is moving from strength to strength. Increasingly, all three branches of the federal government are ranged against gay people, and the situation in many statehouses is not much better. In some it is worse. Not since the days of segregation has a whole community faced constitutional amendments branding them as noncitizens—nineteen passed and counting. "Abstinence only" and other faith-based boondoggles are lavished with tax dollars, while scientifically proven health programs associated with lesbian, gay, bisexual, and transgendered people get defunded, staffs are slashed, and the health of thousands needlessly threatened. A few years ago one would have thought that fantasies like Intelligent Design and other measures designed to marginalize gays and non-Christians were outlandish relics of another century, but increasingly gay people have to fight these battles all over again.

Even before the latest right-wing offensive, LGBT people were not citizens in this country. Citizens by definition have equal legal rights with others. Not just with respect to the right to marry, however, but also in employment, housing and public accommodations, adoptions, access to medical care, and anything else the Religious Right can dream up, LGBTs are not citizens. Congress, the presidency, and increasingly, the Supreme Court, are all in the hands of sworn foes of the gay community, while most of the elected opposition prefers not to be openly associated with the gay community, let alone to be taking leadership on its issues. This situation will not change until there is a public opinion groundswell of opposition to the Religious Right and in favor of LGBT rights.

A targeted lobbying visit here, a clever use of the law to stall a constitutional amendment there, might work to improve the immediate tactical situation the community faces, but it will not change the overall course of the struggle for gay rights. We need a radical reshaping of the terms of the debate. No legislative victories will be secure until there is a wholesale shift in public opinion.

Not just in the marriage struggle, but in all arenas of LGBT activism for the last several years, the community has relied far too heavily on legal or legislative approaches to win its rights. History is filled with examples in which activists attempted to win gains by relying mainly on the courts or legislative process; while they sometimes "won" the legislation or court decision they desired, in the end they had little to actually show for their victory.

In the worst-case scenario, gay rights activists have quietly passed rights bills with little advance publicity, thus allowing our opponents to accuse us of bypassing the "will of the people," giving them reasons to organize a backlash movement. Such was the history of the 1977 gay rights bill in Dade County, Florida, that gave Anita Bryant the excuse she needed to launch her infamous "Save Our Children" crusade. Her crusade was eventually stopped on the West Coast, but not before many people were hurt. For example, city after city in which Bryant campaigned reported huge spikes in antilesbian and antigay violence in her wake. In the year following the 1992 passage of Colorado's Amendment 2, which outlawed municipal LGBT rights bills, the Gay and Lesbian Community Center of Colorado reported a 129 percent increase in anti-LGBT violence over the previous year—a figure corroborated by the Denver Police Department. Amendment 2 was overturned by the Supreme Court's *Romer v. Evans* decision in 1996.

Another example of a Pyrrhic legal victory comes from the history of the civil rights movement of the 1950s and 1960s. One of the great myths taught to our nation's school students is that the Supreme Court's 1954 decision, *Brown v. Board of Education of Topeka, Kansas* desegregated the nation's schools. The truth is that very little desegregation occurred because of *Brown*. Real change did not begin to take place until the civil rights movement gained momentum in the early 1960s, and acquired such strength that it could begin to *force* the changes that the government had promised. Certainly the *Brown* decision served as a tremendous impetus to the movement; initially it gave inspiration to activists and later caused them to seethe over the federal government's broken promise of desegregation "with all deliberate speed." But it was the movement itself, not the Court, that was the main engine of desegregation.

Recent court victories like the Massachusetts Supreme Judicial Court decisions on marriage and the United States Supreme Court's *Lawrence v. Texas* decision on sodomy law have encouraged a dangerous complacency among some in the gay community. For several years, most LGBT rights bills have been passed with little advance educational work outside of our community, apparently due to fear that this activity would prompt our opponents to mobilize. This decision is a pity, as it means that relatively few nongay people know when our bills pass, thus missing an important educational opportunity and leading to a situation in which the bills themselves have negligible impacts on the actual level of anti-LGBT bias and discrimination that the community experiences.

Winning legal battles is important, but if the victories occur in a vacuum of little or no public education, they accomplish relatively little from the perspective of the average LGBT person in the street or the young person growing up in a homophobic school system. We need to change the social climate in which everyday LGBT people live. When public opinion shifts in concert with legislative advances, then that legislation takes on far greater power and also is much more impervious to reversal. Changing public opinion is the key to defending and advancing the civil rights of the gay community.

But how do we change public opinion? Certainly, letters to the editor, coming out to those around us, not remaining silent when an antigay remark is made—all of these have their place. But how do we change opinion on a *massive* scale?

## MASS MARCHES IN SOCIAL CHANGE

In 1963 the African American community faced a situation more dire than the LGBT community faces today. In a country in which most of the black community could not even vote, the idea of lobbying politicians was even more quixotic than an LGBT person thinking we could persuade Bill Frist or Tom Delay to do the right thing by gay people. But in spite of the apparent powerlessness of African Americans in the electoral arena, the strategy of Dr. King and others was about to produce a wholesale change in public opinion and in turn bring about sweeping legislative victories.

The preceding years had seen increasing numbers of African Americans and their allies marching in the streets of America's cities, and the images of dignified people standing up for their rights in person began to produce a sea change in public opinion. A liberating feeling of self-worth flooded through the African American community as thousands no longer consented to "take it" from racists. In turn, even many staunch racists were forced to grudgingly respect the courage of the marchers who bravely stood up in public to their abuse, and grudging respect is the first step toward tolerance and acceptance. Public opinion began to change.

The key to this change was the vision of thousands of African Americans taking the struggle for freedom directly into their own hands. The Internet and writing a check to one's favorite LGBT group, as important as these are, are no substitute for large-scale personal advocacy of one's own legal equality and dignity.

The LGBT struggle has itself seen instances in which this sort of personal advocacy in the streets has led to a radical reshaping of the public debate about the LGBT community. Most famously, the Stonewall Rebellion of 1969 produced a surge of self-worth in the gay community. Whereas previously most LGBT leaders—not to mention regular community members—behaved like gay people were a defective group of people to be pitied and given "help" by straight homophobic "experts," three days and nights of protest in Greenwich Village spurred a radical reshaping of our community's self-image—the first step toward becoming a force that could produce later legislative victories.

Fast-forward closer to the present. Nineteen ninety-eight was the height of the "Republican Revolution." Newt Gingrich and his "Contract with America" were riding high in the saddle, and despite signing "Don't Ask, Don't Tell" and the Defense of Marriage Act, every appeasement to bigotry by the Clinton administration just whetted the Religious Right's appetite for more. But then a Wyoming college student was strung up on a fence and left to die in what clearly was a hate crime. Matthew Shepard was by no means the first nor the last LGBT person murdered in a hate crime, and certainly there are nasty racial and gender dynamics in the fact that the hate murders of many other people have not drawn the same level of attention. Nonetheless, Shepard's murder spurred an outpouring of LGBT people and their allies into the streets of America.

For years previously, groups like the National Coalition of Anti-Violence Programs had valiantly tried to draw public attention to the epidemic of violence against the gay community but had been unsuccessful. Now the wave of Matthew Shepard vigils and protests put the issue of antigay hate crimes on the national political agenda in a matter of days. Bigoted politicians who had been crowing about their successes just weeks earlier were suddenly pushed back on their heels.

The Shepard marches and vigils transformed the gay community in ways that even many within it still do not recognize. LGBT youth took the activism related to the Shepard case to heart and began the kind of local grassroots organizing that can transform the political climate. At the time of Shepard's murder there were only about a half-dozen gay-straight alliances in the nation's schools. Within six months of his murder, there were over a thousand. For LGBT people who came of age before 1998, the idea of progay youth groups to support them while they were in high school seemed like an impossible dream. The Shepard protests marked the coming out of the LGBTQ (lesbian, gay, bisexual, transgender, and queer) youth movement.

## GOOD MASS MARCHES AND BAD

As important as large-scale community mobilizations are for changing public opinion, if they are not combined with a savvy political strategy, legislative results may be minimal, the hopes of the affected community dashed, and major defeats reaped instead. The 1993 LGBT March on Washington was a classic example of this lack of strategy. Our community focused all of its fire on the bigoted Republicans who opposed the gay presence in the military while putting no pressure on Clinton and the Democrats. This narrow focus meant that the march's implicit message was that the Democrats could do virtually anything they pleased and the LGBT community would not make them pay a price if they crossed it. Just weeks after the march, the community's reward was "Don't Ask, Don't Tell"—a measure introduced into Congress by none other than Representative Barney Frank.[22]

A *positive* example of large-scale community mobilization combined with an intelligent political strategy was the classic 1963 March on Washington. Part of the little-known history of that landmark event was that it was a march which the Kennedy administration initially *opposed*—vehemently. Over and over again they attempted to get Dr. Martin Luther King to call it off, but he refused. Even though the Kennedy administration appeared to be more amenable to civil rights than the preceding Eisenhower administration, Dr. King was not going to sacrifice the civil rights of his community to the political alliances he had developed with the Democratic Party. Kennedy was faced with a choice: either openly ally himself with the goals of the 1963 march or risk, in the words of one of his aides, the event's becoming "an anti-administration march." Kennedy made the right choice, and while racism has proven much more resilient than that generation of civil rights leaders hoped, few would deny that the 1963 march had a sweeping impact on both public opinion and legislation.

## STRATEGIES FOR LGBT CIVIL RIGHTS

Amidst the civil rights crisis facing the LGBT community in the early 2000s, it needs to make a sober reassessment of the allocation of its civil rights resources. It is not a wise strategy to say that everything is good, that we can afford to spend money and labor on every strategy and just hope that everything works out for the best, especially when our opponents often have much greater resources than we do. Any good business, military, or political tactician facing a difficult task will assess the objective situation with an eye to determining where he or she "will get the most bang for the buck," and then concentrate his or her resources in that area.

In the struggle for civil rights, the opponents of the gay community are generally able to outspend it many times over. Relying on a huge constellation of right-wing megachurches and foundations developed over many years, they have an institutional infrastructure that gay people can't hope to match any time within the next few years. In a capital-intensive political campaign relying on large media buys, not only can the opponents easily outspend the gay community and dominate the airwaves of commercial broadcasting stations, they also have a sizable stable of right-wing Christian radio and television networks and syndicated shows saturating most parts of the country. In all nineteen states where gay people have had open battles, including relatively liberal Oregon, the capital-intensive strategy to oppose the constitutional amendments has led to sound defeat.

As of 2006, to the extent that the gay community has had any success in blocking these statewide amendments, it has only been thanks to the much more inflexible nature of the amendment process in some states, and by having gay lobbyists and allies use these often-arcane laws and constitutional provisions to bottle up the right-wing assault. But this is just a rearguard action, and not one that is going to radically turn the tide of the struggle in favor of gay rights.

A contrast to the failed capital-intensive strategies was the cash-poor but people-intensive "StopDrLaura" campaign of 2000 and 2001. Over the course of less than a year, gay people defeated one of the rising stars of the Religious Right. The radio hostess Dr. Laura Schlessinger, then the most popular talk radio host after Rush Limbaugh, was scheduled for a one-hour daily television show by the CBS television network. On a national budget of just $18,500 with no paid staff and no office, gay people worked with local volunteers to put together protests at television stations around the country and got a great deal of free news coverage over the issue. The result of the bad publicity was that both Schlessinger's radio and pro-jected television program began hemorrhaging sponsors left and right, including the number-two advertiser in the world and long-time sponsor of her show, the multi-billion-dollar Procter & Gamble Company.

By the time Schlessinger's television show made its debut, she was severely damaged goods. The gay community's strategy was to quote her against herself. After people called attention to her viciously antigay remarks in the past, she was forced into the closet on the issue. Not being able to leverage the routine that had made her the second most popular radio personality, her television program rapidly tanked. It was followed by her radio program, which was pulled from many major markets within months of the demise of the television show. The successful StopDrLaura campaign showed that by leveraging the volunteer enthusiasm of new activists, even a cash-poor campaign can have a dramatic impact on public opinion and ultimately force multi-billion-dollar corporations like Procter & Gamble to do the right thing.[23]

## THE "SIT BACK AND DO NOTHING" APPROACH

Many professional political commentators as well as many in the gay community act as though it is just a matter of time before we see the end of all discriminatory laws, including laws against equal marriage rights. This complacency is dangerous. While the threat of a federal antimarriage constitutional amendment appeared to have receded during the early months of 2005, in November 2005 the amendment passed out of a Senate subcommittee and will be headed for another vote in Congress in 2006. This timing places the Senate and House votes on the amendment right in the midst of a nasty midterm Congressional election, with five more anti-gay amendments on state ballots, and Neanderthal legislators using the circus-like atmosphere to scapegoat the gay community. If a number of additional states pass amendments and join the nineteen already ranged against us, they could contribute to a national political momentum that might make a federal amendment a real threat once again.

The danger to the present gay community and future generations of LGBT peo-ple is very real. Constitutional amendments by their very definition are exceedingly difficult to reverse. Moreover, as we've seen with Anita Bryant's and other antigay campaigns, many people get hurt in the course of the bigotry whipped up during the passage of measures like these. Progress is *not* inevitable. History offers examples of both rapid civil rights progress *and* devastating civil rights routs.[24] There is noth-ing inevitable about the advance of civil rights. History is made by human beings.

The question then is what is the most effective strategy for human beings who want to advance civil rights for LGBT people?

## HOW DO WE MAKE CIVIL RIGHTS PROGRESS TODAY?

To obtain civil rights, gay people need to look at how other communities have won legal equality and attempt to emulate their successes. It was wide-scale mobilizations of people in the streets of the nation—women demanding the right to vote, women demanding freedom of choice, and African Americans demanding voting rights and an end to legalized segregation—that prompted legislatures and courts to act. With these examples in mind, gay people have called for a 2008 March on Washington to advance civil rights for LGBT people, including marriage rights.

Bearing in mind the positive example of the 1963 March on Washington and the negative examples of the 1993 and 2000 LGBT marches, we intend to make the 2008 march one that not only generates large-scale community mobilization but also one that puts the community's demand for equality above all partisan political considerations. Put simply, any politician, Democrat or Republican, who opposes our full legal equality will catch hell. This equality includes the right to marry; there is no avoiding the issue. It is front and center on the political debate about the gay community and we must deal with it. If someone says that they oppose constitutional amendments but *also* oppose "gay marriage," that is not good enough—either they favor equality or oppose it.

The alternative to a civil rights-style strategy of protests in the streets is to stay the course, to continue lobbying politicians who don't give a damn about the gay community—except when it's time to collect money and votes—and who blame it for their own lack of courage in standing up to the Religious Right. If gay people are going to put themselves in a position where the politicians will have to respect them, where lobbying will become effective again, then they must make the community a force to be reckoned with by changing public opinion and sending a strong message to all politicians, steadfast foes, and fickle friends alike.

To get back to the best grassroots traditions of the gay community and other communities, the planners intend to make the 2008 march not just a stand-alone, flash-in-the-pan event, inspiring for one day but leaving no impact. Beginning in 2006, focusing on the "red" states, gay leaders will begin a series of local organizing meetings for the march. The goal is to spur local organizing among different community organizations and individuals with events in 2007. As the community's 1979 and 1987 marches demonstrated, a national march can serve as a tremendous boon to both local and national LGBT organizing, reinvigorating local organizing projects and creating new ones where needed.

If gay people are going to win civil rights, including the right to marry, they must begin acting like a civil rights movement. That means getting back into the streets. That means putting aside partisan considerations and publicly taking on *all* politicians who fail to treat them as full human beings by failing to endorse full legal equality, including marriage rights.

## WHAT THE MARRIAGE STRUGGLE IS AND IS NOT ABOUT

> So the religious radical right says they want to defend heterosexual marriage? Well,
> let's Focus on their Families. In the United States, close to 50 percent of marriages
> end in divorce.[25] One out of three children are sexually or physically abused, and
> 80 percent of the top income-earning spouses, usually men, do not pay their child
> support. If straight marriage is the root of a patriarchal society in which the heads
> of families wish to return to the good old days, when women were property, and
> children were chattel, then, we, gay people, who self-define roles as we live in non-
> hierarchical families, will rot away the foundation of that fantasy, so that in the end,
> their rigid tree will fall. This is their fear, and they are right to be afraid.
> —Robin Tyler, Speech of February 14, 2005, Beverly Hills, CA

Regardless of what faith (or lack thereof) to which one subscribes, marriage is a
legal contract between two consenting adults, with an allegedly nonsectarian government as its arbiter. This contract confers certain legally recognized rights and
responsibilities on its partners. Religious obligations, if any, are additional ones to
which the parties themselves must freely agree; they cannot be imposed on the couple by the government.

In an attempt to evade the Establishment Clause of the First Amendment in the
Bill of Rights, which provides for the separation of church and state, a basic building block of the United States Constitution, the theocrats of the Religious Right
prattle on endlessly about marriage being a sacred institution. For some Americans
it is, and yet for many it is not—which does not make their relationships any less
loving and nurturing. The theocrats hope that endless repetition of the falsehood
that marriage is necessarily "sacred" will induce many to believe it. By sanctifying
an institution about which a large number of Americans already feel guilty because
of their failures to maintain it, the Right is piling on an extra layer of religious guilt
in order to impose its political agenda on marriage.

This guilt is a necessary diversion if the Religious Right is to succeed in winning over more Americans to their cause of enacting discrimination against LGBT
people. Thanks to the lessons taught this nation by the African American civil rights
movement, most Americans today recognize that opposing legal equality for whole
groups of people is bigotry.

To try to deflect Americans from realizing that their legal attacks on LGBT
people are in fact discrimination, Religious Right activists have assiduously promoted the idea that legal measures against gay people *aren't* discrimination,
because they can "change." Even though most LGBT people believe that their sexuality was permanently determined at a very early age, it is not useful to engage the
debate on that level. Whether LGBT people can change is irrelevant. If mutability
is the criterion for whether or not discrimination is permitted, then presumably it
would be acceptable for this nation to pass laws overtly discriminating against religious minorities like Jews, Muslims, or Hindus. After all, those individuals can
"change" by joining the majority religion. So whether a group can change should
be irrelevant to the question of whether they have equal legal rights.

Another stratagem of the Religious Right to divert people from the basic issue
of discrimination has been to try to pit African Americans and Latinos against LGBT
people, forgetting the inconvenient fact that many LGBT people are themselves

African American or Latino. They falsely claim that LGBT activists say that the community's struggles are the same as struggles against racist discrimination, and hence are denigrating those struggles. The strange thing is that people on the Religious Right never seem to be able to find an *actual quote* from any prominent LGBT leader that includes such a statement. Being in part movements for legal equality and recognition of self-worth, they all have *some* similarities and in the broadest sense are all freedom movements, as are the movements for women's equality, the rights of religious minorities, the disabled, and others. It is no accident that this article itself relies heavily on the rich legacies of other movements in order to illustrate how LGBT people can best make progress.

By inventing alleged slanders of LGBT people toward the freedom movements of those fighting racial inequality, the Religious Right is playing a very deliberate game of divide and conquer, pitting gays against blacks and Latinos and vice versa, fanning insecurities by promoting the notion that rights are a finite commodity in which one community's advance necessarily occurs at the expense of another's. It is a particularly galling maneuver, given the Religious Right's rich pedigree of promoting racist inequality. That they would stoop to such a base level of political discourse and pour millions of dollars into the battle of determining whom *other people* can marry shows that they realize that much more is at stake in this battle than marriage equality alone.

For the gay community, the importance of winning marriage equality goes well beyond the 1,138 rights that come with marriage, as important as winning those rights would be to the lives of countless couples. The marriage equality issue has become a national litmus test on whether LGBT people are going to be citizens of this country.

Citizens by definition have equal legal rights with their peers. Lesbian, gay, bisexual, and transgendered people in this country are not citizens yet. The Religious Right wants to keep it this way, and make their noncitizenship virtually permanent by passing constitutional amendments. They have a broad antiequality agenda—not just against LGBT people—but they have determined that LGBT people and the marriage issue are their best ticket to promoting this agenda. This is why LGBT activists who criticize the equal marriage movement are being shortsighted in the extreme. A defeat for any of us almost always carries over into negative ramifications for other progressive issues.

The leaders of the Religious Right really don't care whom we marry any more than we care whom *they* marry. That is not what their campaign is about. What they *do* care about is having the right to openly discriminate. They yearn for an America like the 1950s, when people were afraid to criticize religious and political institutions, when not only gays knew their place but women and African Americans too. The smarter ones among them see their current attack on equal marriage rights and LGBT people as the opening battle in a war to bring about a more repressive United States in which all people have many fewer choices and must conform to rigid theological and political dictates that give greater power to the already powerful. The fundamentalist radical Right is a multi-billion dollar industry. They realize that hate sells. With antichoice rhetoric no longer raising as much money for the fundamentalists, they found that gay hate in the form of "save straight marriage" began to raise millions of dollars.

The equal marriage movement is about promoting *choice* for lesbian, gay, bisexual, and transgendered people, the choice to live their lives as consenting adults with those whom they love, without discrimination or penalty from the theocrats. Those who have not already joined that movement are invited to do so. The freedoms for all of us are what are ultimately at stake.

## DONTAMEND.COM: GRASSROOTS NATIONAL STREET ACTIVISM

DontAmend.com was formed on July 15, 2003, because of a rumor that the federal government would try to amend the United States Constitution to take away a fundamental right that the gay community did not have—the right to marriage. A small group of seasoned activists, most of whom had been part of the successful StopDrLaura campaign in 2000 and 2001, registered the Web domain dontamend.com. The explicit aim, once again, was to leverage the Internet to support grassroots street activism involving rallies, pickets, and other protest events. DontAmend organizers knew that the Internet, when used not as a *substitute for* but rather as an *adjunct to* this face-to-face activism, could be an important tool with which to assist activists on the ground.[26] A 501c4 organization, the Equality Campaign, Inc., was formed to accept donations to support the work of DontAmend. A DontAmend t-shirt with the slogan "Marriage is a Human Right, not a Heterosexual Privilege," was created to help raise funds. All the organizers were and still are volunteers; all donations go directly to organizing.

## "FREEDOM TO MARRY WEEK" GOES NATIONAL

The first set of major rallies across the United States took place between February 9 and February 15, 2004, as DontAmend.com helped local activists in dozens of cities rally for equal marriage rights.[27] Then, as now, the DontAmend.com Web site serves as a practical how-to resource for new activists who want to organize their own rallies but have never done so before. The site contains information on everything from the mass production of inexpensive protest placards to dealing with the media and the police. In addition to providing information brochures and handbills for downloading, the site's production department produces custom-made posters, flyers, and handbills for local activists to use in publicizing their pickets and rallies.

The DontAmend.com Web site itself serves as a clearinghouse to bring local activists' actions to a broader audience and bring national media attention to coordinated local actions around the country, using the site's well-developed media operation. In the short period of its existence, DontAmend.com has organized and coordinated several national days of action around such anniversaries as Freedom to Marry Week in 2004, 2005, and 2006. Dozens of cities also participated in the annual National Tax Day protests on April 15, 2004 and 2005, when the gay community rallied in front of post offices to protest unfair taxation of gay couples. To support the Massachusetts court's promarriage decision, dozens of support rallies were organized around the country.[28]

## PROTESTS AT NATIONAL CONVENTIONS

Almost alone among national organizations, DontAmend.com has distinguished itself by confronting politicians regardless of party affiliation if they oppose gay people's equal right to marry. The group is resolutely nonpartisan; both Democratic and Republican politicians have been the subject of DontAmend.com pickets and protests. Even though both major presidential candidates said very clearly that they opposed "gay marriage," DontAmend.com was the *only* LGBT organization that protested against both the Democratic and Republican National Conventions in 2004 in Boston and New York respectively.

## COURT CASES

While DontAmend.com sees lobbying in the streets as the key factor in pushing the courts and legislatures in a positive direction, the group has not only supported but also encouraged legal challenges to marriage discrimination.[29]

### *Florida*

In Florida, DontAmend.com worked with local couples to file a series of suits challenging the state's discrimination against lesbian and gay couples as well as the federal Defense of Marriage Act.[30] While the lawsuits gave a great deal of positive publicity to our issues, unfortunately a negative decision on the right to adopt forced DontAmend to discontinue those Florida suits lest they reinforce that negative precedent.

### *California*

On a more positive note, DontAmend.com's executive director, Robin Tyler, and her partner, Diane Olson, were the first couple to file a lawsuit in the state of California, on February 24, 2004, for marriage equality. This lawsuit, *Tyler v. City of Los Angeles*, was announced at the Beverly Hills Courthouse at 9 a.m. on February 12, 2004, by their attorney, Gloria Allred. That afternoon in San Francisco, Gavin Newsom began marrying same-sex couples. The City of San Francisco cases were eventually disallowed by the California Supreme Court. Couples from the Bay Area subsequently filed suit, with the National Center for Lesbian Rights (NCLR), Lambda, and the American Civil Liberties Union (ACLU) representing them. All the suits were consolidated, winning a major victory in the San Francisco appellate court, where a Catholic Republican judge ruled in favor of the couples. The suit will reach the state's Supreme Court for what could become a landmark decision not just for the state but for the whole country.

## NOTES

1. Tim Campbell, "Gay Marriage—The Early Years," *Pulse of the Twin Cities*, April 8, 2005, http://www.pulsetc.com/article.php?sid=1015. The original title for Campbell's article

was "How Gay Marriage Got Divorced from Gay Rights," but was retitled upon publication. For Campbell's weblog, which contains several other articles, the reader is referred to http://timcampbellxyx.blogspot.com. At the time that Campbell's article was written, thirty-four years later, he reports that Jack Baker and Mike McConnell are still together and, in their eyes, still married.

2. Martin Luther King, Jr., *Why We Can't Wait* (New York: Harper & Row, 1964), 141.

3. The demand for equal marriage rights has been a demand not only of isolated individuals; it also took on a mass character very early in the gay rights movement. At the first large gay march on Washington, D.C., in 1979, the marchers protested in front of the federal tax office against unfair taxation of gay couples who could not get married. At the second march in 1987, over four thousand couples gathered for a marriage ceremony. At the 1993 march, double that number of couples gathered for a marriage ceremony. In an issues survey conducted with seventeen thousand prospective participants in the 2000 Millennium March on Washington, the right to marry came in third place, only slightly behind demanding an end to violence and the right to work, as the top priority of the movement.

4. According to a 2004 General Accounting Office (GAO) report, some 1,138 benefits are associated with marriage. These include but are not limited to: Social Security and related programs; employment benefits and related laws; federal, civilian, and military service and veterans' benefits; medical, health and illness benefits; estate and taxation benefits; immigration, naturalization and aliens' rights (the right to petition for spouses to immigrate to the United States and family reunification for asylum seekers); trade, commerce and intellectual property rights (the ability to file jointly for bankruptcy protection; renewal and/or termination rights to the copyrighted work of a deceased partner); marital communication privilege (the right not to testify against one's spouse); recognition and guaranteed provision of rights in other jurisdictions; and coverage under federal law prohibiting discrimination based on legal relationship status. This list does not include the few hundred additional benefits that accrue at the local level, depending on one's state of residence. Significantly, even though marriage is legal for same-sex couples in Massachusetts, married gay and lesbian couples in that state still fail to obtain the vast majority of the legal benefits of marriage, as the bulk of these accrue at the federal level where our rights still are not recognized.

5. National Gay and Lesbian Task Force (NGLTF) Policy Institute and the National Black Justice Coalition (NBJC), "Black Same-Sex Households in the United States: A Report from the 2000 Census" (Washington, DC: NGLTF 2004), 2. Another NGLTF study, "Hispanic and Latino Same-Sex Couple Households in the United States," again breaks the antiassimilationists' stereotypes about LGBT families. *Sixty-eight percent* of Latino women living with other Latino women in same-sex couple households were raising children under the age of 18, according to the 2000 census, and 58 percent of Latin men in such couples were raising children. J. Cianciotto, "Hispanic and Latino Same-Sex Couple Households in the United States" (New York: NGLTF, 2005), 51. Emphasis added.

6. NGLTF Policy Institute, "Say It Loud: I'm Black and I'm Proud," (Washington, DC: NGLTF, 2002), 25–6. The report goes on to say "The support for marriage in the sample is especially interesting not only because it was most forcefully embraced by women, but also because it contradicts the position of those, most often on the left, who see marriage as an issue most salient to White GLBT communities." Ibid., 29. With the publicity given to the marriage issue in the years since 2000, when this survey was conducted, it is reasonable to assume that African American LGBT people's ranking of the marriage issue has probably risen even higher.

7. Ibid., 8–19.

8. King, *Why We Can't Wait*, 32–33 (see note 2).

9. As this enumeration of some of the life-and-death issues of the equal marriage struggle shows, there is hardly an impenetrable wall between these issues and those that have

dominated the thinking of AIDS activists for several years. Indeed, one of the coauthors of this chapter is a close friend of a man who is *both* living with AIDS *and* one of his city's most active marriage rights campaigners, in part because he sees how winning legal marriage in Illinois might help secure his husband's future.

10. NGLTF Policy Institute, "Moral Values and Gay and Lesbian Rights Issues Low on the List of Concerns to Voters, Polling Shows," November 4, 2004. http://www.thetaskforce .org/downloads/MoralIssues2004.pdf (accessed October 16, 2006). "Pundits from across the political spectrum and antigay activists are claiming that the gay marriage issue cost John Kerry the 2004 presidential election, particularly because of an antimarriage amendment on the ballot in Ohio. While the issue of marriage equality for same-sex couples was certainly an issue and 11 antifamily amendments were passed on Tuesday, there is no evidence that gay marriage played a decisive role in the outcome. In the 3 battleground states where an antimarriage amendment was on the ballot, Kerry did better than Gore. Three battleground states had antifamily amendments. Kerry won two of these—Michigan and Oregon—even as voters there approved antigay marriage amendments."

11. "Silence equals Death" was the mantra of ACT-UP, the AIDS activist group.

12. See David Mixner's inside account of the Clinton administration's advice to the LGBT community during the dispute over gays in the military in 1992 and 1993. David Mixner, *Stranger among Friends* (New York: Bantam, 1996), 270–71. George Stephanopoulos "urged the community to stay calm, to keep a low profile, and to trust them to manage the matter," writes Mixner. The result was that conservative Democrats and Republicans made the running on the issue, and polls in the summer of 1992 that said a majority of Americans supported gay people's equal right to employment in the military were rapidly reversed over the course of just a few months.

13. *The Pulse*, April 8, 2005, http://www.pulsetc.com/article.php?sid=1015.

14. Ibid.

15. Contrary to the statements of the Religious Right and George W. Bush, Governor Schwarzenegger said at that time that the courts should decide the issue rather than the legislature.

16. For example, Newsom's actions were the direct inspiration for the largest and most dynamic promarriage equality protests Chicago had seen in years, prompting Mayor Richard M. Daley to remark that he "had no problem with gay marriage." A few months later, at a reception attended by hundreds of LGBT people, Daley was publicly challenged by one of this article's coauthors to sign a petition in favor of marriage equality. He did so, becoming perhaps the only mayor of a major city besides Newsom to endorse gay people's legal equality at least verbally.

17. It is not that legal equality is the only thing gay people are demanding, but for the sake of self-respect it should be the bare minimum demanded in order for a politician to be embraced as progay.

18. One of their Chicago recruits infamously proclaimed that "if the Klan is against gay marriage, I ride with the Klan." "Chicago Black Ministers Attack Gay Marriage," *Windy City Times*, June 2, 2004.

19. For example, the *Jewish News Weekly* reported on January 22, 1999, "Last week Falwell told about 1,500 people gathered in Tennessee that he believes Jesus will return within a decade. Before that event can take place, Falwell and others believe, a figure known as the Antichrist will arise and spread universal evil, but will be conquered at the Second Coming of the Christian messiah. Is the Antichrist 'alive and here today?' Falwell asked his parishioners and millions of viewers who see the service broadcast by television and radio during Sunday morning services at his Lynchburg, Va., church. 'Probably,' he said, 'because when he appears during the tribulation period he will be a full-grown counterfeit of Christ. Of course he'll be Jewish'" (Debra Nussbaum Cohen, "Falwell Antichrist Remark Sparks

Anti-Semitism Charges," *Jewish News Weekly of Northern California*, Jewish Telegraphic Agency, January 22, 1999). Among the many rolls of tapes from the Nixon administration are several recorded conversations of Nixon and Robertson exchanging anti-Semitic remarks.

20. An excellent account of this history can be found in Taylor Branch's *Parting the Waters: America in the King Years, 1954–1963* (New York: Simon & Schuster, 1988).

21. See John D'Emilio's *Lost Prophet: The Life and Times of Bayard Rustin* (New York: The Free Press, 2003) for more details of Powell's backstabbing.

22. The Democratic leadership's sellout was not something that could not have been foreseen. One week before the march, Les Aspin, Clinton's Secretary of Defense, used the pages of the *New York Times* to float the idea of *segregating* gays in the military!

23. For more information about the StopDrLaura campaign, the reader is referred to the archived Web site, http://StopDrLaura.com (accessed October 16, 2006).

24. The most dramatic example of the latter is the situation of lesbians and gays in Germany in the early 1930s. In the space of just a few years, the country that was universally recognized as the center of the world gay movement, a place where lesbians and gays were most free, rapidly turned into the most repressive country on the planet for them, not to mention for almost everyone else.

25. In fact, the state with the *lowest* rate of divorce is relatively liberal Massachusetts. The states with the highest rates of divorce are concentrated in the Bible Belt, with Arkansas leading the way with the highest rate of divorce in the country. The alleged defenders of the family prefer to ignore inconvenient facts like these.

26. See http://www.dontamend.com/DontAmendAbout.htm (accessed October 16, 2006).

27. Christopher Curtis, "Activists Prepare Mass Valentine rallies," Gay.com/PlanetOut .com Network, January 8, 2004, http://www.gay.com/news/article.html?2004/01/08/5 (accessed October 16, 2006).

28. See http://www.dontamend.com/photos.html (accessed October 16, 2006).

29. See http://www.dontamend.com/lawsuits.html (accessed October 16, 2006).

30. See "Florida Attorney Ellis Rubin Joins DontAmend.com—The Equality Campaign as Senior Legal Counsel," http://www.dontamend.com/DAPREllisSeniorCounselJuly27.htm (accessed October 16, 2006).

# 3

# LAYING THE GROUNDWORK: EARLY ORGANIZING IN VERMONT

*Susan M. Murray and Beth Robinson*

## THE INSPIRATION: HAWAII, PENNY, AND PASHA

Our first gay marriage case in Vermont was the one we *didn't* litigate. In July 1994, Susan Murray and I shared a law practice in Middlebury, Vermont. The receptionist buzzed Susan to say that a woman was calling who wanted to talk about her marriage. Since Susan practices family law, she assumed the call was about a divorce; she was wrong. Susan picked up the telephone; a breathless, insistent woman got right to the point: "My name's Pasha. My partner Penny and I are getting married in September, and we want you to represent us in case they won't let us."

A little over a year earlier, in May 1993, the Hawaian Supreme Court had taken the nation by surprise when it sided with three gay couples who had sued after being denied marriage licenses. In that case, *Baehr v. Lewin*, the Hawaii court ruled that denying marriage licenses to gay and lesbian couples is sex discrimination. The Supreme Court then sent the case to a lower court for trial to see whether the Hawaii Attorney General could present a sufficiently compelling reason to allow the state to discriminate against same-sex couples.

The Hawaii Supreme Court's decision in *Baehr* had come without warning. No gay or lesbian couple had ever successfully sued for the right to marry before 1993, and no appellate courts had addressed the issue since a handful of cases in the 1970s.[1] But *Baehr* had suddenly reopened the issue, and the possibility of filing a similar suit in Vermont was intriguing. If the Hawaii court could rule that denying marriage licenses to gay couples constitutes sex discrimination under its state constitution, might the Vermont Supreme Court be persuaded to rule likewise?

Several meetings and several months later, Pasha called again; she was ecstatic. She had gone to her town clerk's office, identified herself and her female partner, and asked for a marriage license. Without hesitation, the clerk pulled out the form, signed the license, and gave it to Pasha. We were stunned; we hadn't expected that the town clerk would *give* Penny and Pasha a license without a legal fight. Did this mean that they would be legally married when they said, "I do," at their ceremony in less than two months' time? If so, *then* what?

We needn't have wondered. The next day, the town clerk sent Pasha and Penny a letter telling them that she had issued the license in error. She asked them to return the license so that it could be voided. Pasha and Penny refused. They found a minister who agreed to marry them and sign the license.

Not surprisingly, the town clerk refused to record the marriage license that Penny and Pasha's minister signed on their wedding day. Recording the license in the town's record books would have made the marriage official, and the town wanted no part in sanctioning their union. Instead, the clerk sent the signed license to the Vermont Attorney General's office and asked for an opinion. Basing the decision on an opinion letter on same-sex marriage written by a lawyer in the Attorney General's office in 1975, the Attorney General told the town clerk not to record Penny and Pasha's marriage license because their marriage was invalid.

Undaunted, Pasha kept up the pressure. She called a daytime talk show to inquire about appearing on the show, and she convinced the local paper to write a comprehensive article about the wedding and Penny and Pasha's family, complete with pictures. Reporters started calling, asking for interviews with Susan and her clients. Penny and Pasha's story jolted us both. From then on we couldn't sit back and idly contemplate the significance of Hawaii's groundbreaking court decision. We had to act.

It was early 1995 by then. Given media interest in Penny and Pasha's wedding and the buzz the Hawaii court decision had created, it had become abundantly clear to us that we couldn't dive pell-mell into a lawsuit. Before filing case, we needed to prepare carefully. This was not an issue that would be decided solely in the courtroom. If we were going to be successful, we needed to enlist the support of gay, lesbian, and bisexual Vermonters and straight allies, including members of the clergy and lawmakers. We needed to craft our message for the media. Most of all, we needed volunteers to go out and talk to Vermonters of all stripes in every corner of the state, to put a human face on the issue. We not only needed to win the legal case in the courts, we needed to win the hearts and minds of ordinary citizens.

## AMBIVALENCE IN THE COMMUNITY

To have any chance of succeeding in our quest for marriage, we needed widespread support from the gay and lesbian community. We couldn't afford any significant disunity. Based on our initial experiences, we were worried that many gay and lesbian Vermonters would be indifferent to the idea of equal marriage rights or even worse, actively opposed.

In 1993, Susan had joined the board of the Vermont Coalition for Lesbian and Gay Rights (VCLGR)—an eight-year-old, recently revitalized statewide lesbian and gay rights group. That fall, VCLGR organized Vermont's first statewide town meeting, drawing hundreds of enthusiastic gay and lesbian Vermonters from all over the state to attend workshops on a variety of topics. That 1993 town meeting took place just a few months after the Hawaii Supreme Court's same-sex marriage ruling; however, the only discussion of marriage at the town meeting was a lunchtime presentation led by Paula Ettelbrick, then a lawyer with the New York–based Lambda Legal Defense and Education Fund, and David Chambers, a law professor at the University of Michigan. Although billed as a debate on the pros and cons of marriage rights for same-sex couples, the two debaters agreed that gays and lesbians should not focus on marriage but on securing health insurance and other basic legal protections for people who share a household, regardless of whether they are a gay couple, an unmarried elderly man and woman, two adult siblings, a woman and her young grandson, or any other combination of people.

A year later, at our second town meeting, held at Middlebury College in November 1994, same-sex marriage inspired a similarly tepid response. Although VCLGR had reserved a large lecture hall for the workshop, fewer than twenty people showed up. Susan and her fellow panelists took turns making short presentations and then took questions.

Although a few people expressed support, the majority were lukewarm at best to the idea of fighting for marriage rights. Some feared a social and political backlash that would undermine all the hard-fought rights which had been so recently gained, including the 1992 Vermont law prohibiting employment and housing discrimination against gays and lesbians—a law for which VCLGR had lobbied hard for many years. Others thought it would be wiser to work for discrete rights one at a time, such as hospital visitation rights, inheritance rights, health insurance, or domestic partnership benefits. Finally, some in the audience argued that marriage is an inherently patriarchal institution that devalues women. They wanted no part of such a flawed institution. Instead, they wanted to create a new legal entity with equality at its core.

Finally, toward the end of the workshop, panelist Jan Platner, then executive director of Gay & Lesbian Advocates & Defenders (GLAD), stated the obvious: regardless of what those in the audience thought, clearly there were gay and lesbian couples in every state in the country who wanted the right to marry, and these couples were likely to begin filing lawsuits to obtain that right. Such gay and lesbian legal organizations as GLAD could not control or stop the suits, nor could activists in organizations like VCLGR. As Jan bluntly quipped, "This train has left the station; it's too late to stop it. The only thing we can do now is jump on board." We left that workshop discouraged. We worried that without the gay community's support for equality in marriage, we would not be able to build the grassroots network we desperately needed.

VCLGR's nascent interest in the marriage issue in 1995 was derailed by several other political crises—most notably, by a debate over gay and lesbian adoption rights. The Vermont legislature was in the process of overhauling the state's antiquated adoption laws. In February 1995, an influential legislative committee dropped a bombshell by unexpectedly voting to insert a provision in the adoption bill that would overturn the 1993 Vermont Supreme Court's ruling allowing unmarried gay and lesbian couples to adopt. The amendment had a good chance of passing, and VCLGR launched an aggressive campaign to defeat the amendment.

Susan set aside her focus on marriage and spent much of 1995 and early 1996 working with a core of VCLGR volunteers to fight the amendment. Susan testified at legislative committee hearings, provided legal research and background information, and helped draft language for the bill. With other volunteers, she organized meetings between gay and lesbian parents and small groups of legislators. For many lawmakers, it was the first time they had ever met a gay or lesbian parent. VCLGR also arranged for some senators to meet privately with a prominent psychologist, who presented the results of myriad psychological studies that showed that children raised by gay and lesbian parents are well adjusted and psychologically healthy. Legislators were impressed by our grassroots organizational skills. The overwhelming majority of the witnesses testified in support of gay adoptions at a public hearing. The legislators were clearly moved by the accounts of the many gay and lesbian Vermont families affected by the state's laws.

All the hard work paid off during the next legislative session: the legislature passed a sweeping adoption reform law that explicitly provided for adoption by unmarried partners, including gay and lesbian partners. This experience offered us a chance to talk with our legislators and the broader Vermont community about gay and lesbian *families*. It was our first exposure to the same-sex marriage debate.


## CHANGE IN THE AIR

By late 1995, when VCLGR hosted a third workshop about gay marriage, it became obvious that sentiment had changed. Since so few people had bothered to attend the workshop the year before, we booked a small classroom this time. When we arrived, there were at least seventy-five people crammed into the room. This time, however, no one asked whether fighting for marriage was a wise strategy. People were clamoring to help. They wondered whether there was a Vermont organization they could join that focused exclusively on gay marriage. They wanted to sign a resolution, volunteer their time, and contribute money.

It was an astonishing turnaround from just one year earlier. We played devil's advocate several times during the workshop, asking whether anyone thought it might be wiser to try to work for discrete rights one at a time, such as inheritance or health insurance. The group dismissed that notion. They wanted the full panoply of rights that come with marriage, not just some of them. We asked whether anyone thought we should reject marriage, given its flawed and demeaning history in regard to women, and work instead to establish a completely separate institution. Again the audience rejected the idea; they wanted marriage, not some lesser counterpart. They also recognized the critical distinction between the question of whether we *should* marry and the question of whether we should have the *choice* to marry. Regardless of how people felt about the institution of marriage, they believed that gay men and lesbians are entitled to be a part of that institution. Most significantly, they believed that now was the time to begin the fight.

The energy and enthusiasm generated at that town meeting in the autumn of 1995 exceeded our wildest expectations. We quickly agreed to meet again.

## GETTING STARTED

We passed the majestic golden dome of the statehouse on the hill overlooking State Street and the Vermont Supreme Court building next door before parking in front of Christ Episcopal Church in Montpelier. The church basement was dark and quiet on that cold Monday evening late in November 1995. We'd been buoyed by the interest in the marriage issue at the VCLGR town meeting a few weeks earlier; now we would discover whether that interest translated into activism.

As a handful of people trickled in, we realized that we weren't drawing the usual activist suspects. None of the five other women in the room had been meaningfully involved in prior gay rights efforts or organizations. Perhaps our goal seemed too ambitious for those who had had experience in the gay and lesbian civil rights struggle. Or perhaps, as evidenced by Susan's experience with the VCLGR board, the marriage issue didn't resonate among experienced gay rights activists as forcefully as it did with others who hadn't been active in prior gay rights struggles.

We went around the small circle and introduced ourselves, talking a bit about who we were and why we'd come. The only two we hadn't previously met were a couple in their fifties who had been together since 1972. Lois Farnham was tall and sturdy, with a head of short-cropped, distinguished-looking white hair. Her waste-no-words speaking style and dry wit quickly gave away her Vermont roots. As it turned out, she was a seventh-generation Vermonter, raised in a family of twelve children. Her partner, Holly Puterbaugh, was short with bangs, glasses, and a brown ponytail. Holly was an instructor in mathematics at the University of Vermont, and her more ebullient demeanor complemented Lois's New England reserve.

As Holly and Lois told their story and described their twenty-three years together, we could tell this was a new experience for them. They had been a couple for the bulk of their adult lives, but their circle of fellow-travelers had been small, and they had rarely acknowledged the central relationship of their lives to the outside world. They didn't seem completely comfortable using terms like *gay* or *lesbian*, and relied more on our implicit understanding that they were life partners. By showing up at our meeting and telling their story to a handful of new acquaintances in that church basement, Holly and Lois "came out" on an entirely new level for them. Their endurance as a couple through such different and difficult times for gay couples impressed everyone.

Amelia Craig, a representative from GLAD, had traveled up from Boston to fill us in on the national picture to provide a better context for our work. The national legal organizations actively discouraged litigation, recognizing that an ill-advised lawsuit resulting in a bad court decision could sap some of the momentum the Hawaii court decision had generated. These organizations strongly encouraged activists around the country, however, to begin the long and difficult process of organizing and educating friends, neighbors, coworkers, and elected officials about the injustice of laws denying same-sex couples the right to marry. Although not completely convinced that litigation in Vermont was a bad idea, we wholly agreed that we had to do the groundwork first. We had come to Montpelier to begin the core organizing work in earnest.

At our second meeting in January 1996, we had agreed to form the Vermont Freedom to Marry Task Force. Seven new volunteers had joined our ranks at that meeting. Our to-do list included training volunteers to speak around the state, identifying and contacting audiences to host those speakers, producing a brochure, and contacting the dozens of organizations we had identified to solicit their support for the same marriage resolution that Susan had presented to VCLGR the preceding spring. We decided not to announce our new group in Vermont's gay, lesbian, bisexual, transgender, and queer (GLBTQ) monthly newspaper, *Out in the Mountains*, until after the legislature had voted on the pending adoption reform bill in which the legislature ultimately codified the allowance of second parent adoptions in Vermont. We drafted a proposed master plan to guide our collective efforts. Susan and I facilitated the meetings, but the organization operated essentially by consensus, without a formal structure or elected leaders.

## SPREADING THE WORD

"Nobody should *ever* hear the two of you speak without learning up front that you've been together for twenty-three years and that Lois is a seventh-generation Vermonter; those are critical pieces of your story," Beth coached Holly and Lois during one of our first speaker's training sessions. "And talk about the dozen-plus foster children you've cared for, the cross-country bike trips you've taken to raise money for charity, your work on the local public library board, and your positions as deacons of your church. People need to understand your long history of volunteerism and community service."

We used several of our early task force meetings in 1996 as speaker training sessions—taking turns telling our stories, responding to questions, and critiquing one another. The basic guidelines were simple: First, remember the audience. Roughly a third of the population is already with the gay community, and roughly a third of the population never will be; the target is that winnable middle. Once those people understand that gay people are seeking equal treatment for their families, they will be with us. They just need the opportunity to hear from the community in a safe, nonadversarial environment.

Second, don't lose self-control. Listeners remember a speaker's demeanor long after they have forgotten the specifics of what was said. Gay persons will never change the mind of someone who publicly attacks them; but if they respond calmly, thoughtfully, and honestly, they are much more likely to win over the listeners from that winnable middle.

Finally, speak to people's hearts as well as their heads. There is nothing a speaker knows better than their own story, and that is far more compelling than facts, figures, and academic generalizations. The trick is to identify the key features of one's story and articulate them. Through the process of practicing with new volunteers as they came on board over the ensuing months and years, we heard more and more stories about families who had suffered genuine harm because the laws refused to recognize a family when the reality was otherwise.

For example, Janice, a volunteer from Rutland, had been with her partner Suzie for eighteen years. Janice had been close to Suzie's brother. After the brother's death, Janice assumed that she would be eligible for bereavement leave from her manufacturing job; after all, the company had a policy allowing employees paid leave upon the death of a family member, including an in-law. The company refused to give Janice bereavement leave. In their eyes, Suzie's brother was a legal stranger to Janice, even though in effect he had been Janice's brother-in-law. Janice explained that it wasn't the loss of money or the vacation day she had to take to attend the funeral that stung—it was the suggestion that her family somehow didn't count as a "real" family that hurt, especially in their time of grief.

One story hit particularly hard. We read it in a newsletter from a legal advocacy organization. Two men from a neighboring state had been partners for years when one of them died. The grief-stricken survivor buried his longtime partner in the double plot they had bought together. One day when the survivor came to visit the grave, he encountered a hole in the ground where his partner had lain—and where both of them had planned to lie together for eternity. The deceased partner's biological family—his *legal* family—had removed the body to bury it in the "family" plot. What's more, the family had every legal right to do that.

These were the stories we heard, and the stories that volunteers like Holly and Lois told whenever they spoke about marriage to communities of faith or Rotary Clubs or other public forums: real stories about real people, real *families*, who needed the same protections and supports that so many of their friends, neighbors, and coworkers took for granted.

## HOLLYWOOD, VERMONT

A stunned silence filled the conference room in our law firm as the video ended with the narrator imploring viewers to show "strength and courage in withstanding the forces determined to lay claim to one of our culture's most sacred institutions."[2] Some of the four men and fourteen women who had come to that meeting in May 1996 looked wounded. We had brought a video of a right-wing program condemning the same-sex marriage movement in Hawaii because we thought seeing what the opposition was saying about us would be helpful. What we found out shocked us.

The film juxtaposed warm, fuzzy pictures of brides in white wedding dresses and their tuxedo-clad grooms with images of an urban gay "cruising" scene and pages of gay sex-solicitation advertisements. It featured young men at a drop-in center for at-risk gay youth graphically describing their sexual activities to an unseen interviewer. Ominous-sounding music played in the background while, over footage of shirtless gay men dancing on a crowded dance floor, the voiceover asked, "With over ten years of AIDS education, does this not demonstrate an almost pathological inability of the gay community to exercise self-restraint? Should homosexuals be entrusted with teaching our young people about sexual expression? Should anything that legitimizes their behavior, particularly marriage, be embraced by society?"

Spokespeople from a half-dozen right-wing organizations decried the "normalization" of homosexuality, described marriage as "the ultimate target of the gay agenda," and talked about the inevitable consequences of allowing same-sex couples to marry in Hawaii—including inviting people who practice "other aberrant sexual behaviors" to flock to Hawaii and demand recognition for their ways of life. One declared that what homosexuals want is not relationships but unrestricted sex. He went on, "We look at the homosexual publications and they are dripping literally [*sic*] of sexual deviancy, sexual perversity, the desire for open sex without any boundaries. The underlying philosophy of homosexuality is hedonism. It is all about self-gratification from a sexual perspective. It is the kind of lifestyle that wants to eliminate all sexual boundaries."

The film's tactics—demonizing gay people, equating homosexuality with anarchic and anonymous sex, predicting a proliferation of deviant sexual behaviors if same-sex couples are allowed to marry, raising the specter that schools will be forced to instruct schoolchildren on the mechanics of gay sex, and painting a frightening and narrow picture of what it means to be gay—became all too familiar to us over the coming years.

Painful as it was, watching the video was helpful. If we were going to get anywhere, we needed to have pretty thick skin. This example certainly was not the last offensive thing we'd see or hear, and probably not the worst.

Ironically, the hateful video also inspired us. We had considered the possibility of creating a video, and watching this fiercely antigay piece of propaganda convinced us to proceed with that project. Ours would be the opposite of what we'd just seen in every way. It would not be mean and it would not attack others; we would just tell our stories—real stories about real families.

Joseph Watson, who volunteered for a local public access television station, offered to take the lead. Although he had minimal experience in media, he had enthusiasm, determination, and a willingness to devote the time needed to complete the video. A handful of others offered to contact potential subjects or help with a few interviews. We had no budget, little background in video production, and a vision short on specifics. Fortunately, we did not know enough to be deterred.

A few weeks later, Beth joined Joseph as he drove up the steep windy roads of Waterbury, Vermont, to meet with Chuck and Robert for one of the sixteen interviews that would comprise the video. The two men, who had shared their lives together for over a dozen years, lived in a tasteful and comfortable home in the hills with stunning views of the Green Mountains. Joseph did the filming and Beth sat off camera asking questions to get them talking. Robert talked about his fears that if Chuck were hospitalized, he might not be able to make decisions for his longtime partner if Chuck could not speak for himself. "No one knows him better than I do. None of his family do. *I* know what his wishes are." Robert's fears were well founded: several years later, well after the video was completed, Robert had to go to the hospital emergency room. Chuck was not allowed to sign him in because he was not a relative; a nurse had to do it.

Robert described the ways their lives were financially intertwined. He noted that everything they owned, they owned together. Chuck explained that they were fully integrated into one another's families and were one of the more stable long-term couples among their various siblings. The interview generated good material. Joseph's challenge would be to edit it down to the thirty to sixty seconds that would be allotted to this couple.

## COMING OUT

Gay Pride '96 was our fledgling organization's "coming out" party. The annual mid-June march through the streets of Burlington, followed by a rally, was the task force's first opportunity to introduce ourselves to the broader gay community and the public. We'd prepared for weeks, painting a "Vermont Freedom to Marry Task Force" banner, assembling brochures and literature, and rallying the growing corps of volunteers to march together.

Joseph Watson reported that morning that his partner, Michael, had refused to leave the house. Joseph and Michael, with two other couples, had agreed to be "poster couples," speaking to the *Burlington Free Press*, an important local daily, about their relationship, their family, and their lives. Michael was shy but participated for the good of the cause. He apparently had not expected that their picture would appear on the front page of the newspaper above the fold on the morning of the Pride march, alongside a lengthy article focused most prominently on them. Michael was apparently stunned, but the honest and humanizing profile of the two men who had generously opened their lives for the world to read was inspiring and helpful. At their commitment ceremony a few years earlier, they had promised to share equally the responsibility and the exhilaration of the commitment they are making as life's partners, today and forever. How could anyone feel threatened by this pledge?

## THE DOMA FIASCO

We were surprised that Senator Jim Jeffords agreed to speak with us himself. It was early in September 1996. The vote in Congress was less than a week away, and we were lobbying him hard to vote against the Defense of Marriage Act (DOMA).

Recognizing the imminent breakthrough for same-sex marriage in Hawaii, and spurred on by the conservative activist Gary Bauer's presidential candidacy, the right wing had gone on the attack around the country. With minimal debate or opportunity for gay and lesbian citizens to plead their case, state legislatures around the country had begun passing Defense of Marriage bills. Legislatures designed these bills not only to prohibit same-sex marriage in their respective states but also to prevent recognition of valid same-sex marriages from other states.

Opponents of same-sex marriage did not limit their efforts to state legislatures. In the spring of 1996, Representative Robert Barr, a Congressman from Georgia who had been married three times, introduced a federal Defense of Marriage Act. The Defense of Marriage Act denied federal benefits to same-sex couples even if they were legally married. DOMA also purported to permit states to refuse to recognize valid same-sex marriages contracted in other states.

It was no coincidence that DOMA had been introduced during an election year. Many of our allies in Congress were afraid to align themselves in any way with gay marriage. President Clinton was still smarting from the political fallout of his botched attempt to end discrimination against gays in the military, so he had announced that he would sign DOMA if it reached his desk. After a summer of hearings and demagogy, the House passed the DOMA bill. Vermont's lone Representative, Independent Bernie Sanders, voted against the bill. We had met with Representative Sanders in his Burlington office at one point before the vote. We couldn't tell whether Sanders was at ease with the issue, but as an outspoken and unabashed advocate for farmers, veterans, and the working class in general,

Sanders cast his political lot with the underdogs of the world. We were nothing if not underdogs.

The Senate vote was scheduled for early September. David Curtis, an openly gay man who was the former Defender General of the State of Vermont and a friend of Senator Jeffords, arranged for us to speak directly with Senator Jeffords by telephone. We had drafted a lengthy script to try to persuade Senator Jeffords that DOMA was wrong, but he quickly acknowledged that we were right on the merits. He also conceded that Vermonters probably would not react badly if he opposed DOMA. But he had decided to vote for the bill to show loyalty to his Republican party. As a matter of intra-Senate politics and procedure, the DOMA vote would be a vehicle for ensuring a vote on the gay-positive Employment Non-Discrimination Act (ENDA). Jeffords was a lead sponsor of ENDA, and his support for that bill had irritated his Republican Party leaders. He was already opposing his party by supporting ENDA. "Don't make me stick my neck out on DOMA too," he said.

We did not talk directly to Vermont's senior senator, Senator Patrick Leahy, but we had a lengthy conversation with a member of his staff. We made our arguments, but without result. This was a matter of conscience for Senator Leahy, according to his staffer. We couldn't decide which was more troubling—Senator Jeffords' vote for DOMA even though he seemed to know that it was wrong, or Senator Leahy's belief that voting for it was the right thing to do.

DOMA overwhelmingly passed the Senate and President Clinton signed it. The first major political test of our novice freedom-to-marry organization had ended, and we had failed miserably.


THE PREMIERE

What a contrast to the mean-spirited, fear-inspiring video we had viewed together the prior spring! From the very beginning, the task force's newly completed video conveyed exactly what we wanted—honest images and conversations with real Vermonters. Over pictures of Vermont's Green Mountains, the narrator, Stan Baker, who had been chosen for his mellifluous voice, began describing the core values of independence, individual rights, and respect for differences that characterize Vermont's people. As we saw the footage of various families in different homey settings, Stan introduced the video: "Lesbian and gay people abide throughout the heart of Vermont: living, loving, working, making homes, and creating families.... These people are your neighbors."[3]

Howdy described growing up on a farm in Vermont, while his partner Brian described the importance of their home and their investment in their community. Carol and Deb shared their commitment to sitting down to dinner together every night with their two small daughters. John surmised that some people who are not close to gay people might not fully understand that he and Marshall love one another. "I can't imagine how he could put up with me for ten years without it being true love!" With a grin, Marshall concurred. Janice said she had a daughter and granddaughter, and that Suzie, her partner of thirteen years, was fully woven into her family, just like any other family member or in-law. Erin affirmed that although she had been raised by a lesbian couple, she had turned out just fine; she reported that her childhood had been happy and healthy.

Many of the couples in the video described the ways in which their inability to marry had harmed them. Deb mentioned the tax that she had to pay for the privilege of putting Carol's name on the deed to their home. Janice noted that if she were to die first, Suzie would get neither a penny of her pension nor Social Security survivor's benefits. And Jill spoke of the thousands of dollars in medical bills that she and Ellen had spent years paying off because Jill was unable to obtain health insurance through Ellen's employer.

The only indignant words in the video came from the mouths of heterosexuals. Ian expressed his anger that he could legally marry his life partner but his gay friends could not do the same. Marion, sitting with Hall, her husband of forty-six years, noted the importance of the social and community support that marriage offers. She declared, "I'd like my son to have that." Roddy, a minister, looked directly into the camera as she said simply, "To limit marriage to heterosexual couples is bigotry—not even disguised bigotry." Her words, though blunt, did not seem harsh. Perhaps her unwavering smile, her slight figure, and her white hair (which looked blue in our low-budget production), made her seem unthreatening.

Joseph and his small group of assistants edited sixteen interviews with various Vermonters into a compelling and unpretentious thirteen-minute video—and did so with minimal resources. We found a local video producer who, recognizing that we were a ragtag bunch with no funds but filled with passion for a good cause, generously agreed to help produce the final product at a reduced rate. Since the task force had not actually done any fund-raising, our small group of volunteers covered the four-hundred-dollar cost of the video from our pockets. In November 1996, the video began running on Public Access Television around the state. We immediately mailed copies to various elected leaders with whom we had met during the preceding months. The video, completed in about six months, proved to be the cornerstone of our efforts for years to come.

## COURAGE IN THE CONGREGATION

Our first venture into unknown territory was the United Church of Christ (UCC) congregation in Manchester, Vermont. It was one thing to talk about this issue with gay men and lesbians or supportive straight groups like Parents, Families and Friends of Lesbians and Gays (PFLAG); it was another thing to stand up and make a presentation to an audience whose support was by no means guaranteed.

Sandi Cote and Roberta "Bobbi" Whitacre, a couple who were active members of the church as well as the owners of a small retail business in Manchester invited Susan to speak. The event would be their "coming out" to their fellow parishioners. Susan met Bobbi and Sandi at the restaurant of the elegant Equinox Hotel to have a quick dinner before walking over to the church. Both women were in their fifties. They had met while each was in the Army during the Vietnam War, and had been together almost thirty years. Throughout their long relationship they had led private lives and had closely guarded the nature of their relationship—their job security depended on it. It never occurred to them that they might someday have the chance to legally marry, but when they found out about the marriage task force, they decided to sign up as volunteers. One of their first tasks had been to arrange Susan's speaking engagement at their church.

Bobbi and Sandi were usually gregarious women, but as Susan joined them at the restaurant, they were quiet. Susan reassured them, "These folks know you and respect you; even if they don't like what I have to say, that doesn't mean they will somehow take it out on you!"

Sandi then revealed something that momentarily left Susan speechless: "Well, you see, Susan, we've never actually come out to anyone. No one knew we were gay—until today." Then she pulled out a copy of that day's edition of the local newspaper. There they were, both of them, in a large picture on the front page. The accompanying article boldly proclaimed that Bobbi and Sandi were a long-time lesbian couple and that they had arranged for Susan to speak about gay marriage to the congregation of the local UCC church.

Just like that, Sandi and Bobbi had "come out," not only to a few trusted friends, but also to the entire Manchester community, including their business customers and all of their church's congregants. Since the paper was only a few hours old, they had not yet received any feedback and had no idea how their customers or fellow church members would take the news. Their nervousness was palpable. Neither had the stomach to order anything to eat.

As Susan, Sandi, and Bobbi walked slowly across the street to the church, they anticipated the complex emotions that likely awaited them. Some of Bobbi's and Sandi's friends at the church might be upset that the women had not confided in them. Others might be bemused or dismayed to have learned that two active members of their church were homosexuals. Still others were likely to be harboring much stronger and more negative emotions. And here they were, coming to talk about the volatile issue of gay marriage. It was going to be an interesting night.

When the threesome entered the church, Sandi walked without hesitation to the small podium. The crowd grew quiet. In a halting voice, she thanked everyone for coming. Then, before introducing Susan, she told the crowd that she and Bobbi had been very nervous about revealing their sexuality to the newspaper reporter, knowing that it would be published and that all of their fellow townspeople would now be aware of their long-held secret. She wanted them to know, however, that neither she nor Bobbi regretted the decision and that they felt freer than they ever had before.

As Susan took the podium to begin her talk, she remembered why Sandi and Bobbi had become so active in the marriage task force: a few months earlier, Sandi had gone to her doctor and been told that she had a potentially fatal illness. Devastated, she asked the doctor to schedule another appointment so that Bobbi could be there and participate in the discussion of treatment options. The doctor, however, refused to reschedule the appointment. He did not see any need for Bobbi to be there. Sandi protested, pointing out that she had signed a legal document naming Bobbi her health care agent. Again the doctor demurred, saying that the legal document did not matter because Sandi was still able to make decisions for herself, so that Bobbi did not need to be involved.

Fortunately, the doctor's diagnosis turned out to be incorrect: Sandi did not have a fatal illness after all. Her experience with the doctor was a painful reminder, however, that her relationship with Bobbi was not legally recognized. Although they had been together for nearly three decades and had been through much together, the doctor did not recognize them as spouses because the law itself did not recognize them as spouses. This frightening and humiliating experience had given these two women the courage to come out so publicly despite the potentially negative ramifications for their friendships and livelihoods.

After a short introduction, Susan played the task force's video; the room was quiet as the participants watched the short tape. The question-and-answer session that followed Susan's "Marriage 101" presentation was lively, thoughtful, and respectful. There was none of the vitriol we had feared. When the forum started, Bobbi had taken her glasses off and covered her face in her hands so she couldn't see anyone. Now her glasses were back on, and she smiled broadly. Susan felt relieved, even mildly triumphant as the presentation ended. The evening had gone exceedingly well.

As Susan put on her coat to leave, a smartly dressed elderly woman approached her. Susan stiffened, thinking that this, finally, was the sour note she had been expecting all evening. The woman introduced herself, said she was there with her husband, and had been listening carefully. She told Susan that she'd had no idea that she and her husband were entitled to such a broad range of legal rights merely because they were married. It also shocked her to learn that Bobbi and Sandi and other gay couples had no access to those same legal rights. "It was like a light bulb going off in my head; this is an enormous legal problem, a huge inequality, and I had no idea that it even existed!" She thanked Susan profusely for coming and promised to write a letter and sign a petition supporting marriage for same-sex couples.

Susan watched the woman for a moment as she walked away, her white hair complementing her blue dress. This woman was a wife, a mother, a grandmother, and a churchgoer, and she had "gotten" it. She was exactly the kind of person we needed to reach and persuade. At that moment Susan wished we could drive around Vermont full-time, making the same presentation to every grandmother and churchgoer in the state. In the future, whenever and wherever we talked to groups of people about gay marriage, we kept this woman's remarks in mind; they gave us hope and courage.

## EDUCATING OUR LEGISLATORS

Our friend Mary Hurlie loves politics and likes to throw a good party. So she jumped at the chance to host a small gathering for the newly elected state senators from her home county to talk about gay marriage. She sent elegant invitations on thick card stock. Four of the six senators—two Democrats and two Republicans—agreed in late 1996 to come to hear Susan speak about the issue. Unlike some states, Vermont has a part-time citizen legislature. Senators and representatives do not have entourages or staffs or even offices in the statehouse. They are remarkably approachable and genuinely interested in hearing what their constituents have to say.

Given the rash of antigay DOMA laws that other states had passed in the previous months, we were worried about a potential political backlash in Vermont if we filed a marriage lawsuit. We needed to be sure we had the votes in the Vermont legislature to fight back a Vermont DOMA, or worse yet, a state constitutional amendment banning gay couples from marrying.

Amending the Vermont Constitution isn't easy: constitutional amendments may be proposed only once every four years, and twenty of Vermont's thirty senators and a majority of the 150-member House must approve a proposed amendment. Then there must be another election. The Senate and House must approve the amendment again before it finally goes to the voters for an up-or-down vote. We knew that the earliest a Vermont senator could propose an antigay marriage amendment was 1999, and the earliest it could reach the voters was 2001—a full five years away. Given all this, we assumed that we didn't have to worry about a constitutional amendment any time soon—but we still wanted to gauge the level of support in the Senate for such an amendment.

We also wanted to know whether a DOMA statute could pass the legislature. Unlike a constitutional amendment, a DOMA statute needed only a simple majority in the House and Senate and the governor's signature to become law. Although a statute would not override the constitution's nondiscrimination protections, it might influence the Vermont Supreme Court as it considered a future case. The Democrats, who were in control of both the Senate and the House, had indicated that they had no intention of taking up a DOMA bill. We were not taking any chances. We wanted head counts; hence the party at Mary Hurlie's house.

Susan began by discussing the panoply of benefits and obligations that come with marriage. One senator raised an issue we'd heard frequently during our speaking engagements: Isn't marriage by definition a union between a man and a woman? Susan pointed out that the institution of marriage had changed in many ways over the years. For instance, it had been only about a hundred years since married women had gained the right to own property or sign contracts. Before that, women had forfeited their legal rights when they married. And interracial marriage had been forbidden in many states until the prohibition was overturned by the United States Supreme Court in 1967. These kinds of fundamental changes in the meaning of marriage had not undermined the institution but had strengthened it, bringing it in line with the times. Allowing gays to marry would be a change that would strengthen the institution of marriage as well as provide needed protections for gay and lesbian families.

Throughout our talk, the senators seemed friendly but wary. Finally, one asked whether we wanted the legislature to pass a gay marriage law. Susan assured them that we didn't want them to do anything; in fact, we wanted them to agree *not* to do anything. Susan told them that this was a constitutional issue and was likely to be resolved by the courts. We wanted the senators to refrain from doing something (such as passing a DOMA or proposing a constitutional amendment) that might undermine or preempt a claim in the courts. That brought a palpable sense of relief to the room. The lawmakers assured us that they would be more than happy to sit back and let the courts decide the issue.

## TAKING IT TO THE TOP

Throughout 1996 we met with several political heavyweights in Vermont, including our Congressional delegation, Lieutenant Governor Doug Racine, a handful of state senators and representatives, and, prior to the election, several candidates for state and federal office. The obvious next step was to meet with Vermont's then governor, Howard Dean. Keith Goslant, a longtime gay political activist, agreed to set up the appointment and join us for the meeting that November morning. Our goal was to introduce ourselves, let Governor Dean know that Vermont might soon see a marriage case like Hawaii's, and make the same points that we had already made in countless small groups around the state.

Governor Dean greeted us heartily and introduced us to Janet Ancel, the governor's counsel, who was joining our meeting. We spent a few minutes bantering, sizing each other up as we made small talk. After a few minutes, when it was time for the conversation to transition, the governor abruptly asked us to begin. We started with our by-then familiar routine, giving him examples of Vermonters who had suffered real hardships because they were prevented from marrying. Governor Dean readily agreed that denying basic protections to same-sex couples is unfair. He wanted to know what we were planning to do about it.

We then turned to politics; at that point, we had the governor's full attention. We told him that the Hawaii trial court was likely to rule any day now that same-sex couples can marry, and that it was just a matter of time before the issue hit Vermont. We knew we were not ready to file a lawsuit yet, so we didn't want to come right out and say we were going to file. On the other hand, we did want Dean to know our intentions. We told the governor that the forum for this debate would likely be the courts, not the legislature. Dean was keenly interested in this information. We told him it made sense for the judicial branch to deal with this matter, since the courts are the branch of government through which citizens enforce their constitutional rights.

We explained that we were worried that our opposition would take the issue to the Vermont legislature. Our greatest fear was that before we had had an opportunity to do our public education work, and before the Vermont courts got the chance to weigh in on the constitutional question, the legislature would get swept up in the antigay backlash and would pass a DOMA. Dean dismissed our fear, saying, "You won't see a DOMA coming out of this legislature, I can assure you." He knew the players at the statehouse better than we did, and knew the legislature's makeup. He was not worried that a DOMA bill would emerge. We hoped he was right.

Then, with his eyes upon both of us, Dean waited to hear what we were going to ask of him. We had agreed that we did not want to push Governor Dean to take a public position prematurely. We were afraid of what he might say if pressed for his views too hard and too soon. So, as he looked at us expectantly, we suggested that if a lawsuit were filed, he could simply say that it was an important constitutional matter and that the courts should be given the freedom to decide it without interference from politicians. Dean smiled and leaned back in his chair, visibly relieved; he told us he was perfectly comfortable taking that position.

The meeting ended pleasantly after about a half hour with handshakes all around. The governor certainly had not agreed to support equal marriage rights for gay couples, but he was too much of a politician to denigrate or dismiss the idea outright. Our entrée, our initial introduction to Howard Dean, had seemed a success.

## MILES TO GO

Vermont looks like a small state on a map. You wouldn't think it could take that long to get from our office in Middlebury to any other place in the state. But the Green Mountains form a ridge down the middle of the state; there are no interstate highways on the western side of the mountains; and there are few major roads running from east to west. Hence the expression, "You can't get there from here." The drive to Brattleboro on that cold November night in 1996 took close to three hours.

During our first year of organizing we had recruited and trained over thirty volunteer speakers. Our organization had made about two dozen presentations to diverse audiences, ranging from the Governor's Commission on Women to a conservative synagogue in Burlington. We had received good media coverage in the press and on the airwaves. We had done virtually nothing, however, outside of northwestern and central Vermont, where Burlington, Montpelier, and Middlebury are located. It was high time we reached out to other parts of the state.

Fortunately, Bari Shamas, an activist and mother of two in the Brattleboro area, had taken action by convening over a dozen key people, including several local ministers, a rabbi, and members of the local Quaker community as well as various gay rights activists, to meet with us. Although our themes and stories had come to feel repetitive to us, the group was clearly interested and motivated, and many would go on to be important volunteers in our freedom to marry movement. From that day forward, Bari assumed responsibility for southeastern Vermont, training speakers, organizing grassroots volunteers, and dealing with the media.

At 9:30 that night we finally got back into the car for the three-hour drive home; we were tired and very hungry because we had not eaten any dinner. We stopped at one of the few places that was still open at that hour: a gas station and mini-mart. By then, we were used to this life. In the year since our first Vermont Freedom to Marry Task Force meeting, the two of us had traveled to countless meetings, speaking with gays and lesbians, gay-friendly organizations, and supportive religious and community leaders as well as a variety of politicians. We both felt good about our progress but also knew that life was only going to get busier.

As we drove home that night, we reeled off a list of all the things we needed to do quickly. At that hour of the night, the list only raised our anxiety levels. Slouched in the passenger seat, staring into the dark night, Susan reminded me: "Remember, it's a marathon, not a sprint." Her admonition would become our mantra in the coming months and years.

After two years of grassroots organizing, Susan and Beth, along with co-counsel Mary Bonauto from Gay & Lesbian Advocates & Defenders, filed a lawsuit, *Baker v. State*, on behalf of three same-sex couples who had been denied marriage licenses. The Vermont Supreme Court ultimately ruled that Vermont's denial of the protections and obligations of civil marriage to same-sex couples was unconstitutional, and deferred to the Vermont Legislature to pass a law consistent with the court's decision. The court did not decide whether denying same-sex couples marriage licenses themselves, even while making the benefits of marriage available, would be unconstitutional. In April 2000, after four months of intense debate, the Vermont legislature passed the then groundbreaking civil union law, providing all of the tangible legal benefits of marriage defined in state law to same-sex couples joined in civil union. That law fell short of the goal of full equality but represented a significant step forward. The grassroots organizing and outreach of the Vermont Freedom to Marry Task Force continued throughout the *Baker v. State* litigation, the lobbying that led to the civil union law, and through the present. It will continue until Vermont affords full marriage equality to same-sex couples.

## NOTES

1. See, for example, *Baker v. Nelson*, 191 NW.2d 185 (Minn. 1971); *Singer v. Hara*, 522 P.2d 1187 (Wash. Ct. App. 1977); *Jones v. Hallahan*, 501 S.W.2d 588 (Ky. Ct. App. 1973).

2. *The Ultimate Target of the Gay Agenda: Same Sex Marriages*, The Report, VHS (Lancaster, CA: The Report, 1996).

3. *Freedom to Marry: A Green Mountain View*, Vermont Freedom to Marry Task Force, VHS (Middlebury, VT: Vermont Freedom to Marry Task Force, 1996).

# 4

## GRASSROOTS ORGANIZING: LESSONS FROM THE GARDEN STATE

### Laura E. Pople

I know that those of us in New Jersey are among the lucky ones, at least after a fashion. Today, as a lesbian living in New Jersey, I can enter into a legally recognized relationship with my significant other. Twenty-eight dollars and our signatures on a couple of forms for the state is all it would take. Of course, we would need to demonstrate that, in some tangible ways that the state has decided are relevant, we are a couple. Ironically, although I cannot marry the person of my choosing—a woman—if I were chosen to be the bride in a current "Two Strangers and a Wedding" contest on one of New Jersey's radio stations, I could legally marry the perfect stranger they chose to be my husband. Marriage between two people who love each other and want to enjoy and honor the privileges and obligations of marriage, no. Marriage as a publicity stunt for a radio station, sure. Then, as they say, I could "kiss the bride." Well, not a bride exactly, because both the federal government and the state of New Jersey still maintain, at least for the moment, that two people of the same sex cannot marry. But I could kiss my domestic partner. My domestic partner may legally visit me in the hospital, make a few decisions—but by no means all—on my behalf, and would be spared state inheritance tax on anything I choose to leave her in a will. She would, however, still be denied more than eight hundred state-conferred spousal rights, responsibilities, and privileges, and her receipt of the 1,138 spousal rights conferred by the federal government isn't even on the table. Ironically, if after being partnered, we choose to end our relationship, severing the legal partnership would be as complicated as divorcing a spouse of the opposite sex.

While marriage isn't an option for us yet, the outcome of *Lewis v. Harris*, the same-sex marriage case currently awaiting a decision by the New Jersey Supreme Court, might just give us that right. Lambda Legal, the group that filed the case in

2002 on behalf of seven gay and lesbian couples, maintains that the state, by exclud-
ing gays and lesbians from marriage, violates the equal protection guarantees of
New Jersey's state constitution. In effect, the plaintiffs in that case are saying that
the state's constitution provides them with the fundamental right to enjoy the protections and benefits of marriage and to be married to the person of their choosing.

Given the limitations of domestic partnerships, and the possibility of marriage
on the horizon, why then might we or any of the thirty-three thousand gay men or
lesbians that the 2000 census records as living as couples in New Jersey choose to
enter into a domestic partnership? And why did the organized lesbian, gay, bisexual, transgendered, and intersex (LGBTI) community in New Jersey pursue domestic partnerships at all?

To answer these questions, let us first consider several others: How did New
Jersey become one of the battlegrounds for same-sex marriage? How have the
events of the past thirty years helped shape this fight today? And ultimately, what
lessons can we learn from this and other efforts at LGBTI grassroots activism in the
Garden State?


KNOWING THE VENUE

When one thinks about New Jersey, what generally comes to mind? Its official
moniker is the "Garden State," although it might as well be the "Turnpike State."
Those of us who are lucky enough to call New Jersey home endure a fair amount of
teasing. "What exit are you from?" we get queried. "I learned all I need to learn
about New Jersey by watching *The Sopranos*," we often hear. But the reality is that
New Jersey is a diverse state. We have oceanfront boardwalks and large rural
expanses. The Mason-Dixon Line runs through the southern part of our state, and
the Appalachian Trail cuts through the northern part. We are the home of Jersey
tomatoes and Atlantic City casinos, Thomas Alva Edison and Bruce Springsteen.
We were one of the thirteen original colonies, and the Bill of Rights to the United
States Constitution was first signed in Perth Amboy. Today giant telecommunica-
tions, pharmaceutical, and financial companies are major employers in the state.
Although not officially recognized as such, New Jersey hosts the Statue of Liberty,
the "New York" Giants, and many of New York's radio stations.

I do not review these aspects of New Jersey as an idle exercise. Rather, I linger
on New Jersey's nature specifically to introduce one of my principal themes of
grassroots activism. One must understand the political and social environment in
which one functions in order to craft one's efforts and message appropriately.

That begs the question—what does queer New Jersey look like? Despite the
absence of a thriving metropolis in which a gay Mecca could develop, LGBTI
organizations have flourished, albeit in a decidedly suburban way. According to
the 2000 census, gay and lesbian couples reside in 548 of the state's 566 cities,
towns, and boroughs. Of special note, the towns of Highland Park, Montclair,
Asbury Park, Plainfield, and Cape May all have booming gay residential areas.
The same census finds that approximately 30 percent of those gay and lesbian
coupled households have children in the home. Over time, New Jersey has witnessed the rise—and sometimes fall—of LGBTI-oriented political groups, social

groups, religious groups, community centers, bars, and professional organizations. Yet political groups like the New Jersey Lesbian and Gay Coalition and regional groups like the Gay Activist Alliance in Morris County have both now passed their thirty-year anniversaries.

On the political front, for more than thirty years New Jersey has been in the forefront in its pursuit of rights for its gay, lesbian, bisexual, transgendered, and intersex citizens. New Jersey's state constitution guarantees that every citizen will be treated equally. Gradually, steadily, the gay, lesbian, bisexual, transgendered, and intersex community has been making inroads toward achieving the promised equality. The state's sodomy laws were repealed in 1973. In the early 1990s, sexual orientation was added to the Hate Crimes Law and the Domestic Violence Law. In 1992, Public Law 519 went into effect, prohibiting discrimination based on sexual orientation in the areas of employment, public accommodations, housing, and credit. In 1999, a unanimous New Jersey Supreme Court struck down the Boy Scouts' right to discriminate against a gay Eagle Scout—although the decision was subsequently reversed by the United States Supreme Court. We have had favorable second-parent adoption decisions, a favorable judicial decision prohibiting discrimination in employment based on gender identity, and a Safe Schools Law that includes youths of all perceived or actual sexual orientations and gender identities. It was in this atmosphere that Lambda Legal determined in 2002 that a same-sex marriage lawsuit might succeed.

While one can applaud these advances and appreciate that they have helped award New Jersey a Human Rights Campaign rating as one of the more livable states in the country, they did not appear out of thin air. These laws owe their origin in part to New Jersey's political reputation as a socially liberal state. We have seen progress in extending LGBTI rights under both Republican and Democratic administrations and legislatures as well as in courtrooms overseen by justices appointed by Republicans and Democrats. And more than that, time and again polls show that popular opinion in New Jersey favors equal rights for all. In short, to quote a phrase in use right now, "New Jersey is the state that doesn't hate."

Look at any nationwide LGBTI publication—on the Internet or in print—and you will quickly realize that the red/blue divide extends to queer progress as well. Notice how disparate the states in this country are with regard to LGBTI protections. At the end of 2005, only fourteen states and the District of Columbia protected people against discrimination based on sexual orientation. Fewer still have made any progress in offering protections against discrimination based on gender identity. More than two-thirds of the states have some kind of statewide prohibition against same-sex marriage—and as of this writing, only one state allows same-sex marriage. In fact, only a handful of states provide any kind of legal recognition of same-sex relationships.

Nonetheless, each year the struggle is waged in statehouses and in Washington to gain this protection, and slowly more states come on board. More states are seeing legal challenges to their prohibitions of same-sex marriage; some states are extending partner rights of some kind. In the workplace, more employers are extending domestic partner benefits to their gay and lesbian employees. In many states, gay men and lesbians will not hold hands in public, fearing reprisal, often violent, if they were to do so. And yet some do take that tentative step. Although some

statewide pride festivals in the Bible Belt draw only hundreds to their day of celebration, in New Jersey, fifteen thousand people flock to Asbury Park on the first
weekend in June for the state's annual LGBTI Pride Celebration. In short, progress
as regards LGBTI issues varies on a state by state and town by town basis.
Dramatically underscoring that point, that variation is making news across New
Jersey in 2006, as towns and counties across the state now take up the issue of
extending domestic partnership rights to those in their employ. In our newspapers
and at town halls, relationship equality is being debated with differing levels of
respect and rancor. In New Jersey, our efforts are distinctive for both their tentative
success and diverse nature.

## ALL ROADS TO JUSTICE: WHY SETTLE FOR ONE DIRECTION?

In activism there is no silver bullet, no one right answer. Because there are no guarantees, activists must be aggressive and creative to win rights and secure victories.
They need to embrace every ally and explore every option. Why? First, gay activists
never know when one avenue will be blocked, either temporarily or more permanently. Engaging in several activities simultaneously allows quick redirection of
efforts and continuation of the fight. Second, one should consider for a moment how
many people are currently working on these efforts—and how many more there are
who would like to be. Gay people are at their strongest and most effective when they
can maximize everyone's contributions, matching their efforts to their interests and
skills. Third, each time gay people take a step toward equality, it can have a ripple
effect on future, often seemingly unrelated, efforts. For example, the groundwork
laid with the governor for syringe exchange may help strengthen our relationship
with that office so that a later governor feels more comfortable promising to veto
defense-of-marriage legislation should it get that far. Legislative meetings about
safe school bills can introduce politicians to the same people who will be asking
them to vote to amend the Law Against Discrimination to include gender identity
and expression. The presence of activists at PTA meetings to discuss gay-friendly
curricula may help to elect the next gay or lesbian school board member. Finally, this
strategy enables activists to make full use of all allies, and promotes the idea to
everyone in New Jersey that gay, lesbian, bisexual, transgendered, and intersex people deserve the same rights that everyone else in New Jersey enjoys.

At this point I should talk specifically about relationship equality in its many
flavors. It is tempting for many activists to focus on achieving marriage equality,
viewing it as the Holy Grail. And it is not just a desire for matching wedding dresses
or tuxedoes that drives that point of view. There are literally thousands of spousal
rights, responsibilities, and privileges that are currently unavailable to same-sex
couples. More than a thousand of these benefits are granted by the federal government, and each state usually confers another thousand or so state-specific rights.
Moreover, each year Congress and state legislatures pass laws that amend or expand
existing spousal rights legislation. Extending marriage at the state level to same-sex
couples would automatically extend to same-sex couples access to all the state-
secured rights in that state. So if the New Jersey Supreme Court decides in favor of
the plaintiffs in *Lewis v. Harris*, same-sex couples who marry will obtain more than

eight hundred rights, responsibilities, and privileges in New Jersey. That decision would not qualify them for the 1,138 federal rights that will continue to be denied to them. Moreover, it does not automatically mean that their marriage will be recognized in any other state, although it likely will be in Massachusetts and any other states that eventually allow same-sex marriage.

So back to the question—why pursue any goal other than marriage? Domestic partnerships and civil unions are at times referred to as "marriage-lite." And certainly, as they are implemented, they do not provide all the rights that marriage does. Are they worth our attention and resources?

In New Jersey, the answer has been and remains a resounding *yes*. Even as the *Lewis v. Harris* case began working its way through the New Jersey court system, with disappointing defeats at the trial and appellate levels, bills to create domestic partnerships and civil unions were crafted; and ominously, bills to narrow the definition of marriage to one man and one woman were reintroduced. Ultimately, a narrow domestic partnership law was passed in 2004. This law establishes a domestic partnership registry, defines domestic partnerships, and provides a handful of rights—among them hospital visitation, relief from state inheritance tax, and access to health and pension benefits for state employees. Among the hundreds of rights it excludes, however, are legal redress in cases of a domestic partner's wrongful death, automatic second-parent adoption rights, and access to family leave time to care for a sick partner. Two more rights were added cafeteria-style through legislation in 2005. Adding rights piecemeal and monitoring new spousal legislation as it is introduced to ensure that domestic partners are included is a painfully slow and tedious process. Moreover, a New Jersey domestic partnership would not be recognized in states without any kind of legal same-sex relationship, nor is it clear what rights would be granted to a New Jersey domestic partnership by any of the other states with legal relationships for gay and lesbian couples. Even within New Jersey, the relatively new concept of a legal relationship called a domestic partnership has left some hospitals struggling with the management of conflicting demands when a domestic partner and other family members are present for visitation. Domestic partnerships can be far from straightforward or satisfying.

Most same-sex couples look at the list of rights and feel that it is a far cry from marriage. So why did they even pursue this option? It was and is not certain how *Lewis v. Harris* will ultimately be decided, or whether a decision in favor of gay people might not be overturned. At the very least, it is clear that the judicial process is a long one. In the meantime, gay men and lesbians who were living as couples and wanted to enjoy marital rights and protections had no legal relationship to each other. They hoped, and indeed found, that a legislative solution would give them some kind of legal status more quickly than the judicial solution. Pursuing domestic partnerships through the legislature did not obviate the need for a court case. Therefore, it seemed logical to pursue both the court case and domestic partner status. Doing so built on preliminary work done for domestic partnerships that was begun in the mid-1990s. Moreover, domestic partnership legislation eased the New Jersey legislature into a debate about the reality and validity of same-sex couples' relationships. Prior to the 2004 law, same-sex partners had no legal standing vis-à-vis their partners and were forced to rely on a patchwork of legal documents for basic protections. When considering the merits of the domestic partnership bill, its proponents, including the bill's sponsors, developed a deep understanding and articulate defense of same-sex couples' relationships. This development has changed the dialogue going forward. More and more people are aware that gays and lesbians have valid relationships deserving the same rights and protections that opposite-sex couples can enjoy with marriage. Educational efforts about spousal rights, same-sex couples' relationships, and the legislative process have provided everyone with a tremendous learning experience. Now the discussion is focused on the best way to go about achieving those rights.

Well before *Lewis v. Harris* was filed in 2002, New Jersey's LGBTI community was already agitating for relationship equality. In 1997 five professors at Rutgers, the state university of New Jersey, filed suit for benefits, citing the state's Law Against Discrimination. They claimed that denying them access to the same benefits provided to married heterosexual couples amounted to discrimination on either marital or sexual orientation status. Although ultimately failing to convince the court, this case was a catalyst for work on domestic partnership legislation. Since the bill had been originally conceived as an omnibus measure that would update each spousal rights law to include domestic partners, early work on the bill involved identifying sponsors and building a broad coalition of support. Consistent with the latter goal, domestic partners were defined as any couple who were living together and satisfied certain criteria of financial and emotional interdependence regardless of gender or the familial relationship between them. That is, opposite-sex couples who choose not to marry, or family members like a brother and sister or an elderly parent and child who share a domicile and are financially interdependent, could be characterized as domestic partners by these criteria. This broad definition was later narrowed as the bill neared final passage.

When Lambda Legal approached the New Jersey LGBTI community in early 2002 about their plan to introduce a same-sex marriage lawsuit, they joined the domestic partnership efforts already underway by the New Jersey Lesbian and Gay Coalition (NJLGC), the newly formed Family Equality Coalition (FEC), the New Jersey Educators Association, the American Civil Liberties Union (ACLU), and other local organizations. Lambda Legal's strategy was intended to complement the work already being done in the state and to work with local entities in doing so. Lambda Legal did not want to be seen as outsiders; rather they recognized the merits of working within the existing LGBTI community structure. They were adamant, though, about not repeating their experience in Hawaii, where a favorable marriage decision in the courts in 1996 was defeated in the court of public opinion. In Hawaii a marriage amendment was introduced and passed by the state legislature, enabling it to restrict marriage to opposite-sex couples. Lambda Legal reasoned that if they were to succeed in New Jersey, they would need to persuasively argue their case in the courts and make their case to the public. To this end they hired a professional consultant to work with the existing organizations and develop an education campaign to help persuade people from all walks of life to support relationship equality. The centerpiece of this educational effort was a series of town meetings. More than five thousand people attended the first year's town meetings, which were held in towns up and down the New Jersey Turnpike.

The town meetings were extremely effective in many ways. They were structured with four goals in mind: disseminating information; personalizing the gay and lesbian plaintiff couples and putting a face on same-sex relationships in general; educating elected officials; and garnering media attention. Representatives from Lambda Legal would usually begin the meetings by briefing the audiences, which ranged in size from 250 to 650 people, about the status of the case. A representative from the NJLGC, FEC, or ACLU would then provide an update on domestic partnership legislation. After that, the couples would introduce themselves and tell their stories. Each couple's unique story never failed to engage the crowd. At times some of the couple's children would join them on stage, bravely taking the microphone to entreat the powers that be to let their parents marry. At times, special guests like Mayor Jason West of New Paltz, New York, would lend their presence and unique perspective to the proceedings. Some town meetings were treated as specialty meetings: one town meeting focused exclusively on religious support for same-sex marriage, and more than two dozen clergy each gave a two-minute sermon on why this issue was important to them. The meetings were always organized in conjunction with the local LGBTI groups. During the course of this first wave of town meetings, more than one hundred groups signed on as cosponsors of the events. Local legislators and other elected officials were invited to the meetings, sometimes addressing the crowd, at other times watching quietly from the back, but invariably walking away with their perceptions and preconceptions slightly changed. The town meetings were a win/win/win/win. The rooms were crowded to capacity, the stories riveting, the politicians attentive, and the media coverage exceptional.

On the heels of the last town meeting of the first series, during New Jersey's thirteenth annual gay, lesbian, bisexual, transgendered, and intersex Pride Celebration, Governor James McGreevey stood on the rally stage and, pumping his arm in the air, promised the throng of more than ten thousand people that domestic partnership legislation would pass on his watch. Critics within the community are quick to counter that this same governor was at the state's helm when the state's Deputy Attorney General argued effectively at the trial and appellate levels that same-sex marriage is not guaranteed by the state's constitution. Nevertheless, McGreevey's support for domestic partnership was on record and was one of the critical components in getting the legislation passed.

The domestic partnership bill, introduced the day after the governor's impassioned promise, languished in committee during the next several months. Continued discussions with the governor and the legislative leadership pointed to a so-called lame duck strategy. This approach was used effectively in 1991 to secure passage of the amended Law Against Discrimination to include sexual orientation. The strategy involves holding off on a full-scale campaign for passage of a particular bill until after elections in November. Conventional wisdom holds that this is an effective strategy for controversial bills because a legislator's support for a bill will not be held against them, potentially costing them an election. And it enables people who would not go on record as supporting the bill if pushed to do so before the election, to come on board afterward without seeming to contradict themselves. Through the fall, public education efforts continued as more town meetings were scheduled. Lambda Legal added more intimate gatherings to the mix. At these gatherings a limited number of constituents could enjoy dinner with their legislators and some of the plaintiffs.

Meanwhile, taking a page from the NJLGC's successful campaign to amend the Law Against Discrimination to include sexual orientation, the Domestic Partnership Task Force of NJLGC began preparing lobbying materials for distribution to legislators. These materials were intended to address all the questions that a legislator might want answered before agreeing to vote for the bill. The materials also had the added benefit of making sure that those who were talking to legislators and the public were all on the same page. The task force wanted to achieve a "thud factor"—lots of material, yet professional in presentation. It created binders for each legislator, personalized to reflect the number of gay and lesbian couples reported in their district by the 2000 census. In addition to an enjoinder from then Senator (now Governor) Jon Corzine to vote for this bill, the task force sought to provide the following information in the binder: the bill and all its amendments; evidence for its need; relevant fiscal data; evidence of support from corporations, clergy, professional organizations, unions, political leaders, and the general public; and personal testimonials. It commissioned a fiscal impact analysis by economists at the Institute for Lesbian and Gay Strategic Studies, one of the leaders in this field. By analyzing national data and employer Web sites, the task force was able to provide a comprehensive list of hundreds of employers in the state who already provided domestic partner benefits to their employees. It provided documentation from the American Medical Association and the American Psychological Association that enumerated the public and mental health arguments in favor of domestic partnership.

By December 2003, the bills began to move in both the Senate and Assembly. Both bills had hearings in their chambers' Health Committee. In the Assembly, the bill also had to pass through a financial committee. The LGBTI community prepared to testify in both chambers. Working together, the community identified the broad classifications of testimony that would be necessary. The activists knew from the varied lobbying efforts with legislators the kinds of questions that were likely to arise during the hearings. The lawmakers' concerns would likely focus on financial issues, the merits of same-sex relationships, community support, and personal stories. One young woman, whose partner died after a car accident and whose partner's family refused her access to her dying partner in the hospital, was both poignant and powerful as she recited her painful story. The activists anticipated opposing testimony from clergy, so their clergy supporters came out in force. So many clergy prepared testimony that they had to be combined into panels when testifying. Even as the bill was introduced for consideration by the committees (and indeed, well before that point), behind-the-scenes changes to its language were hotly debated. To the dismay of the LGBTI community, the bill's comprehensive coverage was reduced to a limited range of rights and its broad definition of the criteria for qualification as a domestic partner was also narrowed. Even so, the activists were able to successfully overturn some of the most offensive changes.

It was still largely a stealth campaign; even as the legislative session charged to its conclusion, media coverage of the legislative progress was kept to a minimum. Several of the usual antigay organizations came to testify at the hearings and a small protest was held in a courtyard at the statehouse. The organized LGBTI community, however, showed up in force for the hearings, for *ad hoc* lobbying of legislators in hallways and committee rooms, and for the votes in the Senate and

Assembly. Respectfully lining the galleries of both houses, members of the community listened to impassioned testimony from the floor prior to the main votes with great anticipation. Having canvassed the legislators, working with the governor's staff to reach legislators who were on the fence, the activists were cautiously optimistic that they had the necessary votes. With several Republicans joining their Democratic colleagues, the bill passed in both Assembly and Senate. Signed on January 12 by a jubilant Governor McGreevey, with the prime sponsors and main supporters in attendance, the domestic partnership law went into effect on July 10, 2004. Since that date more than three thousand couples have registered their partnerships in the state.

Almost immediately, and nearly continuously in the time since the law went into effect, its limitations—resulting in large part from last-minute tinkering with its language—have become the basis of legal battles, legislative updates, public outcry, and quiet pressure. Domestic partnership in New Jersey is far from a settled matter. A favorable and sustained outcome to *Lewis v. Harris* will undoubtedly see more same-sex couples choosing marriage rather than domestic partnerships. If domestic partnership remains a viable option as a relationship alternative, it will likely go through changes as it is expanded to include more rights and more types of eligible couples beyond the same-sex couples and opposite-sex couples over the age of sixty-five that it currently allows. In the meantime, cases like *Hennefeld v. Township of Montclair* (N.J. Tax Court, March 15, 2005) will continue to use the domestic partnership act to achieve limited rights heretofore afforded only to married couples.

The case for relationship equality obviously did not end with the signing of the Domestic Partnership Act (DPA), nor has it been dormant as the New Jersey gay community awaits a Supreme Court decision in *Lewis v. Harris*. In March 2004, the city of Asbury Park began accepting marriage license applications from same-sex couples but was shut down by the state after granting the first same-sex marriage license. Amid such local and other statewide activism, educational efforts continue, including the popular town meeting series. The series is now spearheaded by Garden State Equality (GSE), an advocacy group originally founded as a political action committee in New Jersey. Highlighting one of the shortcomings of the Domestic Partnership Act, GSE's recent pressure to secure health and pension benefits for an Ocean County employee (something the DPA renders at the discretion of the county) succeeded in achieving these benefits for the dying police officer's domestic partner. It also encouraged other counties to extend these benefits to their employees as well.

So what does the short-term future look like for relationship equality in New Jersey? The Supreme Court will have heard arguments in the case by the time this chapter is published, and in fact may have issued a ruling. The New Jersey Supreme Court should have the final say on this matter—the arguments in the case preclude appeal to the United States Supreme Court. If the gay community obtains a judicial victory, it also may see the opposition attempt to pass a constitutional amendment to restrict marriage to one man and one woman. If the community gets an unfavorable decision, it will likely see efforts to introduce a civil union bill or more comprehensive domestic partnership legislation. Even as the community waits, public education efforts must continue. And gay people must continue to address the limitations of the existing domestic partnership bill through all available legislative and judicial channels.

Relationship equality will continue to be on New Jersey's radar for the foreseeable future. With marriage, civil unions, and/or strengthened domestic partnership laws possible, gay activists must continue with a strategy of "All Roads to Justice" in its broadest sense. They need to ensure that same-sex relationships are safeguarded as much as they can, in whatever ways they can. Gay people need to keep their legislators' ears and maintain the good working relationship they have with the governor. And they need to keep pressing forward on all the other gay, lesbian, bisexual, transgender and intersex issues as well. Elected officials need to hear that the gay community wants a federal Employment Nondiscrimination Act—one offering protections for both sexual orientation and gender identity. They need to know that a more inclusive Hate Crimes bill is a priority on the state level. HIV/AIDS issues in New Jersey cannot be ignored. As activists proceed on all these fronts, they help to establish a strong foundation upon which eventual relationship equality can be achieved.

## EVERYTHING I LEARNED ABOUT LIFE
## I LEARNED FROM ACTIVISM

One of the things I am most grateful for is the civics practicum my gay activism has given me. I do not think that I was unlike most of my fellow New Jerseyans when I first got interested in activism. I voted and served jury duty when called—less grudgingly, perhaps, than some. Beyond those activities, though, I had very little sense of the political process and what civic responsibility really meant. I knew that my state capital was Trenton, and of course, I had at times visited Washington, D.C. The floor of the assembly chambers seems in many ways different when one is standing on it doing last-minute lobbying of assembly members rather than seeing pictures of it on the local cable news network. One can have an intellectual sense of the separation of powers among the executive, legislative, and judicial branches of government, but that academic understanding changes quickly when making practical determinations of what will most effectively move one's issue along: pressuring the governor for an executive order, pushing the legislature to introduce or pass legislation, or bringing suit before a trial court for satisfaction under an existing law. What will persuade legislators? How does one reach them? Who in the capitol are the movers and shakers, and whom can you bypass? How does an idea become a law? I'm not talking about the high-school civics class answer to these questions— I'm talking about the minutiae. Who drafts the bill? What is the sponsors' role? What about the different chambers? So much to know, and most of us don't walk into this process as experts. But anyone can become one, and it is hard to imagine a more satisfying experience.

While people may reach adulthood knowing that they elect individuals to municipal, county, state, and federal office, they often don't have a good grasp on the differences among those various levels. How are laws passed at the state level related to those passed at the federal level? What falls within the jurisdiction of a city manager, or the local assembly member? Is that the governor's call, or the congressman's? Who are one's most important allies and why? Surprisingly, at times the most important allies (or most frightening opponents) aren't the people elected to office but the people they bring with them—just think about Karl Rove as an example. A senator's legislative director can get a bill on the senator's radar or obtain that sought-after five-minute meeting with the senator. In New Jersey there are special constituency liaisons, chiefs of staff, and legislative directors, whose dedication and persistence cannot be overstated. One cannot overestimate how important it is to have a legislative champion for a bill. In this case, the assembly's prime sponsor of the bill, Assemblywoman (now Senator) Weinberg, did a lot of heavy lifting for the domestic partnership legislation. Through repeated meetings with the gay community, she helped to develop its strategy. Throughout the entire process, she was there for this bill, moving it along in every way and reaching out with advice or requests for assistance as necessary. She, like Governor McGreevey, had made this bill's passage a personal mission; both of them, in their own ways, worked closely with the LGBTI community to see that happen.

In the gay community's fight for relationship equality, it has and must continue to take advantage of every aspect of the political and judicial process if it is to succeed. The obvious legislative efforts—passing domestic partnership legislation, expanding domestic partnership definitions, and preventing DOMA legislation—have been matched with judicial cases like *Lewis v. Harris* and *Hennefeld v. Township of Montclair*. Gay people have challenged the state's prohibition of marriage licenses at the state and city levels with the Asbury Park marriage. Once domestic partner benefits became an option for county and municipal employees, as the domestic partnership bill allows, city and county employees began demanding that their county freeholders and city councils extend the benefits to their partners. Gay people remind their federal representatives—members of both the House and the Senate—that a federal marriage amendment is plainly and simply wrong and that they must not allow discrimination to be written into that constitution. And we tell them that the Domestic Partners Benefits and Obligations Act and the Uniting American Families Act, both currently introduced, are priorities for their constituents.

I can also thank social activism for my increasing awareness of the social environment in which gay people live and operate. Or rather, the fight for relationship equality has underscored for me how the community cannot hope to win if it ignores that social reality. Gays and lesbians need other people and they need us. I mean this in both the broadest and the narrowest senses. The community has had its greatest successes when it builds and works within coalitions. On the other hand, some of its most striking breakthroughs come when it influences that one right person who, like Senator Weinberg, can make the difference needed in that moment.

Every indicator of successful social strategizing pointed to developing, early and often, strong support for relationship equality among New Jersey's religious community. Gay people saw how effective strong clergy support could be in the halls of the statehouse during the campaign to pass an amended Law Against Discrimination. It becomes that much more important to demonstrate the clergy's support for relationship equality because in the process, clergy can, often more effectively than laypeople, explicate the differences between civil and religious unions, with an emphasis on the civil rights issues inherent in the pursuit of the former. The gay community knows that the conservative Catholic Conference usually sends a lobbyist to Trenton to testify against pro-LGBTI legislation. It knows that some clergy use their pulpits to specifically promulgate antigay marriage platforms and denigrate gay people in general. It knows that its opponents try to characterize same-sex marriages as the antitheses of traditional religious and moral values, and it knows the best counterargument comes from clergy standing arm in arm with gay people.

Fortunately, gays and lesbians in New Jersey didn't have to start from scratch to build a religious coalition of support. When GAYPASG, a marriage advocacy organization, first began its efforts in the early 1990s, its strategy included compiling a compendium of supportive religious institutions and clergy members in the state. Both Jersey Pride and the NJLGC made subsequent efforts to develop directories of welcoming congregations. As Lambda Legal began its outreach to the religious community, there was ample foundational work upon which to build. Clergy-oriented town meetings in particular helped generate a list of clergy supportive of same-sex marriage that now includes more than two hundred persons and represents nearly every major religious denomination. Among them are clergy who have personally lobbied legislators and members of Congress on behalf of gay people, written editorials and articles in mainstream and community publications, hosted town meetings in their churches, provided testimony in committee hearings, and counseled stricken couples who cannot yet marry.

Outreach within the LGBTI community is as important an effort as coordinating the religious community. An early concern of Lambda Legal was efficiently addressed when it decided to coordinate its work with local organizations. Lambda Legal recognized that even at a state level, relationship equality campaigns are most effective when they make use of the resources and talents that local organizations afford. New Jersey's suburban nature has been a particularly fertile environment for the development of local groups. Here, Lambda Legal's nascent same-sex marriage effort was able to work with other initiatives underway, and gain community access through the various organizations. As previously discussed, state groups were already working on passage of domestic partnership, and organizations like GAYPASG had been advocating same-sex marriage for over a decade. The New Jersey chapters of the Stonewall Democrats and the Log Cabin Republicans, although each is partisan in nature, have decidedly better access to their parties' representatives than most groups do. They facilitated meetings strategizing with party leaders. The NJLGC had used a donation from the national Human Rights Campaign (HRC) to invest in legislative access software that deluged senators and assembly members with e-mails from their constituents urging passage of domestic partnership legislation and support for same-sex marriage. Local groups have mailing lists, membership databases, and, in some ways most important, credibility with their membership. Every organization in the state has helped to carry this effort along; from Parents, Families and Friends of Lesbians and Gays (PFLAG) chapters and campus student groups to LGBTI employee groups and neighborhood social groups. Complementing local efforts were the contributions from national organizations like the HRC, the Gay and Lesbian Alliance against Defamation (GLAAD), the National Gay and Lesbian Task Force, and others. The HRC, for its part, funded a fiscal impact analysis, disseminated action alerts through its lists, and cosponsored training for legislative lobbying.

In some ways, developing the relationship equality campaign at the individual level was as challenging as working with the organizations. Many people regard relationship equality as a couples' issue. Single gay men and lesbians may not see its relevance. In fact, in New Jersey there are many individuals within the LGBTI community who are explicitly antimarriage. Why should they support this effort? Why not oppose it? The task force's answer to this question is that relationship equality is a civil right, and as such is relevant to every person. Marriage entails rights that all should have the opportunity to avail themselves of. Gay men and lesbians who are not currently coupled or not actively interested in marrying should still have the option of securing the rights of marriage if at some point they decide in favor of matrimony. This argument silenced the critics. Similarly, although this issue focused on gay and lesbian couples, bisexual and transgender members of the community were stakeholders as well. Bisexual individuals may find themselves in same-sex relationships but denied the possibility of marrying their same-sex partner. Relationship issues for members of the transgendered community are often complex. At times perceived to be in a same-sex relationship, transgendered men and women can also find their relationships in jeopardy. One can see the bisexual and transgendered community's commitment to relationship equality through the strong contributions of groups like Bizone and the Gender Rights Advocacy Association of New Jersey to same-sex marriage and domestic partnership campaigns. Most broadly, equal rights for everyone creates a culture of acceptance in society. This benefits everybody—each individual within the gay community and their allies across all walks of life.

Finally, the task force cultivated relationships with professionals of every kind. Of course, one obvious sector is the political. Developing relationships with elected officials, their staffs, and aspiring candidates all help further the cause. Beyond this arena, professional organizations provided powerful arguments in favor of same-sex relationships. Organizations like the American Psychological Association and its New Jersey chapter, the National Association of Social Workers, the American Bar Association, the New Jersey Educators Association, and unions of all varieties have taken positive positions on same-sex relationships and the quest to achieve legal recognition of the same. This list of supporters grows daily. One caveat to this, though, is that at times opposition comes from unlikely sources. After Asbury Park entered the marriage controversy by allowing gay and lesbian couples to file marriage applications, the town council opened up the next council meeting for debate about the action. A handful of speakers at the meeting protested not same-sex marriage itself, but characterizing the issue as a civil rights matter analogous to the debate about interracial marriage. They objected to gay people's coopting that language, maintaining that it trivialized their efforts.

While framing the issue as a civil rights matter has not resonated with some Asbury Park residents, it has proven to be generally an effective strategy. As the linguist George Lakoff contends in his book *Don't Think of an Elephant*, too often liberals cede the terrain of acceptable language. For this reason gay activists have made an effort to recognize their values and frame the issues in language of their choosing. Rather than gay marriage, the New Jersey task force characterized the issue as relationship equality. Its members talked about their own family values. In speaking with different audiences, the presenters changed the message somewhat.

At the town meetings, the plaintiff couples spoke of paying first-class taxes for second-class citizen status. One prominent senator reacted more favorably to handwritten communications than to typed ones, so he received handwritten letters. To those legislators emphasizing a bottom line, the task force provided fiscal data. One senator, during the caucus prior to the domestic partnership vote, came scurrying into the hallway seeking employer data—how many New Jersey companies offered domestic partnership benefits? For her, that was the most pertinent message. For others, relationship equality mattered most.

In the Internet age, the world is much smaller. E-mail and Internet postings as well as snail mail and meetings can all convey messages. Because the New Jersey task force was able to build a broad e-mail address base, it can now reach many people at once. One challenge of immediate and broad access to a given population is to discern what the nature of any communication should be. At times, activists need to update the gay community about progress and educate them about what that progress means to them. At other times, the community's help is needed. How best to use and not abuse community contacts is something with which the task force still struggles. As New Jersey continues its work toward relationship equality, the members of the group continue to adjust the frequency, quantity, and language of its persuasive communications.

## PARTING THOUGHTS

When I look around New Jersey, I am humbled by the people who stand shoulder to shoulder, working toward equal rights for LGBTI people: the old and young, those of every gender identity and sexual orientation. Some donate their time, others donate resources. They work within big corporations or in the statehouse, in hospitals, and in the PTA. Some volunteer with local or statewide organizations, some with the national groups. They offer ideas and energy—myriad avenues to pursue. Every one of these brave souls is helping to change the world for the better. The story of LGBTI success in New Jersey is not the story of any one person, any one organization, or any one effort, but rather an epic saga involving an ensemble cast whose efforts build on those who came before. Gay people in the state are committed to a long-term strategy that requires patience, patience, and more patience.

# 5

# THE WEDDING PARTY

*Renée Rotkopf and Anthony M. Brown*

Leading the charge since June 2000, The Wedding Party has created one of the most visible expressions of the marriage movement. For five years in a row, The Wedding Party ceremonies have kicked off the New York City gay pride march, celebrating commitment, honoring relationships, and introducing ordinary people to the issue of gay marriage. These landmark ceremonies have brought to the forefront the existing inequality that committed same-sex couples endure while creating a positive and realistic face for same-sex couples across the nation. The Wedding Party events consistently provide high-profile media coverage to local, national and international networks and their affiliates.

The Wedding Party is an all-volunteer nonprofit organization that supports and celebrates same-sex partnership and educates the public about the need for equal marriage rights. The Wedding Party comprises skilled professionals in the areas of marketing, media, special events, and the law. We produce unique, high-profile events that bring the community together to give testimony on a national level to the importance of family, commitment, and equality.

Our vision is the creation of an educated world, free from hatred and fear, in which all couples, gay or straight, are treated with respect and given equal rights under the law. We envision a world in which honoring commitment in relationships empowers and inspires the gay community to live a life of dreams fulfilled. Our goal is to foster understanding and tolerance of same-sex unions. To this end, The Wedding Party seeks to educate the public on the need for same-sex couples to have the freedom to enter into legally recognized marriages and obtain all the 1,138 federal benefits, legal protections, and rights conferred by civil marriage. We plan to change the social climate of our country by ensuring equality for all lesbian, gay, bisexual, and transgendered people.

## HOW IT ALL BEGAN

*Renée*

The Wedding Party started with a vision: wouldn't it be great if the gay community had a huge wedding ceremony to celebrate love, life and equality? At the time, the only celebration the community had was Gay Pride, which showcases a fabulously colorful spectrum of the lesbian, gay, bisexual, transgender, and intersex (LGBTI) community. It needed more, however. Who was honoring gay role models? Who was honoring the couples who have maintained successful loving relationships for ten, twenty, or fifty years? Society at large didn't recognize them, so the community needed to.

I came out in 1992, after being married to the man I loved. When I realized that I was gay, it was very difficult for me to accept that I no longer had the same rights and was not allowed to marry another woman. Marriage was something I understood from experience. And many couples choose to get married after they have been together for some years. The Wedding Party provided me the opportunity to fulfill my dreams by fulfilling the dreams of others and taking a stand for everyone's right to marry.

In September of 2000 I took a series of courses with Landmark Education. Their courses are designed to inspire people to realize their potential. The work I did in those courses helped me to understand that anything in life is possible. I was able to move beyond my fears and limitations and imagine a world that recognizes that all people are created equal, where families accept their gay and lesbian children, where all families are honored and get the respect they deserve.

One day I thought to myself, "Wouldn't it be great if there was a huge wedding ceremony in Central Park to kick off the gay pride parade? There will be hundreds of couples, gay and nongay, including their supporters. We will celebrate love, honor commitment, and take a stand for equality." I shared this idea with a few of my very close friends—Susan Burdian, Gabriella Messina, Anthony Brown, Gary Spino, Anita Visser, Penny Goodwill, and Karen Gracianette. And from that inspiration, together we founded The Wedding Party.

Each of us had our unique talent that we brought to the table. With a shared vision and a common goal, we worked together to produce the big event. The group started in the winter of 2000, and in less than four months we celebrated our first Wedding Party ceremony on June 25, 2000. The event was held in Grand Army Plaza on the corner of Fifth Avenue and Fifty-ninth Street. It was a perfect spot, just two blocks above the start of the pride parade. The gods must have been with us: there was not a cloud in the sky and the event was magical. Everything ran smoothly. We started at ten a.m. and ended at noon, just in time to join the lineup for the parade. Harvey Fierstein was our master of ceremonies, and our guest speakers included Ruth Berman, Connie Kurtz, Senator Tom Duane, Public Advocate Mark Green, Evan Wolfson, and many others. As 2000 was a mayoral election year, The Wedding Party was able to attract every conceivable media outlet, from international and local television stations to every major newspaper in New York City. We wanted to create an educational atmosphere, a way to show our community what was happening and who was doing it, and we were successful beyond our wildest dreams.

The real power came from the ceremony itself. With the divine inspiration of the Reverend Pat Bumgardner from Metropolitan Community Church, New York, the Reverend Rob Williams of Marble Collegiate Church, and Rabbi Michael Feinstein, we created a spiritual ceremony that welcomed everyone. No one had seen leaders from the spiritual community stand up for same-sex commitment in such a powerful way before. The officiating clergy worked well together and composed a ceremony that transcended politics and hate, a ceremony that was pure love.

Hundreds of people came. It was an incredible experience to witness. We had over sixty couples: male-male, female-female, and nongay couples, all of whom carried signs with the number of years they had been together. We also had over a hundred friends, family, and strangers who came out to support the unions. It was a huge wedding ceremony and there was not a dry eye in the park. Love was in the air and one could feel it. The couples' love for each other was as strong as ever, and they were there to share their vows and unite for equal treatment in the eyes of the world. Like any other group of human beings, they simply wanted to be recognized, honored, and respected. They participated in the ceremony because they already had the same kind of responsibilities as any other married couple and deserved the same rights.

The most inspiring couples were those that were nearing their retirement years. Their fears were very real, as their needs were a matter of life and death. To them, equality means that they can protect the life they have built together. It also means that they have the legal power and ability to care for each other as the years take their toll.

Looking back on the history of The Wedding Party, while each successive year's ceremony grew larger and grander, the first year was magic in action. For me personally, it was an honor to be in the presence of so much unity and so much love.

## THE FIRST CEREMONY

*Anthony*

I will never forget the first Wedding Party ceremony in June 2000. Not only were my husband Gary and I participating, we were witnessing the realization of a dream. About six months earlier, Gary had invited me to come to the planning meeting of a new project he and his friend Renée were working on. He described it as a labor of love that was right up my alley. I was in law school and my time was precious, but he insisted that I come. I am grateful every day that he did.

I met a group of people who would become my family. People from all walks of life, with very different professional backgrounds, shared one common goal: to change the way that the media looks at the LGBTI community. We didn't even know how to proceed at first. We trusted our instincts and decided to create a celebration for people who are often overlooked: gay and lesbian couples in committed relationships who do not have the opportunity to profess that love publicly. Let me tell you, we hit the jackpot.

When two people stand before their family and chosen community to declare their love for one another, the community celebrates the love they share for each other and commits itself to keeping them together as a couple. In effect, the community takes a vow to support them and to honor their marriage. It is something that many gay people don't understand, simply because they have never had the opportunity to experience it.

The anti-equality opposition does not want gay people to feel that support. They do not want gays and lesbians to stay in committed relationships, because if they do, the opposition's argument that gays are undeserving of the benefits of marriage falters. The opposition is scared that if gays and lesbians feel the support of their loved ones in marriage, they will not be so different after all. That support is indescribably good and everyone deserves it.

Gary and I stood front and center at that ceremony and were subsequently featured in the barrage of media coverage that the event received. The response to The Wedding Party's first ceremony was overwhelming, to say the least. Every major news organization from the local newspapers to the national television networks was represented. I even got a call from a friend who said that he saw Gary and me on CNN International in the Manila airport. The Wedding Party was visible even in the Philippines! Gary and I then traveled to Montreal, Canada, in the summer of 2005, and were legally married before seventy of our closest friends and family members. It was the greatest day of my life and The Wedding Party played a role in making that happen.

## MAKING THE POLITICAL PERSONAL

*Renée*

Over the past five years, The Wedding Party has successfully given real faces to the issue of gay marriage. We were pioneers at a time when very few organizations were even discussing this issue. No one was issuing marriage licences to same-sex couples in San Francisco or New Paltz. Our group was the first, and we took a political issue and made it personal because our focus was on the celebration of life and love. Luckily for us, the press thought this issue was as important as we did. So with their help, footage from our event has now been seen on televisions across this country and around the world.

Getting people to the ceremony is the key to having a successful event. Being in the advertising business, I knew the importance of direct marketing. So we created a print campaign that ran in local newspapers and magazines, including *Max Racks*. To pay for this campaign, we held fundraisers and did a lot of bartering.

But the best things in life are free—so we went to the streets for some one-to-one marketing. We traveled from neighborhood to neighborhood, the East Village to Hell's Kitchen, handing out postcards while simply talking to people. Gary Spino, one of our founding members, would find couples and approach them. Then he would have the most amazing conversations about love, relationships, and possibilities. He was able to relate to and connect with each of them. Gary would say that talking to people was the most powerful way to enroll them in our event. Upon talking to these couples, I discovered that they all wanted the same thing—just to be heard and be recognized.

The word quickly spread; couples came from all parts of the country and the world just to be able to share their vows. We had couples from Chicago, New Mexico, and London. They had already come to New York City for our Gay Pride celebration, but when they heard about our ceremony they wanted to be a part of it. The Wedding Party has been covered by all of the major news affiliates, including the *New York Times*, the *Daily News*, WABC News, WNBC News, WCBS News, United Press National, CNN, CNN International, and many, many more.

As the event gained popularity, The Wedding Party enrolled celebrities to join its honorary Host Committee. Those who accepted included Alan Cumming, Sharon Gless, Harvey Fierstein, Gloria Steinem, Lily Tomlin, Marianne Williamson, Valerie Harper, Mary-Louise Parker, Susan Sarandon, and many others. Their support is a tremendous affirmation of the work we are doing and a testament to how many amazing people support this issue. As time passed, it became clear that same-sex marriage is not merely a gay issue but a societal issue. Whether people choose to recognize it or not, everyone is affected when same-sex couples cannot legally marry. It not only affects the couples' lives directly but also their friends and families who love them. It is time for everyone to come out of the closet—gays as well as those who love them.

## BEYOND THE CEREMONY

*Anthony*

After its first year, The Wedding Party incorporated and received its 501(c) (3) nonprofit status. That initial group of friends became its board of directors and decided to expand the organization into something more than the production of a one-time event. Our next venture was to reach out to the business community with the production of a Same-Sex Wedding Expo. An amazing group of dedicated activists known as Marriage Equality, under the direction of Harlan Pruden, Connie Ress, and James Loney, had previously produced the first-ever Same-Sex Wedding Expo on Long Island. Our board member Anita Visser, currently working in Washington, D.C., with the Government Accounting Office (I cannot think of anyone else I would want in Washington holding the government accountable), approached Marriage Equality and we moved the exposition into a popular Manhattan dance club called The Roxy. The businesses followed. Working together with Marriage Equality, we created a beautifully produced event and a highly effective media opportunity.

Ron Ben-Israel, the cake maker extraordinaire, was our host. Again the news media came in droves. I was even invited for an interview on Fox News for a piece they were doing on the gay wedding industry. They wanted to talk about what cute little things companies were doing to take advantage of our community's desire to get married. I shocked them when I responded with the most recent studies that had just been released, showing the net economic benefits if marriage were made available to gay and lesbian couples. The reporter wanted to talk about pink place cards and I wanted to talk about equality. Fox News was not happy; I was never asked back. As a footnote, I subsequently went on to head the Nontraditional Family and Estates division of the first law firm ever to participate in the Same-Sex Wedding Expo.

After our event at The Roxy, we were invited by the producers of the largest LGBT business exposition, held annually at the Javits Center in New York City, to recreate our exposition within their space. We produced a magical island of equality called Love Land in the midst of the exposition's chaos. We named the aisles Mayor Gavin Newsom Way and Mayor Jason West Boulevard, among others. Again all the press came to see us. We had documentary producers from around the world wanting to shoot footage in Love Land. Even Fox News was there, but they steered clear of me this time.

During these years, The Wedding Party continued to produce bigger and better wedding ceremonies in Central Park to coincide with the New York City Gay Pride event. Our events included a huge wedding procession in the Gay Pride March, with floats, bicycle cabs, flaggers, and marchers. Since our first event we have united over two hundred couples at our ceremony and spread our message to hundreds of thousands.

When we started our organization, same-sex marriage wasn't on anyone's radar screen. We managed to produce our first three events with little or no backlash from the right-wing Christian activists. This was not the case for our last Wedding Party in 2004. Religious traditionalists came out in force and they did not protest quietly. I cannot imagine Jesus ever saying any of the things that they did. What was most inspiring was the crowd's reaction to their taunts. My husband Gary approached the small group of protestors and calmly asked whether they would like someone screaming at their wedding. When the screamers wouldn't quiet down, Gary, inspired by the "wall of angels,"[1] rallied our crowd to form our own "wall of love." Hundreds of people stood arm in arm with rainbow flags, American flags, and posters saying, "Leave No Family Behind," "Love Will Transform Law," and "Love Makes a Family." Our wedding guests blocked from view the uninvited intruders and protected our sacred space. I cohosted the event that year with Renée Rotkopf, the executive director of The Wedding Party. We both cried when we looked from the stage and saw the posters and heard the supporters singing to drown out the horrible things being said behind them. Our couples were going to have their wedding day and no small-minded individuals were going to take that away. Love really does conquer all!

The Wedding Party put a face on the marriage issue for the first time, with minimal resources and a skeleton crew. Almost at once, this small group of like-minded friends became respected for a contribution no one had previously thought of making. By that point we had been working so hard to produce "perfect events" that many of us, including me, simply burned out. We were working for love, not money, which anyone in New York City will tell you is an approach impossible to sustain for any length of time. We had achieved our purpose. By this time, images of same-sex couples were pouring into the media from San Francisco, New Paltz, New York, the Netherlands, and Canada.

We then made one of the most important decisions of our activist lives; we decided to stop being event planners and became "awareness planners." This change involved a new concept; as many of our board members worked in advertising, we knew we had to sell that idea as a brand. We came up with a very effective strategy: we created the educational outreach arm of The Wedding Party. Basically, I would go out to churches, political meetings, medical centers, and anywhere else I could, and speak about why making marriage available to gay couples is so important to our world. Most audiences were receptive; some were not. My favorite experience was speaking to psychiatry students as part of a two-sided panel at Stony Brook School of Medicine in Long Island, New York. My side of the panel included the president of the Long Island chapter of Parents, Families and Friends of Lesbians and Gays (PFLAG), a lesbian mother, a clinical social worker, and me as the legal expert. On the other side of the table were an angry young mother; Frank Russo, the head of the Long Island chapter of the American Family Association (AFA); and two confused ministers. Gary suggested that I prepare for Mr. Russo by studying his resumé and looking at the AFA website. Thank God I did, because I learned more than I ever wanted to know about the anti-equality opposition's misuse of science and psychology, and that prepared me for a memorable confrontation.

I knew that the AFA relied on certain studies dealing with the life expectancy of gay men and child abuse to build their false case against same-sex marriage. I also knew, after a little research, where, when and by whom those studies were created and how the mainstream scientific community responded to them. These studies were severely limited in their scope, outdated, conducted in other countries, and in one case, written by biased scientists.

Frank Russo was so unprepared for my attack on his data that he lost his focus and composure and yelled, "Anal walls were not made for sex!" Yes, my friends, when they resort to yelling about anal anatomy, they have lost. Russo did this because he knew that the only way he could do damage control against my deconstruction of his argument was to change the subject from equality to sex. One of the ministers on his side of the panel actually looked at me and mouthed, "I'm so sorry." I later saw that minister at a LGBT fellowship event. I will always be grateful for that experience. I have subsequently appeared on local television shows and enjoy retelling that story.

Since that first year, The Wedding Party has been recognized among the major equality organizations, and I have met regularly with Evan Wolfson, the executive director of Freedom to Marry, to discuss strategy for the movement.

## EDUCATIONAL OUTREACH

*Anthony*

Our current educational outreach agenda includes interactive web development and a billboard campaign that uses inspiring images of families and children to help keep people talking. I recently proposed a new media campaign idea to Matt Foreman of the task force that Renée and I have been working on. Movement leaders realized that it is easier to move people when they know who gay couples are, what they look like, and what their personal stories are. That's precisely what we set out to do.

Inspiring conversation has always been The Wedding Party's goal. Whether it is sharing opinions online in our first-ever same-sex marriage web forum, using our Media Watchdog 101 materials to help write letters to newspapers and organizations, or simply receiving our e-mail newsletter, which covers all major marriage news and opinion to stay informed, the core of The Wedding Party will always be communication. One cannot see an image of love or read a committed couple's story and remain uninvolved.

The Wedding Party recently produced, under the direction of a board member, Jason Kadlec, and the musical guru Mykel, a compilation CD titled *From the Heart*. It features musicians from around the world singing about love and fighting for what is right. The songs are interspersed with spoken interviews of mothers talking about their gay daughters, nongay friends speaking out for their gay and lesbian brothers and sisters, and gay partners explaining why marriage matters to them. The CD is an entirely new concept and a powerfully moving testament to love. We have also created a marriage awareness ribbon, crafted by Richard Resnik, a New York jewelry designer, giving one more visual image to our fight and designed to spark conversations about our goal of full equality in marriage. This idea led in turn to the production of silver and enamel pins as well as car magnets.

We are always on top of the messages that are being produced about our community. Without those first images from the June 2000 Wedding Party ceremony, we would not be where we are today. We now live in a world in which five countries recognize full marriage for gay and lesbian couples, where Massachusetts recognizes same-sex marriages, and where other states are creating legal protections for LGBT families with names like *civil union* and *domestic partnership*. If readers think that they might have something to offer, remember our story. Everything is possible.

## TAKING ACTION

*Renée*

The Wedding Party is a different kind of organization. We are a small group who believe in making a big difference; we are founded on the understanding that love is the most important influence in the world. While fear and hatred will create separation, love has the power to unify. Love is a transforming force that builds families, communities, and societies. And love is the driving force behind everything The Wedding Party stands for. Love is the reason why we fight for equality.

Marriage is the turning point in the gay community's fight for equality. When that door opens to all people regardless of gender and sexual orientation, love will conquer fear and there will be no separation. Then the gay community will not be considered different, strange, or even evil. Gays and lesbians will be like everyone else, they will be treated like everyone else, and the walls of discrimination will come tumbling down.

The Wedding Party is just a group of people who want to take action. We have creative ideas, we come from a place of possibility, and we are focused in our actions. We have given birth to many ideas and have touched thousands of lives. We encourage everyone to do what they can and be a part of this movement. This movement is still evolving, and it will eventually end discrimination against gays and lesbians.

Here are a few tips for readers:

1. Come from a place of possibility.
2. Generate positive energy.
3. Enroll leaders in your vision.
4. Make your point relevant.

5. Make your idea original.
6. Don't be afraid.
7. Don't let ego stand in the way of integrity.
8. Trust your instincts.
9. Love what you are doing.
10. Think larger than ever before.

And be unstoppable in your vision of equality, truth and justice.

## NOTE

1. Citizens of Laramie created a "wall of angels" to block homophobic protestors after the murder of Matthew Shepard. There are apparently many such walls. People create similar walls at the funerals of soldiers killed in Iraq.

# Part II

## EDUCATION AND MEDIA

# 6

# DECONSTRUCTING ARGUMENTS AGAINST SAME-SEX MARRIAGE

—————————— · ——————————

*Michael R. Stevenson and Markie Oliver*

———————

Arguments against same-sex marriage often focus on the belief that allowing such unions would weaken the institution and have deleterious effects on children. Documents available via the Internet from the Family Research Council (FRC), the Heritage Foundation, and other religiously conservative groups and like-minded people, however, demonstrate that the debate over gay marriage is not only about marriage. At its core, this debate represents the most recent battle in a culture war over the extent to which fundamentalist Christian beliefs should serve as the basis for civil law.

According to the Family Research Council, its view of marriage and family must be the basis of civil law because it is rooted in "the order of creation itself."[1] As the Reverend Dr. Mel White, justice minister of the Universal Fellowship of Metropolitan Community Churches, suggests, over and above "denying gay, lesbian, bisexual, and transgendered people the basic civil rights and protections that go with loving someone else," the current debate around gay marriage "is not about marriage. It's about a fundamentalist takeover of America."[2] The primary purpose of this chapter is to deconstruct this worldview in hopes of providing insights that might lead to more effective advocacy of lesbian, gay, bisexual, and transgender (LGBT) issues.

## THE RISE OF THE RELIGIOUS RIGHT

The organizational foundation of the religious conservative movement, later known as the Religious Right, was laid during the 1964 Republican presidential campaign for Barry Goldwater. During that campaign, religious conservatives like Phyllis

Schlafly worked at the grassroots level for a national candidate and learned political skills that would later be applied in other contexts. Although Goldwater lost the
election, his supporters learned many lessons and gained confidence. Later, religious conservatives thought they had a friend in Richard Nixon but were disap-
pointed with the Watergate scandal and Nixon's resignation in 1974. As a result, the
religious conservative movement developed a distrust of government.[3]

The Religious Right first successfully used its grassroots organizing skills to
address the issues of abortion and secularism in school textbooks.[4] Homosexuality
and gay rights were added to the conservative agenda during the 1970s as gay-
affirming activists began to bring antidiscrimination ordinances and policies to the
attention of city councils and private businesses. In 1976, Anita Bryant successfully
led a counter-campaign to overturn the county commissioner's decision in Dade
County, Florida, to prohibit discrimination against gay and lesbian people in housing, public accommodation, and employment. Bryant's campaign became the first
organized religious opposition to gay rights.[5]

In the first year of the Clinton administration, the Religious Right became
uneasy about the possibility of lesbian and gay people serving openly in the military. According to Michael Horton, an evangelical theologian, "If your religion is
basically political you have to have a nemesis. After the collapse of the Berlin Wall
you still need a nemesis. That nemesis shifted from the Soviet Union to the United
States... Other Americans become the nemesis." The Reverend Dr. Mel White
echoed that view: "What do we need to keep people going? The Religious Right
pushes the fear button."[6]

As the struggle against discrimination continued into the early 1980s, the
Religious Right intensified its focus on gay-related concerns with the emergence of
the human immunodeficiency virus (HIV) infection. The Religious Right also
gained influence in the Reagan White House and hoped to amend the Constitution
to allow prayer in the public schools and overturn *Roe v. Wade.*

The Religious Right perceived acquired immunodeficiency syndrome (AIDS),
first diagnosed in 1982, as a punishment from God. The Reverend Jerry Falwell
suggested "that AIDS could be God's judgment on homosexual persons and society," that "AIDS is a lethal judgment of God on America for endorsing this vulgar,
perverted and reprobate lifestyle," and that "[male homosexuals] are scared to walk
near one of their kind right now. And what we preachers have been unable to do with
our preaching, a God who hates sin has stopped dead in its tracks by saying do it
and die. Do it and die."[7] Although a few laws were passed requiring partner notifi-
cation or making the knowing transmission of HIV a criminal offense, the Religious
Right was not successful in creating political capital out of the pandemic.

In contrast, Colorado's ballot initiative (Amendment 2) of 1993, the federal
Defense of Marriage Act of 1996, the passage of same-sex civil unions in Vermont
in 1997, and the State Supreme Court of Massachusetts' legal recognition of same-
sex marriage in 2004 provided greater opportunities for mobilizing religious conservatives. As a result, same-sex marriage has become one of two issues—abortion
is the other—at the top of the Religious Right's agenda.

Phyllis Schlafly of the Eagle Forum had hinted at the possibility of same-sex
marriage in the 1970s when she attacked the Equal Rights Amendment (ERA) and
suggested that its ratification would lead to legalization of same-sex marriage.[8]

Several same-sex couples attempted to obtain marriage licenses in the 1980s, but this issue did not monopolize the attention of the Religious Right until the Hawaii State Supreme Court considered such a case in 1990. Before the Hawaii case, gay and lesbian activists had won domestic partnership benefits with some private corporations and in some municipalities.[9] They had achieved recognition for holy unions in a few religious denominations, including the Unitarian Universalist Association and the Metropolitan Community Church.[10] But the possibility of a court decision in Hawaii that would allow same-sex couples to marry legally intensified the Religious Right's efforts to portray gay-affirming policies as a threat to traditional values and families.

## THE FUNDAMENTALIST VIEW OF MARRIAGE

For many Christians, marriage is a union between a man and a woman; it has remained unchanged for approximately five thousand years; it predates the church and all forms of government; and was ordained by the Christian God.[11] From this viewpoint, marriage is the defining characteristic of a family and assumes that men and women are inherently complementary. It also takes for granted that heterosexual married couples are most productive (or rather, reproductive) and happiest when they follow traditional gender roles; that is, when they "complete" one another. As James Dobson explains in *Marriage under Fire*, "One reason the preservation of the family is critical to the health of nations is the enormous influence the sexes have on each other. They are specifically designed to 'fit' together, both physically and emotionally, and neither is entirely comfortable without the other. There are exceptions, of course, but this is the norm."[12]

Besides its exclusive heterosexuality, marriage has four defining features for fundamentalists. Marriage is monogamous; sexually exclusive; permanent; and provides the only morally legitimate context for raising children.[13] Writing for the Family Research Council, Gerald Bradley argues that before *Lawrence v. Texas*, the Supreme Court case that overturned all remaining sodomy laws at the state level, laws against nonmarital and extramarital sex had been used to limit sex to married couples and increase the likelihood that children would be born only to married couples.[14] From this point of view, defending marriage means not only legally defining it in biblical terms but also making divorce more difficult. It also means finding other ways to ensure that legally married heterosexual couples retain a monopoly on parenting and are the only parents privileged by government. Similarly, the Heritage Foundation's Matthew Spalding wrote: "Expanding marriage supposedly to make it more inclusive, no matter what we call the new arrangement, necessarily ends marriage as we now know it by remaking the institution into something different: a mere contract between any two individuals."[15] It may be useful to point out that from a legal perspective marriage always has been a "contract between two individuals" for those persons who meet specific requirements.

According to the Family Research Council, the universal purposes of marriage include companionship, regulation of sexual behavior, procreation, and childrearing. From this perspective, a partner of the same sex is a poor substitute for a companion of the other sex because "marriage unites opposites, each of whom has what the other lacks, and only in this way does it resolve the incompleteness that each feels when alone."[16]

Marriage supposedly regulates sexual behavior by confining it within specific boundaries. Outlawing sexual behavior outside marriage is therefore seen as supporting marriage. The fact that same-sex couples are incapable of reproducing without assistance is taken as evidence that such relationships are unworthy of recognition by governments or religious institutions.

From this viewpoint, a government's primary interest in marriage is the welfare of children. Interestingly, childless couples (whether their childlessness is voluntary or not) are recognized as legitimate because "it would be an invasion of a heterosexual couple's privacy to require that they prove their intent or ability to bear children."[17]

In another FRC document, "Questions and Answers: What's Wrong with Letting Same-Sex Couples 'Marry?'," Peter Sprigg, Vice President for Policy at the FRC, suggests that it is necessary to "defend marriage" because same-sex couples who wish to marry are likely to be in heterosexual marriages that would have to end before the same-sex marriage could occur.[18] Apparently, gay sex is perceived to be so tempting that otherwise content husbands and wives will engage in it if not for the preventive powers of heterosexual marriage. For whatever reason, the underlying fear appears to be that heterosexual relationships have little chance of survival if same-sex relationships are considered lawful.

The attractiveness of a same-sex relationship is not the only threat. Sprigg continues:

> The most significant impact of legally recognizing same-sex unions would be more indirect. Expanding the definition of what "marriage" is to include relationships of a homosexual nature would inevitably, in the long run, change people's concept of what marriage is, what it requires, and what one should expect from it. These changes in the popular understanding of marriage would, in turn, change people's behavior both before and during marriage… So if same-sex relationships are legally recognized as "marriage," the idea of marriage as a sexually exclusive and faithful relationship will be dealt a serious blow. Adding monogamy and faithfulness to the other pillars of marriage that have already fallen will have overwhelmingly negative consequences for Americans' physical and mental health.[19]

The underlying message is that such changes are assumed to lead to disaster.

Likewise, in a series of columns for Family.org, a Web site sponsored by Focus on the Family, James Dobson outlined eleven arguments against same-sex marriage: if same-sex couples are allowed to marry, the family as he conceives it would be destroyed. Children would suffer. Public schools would teach that same-sex marriage is the moral equivalent of heterosexual marriage and children would be exposed to positive depictions of LGBT families in their textbooks.[20] Adoption laws would become obsolete. Foster care programs would suffer. Health care and insurance systems would be bankrupt under the weight of all of the HIV-positive gay men who will find partners and subsequently be covered by health insurance. Social Security benefits would be at risk because of the millions of new, eligible dependents. Religious freedom would be jeopardized because churches will no longer be able to preach against homosexuality. The gospel of Jesus Christ will be severely curtailed (apparently because religious teachings can be successfully passed to the next generation only within traditional families). The family would disintegrate worldwide. And the culture war would be lost.[21]

Some of the consequences outlined above would be true by definition under the assumptions held by Dobson and other like-minded political figures. For if the definition of *family* is limited to a man and a woman joined in marriage, both enacting traditional roles for their children while benefiting from government-conferred privileges, then from this perspective the family would no longer exist if gays and lesbians were offered access to marriage or included under the rubric of family.

If someone's worldview leads them to believe that it is impossible for children to live happy, healthy lives and become productive adults in any context other than a traditional family, then fear of other kinds of families is understandable. Likewise, if same-sex couples were given access to the opportunities and responsibilities marriage currently affords heterosexual couples, straight two-parent families could no longer hold a monopoly of adoption and foster care. Besides protecting a religious ideal, these arguments are aimed at ensuring that the privileges now afforded to heterosexual married couples by the government remain their exclusive domain.

A federal constitutional amendment that would define marriage as a heterosexual institution was proposed by religious conservatives as their last hope of achieving these goals. Jerry Falwell claimed:

> It is imperative that we remove the sacred biblical definition of marriage from the reach of unelected and valueless federal judges who would seek to protect newly fashionable sexual trends by recklessly affording them with legal protections.... We must not allow our children and children's children to grow up in a nation with legalized polygamy, common law marriage and same-sex marriage. The only way to put the traditional and biblical family form of one man married to one woman safely out of the reach of future courts and legislatures is to pass an amendment to the U.S. Constitution.[22]

James Atticus Bowden, a Defense Department consultant who is active in the Republican Party in Virginia, claimed that a federal marriage amendment is "the only way to stop our mighty judges from forcing homosexual 'marriage' on America. Homosexual 'marriage' dismisses, forever, the moral authority of the Ten Commandments for American laws. It destroys the legal wrongness of adultery. Marriage and family are whatever a judge says they are. Every Judeo-Christian value and institution is 'arbitrary.'"[23] Beyond concerns about the impact of "activist judges,"[24] Senate debate on the proposed amendment focused on the well-being of children,[25] a topic we will return to shortly.

In addition to the election-year politics surrounding the federal marriage amendment, the Vatican launched a global campaign against gay marriage. Pope John Paul II stated:

> This is a time in which there is no lack of attempts to reduce marriage to a mere individual contract, with characteristics very different from those that belong to marriage and the family, and that end up degrading it as if it were a form of accessory association within the social body.[26]

According to the Congregation for the Doctrine of the Faith, the Pope's guardian of orthodoxy, "There are absolutely no grounds for considering homosexual unions to be in any way similar or even remotely analogous to God's plan for marriage and family.... Marriage is holy, while homosexual acts go against the natural moral law."[27]

Despite the endorsement of President George W. Bush, attempts to amend the United States Constitution failed in both houses of Congress in 2004,[28] and the president turned his attention to such other pressing issues as the war in Iraq. Religious conservatives, however, had considerably more success at the state level. According to the Heritage Foundation,[29] forty-four states have statutory and/or constitutional language restricting marriage to heterosexual couples. During the November 2004 election alone, thirteen states placed constitutional amendments on the ballot and all thirteen measures passed.[30]

In sum, religious conservatives see same-sex marriage as the final battle in an assault on marriage and a significant defeat in their plan to base civil law on church doctrine. Consistent with this view, the strongest opponents of same-sex marriage also call for divorce and custody reform. They see no-fault divorce as a weakening of marriage and wish to return to faultfinding, arguing that it is better for the family—especially the children—for a bad marriage to remain intact than for one or both spouses to seek a divorce. As an alternative to no-fault divorce, Stephen Baskerville, a member of the political science department at Howard University, suggests that the party seeking the divorce should be expected to abandon everything, leaving the household and children with the person wishing to keep the family together.[31] If this solution were made mandatory, he argues, there would be fewer divorces. In spite of a vast research literature that says otherwise,[32] Baskerville appears to assume that one-sided surrender would produce a family environment conducive to rearing healthy children. He also argues that lawyers and therapists are the biggest supporters of the "divorce industry," as the legal and psychological problems associated with divorce provides these professionals with the means to earn a high income.

It should be clear at this point that religious conservatives attempt to justify at least five interrelated assumptions that require scrutiny.

## GOVERNMENT AND RELIGIOUS FREEDOM

- Religious freedom requires that civil law be based on fundamentalist Christian beliefs and therefore privilege heterosexual couples.
- Marriage is a monolithic institution that has remained unchanged for thousands of years.
- Same-sex marriage will weaken the institution of marriage and disrupt the social order.
- The well-being of children hinges on parenting that can only be provided by heterosexual married couples.
- Protecting marriage and putting it out of the reach of the courts requires constitutional amendments at the federal and/or state level.

The protection of religious freedom should be of utmost concern to government. Enshrining a particular religious view in civil law, however, does not ensure religious freedom. Rather, it privileges one religious viewpoint over others. In fact, religious freedom will be circumscribed further if civil definitions of marriage and family are not made more inclusive. Religious freedom, including the right to share the message of Jesus, cannot be successfully defended when other moral viewpoints are marginalized. The government's interest, economic and otherwise, is in supporting loving and committed couples regardless of whether they expect to raise children, not in supporting a specific religious belief and privileging a particular form of relationship.

To understand this distinction, it is essential that we disentangle the civil and religious dimensions of marriage. For example, when the Pilgrims first established marriage after landing at Plymouth in 1620, its status was understood as a civil matter. Not until the Plymouth Colony was merged into the Massachusetts Bay Colony in 1692 were clergy authorized to solemnize marriage in that region.[33]

Despite claims that "marriage is not about perks from the government,"[34] marriage is no longer considered a status relationship in which marital roles are assigned by the state.[35] As a result, it is no longer "an eternal union of love benevolently presided over by the husband."[36] Instead, under current United States law, marriage is a contractual and economic partnership.[37] As a civil contract, marriage currently entitles couples to over eleven hundred federal rights.[38] Depending on the state, there are an additional 170 to 250 state laws prescribing rights and responsibilities to married spouses.[39] Moreover, the United States Supreme Court considers marriage a fundamental right. Therefore, a state's power to regulate an individual's right to marry is limited.[40]

As a religious construct, marriage is neither monolithic nor immutable even among Jewish and Christian denominations. The biblical Abraham had two wives. St. Paul considered marriage a lesser estate. Certain religious traditions require couples to meet religious qualifications before their marriages are recognized, while other religious traditions already bless same-sex unions without requiring a civil license. As the Reverend Howard Moody suggested, "[i]t is clear that there is no single religious view of marriage and that history has witnessed some monumental changes in the way 'husband and wife' are seen in the relationships of marriage."[41]

Far from harming marriage or disrupting the social order, encouraging same-sex couples to share legal and emotional responsibility for one another through a government-licensed commitment would only strengthen marriage and increase social stability. As Richard Cohen, a syndicated columnist, observed, "If opponents [of same-sex marriage] were not so blinded by bigotry and fear, they would see that homosexuals provide the last best argument for marriage: love and commitment.... Just as gays are renowned for moving into urban areas that others have fled, for refurbishing neighborhoods and making them attractive, so they might rehabilitate marriage."[42]

More importantly, a government's recognition of same-sex marriage need not affect the decisions of religious institutions. Given the principle of religious freedom, the government cannot force a church or synagogue to perform or affirm same-sex marriages any more than it can force a religious body to recognize divorce or approve abortion. Whether congregations nurture their gay and lesbian members by celebrating their relationships is a decision that must be left to the religious body in question while the government tends to civil matters. To ensure religious freedom, it is of the utmost importance to prevent government endorsement or adoption of a particular religious viewpoint for the definition of marriage or any other matter of public interest.

Government recognition of same-sex relationships would strengthen families headed by same-sex couples and assist those who choose to become parents in providing and caring for their offspring. If marriage promotes stability, commitment, and responsibility in heterosexual couples, it should do the same for same-sex partners. From this perspective, same-sex couples who wish to marry also wish to contribute to the social order, not destroy it. As religious conservatives fear, however, granting access to the privileges and responsibilities of marriage may well change expectations about marriage—but those changes are likely to strengthen the institution rather than harm it.

Despite claims to the contrary,[43] evidence from Scandinavia and the Netherlands, countries that have granted many benefits of marriage to same-sex couples, shows that providing marriage rights to same-sex couples has no impact on heterosexual marriage. Comparing data from periods before and after same-sex couples were granted marriage rights, one finds that divorce rates and commitment to children remain unchanged. Moreover, none of the extant evidence demonstrates that same-sex partnership laws have an impact on heterosexual marriage rates.[44] As the American Anthropological Association asserts:

> Anthropological research on households, kinship relationships, and families, across cultures and through time, provide[s] no support whatsoever for the view that either civilization or viable social orders depend upon marriage as an exclusively heterosexual institution. Rather, anthropological research supports the conclusion that an array of family types, including families built upon same-sex partnerships, can contribute to stable and humane societies.[45]

Besides data from cultures that recognize same-sex relationships, a considerable body of psychological research on gay and lesbian parenting provides ample justification for government support for same-sex couples who choose to become parents. The American Psychological Association (APA) recognizes that "the scientific literature has found no significant difference between different-sex couples and same-sex couples that justify discrimination."[46] Psychological research has also documented that the absence of access to the benefits of marriage—for example, property rights, health care decision making, estate planning, tax consequences, spousal privileges in medical emergencies, and coparental adoption of children—constitutes a significant psychosocial stressor for lesbians, gay men, and their families.[47]

The APA's *Resolution on Sexual Orientation and Marriage* and its *Resolution on Sexual Orientation, Parents, and Children*[48] affirmed the Association's opposition to discrimination against adoption by lesbian or gay parents, child custody and visitation, and foster care and reproductive health services. They also make explicit the Association's position that prohibiting same-sex marriage is discriminatory as it unfairly denies such couples, their offspring and their families, the legal, financial, and social advantages of civil marriage. In the same way the American Psychiatric Association (APA) has observed:

> Same sex couples experience several kinds of state-sanctioned discrimination that affect the stability of their relationships. The children of gay and lesbian parents do

not have the same protection that legal marriage affords the children of heterosexual couples. Adoptive and divorced lesbian and gay parents face additional obstacles. An adoptive parent who is lesbian or gay is presumed unfit in many United States jurisdictions. When couples do adopt, usually one parent is granted legal rights, while the other parent may have no legal standing. These obstacles occur, though research has shown that the children raised by lesbian and gay men are as well adjusted as those reared within heterosexual relationships.[49]

Furthermore, based on a comprehensive review of the relevant literature, Charlotte Patterson, a professor of psychology at the University of Virginia, has confirmed that not a single study has found children of lesbian or gay parents to be disadvantaged in any significant respect relative to children of heterosexual parents.... The evidence to date suggests that home environments provided by lesbian and gay parents are as likely as those provided by heterosexual parents to support and enable children's psychosocial growth.[50]

Contrary to critics who claim that the only good parents are heterosexual couples who enact traditional gender roles, the social sciences have clearly demonstrated the value to children of strong, positive, and stable relationships with competent and caring adults regardless of their genders, their sexual orientations, their biological relationship to the child, or whether they practice traditional gender roles.[51]

Other than those couples who seek only civil marriage—for instance, those who have their marriages solemnized by a justice of the peace—marriage as it is currently carried out in religious institutions is a conflation of two processes. One is claimed by religion; the other is a civil contract. To the extent that marriage is a religious institution, one could consider the truly conservative notion to be that governments have no specific interest in marriage per se. That is, a government's interest is in a legal contract that promotes health, protects money, and supports the welfare of children.[52] The Reverend Moody explains:

> The state is not interested in why two people are 'tying the knot,' whether it's to gain money, secure a dynasty or raise children.... The state doesn't care what the commitment of two people is, whether it's for life or as long as both of you love, whether it's sexually monogamous or an open marriage. There is nothing spiritual, mystical or romantic about the state's license to marry—it's a legal contract.[53]

In contrast, religious institutions should be able to choose which kinds of relationships they will encourage and which they will ignore or condemn. The government, however, cannot give preference to one religious viewpoint over another. Conservatives who wish to limit the size and influence of government might more readily attain that goal by limiting the reach of the federal government and not by creating obstacles to equal treatment. They could give the word *marriage* to the church while using other terminology in civil law. If the government got out of the marriage business, religious institutions could choose for themselves what kinds of relationships they wish to recognize, whose relationships they wish to encourage, and whether or under what circumstances religious unions may be dissolved. The government, on the other hand, could adopt its own rules without giving preference to a belief system that is embedded in a religious institution. Legal recognition of such unions (for example, civil unions) could therefore be sought by adult couples regardless of their genders or sexual orientations, whereas marriage would be construed in purely religious terms.

Clarifying the roles of the church (or synagogue) and the government would certainly not prevent religious LGBT people and other advocates from agitating for recognition from within their own religious institutions. It would, however, allow the government to act according to the secular nature of the United States Constitution by providing all adult citizens the opportunity to benefit from legal recognition of their relationships. In short, constitutional amendments that limit marriage to heterosexual couples and prevent government-sponsored recognition of same-sex couples will be ineffective in protecting marriage. One alternate route is to construe marriage as an explicitly religious institution while governments reconsider their interests in the relationships of adult couples, regardless of their genders, sexual orientations, or their procreative intentions.

In the words of the Reverend Peter Gomes, Plummer Professor of Christian Morals and Pusey Minister in the Memorial Church at Harvard University, "To extend the civil right of marriage to homosexuals will neither solve nor complicate the problems already inherent in marriage, but what it will do is permit a whole class of persons…heretofore irrationally deprived of a civil right, both to benefit from and participate in a valuable yet vulnerable institution which in our changing society needs all the help it can get."[54]

In closing, it is important to note that there are institutions that are threatened by same-sex marriage. Contrary to some of the arguments considered here, however, marriage and the family are not at risk. In truth, the institutions that are threatened by same-sex marriage are bigotry, prejudice, and discrimination. These are institutions that we can live without.

## NOTES

1. Family Research Council, "One Flesh: Sample Sermon Outline for Marriage Protection Week 2003" (Washington, DC: Family Research Council, 2004), http://www.frc.org/get.cfm?i=PD03j02&v=PRINT (accessed June 29, 2004).

2. Wendy McDowell, "White Makes Case for Gay Marriage: Argues for 'Basic' Civil Rights…That Go with Loving Someone Else," *Harvard University Gazette*, April 4, 2004, http://www.news.harvard.edu/gazette/2004/04.22/09-white.html (accessed June 30, 2004).

3. Calvin Skaggs and David Van Taylor, *With God on Our Side: George W. Bush and the Rise of the Religious Right*, DVD, episode 6 (Brooklyn, NY: First Run/Icarus Films, 2004).

4. Jean Hardisty, "The *Roe v. Wade* Decision, 1973, and the Charleston, W.Va., Textbook Controversy," *The Public Eye* (Somerville, MA: Political Research Associates, 1993), http://www.publiceye.org/magazine/conshomo.htm (accessed November 10, 2005).

5. Jean Hardisty, "Constructing Homophobia: Colorado's Right-wing Attack on Homosexuals," *The Public Eye* (Somerville, MA: Political Research Associates,1993), http://www.publiceye.org/magazine/conshomo.html (accessed November 10, 2005).

6. Skaggs and Taylor, *With God on Our Side* (see note 3).

7. Earl Shep and Ronald Sutherland, *AIDS and the Church* (Philadelphia: Westminister John Knox Press, 1987), 23.

8. Jean Hardisty, "Constructing Homophobia" (see note 5).

9. As of 2003, the only Fortune 500 company that did not offer domestic partner benefits was the ExxonMobil Corporation. See http//hrc.org/Template.cfm?Section=Home &Template=/ContentManagement/ContentDisplay.cfm&ContentID=18678 (accessed November 10, 2005) for further details.

10. Currently, many Quakers, especially those in England, as well as some Anglican (Episcopalian), Methodist, American Baptist, and United Church of Christ congregations also support LGBT persons in same-sex couples.

11. See Genesis 2:24.

12. James Dobson, *Marriage under Fire* (Sisters, OR: Multnomah Publishers, 2004), www.familyorg/docstudy/bookshelf/a0032438.cfm (accessed June 29, 2004).

13. Gerard Bradley and William Saunders, "DOMA Won't Do It: Why the Constitution Must Be Amended to Save Marriage" (Washington, DC: Family Research Council, 2004), http://www.frc.org/get.cfm?i=BC04D03 (accessed June 29, 2004).

14. Ibid.

15. Matthew Spaulding, "A Defining Moment: Marriage, the Courts, and the Constitution" (Washington, DC: The Heritage Foundation, 2005), http://www.heritage.org/ Research/LegalIssues/bg1759.cfm (accessed October 26, 2005).

16. Family Research Council, "One Flesh" (see note 1).

17. Ibid.

18. Peter Sprigg, "Questions and Answers: What's Wrong with Letting Same-Sex Couples 'Marry?'" (Washington, DC: Family Research Council, 2004), http://www.frc.org/ get.cfm?i=IF03H01&v=PRINT (accessed June 29, 2004).

19. Ibid.

20. According to Dobson, these depictions would confuse children, as he believes them incapable of understanding anything other than traditional families.

21. James Dobson, "Eleven Arguments Against Same-Sex Marriage (Part 1 of 5)," 2004, http://www.family.org/cforum/extras (accessed June 29, 2004).

22. David F. Brown, "Gay Parenting at Heart of Marriage Debate," *United Press International*, July 13 2004, http://www.365gay.com/NewsContent/080703falwellMarriage .htm (accessed June 30, 2004).

23. James A. Bowden, "The Ten Commandments, Partial-Birth Abortion, Terri Schiavo, Homosexual Marriage, CHRISTmas, and the Confederate Battle Flag," *The American Daily*, December 17, 2003, http://www.americandaily.com/article/1771 (accessed June 30, 2004).

24. Thomas Frank, "Failure Is Not an Option, It's Mandatory," *New York Times*, July 16, 2004, http://www.nytimes.com/2004/07/16/opinion/16FRAN.html?th=&pagewanted=print &position= (accessed July 16, 2004).

25. Brown, "Gay Parenting at Heart of Marriage Debate" (see note 22).

26. Nicole Winfield, "Pope Says Same-Sex Unions Degrades Marriage, Says Authorities Must Defend True Marriage," Associated Press State and Local Wire, February 28, 2004.

27. Josef Cardinal Ratzinger and A. S. D. B. Amato, "Considerations Regarding Proposals to Give Legal Recognition to the Unions of Homosexual Persons," 2003, http://www.vatican.va/roman_curia/congregations/cfaith/documents/rc_con_cfaith_doc_200 30731_homosexual-unions_en.htm (accessed December 7, 2005).

28. David Espo, "Senate Scuttles Gay Marriage Amendment," *Associated Press/Yahoo*, July 14, 2004, http://news.yahoo.com/new?tmpl=story&u/ap/20040714/ap_on_co/gay _marriage. (accessed July 14, 2004).

29. Heritage Foundation, "Marriage in the 50 States," http://www.heritage.org/ Research/Family/Marriage50States.cfm (accessed October 26, 2005).

30. Those states included Arkansas, Georgia, Kentucky, Louisiana, Michigan, Missouri, Montana, North Dakota, Ohio, Oklahoma, Oregon, and Utah.

31. Stephen Baskerville, "Strengthening Marriage Through Divorce and Custody Reform," *The Family in America* 18, no. 5 (2004), http://www.profam.org/pub/fia/fia_1805.htm (accessed June 28, 2004).

32. Michael R. Stevenson and Kathryn N. Black, *How Divorce Affects Offspring: A Research Approach* (Boulder, CO: Westview, 1996).

33. Peter Gomes, "For Massachusetts, a Chance and a Choice," *Boston Globe*, February 8, 2004, H11; Howard Moody, "Sacred Rite or Civil Right?" *The Nation*, July 4, 2005, 28–31.

34. James A. Bowden, "Anti-Sodomy = Hate Speech," *The American Daily*, August 20, 2003, http://www.americandaily.com/article/1785 (accessed June 30, 2004).

35. J. Soshanna Ehrlich, *Family Law for Paralegals* (New York: Aspen Law & Business, 1997).

36. William Statsky, *Family Law: The Essentials* (Clifton Park, NY: Delmar Learning, 2004), 3.

37. Ehrlich, *Family Law for Paralegals* (see note 35).

38. National Gay and Lesbian Task Force, "Marriage and Partnership Recognition," http://www.thetaskforce.org/theissues/issue.cfm?issueID=14 (accessed October 26, 2005).

39. Robin A. Buhrke, "Honoring and Protecting Relationships," in *Everyday Activism: A Handbook for Lesbian, Gay, and Bisexual People and Their Allies,* ed. Michael R. Stevenson and Jeannie C. Cogan (New York: Routledge, 2003), 171–92.

40. Statsky, *Family Law*, 3. (see note 36)

41. Moody, "Sacred Rite or Civil Right?" (see note 33).

42. Richard Cohen, "This May Be Good for Marriage," *Washington Post*, November 20, 2003 (accessed October 26, 2005, on LexisNexis).

43. See Stanley Kurtz, "The End of Marriage in Scandinavia," *Weekly Standard*, February 2, 2004, http://www.weeklystandard.com/Content/Public/Articles/000/000/003/660zypwj.asp (accessed August 28, 2006); "Going Dutch: Lessons of the Same-Sex Marriage Debate in the Netherlands," *Weekly Standard*, May 31, 2004, http://www.weekly standard.com/Content/Public/Articles/000/000/004/126qodro.asp (accessed August 28, 2006); "Unhealthy Half Truths: Scandinavian Marriage is Dying," *National Review Online*, May 25, 2004, http://www.nationalreview.com/kurtz/kurtz200405250927.asp (accessed August 28, 2006); "No Explanation: Gay Marriage Has Sent the Netherlands the Way of Scandinavia," *National Review Online*, June 3, 2004, http://www.nationalreview.com/kurtz/kurtz200406030910.asp (accessed August 28, 2006).

44. M. V. Lee Badgett, "Will Providing Marriage Rights to Same-Sex Couples Undermine Heterosexual Marriage? Evidence from Scandinavia and the Netherlands" Council on Contemporary Families and the Institute for Gay and Lesbian Strategic Studies, 2004, http://www.iglss.org/media/files/briefing.pdf (accessed July 14, 2004).

45. American Anthropological Association, "Statement on Marriage and the Family from the American Anthropological Association," 2004, http://www.aaanet.org/press/ma_stmt_marriage.htm (accessed October 27, 2005).

46. R. U. Paige, "Proceedings of the American Psychological Association, Incorporated, for the Legislative Year 2004. Minutes of the Meeting of the Council of Representatives, July 28 and 30, 2004, Honolulu, HI," http://www.apa.org/pi/lgbc/policy/marriage.html (accessed October 27, 2005).

47. R. F. Levant, "Proceedings of the American Psychological Association, Incorporated, for the Legislative Year 1998: Minutes of the Annual Meeting of the Council of Representatives February 20–22, 1998, Washington, D.C., and August 13 and 16, 1998, San Francisco, CA," and "Minutes of the February, June, August, and December 1998. Meetings of the Board of Directors," *American Psychologist* 54 (1999) 605–71, http://www.apa.org/pi/lgbc/policy/archive.html#legal (accessed October 27, 2005).

48. Paige, "Proceedings of the American Psychological Association, Incorporated, for the Legislative Year 2004" (see note 46).

49. American Psychiatric Association, "Support for Legal Recognition of Same-Sex Marriage: Position Statement" (Arlington, VA: American Psychiatric Association, 2005), http://www.psych.org/edu/other_res/lib_archives/archives/200502.pdf (accessed October 28, 2005).

50. Brown, "Gay Parenting at Heart of Marriage Debate" (see note 22).

51. Michael R. Stevenson and Kathryn N. Black *How Divorce Affects Offspring* (see note 32); C. J. Patterson, *Lesbian and Gay Parenting* (Washington, DC: American Psychological Association, 2005), http://www.apa.org/pi/parent.html (accessed October 17, 2006); C. J. Patterson, "Lesbian and Gay Family Issues in the Context of Changing Legal and Social Policy Environments," in *Handbook of Counseling and Psychotherapy with Lesbian, Gay, and Bisexual Clients*, 2nd ed., eds. Ruperto M. Perez, Kurt A. DeBord, and Kathleen J. Bieschke (Washington, DC: American Psychological Association, in press).

52. Ehrlich, *Family Law for Paralegals* (see note 35); Moody, "Sacred Rite or Civil Right?" (see note 33).

53. Howard Moody, "Sacred Rite or Civil Right?" 29 (see note 33).

54. Gomes, "For Massachusetts, a Chance and a Choice" (see note 33).

# 7

# PERFECTUNION.NET: CYBER-ORGANIZING TO DEMOCRATIZE MARRIAGE

*Eric Rofes*

During March 2004, I found myself ruminating over the idea of creating an activist Web site focused on marriage equality. The notion emerged from the specific context of my life at that particular moment. As a longtime activist working on issues affecting the lesbian, gay, bisexual, and transgender (LGBT) community, I had recently grown restless with the ways the movement for marriage equality was developing. When the movement began gaining traction after judges in Massachusetts cleared the way for that state to become the first in the nation to end marriage discrimination, it felt as if the engines behind this effort were primarily legal groups, occasionally working with legislative lobbies. I wondered where grassroots activists were situated on this issue and why such tactics as street activism and civil disobedience seemed to be virtually absent from this movement.

When I was invited to participate in a conference call of national leaders working toward marriage equality that was scheduled to discuss a strategic response to President George W. Bush's call for a constitutional amendment to prevent same-sex marriage, I was shocked and disheartened by what I heard. When the director of a national gay activist group suggested a planned action—a multiracial group of community leaders chaining themselves to the White House gates—his suggestion was followed by a half-dozen responses from other leaders in the movement explaining why such an action was ill-advised at this particular juncture. I found great irony in realizing that movement leaders who repeatedly embrace the rhetoric and romantic memories of the civil rights era, who refer repeatedly in public statements to marches led by Dr. Martin Luther King, Jr., and actions triggered by Rosa Parks, also believe that such actions in today's world would only harm our cause. This position left me alternately mystified, frustrated, and angry as I watched today's LGBT movement leaders attempt to create a marriage movement that relegated authentic movement activism to the margins.

At the same time, I felt that there was a tremendous amount of untapped rage at the grassroots level at the injustices directed at our community nationwide. When Gavin Newsom, the mayor of San Francisco, flung open the doors of City Hall to marry same-sex couples, thousands stood in the rain waiting for the opportunity to be married. This insurgent act by a heterosexual mayor seemed to tap into a deep spirit of rebellion against the injustice of maintaining marriage as a segregated institution. As television stations around the world captured the San Francisco marriage moment, it seemed as if a formerly staid campaign managed by lawyers and lobbyists had finally found its renegade spirit. It was out of this particular spirit that PerfectUnion.net was born.

## THE FORMATION OF THE PERFECTUNION.NET COLLECTIVE

The early vision for the PerfectUnion Web site was quite ambitious and quite different from what the site has turned out to be. Early confidential conversations with potential organizers discussed a series of campaigns that have not yet come to pass as part of the site. We considered the site as a potential vehicle for catalyzing rapid response to ever-evolving news about same-sex marriage. We envisioned having the capacity to launch direct actions and acts of civil disobedience by simply e-blasting a message to our subscribers, urging them to show up at such-and-such a place, engage in this or that action, and bring specific materials to send a specific message. Hence an early dream was for the site to become the triggering agent for actions that the movement's primary organizations had not yet embraced.

We also saw the site as a central repository for information about upcoming actions spearheaded by local marriage equality groups around the nation. From the outset we knew we did not want to replicate the work of such other sites as those of Lambda Legal Defense and the National Gay and Lesbian Task Force. We visited these sites and found that they contained much useful information, often in an accessible format. At the same time we found very few sites that appeared to support actions that might be considered street activism. We hoped PerfectUnion.net might become the site where such activities were posted.

Some early conversations took place about having a page on the site where people might research and post information about the marriage background of those people who argued that democratizing marriage would somehow undermine or threaten heterosexual marriage. We envisioned a place where mainstream journalists might go to find out how many times a specific opponent of same-sex marriage had in fact been married; under what circumstances these marriages took place; and whether the opponent had ever been convicted of domestic violence. In short, we were envisioning a page on the site that might serve as a "truth squad" about the realities of those public officials, commentators, and activists fighting against ending marriage segregation. This is an idea that we continue to discuss in the collective that is PerfectUnion.net.

During the site's planning stages, I held one-on-one meetings with a series of friends. These were individuals whom I hoped to interest in the project to elicit their participation in the collective that would produce and oversee the site. Because

I imagined that the site would eventually engage in controversial activities that might challenge the existing leadership of the movement, I asked for conversations to be kept confidential. I also entertained the possibility early on of keeping secret the names of collective members from the site's viewers, ensuring that the site would be judged by its value rather than its founders and also creating a kind of excitement and cachet around its mystery. In fact, we began the site anonymously, putting forward the working group of PerfectUnion.net as a group of unidentified people of all sexual orientations and genders, working to democratize marriage.

At this point, a friend and colleague with editing experience took on the task of rewriting the copy for the Web site so that it would not be the voice of any individual member; instead the voice would be that of the working group of PerfectUnion.net, and we discussed the tone and other characteristics of this particular voice. After receiving feedback from national community leaders asking who was behind this effort, however, and wondering whether anti-marriage LGBT people might be spearheading the site, we decided to go public and include basic information on the site about the collective or working group members.

The working group was formed in June 2004 with four members and expanded to six over the next year. The initial members included Diane Sabin, a longtime lesbian activist from San Francisco; Eric Rofes, a longtime gay men's health activist from San Francisco; and two men with design skills—Jeff Brandenburg and Dan Derdula—both from the Bay Area. Jeff is also a technologist, contributing technical expertise to the site. We decided to meet face-to-face monthly over lunch or dinner and make sure that meetings were an enjoyable experience for all working group members. We also decided to divide the costs related to the site four ways and share the work tasks of the site. During the first year, Maria Corral-Ribordy, a bisexual activist from Eureka, California, came aboard specifically to lend her skills in Spanish translation to the site. PerfectUnion.net is one of the few marriage resources translated into Spanish; hence it might serve as a useful resource in parts of the nation with large Spanish-speaking populations—for example, in California. Also during the first year, Gilbert Gonzalez joined the collective to lend his proofreading and editing skills to the effort.

After over a year of working together, most members of the working group know one another well. Some were initially friends or work/activist colleagues. Others have come to know one another through working on PerfectUnion.net. Because five of the six members of the working group live in the Bay Area, they have had opportunities to meet together monthly and also socialize together or take part in other organizing projects, sometimes related to same-sex marriage. The sole member of the working group who does not live in the Bay Area—Maria, who lives three hundred miles north of San Francisco—has come to know the other members of the collective by conversing online, attending one of our dinner planning meetings, and participating in a conference workshop focused on the site.

## CREATING THE SITE

There are two key elements regarding the creation of the PerfectUnion.net Web site: (1) the initial site design, including the logo, site navigation format, and design of key pages, and (2) the creation of copy for the site, particularly the Spotlight—the main feature of the site, which is posted on the first day of each month.

The initial site design took several months to conceptualize, plan, and execute. Both Jeff Brandenburg and Dan Derdula brought expertise in the area of Web site design to the process, yet both sought significant input from Diane Sabin and Eric Rofes before actually designing and producing the site. Jeff gained his design and technology skills as a book designer and an information technology manager. Dan gained his design skills through fifteen years of experience as a graphic designer, illustrator, and art director for editorial print productions and multimedia publishing. Diane and Eric developed their skills primarily through several decades of grassroots organizing in diverse fields, including women's music production, gay media work, LGBT pride organizing, and local political activism.

A range of questions had to be answered before the working group might even begin to create and open the site. What should the pages of the site look like and what impression should this Web site give its viewers? How crowded should the pages be? How much should the site rely on the use of photographs, artwork, and other graphic images? What should be the relationship between the Spanish text and the English text?

A series of meetings was held to discuss these issues. These meetings generally took place over lunch at a San Francisco restaurant. Often Jeff and Dan brought sample pages or designs for the others to scrutinize. After viewing other marriage Web sites, the working group members found it easy to agree that they wanted a site that is user-friendly, easy to navigate, and attractive to the eye. Other matters were not quite as simple. For example, discussion of the creation of a logo for the site lasted many months and involved extensive research and repeated iterations before final approval.

The effort to design the logo illustrates the early workings of the collective and its attempt to function by using consensus in decision making. After a review of existing logos for marriage equality organizations, the working group members agreed to look for an image that put the site's commitment to activism front and center. Rather than focus narrowly on graphic images related to romance (wedding rings) or equality (the equal sign), the working group members wanted to incorporate the raised fist—a popular image from the 1960s and 1970s related to movements for black power, women's liberation, and the liberation struggles of developing nations. Yet the designers were unclear about ways to combine a symbol of revolution or activism with the concept of marriage. After arriving at the idea of putting a prominent wedding ring on the ring finger of the raised fist, the designers then had to struggle with the most appropriate typeface and font for use with the PerfectUnion.net name. Work sessions were interspersed with feedback meetings; finally, after perhaps three months, a logo was adopted for the site.

The general look and feel of the site has continued to evolve. The initial design was very spare; the focus was on legibility and clarity. We started out with small spot illustrations that were eventually changed to photos to make the site look more topical and activist. The inclusion of photos has involved a considerable amount of online research and effort to contact the photographers, gain permission to use their photos, and credit them. All the photographers have donated their work in an effort to support the site. We also modified the navigation and organization of the site several times before arriving at the 2005 design. While the logo has remained unchanged, the look and feel of the pages have changed along with the purpose and vision.

Creating the copy for the site was also demanding. Not only was a significant amount of text needed to fill key pages that comprise the site, but the copy had to be approved by other working group members and changes negotiated. At this stage, we were struggling for clarity about the voice we wanted for the working group on the site. For example, while some of the text initially was created with a scolding or judgmental tone, highlighting what the group saw as the weaknesses of current organizing in the marriage equality movement, others felt that we would gain more readers if we adopted a less strident tone, avoiding harsh critiques and judgmental wording. Hence not only the design of the site but also the text went through a series of iterations.

Once the initial site was created, the working group had to create a process for maintaining and updating the site on a regular basis. Since the site's inception in August 2004, we have developed a regular monthly process for maintenance. On the fifteenth of each month, Eric sends an e-mail to the working group, proposing a schedule for the next two weeks that will ensure that the new Spotlight and other updated materials are posted and available by the first day of the new month. He asks for working group members to suggest topics for the upcoming Spotlight. On the twentieth of the month, working group members begin their work in preparation for the next posting. Members review incoming e-mail messages and consider some for posting on the site. One working group member creates the first draft of the Spotlight. Members of the design team prepare new pages for review by other working group members. On the twenty-fourth of the month, all new materials are circulated to the full working group with a forty-eight-hour turnaround time. One working group member copyedits the drafts of all new text to be posted. Feedback is sought before the final drafts are created. On the twenty-sixth of the month, the revised materials—the final drafts—are sent to the working group for final preparation: second copyediting, Spanish-language translation, and preparation of new pages. Current site materials that are due for replacement are prepared for archiving on the site. An e-mail blast alerting people to the new content on the site is prepared for the site's subscribers. On the last day of the month, posting begins and the final touches are put on design, copy, and the e-mail blast.

The working group's process of identifying key organizing issues may vary from month to month. Sometimes a member of the collective comes up with an idea and sends it to the group as a potential topic for the coming month or a later date. At other times the topic emerges from the deep and rich conversations among members of the group online or around a meal at a restaurant. While disputes and disagreements are common within the working group in regard to political and activist topics, the group generally embraces a similar vision of activism on behalf of democratizing marriage.

The process described above has served the working group well thus far. Because of breaking news about the marriage movement that often seems to occur at the end of the month just as we are working on copy for the site, we have had to rethink our work in midstream from time to time. Likewise, when major news events are capturing the public's attention (for example, Hurricane Katrina), we need to somehow link our new Spotlight to the event. While we have had to make allowances for vacations and other events in the lives of working group members, we have not been late with postings and we have always sent e-mail blasts to subscribers on the first of each month.

## SAMPLE SPOTLIGHTS

A look at a number of the Spotlights published on the Web site captures the site's current primary purposes: to raise important issues related to the marriage movement's values, strategies, and tactics and to provide a space on the Web where activists might engage with critical and reflective thought about the same-sex marriage movement. Below are four different Spotlights that capture the critical issues with which PerfectUnion.net engages:

*"Who Stands with Us?" (February 2005)*[1]

Isn't it amazing that most of the most prominent liberal and progressive organizations, media outlets, and leaders have not come out boldly in support of same-sex marriage? Especially since Election Day, has anyone besides our Working Group noted that those who stand for justice and freedom and human rights are mostly silent on the issue of same-sex marriage? While states are changing their constitutions to mandate blatant discrimination and bigotry, who outside the LGBT community is standing up and saying "This is wrong, unjust, and must be fought"? When an individual or community is attacked in an extreme manner, isn't it simply caring and humane to stand up in visible solidarity? Why isn't that happening now? Where are all those queer-friendly celebrities? Where is a strong and visible liberal religious coalition? Where are all the progressive groups that include lesbian and gay rights in their laundry list of concerns?

   Certainly we have some supporters and there have been a number of elected officials, lawyers, journalists and some groups that have stood up for ending marriage discrimination. Yet as more and more states are targeted, and more and more people are formally relegated to second-class citizenship, we expect much, much stronger and vocal support from our allies.

   The Working Group at perfectunion.net believes this movement needs a concrete organizing plan to marshal support from our allies. We need people with visibility to go public on this issue. We need political leaders who know that our cause is just to state it boldly and unequivocally.

   We are clearly living through, in the words of Suzanne Pharr, the time of the Right. Perhaps now more than ever, it is critically important for all of us to get clear on who we stand with and who stands with us. During a time of such unrelenting attacks on democracy and equality, it's time for all to take a stand. The old union motto rings true today: There is no neutral here.

*"Heterosexuality in Crisis" (March 2005)*[2]

When marriage equality activists debate pro-discrimination leaders, the debate frequently reaches the point where we shake our heads in frustration and say "How does a gay person's marriage pose any kind of threat to your marriage? How does my family undermine your family? How can two women getting married be seen as an attack on heterosexual marriage?" Many of us who are fighting discrimination have a very difficult time seeing how democratizing marriage does anything at all to cross-sex married couples. A casual look at today's television shows suggests that heterosexuality may be experiencing a crisis of meaning. One new popular television show, *Desperate Housewives*, captures the antics of suburban couples and paints a portrait of frustration, deception, infidelity, and unhappiness in lily-white American suburbs. The show makes the recent film *The Stepford Wives* look mild. Reality television shows focus on superficial dating and artificial marriages, wife-swapping, family exchanges, and the plight of poor families who are rendered homeless by our nation's continuing high unemployment rate.

As statistics continue to reveal a high level of failing marriages—especially in the South and other conservative areas—is it any wonder some heterosexuals are skittish about themselves and their marriages? Both the reality (statistics) and representation (television) offer evidence that heterosexuality itself may be a problematic institution.

We believe that current shifts in our nation concerning the economy, sex roles, the role of the state, and education reform have created an era when many heterosexuals of all races and classes are anxious about whether they can fulfill the expectations that were drilled into them since childhood.

We are governed by an administration that continues to discourage women from working outside the home, while promoting economic policies that make it impossible for families with a single wage-earner to thrive. Perhaps we are living through an era when both heterosexual men and women are given very mixed messages about their positions in the workforce, their relationships with one another, and their roles in a partnership called "marriage."

For these reasons, we believe it is important for activists working to democratize marriage to deeply consider the underlying anxieties and fears motivating the movement that opposes marriage equality. While it is never fun to be the scapegoat, our work may be stronger if we recognize some of the underlying social dynamics that are driving our opponents' efforts.

*"Who Should Carry the Message for the Same-Sex*
*Marriage Movement?" (September 2005)[3]*

Recently, useful and productive public conversations have taken place focused on diverse responses to these questions: "What is the best way to articulate the importance of supporting same-sex marriage? What arguments are strongest and which ones will convince the 'mushy middle' of voters to come over to our side?" At PerfectUnion.net, we believe an equally important question involves "Who should carry the message for the same-sex marriage movement?" and we hope to open up discussion about this matter right now.

Many activists believe that LGBT people are the best spokespersons for this issue. These activists see the value of having, for example, Chinese Americans speaking to Chinese Americans on this topic, so they believe that campaigns must specifically identify LGBT Chinese Americans and send them in to talk to their home communities.

While we share in this belief, we go one step further. We believe that it is critical to have the voices of heterosexuals front and center in our movement. In fact, we believe that, in many cases, it may be more strategic and productive to send out heterosexuals to speak to community groups and the media on this topic than to send LGBT people.

We are sure this raises all sorts of questions for many organizers. Don't LGBT people need to keep control of this movement and prioritize our own voices? Can we trust heterosexuals to do the heavy lifting in this movement? Isn't it discriminatory to deliberately identify and deploy straight people in this effort?

We believe that what some see as "discriminatory" might also make for great strategy. And we want to encourage the same-sex marriage movement to put resources and energy behind creating cadres of heterosexuals to go before community groups, neighborhood associations, political clubs, and the media as savvy and bold voices in support of democratizing marriage.

In fact, we believe that we should draw on queer creativity and create really unusual and compelling outreach teams that might surprise people and grab public attention. We want to see teams of "Dames by the Dozen Defeating Discrimination" in every local community. These would be heterosexual women over the age of seventy who would form an affinity group in support of same-sex marriage. They might be white-haired women who have gay pals or elderly women who have worked in the women's movement alongside lesbians for many years. Together they'd go through training sessions in public speaking and in strategic arguments in support of same-sex marriage. We'd love to see these savvy, skilled, and articulate women arrive en masse to an antigay rally and take on the arguments of our opponents with power and style. Plus we'd love to see their coordinated fashions and, especially, their hats!

We encourage the formation of "Family First" teams of public speakers on behalf of same-sex marriage. These teams might be formed like the teams of "Family Feud," and be a group of people who share a gay or lesbian relative and can speak to inclusiveness, love, and true "family values." We'd love to see angry parents of all races, classes, and ethnicities speaking out against anyone trying to make their lesbian daughter's family into second-class citizens. We'd thrill at seeing heterosexual men standing up for their queer brother and insisting that all people receive the right to full participation in the institution of marriage.

We advocate for the formation of special "Kids Say the Darndest Things" teams comprised of ten- to fifteen-year-old children standing up against the antigay bigots and explaining in simple kids' language, why discrimination is wrong. Often children can capture the core spirit of moral questions with much greater impact than many adults. Wouldn't it be wonderful to issue a call, see which young people arrive, and, after training and preparation, set teams of kids off to speak to the media about these important voter ballot questions? Of course we believe that all people putting forward arguments to support same-sex marriage need to be fully prepared with current legal and legislative information and with basic strategic thinking and techniques of effective argument and debate. We also certainly support mixed teams of straight and LGBT people taking on speaking engagements together.

At the same time, we believe that drawing in cadres of volunteer speakers who are not identified as LGBT people might make for very effective organizing and send a very important message: These campaigns are not only about gay people—they are about democracy, human rights, and basic fairness and decency. All people have a stake in social justice campaigns.

*"In This Movement for the Long Haul" (October 2005)*[4]

September brought terrible hurricanes to Louisiana and other Gulf Coast states, but it was also a time for unpredictable storms for our movement to democratize marriage. While waiting for a landmark court decision in Washington State, which many expect to pave the way for same-sex marriage on the West Coast, we experienced a series of dramatic victories and defeats in California and Massachusetts.

California's statewide organization Marriage Equality, working with powerful and strategic lesbian and gay legislators and their allies, won passage of legislation to create gender-neutral marriage in the state. Almost immediately, Governor Arnold Schwarzenegger announced his veto, which came two weeks later despite an intensive lobbying and media campaign that attempted to change his position.

In Massachusetts, activists felt their hearts drop when the State Attorney General, Tom Reilly (running for governor), approved a voter ballot initiative which would attempt to do an end run around the state court decision legalizing marriage and squelch the right of same-sex couples to marry. Just days later, the state legislature, in a lopsided vote, stood firmly against a bill that they'd narrowly approved a year earlier, that would have put same-sex marriage before that state's voters.

Our victories show the value of electing competent leaders to champion our cause and also of the grunt work of grassroots organizing. Both Massachusetts and California stand as impressive case studies in lobbying, constituency mobilization, and collaboration between organizational and legislative leaders. While those of us in the Working Group wish California would adopt some of the more militant direct action tactics that have been used in Massachusetts over the past three years, this does not stop us from praising the legislative and lobbying talents of our state leaders.

This kind of work leaves us vulnerable to a roller coaster of highs and lows as we do the hard but valuable task of changing the hearts and minds of Americans. Central to our effectiveness will be our individual and collective ability to ride the waves of both victories and defeats, keeping our eye on the ultimate objective: democratizing all of our nation's institutions and making marriage an institution that is accessible to same-sex couples. How can we sustain the constant changes without having our hearts broken, our lives wrecked, and our spirits burned out?

We hope to open up a conversation about this topic among same-sex movement activists. Just like sustaining the horrors of Katrina is taking both personal and collective fortitude and hard work, sustaining the roller coaster ride that is our movement, will require at least three things of all of us. First, celebrate and grieve, but place victories and defeats in context. It is so important for all of us—individually and with our fellow activists—to develop meaningful rituals to celebrate achievements and grieve/gripe/moan about our losses. These rituals, if done right, are places where we can unleash our emotions and find our way back to a place of balance. We need witnesses to the emotional upheavals we all experience in this movement. At the same time, effective rituals place victories and defeats in their proper context—on a timeline leading to our ultimate victory.

Second, do not mistake a victory for mission accomplished. If the last twenty years has taught us anything, it is that social change victories remain vulnerable to changing political tides. The erosion of the hard-won gains of the Civil Rights Movement and the movement for women's reproductive rights, presents us with case studies in the need for constant vigilance and the hazards of a populace believing that certain victories have been won and are therefore secure forever.

Third, keep your eye on the prize. Remember that long-term social change takes time. While a veto by a governor might feel cataclysmic right now, keep in mind this is only one chapter in a long story that will ultimately have a happy ending. Keep the faith and keep the ultimate objective in mind.

Our struggle will succeed in the long run, but to do so requires that some of us—many of us—find the way to make a commitment to being activists for the long haul. This isn't only about the current moment, our current romantic relationship, or the current collection of political leaders who either trounce on our humanity or stand tall with us. It's about creating and institutionalizing change and about making room for social justice that will survive the ebb and flow of politics.

## ANALYSIS

The working group at PerfectUnion.net feels it has only started to fulfill its vision of creating a site that would infuse activism into the marriage equality movement. We receive about a hundred visitors to our site each day and we have seventy-five regular subscribers.

After a few months of activity, working group members came to realize that the site is most useful as a space in which activists working to democratize marriage anywhere in the nation might reflect deeply on their values, strategies, and tactics. We came to this understanding through a series of processes. First, those of us who are experienced activists know that social movements—particularly swiftly unfolding movements like the same-sex marriage movement—rarely have time and space for thoughtful consideration of these matters. Instead, it is more common for participants to rush from activity to activity putting out fires but never drawing back and looking at big-picture questions or complex matters. When we queried colleagues in the movement, reflection and analysis were cited as key gaps in the structure of the movement that a Web site might help to fill.

Second, we confronted a serious reality: our ability to use the site to generate acts of civil disobedience or direct action is seriously hampered because of the limited human resources represented by the collective. The six people in the working group do not have additional time and energy to lead major demonstrations; all of our available time and energy is focused on producing the Web site. Hence we have recently begun to search aggressively for additional people to serve as members of the working group.

Finally, we came to recognize that there is something specific to this movement at this particular time that discourages anything that looks like civil disobedience or direct action arising from grassroots community-based groups. While actions by public officials—in this case mayors—in San Francisco, California, and New Paltz, New York, can be seen as a specific form of civil disobedience, the organized, protracted civil disobedience campaigns that were the hallmark of the black civil rights movement are almost absent from the movement to democratize marriage. The PerfectUnion.net working group would like to see extensive, coordinated campaigns blanketing the nation that use civil disobedience as a way to shift public opinion. For example, organized actions by county clerks or justices of the peace providing marriage certificates and ceremonies to couples without regard to the gender mix, or coordinated campaigns in which gay and lesbian couples apply *en masse* for licenses, get turned away, and respond with identical statements about democracy and equal rights, often in front of a media spotlight.

We were recently struck by the limited response to the California governor's veto of a bill permitting same-sex marriage that had been approved by the California legislature. After attending the 2004 and 2005 Creating Change conferences sponsored by the National Gay and Lesbian Task Force, we found ourselves wondering whether those LGBT people most drawn to acts of civil disobedience and direct action were not, in fact, standing on the sidelines looking skeptically at the same-sex marriage movement. We also wondered whether those who were actively involved in the marriage equality movement were not LGBT people more comfortable with legal cases, legislative lobbying, and press conferences than with sit-ins, mass marches, and acts of civil disobedience.

Hence, at this stage in its development, the working group of PerfectUnion.net sees the site as a place to work through complex discussions and debates related to efforts to democratize marriage. For example, when a lesbian activist in Los Angeles issued a call for a march on Washington, D.C., in 2008, the working group devoted a considerable amount of space on the site to the original document—gay newspapers had edited it down considerably—and also researched the perspectives of former lead organizers of earlier LGBT marches. A spirited back-and-forth discussion took place among our readers about the relative costs and benefits of such a march.

A range of cyber-based efforts has emerged over the past decade aimed at promoting one version or another of activism. While we originally embraced a vision for PerfectUnion.net that approximates the activist work of moveon.org or Focus on the Family, and hoped to develop the capacity to serve as a mass organizing vehicle focused on same-sex marriage, this is not where we are, at least at this point in time. Our page now has neither the focus nor intent of these other sites. Instead of serving as an organizing vehicle (like moveon.org on the Left and Focus on the Family on the Right), we focus on promoting dialogue and debate within the movement to democratize marriage. We have become a sounding board for activists working in the trenches of the marriage movement, a place where they might come to raise issues, work through challenging dilemmas, and discuss tough controversies.

As we continue to work on the PerfectUnion.net Web site, the working group continues to struggle with key questions related to the group's original vision. While our initial fear was that a cyber-activist project would cater to a large but privileged group of primarily educated and middle-class activists, we have found that an even greater concern is that activists in grassroots social change movements continue to be preoccupied with putting out fires and handling the next crisis facing their cause and have little time for personal reflection and strategic analysis. When we recently hosted a workshop about the Web site at Creating Change, the National Gay and Lesbian Task Force's annual conference, the assembled participants—activists and leaders working toward marriage equality in different locations in the country—expressed their enjoyment in having a time and space for protracted discussion of some of the key issues highlighted by our Spotlights. We encouraged them to subscribe to the site, just as we do each month in our e-blast. Because we believe that such discussions—involving reflecting, analyzing case studies, critical thinking, mediating disputes, and sharing stories and visions—benefit organizing efforts in any movement, we continue to commit ourselves to our work at PerfectUnion.net.

## NOTES

1. Perfect Union Working Group, "Who Stands With Us?" February 2005 Spotlight, http://www.perfectunion.net/PDF/SpotlightFebruary05.pdf (accessed September 4, 2006).

2. Ibid., "Heterosexuality In Crisis," March 2005 Spotlight, http://www.perfectunion .net/PDF/SpotlightMarch05.pdf (accessed September 4, 2006).

3. Ibid., "Who Should Carry the Message for the Same-Sex Marriage Movement?" September 2005 Spotlight, http://www.perfectunion.net/PDF/SpotlightSeptember05.pdf (accessed September 4, 2006).

4. Ibid., "In This Movement for the Long Haul…," October 2005 Spotlight, http://www .perfectunion.net/PDF/SpotlightOctober05.pdf (accessed September 4, 2006).

# 8

# FROM GAY BASHING TO GAY BAITING: PUBLIC OPINION AND NEWS MEDIA FRAMES FOR GAY MARRIAGE

*Seth Goldman and Paul R. Brewer*

"Gay marriage," said one Massachusetts state senator, "has begun and life has not changed for the citizens of the commonwealth, with the exception of those who can now marry who could not before."[1] That legislator was Senator Brian P. Lees, the Republican minority leader. In 2004, he had cosponsored a state constitutional amendment to overturn the court-mandated recognition of same-sex marriage. The amendment passed its first legislative vote. Just a year later, Lees changed his mind and voted against the amendment on its required second vote. This time it failed.

The legalization of marriage for gay couples in Massachusetts is a clear marker of how far the gay rights movement has come. Unlike Lees, however, many Americans who oppose gay marriage have stuck to their position on the issue. National public opinion polls show clear and consistent majorities against legalizing marriage for gay couples. Moreover, a dozen state constitutional amendments banning gay marriage won at the ballot box in 2004, and another one prevailed in 2005. The public's continued opposition to gay marriage is particularly striking given the impressive increase in tolerance for gay people and the dramatic growth in public support for gay rights in other areas.

In this chapter, we look at how political elites—elected officials, prominent activists, religious leaders, and the like—have attempted to shape public opinion about gay marriage by *framing*, or defining, the issue through the news media. Specifically, we examine progay and anti–gay marriage frames in national news media coverage (and in special cases, local news media coverage) from the rise of the issue on the political agenda in the mid-1990s through the 2004 presidential campaign and beyond. We find that the overt gay bashing of the 1990s is largely absent from more recent mainstream news coverage. Instead of attacking homosexuality and gay people directly, public officials and political candidates who oppose gay marriage tend to frame their position in terms of protecting "traditional moral values" and "the institution of marriage"; they focus their attacks on "activist judges." Conservative activists and religious leaders continue to attack homosexuality in explicit terms, but even their efforts to do so have waned over the years. A new norm of overt tolerance for gays represents a success for the gay rights movement. Nevertheless, opponents of gay marriage still engage in gay baiting, or the use of appeals that may implicitly invoke antigay sentiments.

As for gay rights activists and their allies in elected office—who often endorse civil unions but not gay marriage—they tend to argue their case on the basis of civil equality, emphasizing the principle that gay couples should have the same legal benefits as do heterosexual couples. These activists have done relatively little to build on another theme that appeared in the early years of the debate: namely, the love that partners in gay couples have for each other and their children. Gay marriage supporters sometimes cast their opponents as engaging in political ploys to get votes, but they rarely rebut the anti–gay marriage or traditional morality frame in direct terms.

## PUBLIC OPINION, MEDIA FRAMING, AND GAY RIGHTS

Public tolerance of gays grew substantially from the early 1990s onward. Half the respondents in the 1992 National Election Studies survey openly expressed negative feelings toward "gay men and lesbians"; in 2004, only a third did so. Public support for various sorts of gay rights also grew during this period. The percentages of Americans supporting gay rights in terms of employment nondiscrimination and military service increased by double-digit margins during this period; as of 2004, 76 percent of National Election Studies respondents favored the former and 81 percent favored the latter.[2] Similarly, public opinion on civil unions shifted from clear majority opposition to a roughly even split in just a four-year span. In 2000, Gallup respondents opposed civil unions 54 percent to 42 percent; in May 2004, those percentages were 48 percent and 49 percent respectively. Public support for gay marriage, on the other hand, remained low through 2005. In polls conducted by major polling organizations, including Gallup and the Pew Research Center for the People and the Press, opponents outnumber proponents by as much as a two-to-one margin.[3]

Such variations in public support appear to be rooted in how Americans think about different categories of gay rights. Generally speaking, people base their opinions about political issues on multiple considerations, including abstract principles as well as feelings toward particular groups.[4] In the case of gay rights, the foundations of public opinion include feelings toward gays and lesbians, beliefs about traditional morality, and beliefs about equality.[5] The mental formulas that Americans use to weigh these building blocks of opinion, however, vary from one class of rights to another. For example, Americans think about gay marriage in different terms from those they use to think about gays in the military and employment nondiscrimination laws. Compared to their opinions about the latter, their opinions about the former are rooted more strongly in their feelings about gays and lesbians and their moral beliefs but less strongly in their beliefs about equality.[6] Americans also view civil unions and gay marriage in different terms. In explaining their opinions about the two policies, they are less likely to describe gay marriage as an equal rights issue and more likely to see it as a moral values issue.[7]

With these patterns in mind, we look at the frames transmitted from political elites to the public through the news media. Particular frames for a given issue focus attention on particular ways to think about that issue. For example, an equal rights frame for gay rights suggests that people should base their opinions about the topic on egalitarian principles, whereas a traditional morality frame suggests that they should base their views on their moral values.[8] A frame that revolves around gay bashing highlights antigay prejudice as the appropriate foundation for forming an opinion; a frame that revolves around gay baiting may do the same in a subtler way.

Gay rights supporters and opponents regularly introduce frames into public debate in the hope that the news media will convey these frames to the public and that audience members in turn will adopt the frames in thinking about the issue at hand. Thus the media serve as conduits through which elite frames flow.[9] During the mid-1990s, two of the most common frames in media coverage of gay rights were the progay rights equal rights frame ("gay rights are equal rights") and the anti–gay rights traditional morality frame ("gay rights undermine traditional morality").[10] These frames have also appeared in recent coverage of gay marriage and civil unions.[11]

Exposure to frames in media coverage can shape how Americans think about gay rights issues. One experimental study demonstrated that exposure to a news story framing gay rights as equal rights led participants to describe their own opinions in equality-based language; the same study found that exposure to a news story framing gay rights in moral terms led participants to adopt morality-based language in explaining their thoughts about the issue.[12] Another experiment found that presenting either an equal rights frame for civil unions or a special rights frame for gay marriage shaped the way in which participants discussed legal recognition for same-sex couples.[13]

## NEWS MEDIA FRAMES FOR GAY MARRIAGE

We examine news media coverage to capture the nature and evolution of the frames used in the debate over gay marriage. Given that the issue began to receive attention from the national media in the mid-1990s, we start with that period and end in the fall of 2005. We focus on network television news because the news programs of ABC, CBS, and NBC have the largest audiences of any news sources. We also look at national newspapers with especially large circulations and correspondingly major roles in shaping the national debate—such as the *New York Times*, the *Washington Post*, and *USA Today*. We supplement our examination of the national news media with references to local coverage in states where key events took place—most notably Hawaii, Vermont, and Massachusetts.

As the title of this chapter makes clear, we are especially interested in the transition from gay bashing to gay baiting on the part of opponents of gay marriage. Again, we define *gay bashing* as the use of explicit attacks on homosexuality or gays and lesbians to justify opposition to gay marriage. For example, arguments against gay marriage that revolve around attacks on homosexuality as an abomination or on gays and lesbians as morally unfit to be parents constitute gay bashing. *Gay baiting*, by contrast, uses implicit appeals that do not target homosexuality or gays per se but may trigger antigay prejudice by association. For example, arguments against gay marriage that attack activist judges or cite the virtues of heterosexual marriage may evoke antigay sentiments by implication. The first example casts gay marriage as an illegitimate, even dangerous, creation of the courts; the second draws an implicit— and unfavorable—comparison to gay marriage. Gay bashing and gay baiting differ in that the latter invokes antigay sentiments through language that is more amenable to the growing norms of overt tolerance for gays and intolerance for gay bashing. This distinction between gay bashing and gay baiting parallels the distinction between explicit appeals to racism, which were once common in American politics but have since subsided in the face of changing norms, and implicit appeals to racism, which endure in contemporary American politics.[14]

We also look at two pro–gay marriage frames, one of which is more common than the other. The dominant pro–gay marriage frame is based on the core American value of equality—the notion that everyone deserves equal protection under the law and access to the same opportunities and legal benefits. The second, less prominent, frame emphasizes the love within gay couples and the love of gay couples for their children. These frames often overlap; nevertheless, it is useful to distinguish between them.

## HAWAII: GAY MARRIAGE EMERGES AS AN ISSUE

In 1993, two years after several same-sex couples filed suit against the state of Hawaii because they were denied marriage licenses, the Hawaii Supreme Court ruled that barring gays from marriage might constitute sex discrimination. It thus required the state to show a "compelling interest" for continuing its ban. The court sent the case back to trial court to rehear the state's arguments. In the wake of *Baehr v. Lewin*, Joseph Melilio saw an opportunity to validate the love that he and his partner, Pat Lagon, had shared for fifteen years: "People get married when they love each other and to show other people that they love each other."[15] The Reverend Lou Sheldon, chairman of the Traditional Values Coalition, offered a different view: "The Bible is very clear about licentiousness. You cannot enter the kingdom of God if you're a liar, a drunkard, a murderer, an adulteress, a fornicator or a homosexual."[16] Such conservatives as Sheldon warned that gay marriage was a threat that could spread from Hawaii to the mainland.

National news coverage in 1993 was scant compared to coverage in the late 1990s, particularly when it came to the big three television networks. Nevertheless, this early coverage included all the key frames that appeared in subsequent debate. Such local coverage as that in the *Honolulu Star-Bulletin* tended to explore the issue in greater depth; for example, such coverage included more diverse views from religious leaders. Still, local and national coverage were more alike than different.

Gay marriage opponents showed their willingness to attack gays in direct terms. Robert Knight, the senior director of cultural studies at the Family Research Council (FRC), compared gay marriage to pedophilia: "If states allow two men or two women to marry, why stop there? Why not three men? Three women? A man and a boy?"[17] Even in 1993, however, mainstream coverage suggested that outright name calling was unacceptable. Take, for example, a report on an ABC morning news show:

> Man on beach: Screw those queers. That's what's wrong with this world is these faggots.
>
> John Hockenberry (reporter): So that's what you have to deal with?
>
> Pat Lagon: Oh, that's what we deal with, uh-huh. Some people are just not educated, that's all.
>
> Hockenberry: The possible legalization of gay marriage by Hawaii's courts has produced more than just outrage. There's an organized political effort to stop it.
>
> Mike Gabbard, founder, Stop Homosexuality Now: It is outrageous that a group of judges on our Supreme Court have come along and fanned the flames of this social nightmare.
>
> Hockenberry: Mike Gabbard is a Christian fundamentalist and founder of a group called Stop Homosexuality Now. He goes door to door and says he has the Bible and Hawaii voters on his side.[18]

Although the reporter signaled disapproval of a strikingly overt instance of gay bashing—the reference to gays as "faggots"—he presented Gabbard's reference to a "social nightmare" in more neutral terms, casting this appeal as part of an "organized political effort."

Other gay marriage opponents took a subtler approach: instead of directly attacking gays and lesbians, they argued that heterosexual marriage is the best environment for raising children. For example, the deputy attorney general of Hawaii, Rick Eichor, claimed that a "child raised by his or her biological parents has a better opportunity for development."[19] He added, "This is not a case of gay bashing." A trial court judge, Kevin S. C. Chang, rejected Eichor's logic, ruling that the state had "failed to present sufficient credible evidence…that the public interest in the well-being of children and families, or the optimal development of children would be adversely affected by same-sex marriages."[20]

Gay marriage opponents responded by framing the judiciary as undemocratic. After the 1993 ruling, Hawaii's attorney general, Robert Marks, said, "I'm no homophobe, but I think the issue should be left to the legislature."[21] When the state lost again in 1996, Sheldon called the ruling "another indication of judicial tyranny…. It's almost like an imperial edict from an emperor, against the people."[22] In drafting a proposed constitutional amendment to overturn the decision, state legislators wrote "that the question of whether or not to issue marriage licenses to couples of the same sex is a fundamental policy issue to be decided by the elected representatives of the people and not by judicial fiat."[23]

The news media presented the case for gay marriage through the testimony of gay couples. These couples argued that their love deserved recognition on par with heterosexual relationships; they also cited the legal benefits denied them. Genora Dancel, partner of Nina Baehr, said, "We want to get married like everyone else. When they come to that part in their life, they fall in love, they want to create a family, they want it legalized…and [they want] the 200 benefits that go along with it."[24] David Dudley, who had traveled to Hawaii with his partner in the hope of getting married, said that gay marriage "just means we get the same legal sanctions that all other couples that are married get. If one of us should die, the other would have the right to inherit. If one should get ill, the other could visit in [the] hospital and not be thrown out by family members."[25] Melilio and Lagon argued that domestic partner benefits without marriage would amount to "second-class citizenship."[26]

The news media seldom quoted progay activists. When such activists succeeded in gaining coverage, they tended to frame marriage as an equal rights issue comparable to civil rights for African Americans. Following the 1996 ruling, David Smith, spokesperson for the Human Rights Campaign, said, "We've crossed a very important bridge in terms of treating people fairly as a matter of public policy.... That is the hallmark of American culture, treating people equally and fairly."[27] "Thirty years ago it took courts with courage to tear down racial discrimination in marriage," added Evan Wolfson, who worked on the case. "In that tradition, Judge Chang struck a blow against sex discrimination."[28]

Rarely did anyone challenge the antigay traditional morality frame; indeed, even religious leaders who were in favor of gay rights tended to be silent on this point. The Reverend Jon Bullock, pastor of the Rainbow of Aloha Metropolitan Community Church, argued that gay marriage "has nothing to do with religion.... We take a strong civil rights and social justice stand."[29] Lagon, however, begged to differ: "The Bible to me is of love. Everything that comes out of their Bible is hate: Fear this, hate this."[30]

## DOMA: A CONSERVATIVE RESPONSE TO HAWAII, 1996

In the spring of 1996, United States Representative Bob Barr (R-GA) introduced the so-called Defense of Marriage Act (DOMA). The act mandated that "no State...shall be required...to give effect to any public act, record, or judicial proceeding of any other State...respecting a relationship between persons of the same sex that is treated as a marriage under the laws of such other State." The assumption behind the bill was that the United States Constitution's Full Faith and Credit Clause would require other states to recognize gay marriages performed in Hawaii. The bill also defined marriage under federal law as "only a legal union between one man and one woman as husband and wife." By the fall, the Senate and House had passed the bill by overwhelming margins.[31]

As the name of the bill suggests, DOMA proponents viewed the Hawaii case with alarm. "Out of Hawaii has come Pearl Harbor Two," said Sheldon of the Traditional Values Coalition.[32] With the war metaphor came more gay bashing. Barr engaged in a particularly vivid effort at such, warning that "the flames of hedonism, the flames of narcissism, the flames of self-centered morality are licking at the very foundation of our society, the family unit."[33] Representative Steve Largent (R-OK) argued that "no culture that has ever embraced homosexuality has ever survived," and his colleague, Representative Tom Coburn (R-OK), proclaimed, "We hear about diversity, but we do not hear about perversity. The real debate is about homosexuality and whether or not we sanction homosexuality in this country.... Homosexuality is immoral...it is based on perversion...it is based on lust."[34] DOMA supporters did relatively little to frame the bill in terms of child rearing, although Gary Bauer, president of the Family Research Council, drew the connection: "At stake," he warned, "is nothing less than the future of the nation and the well-being of our children."[35]

For their part, opponents of DOMA cast the bill as an attempt to score political points during a presidential election year (the Republican presidential nominee, Robert Dole, sponsored DOMA in the Senate). They also called it unnecessary and discriminatory. Senator Edward Kennedy (D-MA) said that the bill was "cynically calculated to try and inflame the public eight weeks before the November 5th election."[36] Senator Barbara Boxer (D-CA) added that "we have constitutional experts who say states already have the right not to recognize [gay marriages] from out of state. So I view it as just a very cruel position, an unnecessary piece of legislation."[37] Gay rights activists called the bill a "wedge issue." Candice Gingrich, the lesbian sister of the Speaker of the House, Newt Gingrich (R-GA), said that "the raising of this issue now, at the national level, is nothing more than election-year scapegoating of one group of Americans." To her brother, she said, "Stop this congressional gay bashing."[38]

Two openly gay House members, Barney Frank (D-MA) and Steven Gunderson (R-WI), not only argued against DOMA but *for* gay marriage. "I defend the morality of the position that it's a good thing for two people to love each other, and even better if they're ready to commit to each other," said Frank.[39] Gunderson argued that he and his partner, who had been together for thirteen years, deserved the same health benefits "as individuals around here with second and third wives."[40]

President Bill Clinton's political dance around DOMA anticipated his successor's careful posturing on a federal constitutional amendment to ban gay marriage. First, Clinton said that he would "look carefully" at the bill.[41] After attacking the bill with the same arguments used by opponents of DOMA, he ultimately signed it.[42] A White House spokesman, Mike McCurry, described Clinton's reasoning in vague terms: "He believes this is a time when we need to do things to strengthen the American family, and that's the reason why he's taken this position."[43] Two years later, voters in Hawaii passed a constitutional amendment that allowed but did not require the state legislature to ban gay marriage, thereby removing the right of appeal from state courts and foreclosing, at least for the time, the scenario that DOMA was intended to prevent.

## VERMONT AND THE CREATION OF CIVIL UNIONS

Vermont's debate over legal recognition of gay couples began in 1998, as a case filed by several such couples who had been denied marriage licenses wound its way to the Vermont Supreme Court. In 2000 the court found the state ban on same-sex marriage licenses unconstitutional and ordered the legislature to provide a remedy. Given that the court did not specifically mandate gay marriage, the debate quickly turned to civil unions.

The frames within national news coverage and the *Burlington Free Press* followed similar patterns. Opponents of civil unions often defended themselves against perceived charges of intolerance. State Senator Thomas Bahre, a Republican, simply said, "I don't hate gays and lesbians."[44] After voting against the civil unions bill, State Representative Gary Richardson (also a Republican) said, "I'll believe to the depths of my soul that I discriminate against no one, nor have I ever."[45] "We're tolerant," argued Dick Lambert, a dairy farmer who designed "Take Back Vermont" signs that sprouted up all over the state, "but they've got to see. We don't go into their bedroom and tell them what to do, but don't shove it down our throats."[46]

Despite claims to the contrary, gay bashing reared its head from time to time in Vermont's debate over civil unions. At televised House hearings, opponents cited the Bible as deeming gay sex "an abomination."[47] "God made Adam and Eve," said one speaker, "he didn't make Adam and Steve."[48] In a full-page advertisement in the *Burlington Free Press*, opponents attacked "the insufferable hubris of the narcissistic gay lobby that would place personal pleasures before public order."[49] Rallying with 150 marchers on the statehouse steps, a Republican presidential candidate, Alan Keyes, presented gays as seeking to "indulge their sexual passions."[50] A state representative, Neil Randall, called the passage of the civil unions bill an act of "social rape upon an unwilling citizenry."[51] Protesters with bowed heads and placards reading "SIN is a disgrace to any people" picketed one of the first civil union ceremonies.[52]

As in Hawaii, however, mainstream figures generally shunned name calling. When Fred Phelps, the pastor of the Westboro Baptist Church in Topeka, Kansas, led 10 demonstrators waving signs that read, "God hates fags," he was met by 250 counterprotesters. The Reverend Craig Benson of the Greater Burlington Evangelical Association condemned him: "We can in no way support the self-serving and self-appointed campaign of hatred that Fred Phelps represents."[53] After a Republican state representative, Nancy Sheltra, said on the House floor that civil unions would "encourage anal sex and STDs and AIDS," at least a dozen legislators walked out.[54]

Milder frames trumped blatant gay bashing. Again and again, opponents of civil unions framed the issue in terms of undemocratic court decisions (and later, undemocratic legislative actions). In doing so, they often avoided discussion of homosexuality altogether. "Important public policy," said Vermont's attorney general William Sorrell, "should be debated and decided in the legislature, not the courts."[55] Jim Lake, the pastor of the Bible Baptist Church in Berlin, Vermont, called the court ruling "an abuse of judicial power."[56] Thomas Koch, a Republican state representative who supported a constitutional referendum to overturn civil unions, said that "the real question is whether the people will be permitted to participate in the process or they will be frozen out."[57] "We really feel like this issue should be taken to the people," argued Mary Schroyer, president of the newly formed group Take It to The People.[58] "Let's take it to the people," echoed a Democratic state representative, Oreste Valsangiacomo, on the day that the House approved civil unions.[59]

Opponents also invoked moral values in describing the benefits of raising children with a mother and a father, in warning against the slippery slope to legalizing polygamy, and in calling to protect a traditional institution. The state argued before the Vermont Supreme Court that heterosexual marriage is essential for "furthering the link between procreation and child rearing."[60] "There's a lot to be offered by a mom and a dad," said Schroyer.[61] Bauer—by this time a Republican presidential candidate—argued that the ruling "begins in a fundamental way to redefine marriage. For 6,000 years Western civilization has defined marriage as between a man and a woman, and once you abandon that, all things are possible."[62] He also said, "Unless Vermont is prepared for the first man to show up at city hall with two wives, they should not go down this road."[63]

As before, gay rights advocates rarely attempted to rebut anti–gay rights traditional morality arguments with their own moral and religious arguments. Rabbi Michael Cohen, the leader of the Israel Congregation in Manchester Center, called the text of the Bible "dynamic," and Kenneth Poppe, the dean and rector of the Episcopal Cathedral Church of St. Paul in Burlington, said, "The threat to healthy marriages, I believe, does not come from extending such gifts to our gay and lesbian brothers and sisters. Such extension or civil union has the ability, I feel, to enrich marriage and our ever-expanding sense of what it means to be a family."[64] Their statements, however, were exceptions to the rule.

Some advocates of civil unions invoked the love frame. "People who are loving and caring, I think, should be accepted," argued Lieutenant Governor Douglas Racine. "In a world full of violence and hate and anger, we need more people who are loving and caring."[65] In a speech on the House floor, Democrat William Lippert, the only openly gay Vermont state representative, said:

> We are committed, caring, loving individuals in a time when desire for greater commitment, greater love, greater fidelity is needed in our society, and I find it so ironic that rather than being embraced and welcomed we are seen as a threat. Don't tell me about what a committed relationship is and isn't. There is no love and no commitment any greater than what I've seen, what I know.[66]

Another Democratic state representative, Robert Rusten, who voted for civil unions but was reportedly one of the last legislators to decide, explained that he had "never been able to discern the difference of love between those people who are heterosexual and those who are homosexual."[67]

Gay couples cited not only their love but also concrete examples of legal benefits. "One reason we're in this, besides our having fallen in love, is…to have the same kinds of protections" as heterosexual couples, said Stan Baker, one of the plaintiffs.[68] The *New York Times* illustrated the same theme with a cautionary tale: "When Nina Beck went into labor and frightening complications developed, her lesbian partner, Stacy Jolles, tried to go into the emergency room with her. But she was stopped at the door, she said, and asked, 'Who are you? Do you have legal papers to be there?'"[69]

Still, the most common frame that gay rights supporters presented was one that called for rights similar to those attained by African Americans when courts struck down bans on interracial marriage and desegregation. Evan Wolfson of the Lambda Legal Defense and Education Fund called the Vermont ruling a "legal victory that says that gay people and our families are entitled to full and equal protection under the law."[70] Tom Luce, a former Roman Catholic priest, testified to the House Judiciary Committee that he was there "to urge you to grant gays and lesbians their right to marry…. It is my opinion that same-sex marriage should be defined as a civil right."[71] Richard McCormack, the ranking Democrat in the Vermont Senate, said, "Hundreds of people have told me with such indignation, 'Shouldn't the majority rule?' And the answer is no, not in America. Not in America when it comes to protecting the rights of the minority."[72] Following the Senate passage of the civil unions bill, Democratic Governor Howard Dean called it "a natural extension of what Vermont has stood for for a long time, which is treating everybody the same."[73]

On occasion, opponents of civil unions argued that the issue was not one of civil rights. Republican State Senator Julius Canns, identified in the press as having mixed racial and ethnic ancestry, said, "I don't feel this is a civil rights case. They are asking for...rights because of their sexual habits."[74] In the same vein, Republican Representative Henry Gray said, "This is not a case of civil rights. But this is a case of sexual preference."[75]

News coverage conflated the legal aspects of civil unions and marriage by describing the former as "equivalent to marriage,"[76] "the legal equivalent of heterosexual marriage,"[77] and "the gay and lesbian equivalent of marriage licenses."[78] In one of the rare occasions on which anyone tried to make a distinction between the two, Progressive State Representative Steve Hingtgen said that domestic partner benefits were "not the same" as marriage: "The decision before us is not simply about the financial benefits and rights that a couple gets from marriage. It is about the inclusion of gays and lesbians in the mainstream of our communities."[79]

## THE 2000 PRESIDENTIAL CAMPAIGN

The 2000 presidential election campaign highlighted the strained attempts by Republicans and Democrats to elaborate positions on gay marriage that would appeal to their core constituencies as well as to moderates uncomfortable with both gay marriage and gay bashing. In the vice presidential debate, the Republican nominee, Dick Cheney, said that "people should be free to enter into any kind of relationship they want to enter into," adding, "I don't think there should necessarily be a federal policy in this area."[80] Social conservatives responded to his statement with incredulity and outrage.[81] In a subsequent presidential debate, the moderator, Jim Lehrer of the Public Broadcasting Service (PBS), asked the Republican candidate, George W. Bush, about Cheney's comments. Bush's initial response invoked traditional moral values but avoided gay bashing: "I'm not for gay marriage. I think marriage is a sacred institution between a man and a woman.... I'm going to be respectful, for people who may disagree with me."[82] The Democratic candidate, Vice President Al Gore, agreed but also advocated "find[ing] a way to allow some kind of civil unions." Bush responded by defending his view against the unstated charge of gay bashing: "I will be a tolerant person. I've been a tolerant person all my life. I just happen to believe strongly that marriage is between a man and a woman."

## TEXAS AND MASSACHUSETTS: GAY MARRIAGE MANIA

Dissenting from the majority opinion in *Lawrence v. Texas*, the United States Supreme Court ruling that struck down sodomy laws in June 2003, Associate Justice Antonin Scalia argued that the decision "dismantle[d] the structure of constitutional law that has permitted a distinction to be made between heterosexual and homosexual unions, insofar as formal recognition in marriage is concerned."[83] Following Scalia's lead, all three television networks connected *Lawrence* to gay marriage. Only the *NBC Nightly News* noted the contrary view in the majority opinion written by Associate Justice Anthony Kennedy and the concurring opinion written by Associate Justice Sandra Day O'Connor: both jurists argued that the ruling did not undercut laws prohibiting gay marriage.[84]

Just three days after the *Lawrence* decision, the Senate majority leader, Bill Frist (R-TN), announced his support for a federal constitutional amendment to ban gay marriage.[85] President Bush, however, responded cautiously: "I don't know if it's necessary yet," he said.[86] In July, Bush said that he was looking for ways "to codify" the notion that marriage should only be between a man and a woman.[87] "We're all sinners," he acknowledged, but he did not take this admission to mean "that somebody like me needs to compromise on an issue such as marriage."[88]

In November, the Massachusetts Supreme Court ruled in *Goodridge v. Massachusetts Department of Public Health*[89] that the denial of marriage rights to gays and lesbians violated the state constitution, thereby triggering an unprecedented amount of national media attention. As was the case with Hawaii, coverage in the Massachusetts news media (specifically the *Boston Globe* and *Boston Herald*) provided more diversity in viewpoints from religious leaders; in particular, the local media covered pro–gay marriage religious voices that national coverage largely ignored. In other respects, however, the framing of the issue followed parallel paths in the national and local news media.

In response to the Massachusetts ruling, Lou Sheldon of the Traditional Values Coalition continued his World War II metaphor by proclaiming that "Massachusetts is our Iwo Jima."[90] "We have a freight train coming down the pike, and a federal constitutional amendment is the only way to stop it," said Sandy Rios, president of Concerned Women for America.[91] Bush, by contrast, simply reiterated his support for heterosexual marriage.[92] About a month later, he said that he would support a constitutional amendment "if necessary." Bush called the Massachusetts Supreme Court "a very activist court" while arguing that the country should be tolerant; according to him, tolerance of gays and belief in heterosexual marriage were not mutually exclusive points of view. He also said that the position of his administration was "that whatever legal arrangements people want to make, they're allowed to make, so long as it's embraced by the state."[93]

The widespread efforts to frame the Massachusetts decision as undemocratic began in a dissenting opinion from the court itself. "Although it may be desirable for many reasons to extend to same-sex couples the benefits and burdens of civil marriage," the opinion stated, "that decision must be made by the Legislature, not the court."[94] Kenneth W. Starr, the former independent counsel who had investigated President Clinton, called the ruling "a terrible judicial usurpation of the power of the people."[95] United States Representative Marilyn Musgrave (R-CO), sponsor of the Federal Marriage Amendment (FMA), attacked "activist judges,"[96] and Don Wildmon, chairman of the American Family Association, said that the "judges in Massachusetts...think they are above the law."[97]

With the strong Roman Catholicism of Massachusetts as a backdrop, partisan and religious leaders who opposed gay marriage strove to portray their position as being consistent with their religious beliefs and with tolerance for gays. The chairman of the Republican National Committee, Ed Gillespie, who identified himself as a committed Catholic, said, "I accept people for who they are and love them. That doesn't mean I have to agree or turn my back on the tenets of my faith when it comes to homosexuality."[98] Sean Patrick O'Malley, the Archbishop of Boston, argued, "In no way should this be seen as promoting homophobia or cruel prejudices against members of our community; but we must call on all Catholics to be Catholic and to do the right thing, to safeguard the institution of marriage."[99] The Reverend Raymond Hammond of the Bethel-AMC Church in Boston followed suit: "I, like many other people in this country, don't want to see gay and lesbian people discriminated against. But we don't think that nondiscrimination means that you have the option to redefine the institution of marriage."[100]

Gay bashing played a relatively minor role in the debate, but gay marriage opponents did not completely abandon the approach. An Orthodox Jewish rabbi, Gershon Gewirtz, called gay sex an "abomination."[101] The Vatican issued a directive to politicians stating that legal recognition of gay relationships would mean "approval of deviant behavior"[102] and would be "gravely immoral."[103] Concerned Women for America circulated talking points titled, "Why Homosexual 'Marriage' Is Wrong," arguing that such marriage "is as wrong as giving a man a license to marry his mother or daughter or sister."[104]

In other instances, opponents invoked traditional morality but did not attack homosexuality explicitly. Instead, they argued that heterosexual marriage is important for procreation and childrearing, drawing an unstated but implicit contrast to gay marriage. "The optimal setting for procreation and childrearing is a family with a parent of each sex," asserted Judith S. Yogman, the assistant attorney general of Massachusetts.[105] Maggie Gallagher, the president of the Institute for Marriage and Public Policy, said, "The idea that's at risk here is that children need mothers and fathers."[106] Bishop Gilbert Thompson of the New Covenant Christian Church called heterosexual marriage "the only union that creates life,"[107] and Diane Knippers of the Institute on Religion and Democracy argued that "God made" marriage "that way" because "it's the healthiest environment to rear children."[108]

Gay rights advocates replied in part by emphasizing the separation of church and state. Senator John Kerry (D-MA)—a Roman Catholic, a presidential candidate, and a supporter of civil unions but not gay marriage—responded directly to the Vatican statement: "It is important not to have the church instructing politicians. That is an inappropriate crossing of the line in this country. Our founding fathers separated church and state in America."[109] An openly gay state senator, Cheryl Jacques, said, "The Constitution does clearly say that we will keep our principles about what's good for our country and our constituencies separate from our individual religious principles."[110] David Smith of the Human Rights Campaign emphasized the same theme: "No church is going to be forced to recognize a marriage that they do not want to recognize. The debate in this country is about the civil rights and responsibilities the state confers."[111]

For the most part, however, gay marriage advocates relied on the principle of equality in framing the issue, often including references to the African American civil rights movement. Mary Bonauto, the Massachusetts lawyer from the Gay & Lesbian Advocates & Defenders (GLAD), who represented the gay couples, said, "I very much feel this case has a lot of resonance with what the California Supreme Court did in 1948 when it became the first to strike down a ban on interracial marriage."[112] Evan Wolfson sounded the same note: "We are in a *Brown v. Board of*

*Education* moment right now."[113] Democratic presidential candidate Al Sharpton answered a question about his support for gay marriage by saying, "That's like asking me, 'Do I support black marriage or white marriage.'"[114]

Gay marriage supporters also set forth the equal rights argument by discussing examples of legal benefits from which gays were excluded. Winnie Stachelberg, the political director of the Human Rights Campaign, said that marriage "is a contract that accords to people in a loving relationship certain rights, responsibilities and benefits. It's not one thing, it's a thousand things—it's hospital visitation, it's Social Security benefits, it's joint tax filing, it's passing on your estate."[115] The ruling was "a huge relief," said Stuart Wells. "In the eyes of the law, I can stop carrying all those legal documents in my glove compartment, and if I get hit by a car, Lane can come and see me in the emergency room."[116] Jarrett T. Barrios, a Democrat and the only openly gay member of the Massachusetts Senate, described how a nurse had once stopped him from seeing his hospitalized seven-year-old son: "He could die on my watch, while I was fighting with a nurse over whether I was his parent or not."[117]

Even the religious leaders who supported gay marriage tended to rely on egalitarian rather than moral or religious language in making their case. The Reverend Nancy S. Taylor, president of the Massachusetts Conference of the United Church of Christ (UCC), said, "The court has affirmed that the quest for civil rights for all citizens will not be denied, either by prejudice or by religious doctrine."[118] Similarly, a Reform rabbi, Ronne Friedman of Temple Israel in Boston, said, "Within every religious tradition, they should have the right to define what marriage ought to be. But with the state, there is an obligation to see that all citizens' civil rights and equality are protected."[119] A few religious leaders also observed, however, that equality was a "touchstone of our faith"[120] and "morally right."[121]

Arguments validating the love within gay couples and their families were less common than arguments invoking equality. Still, a few made their way into media coverage. Massachusetts House Majority Leader Salvatore F. DiMasi, a Democrat, defended the court ruling by saying, "These people didn't come from Mars. They live here, they're brothers, sisters, cousins, you know them. They're human, and you have to treat them that way."[122] Bonauto called marriage "the ultimate expression of love and commitment."[123] U.S. Representative Dennis Kucinich (D-OH), another presidential candidate, invoked the love frame as well: "Let people be who they are and love who they love."[124] A *Newsweek* story about Julie and Hillary Goodridge, the plaintiffs in the Massachusetts case, offered a more elaborate version of the frame:

> It was a homey scene. Standing in their warm kitchen on a winter's day in 2001, Julie and Hillary Goodridge, a couple for 16 years, played the old Beatles song "All You Need Is Love" for their young daughter, Annie. Hillary asked Annie if she knew any people who loved each other. The little girl rattled off the names of her mothers' married friends, heterosexuals all. "What about Mommy and Ma?" asked Hillary. "Well," the child replied, "if you loved each other you'd get married."[125]

A Democratic state senator, Robert A. Havern, III, offered a prediction: "Allow people to get married and love each other, see how it works out. And my guess is it will be the biggest nonevent in the history of Massachusetts."[126]

## THE FEDERAL MARRIAGE AMENDMENT AND
## THE 2004 PRESIDENTIAL CAMPAIGN

In his January 2004 State of the Union address, President Bush reiterated his position on gay marriage. He attacked "activist judges," avoided gay bashing—or naming gays at all—and said, "The same moral tradition that defines marriage also teaches that each individual has dignity and value in God's sight."[127] In February 2004, the Massachusetts Supreme Court stated in an advisory opinion requested by the legislature that such legal alternatives as civil unions are not valid substitutes for marriage. A week later, Marilyn Musgrave, the sponsor of the Federal Marriage Amendment (FMA), claimed that Bush privately supported her measure even as White House Press Secretary Scott McClellan said that Bush was "continuing to look closely at this issue."[128]

In national coverage, opponents of gay marriage attacked the judiciary with a passion once reserved for bashing gays. Rios of Concerned Women for America led a chant by antigay protesters outside the Massachusetts statehouse: "For almighty God's sake, let the people vote."[129] After the mayor of San Francisco, Gavin Newsom, began allowing gay marriages in contradiction to California law, U.S. Senator Rick Santorum (R-PA) warned, "We're in a process of vigilantes, of people taking the law into their own hands and changing what marriage is in this country."[130] When Bush finally offered public support for the FMA on February 24, 2004, he attacked "activist judges" in San Francisco and New Mexico who were officiating at gay marriages in violation of state laws—even then, however, he suggested that states should be allowed to provide legal benefits by another name.[131] Bush repeated the "activist judges" refrain after gay marriages began in Massachusetts in May[132] and after the FMA failed in the United States Senate in the summer.[133]

Gay bashing was almost nonexistent in the mainstream debate over the FMA. Proamendment arguments in national media coverage invoked traditional morality but generally avoided targeting gays; instead, they praised heterosexual marriage as the best environment for child rearing. Bush said that "ages of experience have taught humanity that the commitment of a husband and wife to love and to serve one another promotes the welfare of children and the stability of society"[134] and that "changing the definition of traditional marriage will undermine the family structure."[135] During a Senate Judiciary Committee hearing on the FMA, Chairman John Cornyn (R-TX) said, "If the national culture teaches that marriage is just about adult love and not about the raising of children, then we should be troubled but not surprised by the results."[136] Santorum described those results: "A breakdown of the family. Children being born out of wedlock. And communities and cultures in decay."[137]

After Bush endorsed the FMA, such gay rights advocates as Jacques, the former Massachusetts state senator who had become president of the Human Rights Campaign, framed it as "political football, to score some cheap points."[138] Matt Foreman, the executive director of the National Gay and Lesbian Task Force, called it "a declaration of war on gay America...a transparent attempt to use our lives and our families to drive a wedge into the electorate purely for political gain."[139] John Kerry, the eventual Democratic presidential nominee, said, "The floor of the United States Senate should only be used for the common good, not issues designed to divide us for political purposes." He did not vote on the amendment, however.[140]

Still, the equal rights frame, with its analogy to civil rights for African Americans, remained the central tenet of pro–gay marriage arguments.[141] Indeed, the Massachusetts court's advisory opinion proclaimed that anything less than marriage "continues to relegate same-sex couples to a different status. The history of our nation has demonstrated that separate is seldom, if ever, equal."[142] Gavin Newsom offered a similar argument,[143] as did national gay rights leaders.[144] Picking up this theme, some gay marriage supporters sought to differentiate marriage from civil unions. One man in a gay couple raising a daughter said, "There is no explanation needed with the word *marriage*. Paige deserves the right to be able to say her parents are married and not have to explain our relationship to anyone else."[145] A plaintiff in the Massachusetts case concurred: "Marriage is much more than just a good benefit package, it's a huge social recognition of a relationship."[146]

As in the past, there were a few arguments for gay marriage that invoked religion. During the Democratic presidential primary campaign, Howard Dean explained his support for civil unions in such terms: "From a religious point of view, if God had thought homosexuality is a sin, he would not have created gay people.... My view of Christianity...is that the hallmark of being a Christian is to reach out to people who have been left behind."[147] The Reverend Barry W. Lynn, the executive director of Americans United for Separation of Church and State, said, "I am disturbed that even though I can perform a religious ritual to unite a same-gender couple, the state won't recognize it because some different religious group thinks I am theologically wrong."[148] "It's no different than what white fundamentalists did in the South when they took Scripture out of context to justify slavery," concluded Archbishop Carl Bean, the founder of the Unity Fellowship Church of Los Angeles. "They would leave church, put on a hood, find a black person, kill them, take off the hood, go back to church and sing 'Amazing Grace.'"[149] Other gay marriage advocates, however, argued that religion was tangential to the issue. One was Jacques, who said, "No religious organization will be forced to marry same-sex couples." Likewise, representatives from twenty-six religious groups signed a letter that stated, "It is not the task of our government and elected representatives to enshrine in our laws the religious point of view of any one faith."[150]

Gavin Newsom, the mayor of San Francisco, justified his action as a way to put human faces on the issue of gay marriage. Still, these faces were not always accompanied by voices. On network television news, gay couples typically had no opportunity to speak except to say "I do."[151] Print coverage was somewhat more likely to include gay couples' invocations of the love and family frame. One woman who planned on marrying her partner of thirteen years in Massachusetts explained her decision in these terms: "When you're a little girl or a little boy, everybody says when you grow up you'll fall in love and you'll get married. I found somebody who I love, and we couldn't get married."[152] "Small-minded views could never hold out against the tidal wave of love," proclaimed another woman who got married in San Francisco.[153]

Gay rights supporters also pointed to conservative arguments against the FMA. Vice President Cheney revisited the issue in the 2004 vice presidential debate, saying that "freedom does mean freedom for everybody.... People ought to be free to choose any arrangement they want. Traditionally, that's been an issue for the states.... That would be my preference."[154] Former Congressman Barr, the Republican who had introduced the federal Defense of Marriage Act in 1996, said that he opposed gay marriage but did not support the FMA: "I consider the Constitution of the United States of America to be the most profound and important document ever penned by the hand of man. And I think we ought to tread very, very carefully before we start using it as an affirmative tool to dictate social policy in this country."[155]

John Kerry offered a nuanced take on the issue during the presidential campaign. In his third debate with Bush, he said, "I'm for civil union that gives people the rights, the rights of partnership, the rights of inheritance of property, the rights of taxation and so forth, those kinds of treatment that are equal."[156] Allowing such unions would "advance the goal of equal protection," he argued.[157] Kerry also said that he would support an amendment to the Massachusetts constitution to ban gay marriage and simultaneously create civil unions.

Bush continued to send complex signals of his own. Only a week before the election, he offered what appeared to be a qualified endorsement of civil unions:

> I don't think we should deny people rights to a civil union, a legal arrangement, if that's what a state chooses to do so…. I view the definition of marriage different from legal arrangements that enable people to have rights. And I strongly believe that marriage ought to be defined as between a union between a man and a woman. Now, having said that, states ought to be able to have the right to pass laws that enable people to be able to have rights like others.[158]

Bush's comment about people being "able to have rights like others" suggested an equal rights frame for civil unions if not for gay marriage.

## ELECTION POSTMORTEM: THE POLLS AND THE BLAME GAME

Network news coverage immediately following the 2004 presidential election emphasized the notion that the debate over gay marriage had given Bush the margin of his victory, especially in such battleground states as Ohio. On the *CBS Evening News*, correspondent Lee Cowan proclaimed, "In the end, it wasn't the clatter of the war, it wasn't the thud of the economy, it wasn't even the rantings of the world's most wanted terrorist. In the end, what voters say brought them to the polls was much more quiet. The number-one voter motivator: Morality."[159] Print coverage tended to provide more in-depth explanation of just what "moral values" might mean—that is, everything from abortion to embryonic stem cells to sex and violence on television— but the general story was the same in the print media as well. "The marriage issue was the great iceberg in this election," concluded Robert Knight of the Culture and Family Institute.[160] Even U.S. Senator Dianne Feinstein (D-CA) said of San Francisco's unlawful gay marriages, "I think it did energize the very conservative vote. I think it gave them a position to rally around."[161] In some cases, coverage also included those who disagreed with the dominant explanation. For example, Kate Kendell, executive director of the National Center for Lesbian Rights (NCLR), accused Feinstein of looking for "easy scapegoats,"[162] and Foreman of the National Gay and Lesbian Task Force called the blame game "homophobic."[163]

Those who concluded that gay marriage had delivered a Bush victory often cited the National Election Pool exit poll, which gave voters seven choices for the one issue that mattered most for their vote. A plurality (22 percent) of the respondents chose "moral values."[164] There was good reason, however, to be skeptical of the conventional wisdom built on this result. The nonpartisan Pew Research Center for the People and the Press conducted a split-form post-election survey in which half the respondents received the same question and response categories that the exit poll respondents received. Again, a plurality of respondents chose "moral values" (27 percent), but less than a third (29 percent) said in response to a follow-up question that they were thinking of gay marriage or homosexuality in particular. In the other form, respondents received an open-ended question that asked them to describe their top issue in their own words; in this version of the survey, only 14 percent mentioned moral values.[165] Further analysis of post-election survey results suggests that public opinion about gay marriage gave Bush a slight edge across the country as a whole but not in the battleground states.[166]

## CONNECTICUT AND CALIFORNIA: THE RISE OF ACTIVIST LEGISLATURES

After the 2004 election, the national news media turned their attention away from gay marriage. The decline in coverage was particularly pronounced for network television news. Nevertheless, new developments emerged in the politics of gay marriage. In particular, two state legislatures undercut the "activist judges" frame by taking their own actions in advancing gay marriage.

In the spring of 2005, the Connecticut legislature passed a civil unions bill that also defined marriage as between a man and a woman; the governor signed it into law. Apart from California, which had already passed a domestic partner law, Connecticut was the first state to pass such a law without prompting by a state court. "Those who are most adamant about denying these rights say they were being forced on the public by judges," observed a Democratic state senator, Andrew McDonald. "We have elected officials leading the way."[167]

In the fall of 2005 the California legislature became the first to pass a gay marriage bill. Geoffrey Kors, the executive director of Equality California, took the opportunity to rebut one of the leading anti–gay marriage frames: "[The legislature's action] will totally take away the argument that it is just 'activist judges' who are finding for marriage nondiscrimination. It's the people's representatives in the largest state in the nation doing this." California voters, however, had passed a 2000 referendum that defined marriage as a union between a man and a woman under the law. Thus opponents claimed that the legislature's action was undemocratic. "Twenty-one Democrats in the Senate took it upon themselves to redefine marriage…and they're saying that 4.6 million Californians are wrong," said Benjamin Lopez of the Traditional Values Coalition.[168] Ultimately, Governor Arnold Schwarzenegger, a Republican, vetoed the bill; its supporters lacked the votes to override his veto.

## CONCLUSION

Now that we have examined the frames for gay marriage in news media coverage, let us consider the potential consequences of these frames.

*Implicit Appeals and Antigay Sentiments*

Many Americans are probably ambivalent when it comes to gay marriage. On the one hand, they may support traditional moral values and harbor negative feelings toward gays; on the other hand, they may also believe in tolerance for gays and support their equal rights in other domains. An anti–gay marriage appeal that explicitly attacks gays is likely to fail among the majority of Americans who are uncomfortable with overt intolerance of gays. Implicit appeals, by contrast, may evoke antigay sentiments without triggering an aversion to intolerance.

Of course, one could reply that the foes of gay marriage attack judicial activism and praise traditional marriage because they hold sincere philosophical grounds for doing so, not because they seek to play on antigay prejudice. We do not dispute this point; indeed, we make no claims whatsoever about the intent behind such framing efforts. Our concern is with the consequences of these appeals, intended or otherwise. We know that gay rights opponents have moved away from attacking gays in direct terms, choosing instead to make arguments on behalf of traditional marriage and against judges. How, exactly, might the latter approaches trigger antigay sentiments?

Our answer rests with the historical association in public debate between frames explicitly attacking gays and frames attacking activist judges or lauding the virtues of heterosexual marriage. Although explicit attacks waned and milder frames came to dominate anti–gay marriage arguments, these frames often overlapped in news media coverage. Thus ordinary Americans exposed to both sorts of frames at the same time may have internalized the associations between them. By activating these connections in the minds of audience members, gay baiting may evoke the antigay sentiments that gay bashing once triggered.

Although no studies to date have tested the effects of implicit appeals to antigay sentiments on public opinion about gay marriage, research on public opinion about race demonstrates the potential for implicit appeals to work in the way that we have described.[169] This research also shows that when one makes implicit racial appeals explicit, such appeals no longer evoke negative racial sentiments. The implication here is that gay marriage advocates could work to neutralize the impact of gay baiting by calling attention to its implicit appeals.

*Reframing the Issue*

The success of gay baiting offers one possible explanation for the public's continued opposition to gay marriage, but another potential explanation lies with the apparent failure of the equal rights frame in the marriage context. The oddity, of course, is that this frame appears to have succeeded in shaping public opinion about other aspects of gay rights—for example, discrimination in employment, gays in the military, and even civil unions. One thing that sets gay marriage apart from these policies is that many—perhaps most—Americans do not see it as an equality issue. They simply do not make the connection between the principle, which they cherish, and the policy. Instead, they see gay marriage as an issue that has to do with their moral beliefs and their feelings toward gays. Many gay rights activists appear to believe that the key to winning public support is to continue emphasizing the specific legal benefits that gays cannot receive without marriage rights.[170] These activists may be correct; perhaps their approach will work in time. Then again, the equal rights frame may have its limitations when applied to marriage, and alternative or complementary approaches may have their merits.

From the point of view of gay marriage advocates, one potential problem with the equal rights argument is that it allows moderate gay rights supporters, as well as journalists and such moderate gay marriage opponents as Cheney and Bush, to frame civil unions and other legal equivalents as acceptable substitutes for marriage. The reader should recall that around one in two Americans supports civil unions, whereas only around one in three supports gay marriage. Americans who want to support gay rights know that they have a choice: by supporting civil unions, they can satisfy their inclination to favor gay rights without supporting gay marriage. Moreover, gay marriage advocates rarely present arguments that clearly differentiate between marriage and civil unions. Such arguments are difficult to make in a sentence or two, the typical sound bite. To be sure, gay marriage advocates may be able to build public support for gay marriage by first building support for civil unions, but such efforts offer no basis for defeating state constitutional amendments against gay marriage. Moreover, opposition to gay marriage may fuel the passage of amendments that ban both marriage and civil unions.

Given that Americans by and large regard gay marriage as an issue of morality rather than equality, it may be that moral appeals would help gay marriage advocates win the debate.[171] The love and family frame offers one possibility for countering the anti–gay marriage interpretation of morality, but it has been eclipsed—perhaps even crowded out—by the equal rights frame. Nor does the love and family frame offer its own explicit rebuttal to the traditional morality frame, which often has a religious component. The notion that gays deserve marriage because of their love for one another other does not necessarily undermine a frame based on a Judeo-Christian view of the family and homosexuality. Even when progay religious leaders speak out, they rarely challenge theological arguments against gay marriage; instead, they tend to emphasize equality-based arguments. The increase in public tolerance of gays and the decline of gay bashing present a potential window of opportunity for pro–gay marriage morality arguments. Such arguments could challenge antigay assumptions about what is best for children—for example, by exposing the public to gay couples raising children and presenting expert testimony that gays have the same parenting abilities as do heterosexuals.

*Final Thoughts*

Although we have focused on how political elites may influence public opinion by shaping the frames that appear in news media coverage, we do not mean to suggest that such frames are the only factors that influence public support for gay marriage. Furthermore, we recognize that public opinion may also shape news media coverage and the actions of political elites. Even so, our efforts to uncover patterns in how elites have framed the issue through the news media provide starting points for understanding why the American public continues to oppose gay marriage, as well as for thinking about how gay marriage advocates might alter the current landscape of public opinion.

NOTES

1. Pam Belluck, "Massachusetts Rejects Bill to Eliminate Gay Marriage," *New York Times*, September 15, 2005.

2. Paul R. Brewer, "The Shifting and Varied Foundations of Public Opinion about Gay Rights" (paper presented at the annual meeting of the Midwest Political Science Association, Chicago, IL, November 18–19, 2005).

3. Paul R. Brewer and Clyde Wilcox, "Trends: Same-Sex Marriage and Civil Unions," *Public Opinion Quarterly* 69 (2005): 599–616.

4. Donald R. Kinder and Lynn M. Sanders, *Divided by Color: Racial Politics and Democratic Ideals* (Chicago: University of Chicago Press, 1996).

5. Paul R. Brewer, "The Shifting Foundations of Public Opinion about Gay Rights," *Journal of Politics* 65 (2003): 1208–20.

6. Brewer, "The Shifting and Varied Foundations of Public Opinion about Gay Rights" (see note 2).

7. C. Ann Gordon, Barry L. Tadlock, and Elizabeth Popp, "Framing the Issue of Same-Sex Marriage: Traditional Values versus Equal Rights" (paper presented at the annual meeting of the American Political Science Association, Chicago, IL, September 2–5, 2004).

8. Paul R. Brewer, "Values, Political Knowledge, and Public Opinion about Gay Rights: A Framing-Based Account," *Public Opinion Quarterly* 67 (2003): 173–201.

9. William G. Jacoby, "Issue Framing and Public Opinion on Government Spending," *American Journal of Political Science* 44 (2000): 750–67.

10. Brewer, "Values, Political Knowledge, and Public Opinion about Gay Rights" (see note 8); see also Kimberly Gross and Seth Goldman, "Framing Anti-Gay Hate: An Experimental Test of the Effect of Media Framing of Hate Crime on Policy Views" (paper presented at the annual meeting of the American Political Science Association, Chicago, IL, September 2–5, 2004).

11. Gordon, Tadlock, and Popp, "Framing the Issue of Same-Sex Marriage" (see note 7); Frederick Liu and Stephen Macedo, "The Federal Marriage Amendment and the Strange Evolution of the Conservative Case against Gay Marriage," *PS: Political Science and Politics* 38 (2005): 211–15; Vincent Price, Lilach Nir, and Joseph N. Cappella, "Framing Public Discussion of Gay Civil Unions," *Public Opinion Quarterly* 69 (2005): 179–212.

12. Paul R. Brewer, "Framing, Value Words, and Citizens' Explanations of Their Issue Opinions," *Political Communication* 19 (2002): 303–16.

13. Price, Nir, and Cappella, "Framing Public Discussion" (see note 11).

14. Tali Mendelberg, *The Race Card: Campaign Strategy, Implicit Messages, and the Norm of Equality* (Princeton, NJ: Princeton University Press, 2001).

15. Joan Biskupic, "Ruling by Hawaii's Supreme Court Opens the Way to Gay Marriages," *Washington Post*, May 7, 1993.

16. CBS News, *Faith and Politics: the Christian Right*, on CBS Reports, September 17, 1995.

17. Carl Weiser, "Legal Gay Marriage on the Nation's Horizon," *USA Today*, January 2, 1996.

18. ABC News, *Day One*, June 13, 1994.

19. "Arguments Start Again in Hawaiian Case," *Chicago Sun-Times*, September 11, 1996.

20. Joan Biskupic and John E. Yang, "Judge OKs Gay Marriages," *Chicago Sun-Times*, December 4, 1996.

21. Jeffrey Schmalz, "In Hawaii, Step Toward Legalized Gay Marriage," *New York Times*, May 7, 1993.

22. Pete Pichaske, "Years of National Debate Still Lie Ahead," *Honolulu Star-Bulletin*, December 4, 1996.

23. Mike Yuen, "House Tries Again to Ban Gay Unions, Legislators Soften the Wording of Their Proposal in a New Bid for Approval," *Honolulu Star-Bulletin*, April 22, 1996.

24. CBS News, *CBS This Morning*, July 14, 1995.

25. Mary Adamski, "Office Turns Away Gay Marriage Applicants," *Honolulu Star-Bulletin*, December 4, 1996.

26. Alan Matsuoka, "And Now, the Trial…," *Honolulu Star-Bulletin*, May 14, 1996.

27. Pichaske, "Years of National Debate Still Lie Ahead" (see note 22).

28. Linda Hosek, "Judge Grants Delay in Same-Sex Marriage Case," *Honolulu Star-Bulletin*, December 4, 1996.

29. Mary Adamski, "A Haven for Spurned Worshippers," *Honolulu Star-Bulletin*, April 15, 1996.

30. Matsuoka, "And Now, the Trial…." (see note 30).

31. "'Defense Of Marriage Act' 5/96 H.R. 3396 Summary/Analysis," 'Lectric Law Library, http://www.lectlaw.com/files/leg23.htm (accessed October 30, 2006).

32. Elizabeth Schwinn, "House Panel Approves 'Defense of Marriage,'" *Houston Chronicle*, June 13, 1996.

33. Jerry Gray, "House Passes Bar to U.S. Sanction of Gay Marriage," *New York Times*, July 13, 1996.

34. John E. Yang, "House Votes To Curb Gay Marriages," *Washington Post*, July 13, 1996.

35. Carolyn Lochhead, "GOP Bill Targets Same-Sex Marriages, Measure Would Affect Benefits, Recognition," *San Francisco Chronicle*, May 9, 1996.

36. CBS News, *CBS Evening News*, September 10, 1996.

37. Carolyn Lochhead, "Boxer Won't Vote for Gay Marriage Bill," *San Francisco Chronicle*, July 18, 1996.

38. "Gingrich's Lesbian Sister Decries Bill on Same-Sex Marriages," *St. Louis Post-Dispatch*, May 15, 1996.

39. Eric Schmitt, "Panel Passes Bill to Let States Refuse to Recognize Gay Marriage," *New York Times*, June 13, 1996.

40. "House Votes Against Gay Marriages," *St. Louis Post-Dispatch*, July 13, 1996.

41. "Gingrich's Lesbian Sister Decries Bill on Same-Sex Marriages," (see note 38).

42. Alison Mitchell, "Clinton Says G.O.P. Aims to Divide," *New York Times*, May 24, 1996; "House Votes Against Gay Marriages," (see note 40); Yang, "House Votes To Curb Gay Marriages" (see note 34).

43. Dan Balz, "President Opposes 'Same-Sex Marriage,'" *Washington Post*, May 14, 1996.

44. Adam Lisberg, "Civility Vowed in Gay-Marriage Debate," *Burlington Free Press*, January 10, 2000.

45. Nancy Remsen and Adam Lisberg, "House Backs Civil Unions," *Burlington Free Press*, March 16, 2000.

46. Carey Goldberg, "Vermont Residents Split Over Civil Unions Law," *New York Times*, September 3, 2000.

47. Carey Goldberg, "A Kaleidoscopic Look at Attitudes on Gay Marriage," *New York Times*, February 6, 2000.

48. Carey Goldberg, "Forced Into Action on Gay Marriage, Vermont Finds Itself Deeply Split," *New York Times*, February 3, 2000.

49. Carey Goldberg, "In Vermont, Gay Couples Head for the Almost-Altar," *New York Times*, July 2, 2000.

50. Adam Lisberg and Nancy Remsen, "Same-Sex Opponents Rally," *Burlington Free Press*, April 7, 2000.

51. Pamela Ferdinand, "Vermont Legislature Clears Bill Allowing Civil Unions," *Washington Post*, April 26, 2000.

52. Pamela Ferdinand, "Same-Sex Couples Take Vows as Law Takes Effect," *Washington Post*, July 2, 2000.

53. Tamara Lush, "Groups Face Off Over Right to Marry," *Burlington Free Press*, August 4, 1999.

54. Adam Lisberg, "Civil-Union Bill Goes to Dean," *Burlington Free Press*, April 26, 2000.

55. Carey Goldberg, "Vermont High Court Backs Rights of Same-Sex Couples," *New York Times*, December 21, 1999.

56. Adam Lisberg and Nancy Remsen, "Marriage Hearing Packed," *Burlington Free Press*, January 26, 2000.

57. Remsen and Lisberg, "House Backs Civil Unions" (see note 45).

58. CBS News, *CBS Evening News*, December 6, 1998.

59. Remsen and Lisberg, "House Backs Civil Unions" (see note 45).

60. Carey Goldberg, "Vermont Supreme Court Takes Up Gay Marriage," *New York Times*, November 19, 1998.

61. Pamela Ferdinand, "Will Vermont Say 'I Do' to Gays? Supreme Court Could Overturn Ban on Same-Sex Marriages," *Washington Post*, November 19, 1998.

62. Hanna Rosin, "Same-Sex Couples Win Rights in Vermont," *Washington Post*, December 21, 1999.

63. Hanna Rosin and Pamela Ferdinand, "Gays Achieve Breakthrough in Vermont," *Washington Post*, March 17, 2000.

64. Adam Lisberg, "Unions Divide Religions," *Burlington Free Press*, March 30, 2000.

65. Lisberg and Remsen, "Same-Sex Opponents Rally" (see note 50).

66. Adam Lisberg, "House Agonized Over Civil Unions," *Burlington Free Press*, March 19, 2000.

67. Remsen and Lisberg, "House Backs Civil Unions," (see note 45).

68. Lisberg, "Civil-Union Bill Goes to Dean" (see note 54).

69. Goldberg, "Vermont Supreme Court Takes Up Gay Marriage" (see note 60).

70. Ibid.

71. Sally Pollak, "Faith in What They Believe," *Burlington Free Press*, February 20, 2000.

72. Nancy Remsen and Adam Lisberg, "Senate Backs Civil Unions," *Burlington Free Press*, April 19, 2000.

73. Lisberg, "Civil-Union Bill Goes to Dean" (see note 54).

74. Remsen and Lisberg, "Senate Backs Civil Unions" (see note 72).

75. Lisberg, "Civil-Union Bill Goes to Dean" (see note 54).

76. Adam Lisberg, "Panel OKs Marriage Substitute," *Burlington Free Press*, March 2, 2000; see also note 48.

77. Adam Lisberg, "Panel Clears Way for Civil Unions," *Burlington Free Press*, April 14, 2000.

78. Adam Lisberg and Nancy Remsen, "Gay Couples Join Hands with History," *Burlington Free Press*, July 2, 2000.

79. Adam Lisberg, "Panel Backs Gay Partnerships," *Burlington Free Press*, February 10, 2000.

80. Commission on Presidential Debates, "The Lieberman-Cheney Vice Presidential Debate," October 5, 2000, http://www.debates.org/pages/trans2000d.html (accessed September 1, 2006).

81. Michael Cooper, "Cheney's Marriage Remarks Irk Conservatives," *New York Times*, October 10, 2000.

82. Commission on Presidential Debates, "The Second Gore-Bush Presidential Debate," October 11, 2000, http://www.debates.org/pages/trans2000b.html (accessed September 1, 2006).

83. *Lawrence v. Texas* (Scalia, J., dissenting), 2003:20–21, http://www.supreme courtus.gov/opinions/02slipopinion.html (accessed September 1, 2006).

84. NBC News, *NBC Nightly News*, June 27, 2003.

85. "Frist Opposes Gay Marriage," *New York Times*, June 30, 2003.

86. David Von Drehle, "Bush Unsure Ban on Gay Unions Is Needed," *Washington Post*, July 3, 2003.

87. Alan Cooperman, "Sodomy Ruling Fuels Battle Over Gay Marriage," *Washington Post*, July 31, 2003; Ann McFeatters, "'I Believe a Marriage is Between a Man and a Woman,'" *Pittsburgh Post-Gazette*, July 31, 2003.

88. Mike Allen, "Gay Marriage Looms as Issue," *Washington Post*, October 25, 2003.

89. *Goodridge v. Massachusetts Department of Public Health* (2003), http://www.mass .gov/courts/courtsandjudges/courts/supremejudicialcourt/goodridge.html          (accessed September 1, 2006).

90. Thomas Caywood, "Right Wing Revs Up for 'Last Stand' in Bay State," *Boston Herald*, November 21, 2003.

91. Susan Page, "Gay Marriage Looms Large for '04," *USA Today*, November 19, 2003.

92. David Von Drehle, "Gay Marriage Is a Right, Massachusetts Court Rules," *Washington Post*, November 19, 2003.

93. Mike Allen, "Bush May Support Gay Marriage Ban," *Washington Post*, December 17, 2003.

94. Kathleen Burge, "Gays Have Right to Marry, SJC Says in Historic Ruling Legislature Given 180 Days to Change Law," *Boston Globe*, November 19, 2003.

95. Katharine Q. Seelye, "Conservatives Mobilize Against Ruling on Gay Marriage," *New York Times*, November 20, 2003.

96. Charlie Savage, "Frank Sees Referendum for Ruling on Gay Marriage," *Boston Globe*, November 24, 2003.

97. Dennis Cauchon, "Mass. About to Alter Gay-Marriage Debate," *USA Today*, December 26, 2003.

98. Allen, "Gay Marriage Looms as Issue" (see note 88).

99. Frank Phillips, "SJC Solicits Briefs on Civil Unions, Mulls Request by Senate for Advisory Opinion," *Boston Globe*, December 17, 2003.

100. ABC News, *ABC World News Tonight*, July 31, 2003.

101. Jules Crittenden, "Religious Leaders Praise, Curse Court's Gay Marriage Decision," *Boston Herald*, November 19, 2003.

102. Lisa Stein, "Gay Marriage," *U.S. News & World Report*, August 11, 2003.

103. Alan Cooperman and David Von Drehle, "Vatican Instructs Legislators on Gays," *Washington Post*, August 1, 2003.

104. Allen, "Gay Marriage Looms as Issue" (see note 88).

105. Pamela Ferdinand, "Mass. Asked to Allow Same-Sex Marriages," *Washington Post*, March 5, 2003.

106. CBS News, *CBS Evening News*, November 18, 2003.

107. John McElhenny and Donovan Slack, "Gay Marriage Debated at Sunday's Services," *Boston Globe*, November 24, 2003.

108. Cooperman, "Sodomy Ruling Fuels Battle Over Gay Marriage" (see note 87).

109. David R. Guarino, "Kerry Raps Pope," *Boston Herald*, August 2, 2003.

110. ABC News, *ABC World News Tonight*, July 31, 2003.

111. Cooperman and Von Drehle, "Vatican Instructs Legislators on Gays" (see note 103).

112. Charles Lane, "States' Recognition of Same-Sex Unions May Be Tested," *Washington Post*, November 19, 2003.

113. Sarah Kershaw, "Adversaries on Gay Rights Vow State-by-State Fight," *New York Times*, July 6, 2003.

114. Darryl Fears, "3 Support Same-Sex Marriage," *Washington Post*, July 16, 2003.

115. Alan Cooperman, "Sodomy Ruling Fuels Battle Over Gay Marriage" (see note 87).

116. Kimberly Blanton, "The Gay Marriage Ruling. The Legalities," *Boston Globe*, November 19, 2003.

117. Pam Belluck, "Massachusetts Lawmakers, After Heated Debate, Put Off Vote on Gay Marriage," *New York Times*, February 13, 2004.

118. Paulson, "The Gay Marriage Ruling Reaction Pro and Con/Religious Community" (see note 116).

119. Crittenden, "Religious Leaders Praise, Curse Court's Gay Marriage Decision" (see note 101).

120. Brenda J. Buote, "Gay Marriage Debate Splitting Local Clergy," *Boston Globe*, November 27, 2003.

121. Paulson, "The Gay Marriage Ruling Reaction Pro and Con/Religious Community" (see note 116).

122. Raphael Lewis, "In Lawmaker Poll, Few Back Limiting Marriage," *Boston Globe*, December 1, 2003.

123. Ferdinand, "Mass. Asked to Allow Same-Sex Marriages" (see note 105).

124. Bob Dart, "Democratic Field Debates Gay Rights," *Atlanta Journal-Constitution*, July 16, 2003.

125. Evan Thomas, "The War Over Gay Marriage," *Newsweek*, July 7, 2003.

126. Belluck, "Massachusetts Lawmakers, After Heated Debate, Put Off Vote on Gay Marriage" (see note 117).

127. George W. Bush, "State of the Union Address," Address before a joint session of the Congress, Washington, DC, January 20, 2004, http://www.whitehouse.gov/news/releases/2004/01/20040120-7.html (accessed September 1, 2006).

128. ABC News, *ABC World News Tonight,* February 11, 2004.

129. NBC News, *NBC Nightly News*, February 11, 2004.

130. Charles Babington and Helen Dewar, "GOP Uncertain Ban Would Pass Congress," *Washington Post*, February 25, 2004.

131. Elisabeth Bumiller, "Bush Says His Party is Wrong to Oppose Gay Civil Unions," *New York Times*, October 26, 2004.

132. Charisse Jones and Fred Bayles, "First Weddings Intensify Gay-Marriage Debate," *USA Today*, May 18, 2004.

133. Helen Dewar, "Ban on Gay Marriage Fails," *Washington Post*, July 15, 2004.

134. Elisabeth Bumiller, "Bush Backs Ban in Constitution on Gay Marriage," *New York Times*, February 25, 2004.

135. ABC News, *ABC World News Tonight*, July 12, 2004.

136. Carl Hulse, "Gay Official Denounces Amendment," *New York Times*, March 24, 2004.

137. ABC News, *ABC World News Tonight*, July 12, 2004.

138. ABC News, *ABC World News Tonight*, February 11, 2004.

139. Bumiller, "Bush Backs Ban in Constitution on Gay Marriage" (see note 134).

140. Dewar, "Ban on Gay Marriage Fails" (see note 133)

141. In rare circumstances, opponents argued that homosexuality is a choice, not an immutable characteristic such as race, and that gay marriage is therefore not an issue of civil rights. NBC News, *NBC Nightly News*, October 20, 2004; Darryl Fears, "Gay Blacks Feeling Strained Church Ties," *Washington Post*, November 2, 2004. On the other hand, African

American civil rights leaders sometimes rebutted the special rights frame in direct terms. ABC News, *ABC World News Tonight*, March 11, 2004.

142. ABC News, *ABC World News Tonight*, February 4, 2004.

143. Dean E. Murphy, "San Francisco Mayor Exults in Move on Gay Marriage," *New York Times*, February 19, 2004; ABC News, *ABC World News Tonight*, February 13, 2004.

144. Robin Toner and Robert Pear, "State of the Union: Domestic Agenda," *New York Times*, January 21, 2004.

145. NBC News, *NBC Nightly News*, March 11, 2004.

146. NBC News, *NBC Nightly News*, May 16, 2004.

147. Jim VandeHei, "Dean Says Faith Swayed Decision on Gay Unions," *Washington Post*, January 8, 2004.

148. David D. Kirkpatrick, "Religious Leaders Assail Amendment on Gay Marriage," *New York Times*, June 4, 2004.

149. Fears, "Gay Blacks Feeling Strained Church Ties" (see note 149)

150. Alan Cooperman, "Church 'Protect Marriage' Day is Urged," *Washington Post*, June 26, 2004.

151. See, for instance, NBC News, *NBC Nightly News*, May 17, 2004.

152. Jones and Bayles, "First Weddings Intensify Gay-Marriage Debate" (see note 132).

153. Evelyn Nieves, "Gay Couples Rush to San Francisco," *Washington Post*, February 14, 2004.

154. Commission on Presidential Debates, "The Cheney-Edwards Vice Presidential Debate," October 5, 2004, http://www.debates.org/pages/trans2004b.html (accessed September 1, 2006).

155. ABC World News, *ABC World News Tonight*, February 25, 2004.

156. ABC World News, *ABC World News Tonight*, March 27, 2004.

157. Paul Farhi, "Kerry Again Opposes Same-Sex Marriage," *Washington Post*, May 15, 2004.

158. Bumiller, "Bush Says His Party is Wrong to Oppose Gay Civil Unions," (see notes 131).

159. CBS News, *CBS Evening News*, November 3, 2004.

160. Alan Cooperman, "Same-Sex Bans Fuel Conservative Agenda," *Washington Post*, November 4, 2004.

161. ABC News, *ABC World News Tonight*, November 5, 2004.

162. Dean E. Murphy, "Some Democrats Blame One of Their Own," *New York Times*, November 5, 2004.

163. Pam Belluck, "Maybe Same-Sex Marriage Didn't Make the Difference," *New York Times*, November 7, 2004.

164. "Moral values" was followed by "economy/jobs" (20 percent), "terrorism" (19 percent), "Iraq" (15 percent), "health care" (8 percent), "taxes" (5 percent), and "education" (4 percent). National Election Pool, http://www.exit-poll.net/faq.html (accessed October 18, 2006).

165. Pew Center for the People and the Press, "Voters Liked Campaign 2004, But Too Much 'Mud-Slinging'"; "Moral Values: How Important?" November 11, 2004.

166. D. Sunshine Hillygus and Todd G. Shields, "Moral Issues and Voter Decision Making in the 2004 Presidential Election," *PS: Political Science and Politics* 38 (2005): 201–9.

167. Jonathan Finer, "Connecticut Closer to Approving Civil Unions," *Washington Post*, April 3, 2005.

168. Joe Dignan and Amy Argetsinger, "Calif. Senate Passes Gay Marriage Bill," *Washington Post*, September 2, 2005.

169. Kinder and Sanders, *Divided by Color* (see note 4); Mendelberg, *The Race Card* (see note 17).

170. Evelyn Nieves, "Gay Activists Refuse to Bargain Away Rights," *Washington Post*, December 10, 2004.

171. Carlos A. Ball, *The Morality of Gay Rights: An Exploration in Political Philosophy* (New York: Routledge, 2003).

# 9

## INTRODUCTION TO AMERICAN GOVERNMENT: WHAT COLLEGE STUDENTS ARE READING ABOUT SAME-SEX MARRIAGE

*Charles W. Gossett and Elizabeth Bergman*

Persons who are college graduates are more likely to become leaders of community opinion than those who do not attend college. Many state-supported universities and colleges, as well as many private colleges, require students to take a course in American government or politics as part of their general education curriculum; one writer has estimated that as many as one million students enroll in an American government class each year.[1] The textbooks that are commonly used in such courses can be an influential medium through which college students are exposed to information about important political issues. It is thus worthwhile to see whether current textbooks in American government are exposing students to the issue of same-sex marriages, and if so, the ways in which the texts present the issue.

This chapter will examine college-level textbooks in American government with respect to their presentations of the issue of same-sex marriage. A brief introduction to the importance and value of looking at textbooks as sources of political socialization will be followed by a theoretical examination of the possibility of introducing the topic of same-sex marriage into a textbook on American government in terms of the typical chapters one finds. This framework will guide us in analyzing where, in fact, textbook authors have chosen to situate the issue within the broader context of American politics. We will then briefly describe the methodology used in selecting and analyzing the texts, followed by a summary of our findings. The chapter will conclude with some thoughts about what those findings tell us and how they might affect the future of same-sex marriage in this country.

## APPROACH

The scholarly practice of examining the ways in which various issues are treated in college-level textbooks is well established. As is common in this kind of analysis, we examined textbooks in introductory courses. The use of these texts is widespread; moreover, there is a range of texts with different authors but similar content and structure, both of which facilitate comparative study. In addition, students often receive their first impressions of a field of study through these classes and texts. While the first two of these factors are true of courses in American government, such courses are not usually designed as an introduction to the discipline of political science. Compared to other introductory courses in the social sciences, a class in American government usually serves an even wider population of students as either a state-mandated course in many public university systems or as part of the general education program in private colleges. The purpose of the course often extends beyond merely familiarizing students with the structures and activities of the national government in order to prepare them for an active role in civic life. At the same time, this course is often the only opportunity students will have to study and discuss current political events that affect them as citizens. Thus the decisions that textbook authors make about what issues to present and how to present them are important.

Textbooks are regarded as authoritative sources of information by students who are often, at least in introductory courses, encountering ideas and arguments for the first time. While it is true that most college students have been exposed to information about American government in social studies and civics courses in high school, it is not clear how frequently such courses go beyond providing students with such factual information as the number of seats in the House of Representatives to have them engage such controversial and value-laden issues as the appropriate extent of the president's power to engage in foreign affairs or alternative assessments of the success of a particular presidency.[2] College-level texts in American government often identify one or more "controversies" or "debates" in each chapter and specifically encourage students to develop personal positions on the issues that may be at odds with the positions held by classmates. The same-sex marriage issue is clearly one on which the public has diverse opinions, and one might expect to see it included in these textbooks.

Because students see textbooks as authoritative, what the texts include or exclude sends a message to students about what is important and what is not. In particular, scholars who have studied textbooks have often focused on the extent to which issues of race, ethnicity, and gender are addressed by various texts and if included, how they are discussed.[3] Published textbook reviews that discuss whether and how sexual orientation is addressed in textbooks are less common.[4] Another approach has been to examine how textbooks treat particular issues or make use of existing research findings.[5] Because of the nature of the same-sex marriage issue, this chapter will draw on both types of analysis. First, simply because the idea of same-sex marriage cannot be discussed without reference to homosexuality, the study will indirectly provide an assessment of the visibility of gay men and lesbians in these textbooks. In this respect we will be concerned with the inclusion of the topic in the text; the extent of coverage; and the language in text and pictures used to describe the issue. Drawing from studies on the ways in which particular issues are covered in textbooks, we will be concerned with the contextual placement of the discussion, the accuracy of factual information, and fairness in reporting the different arguments used in the debate.

We will begin by using a typical chapter outline of a textbook on American government to suggest ways that an author might use the issue of same-sex marriage to illustrate some of the general principles of American government.

## CONSTITUTIONAL ISSUES

Most American government texts follow their opening chapters with a chapter that focuses on the history and key principles of the United States Constitution. Many of the issues initially raised in this chapters will reappear in later chapters that investigate the principles and institutions of government in more depth. The issue of same-sex marriage as it is currently being debated raises several questions that might be directly addressed in chapters introducing students to some of the key features of the Constitution. First, the Full Faith and Credit Clause (Article IV, Section 1) provides an opportunity to discuss whether the clause requires the recognition of marriages performed in one state by all other states and what would happen if one state did choose to recognize same-sex marriages. Second, the Supremacy Clause found in Article VI might be seen to raise the question of whether the federal courts could force states that did not want to recognize same-sex marriages to do so either through enforcement of the Full Faith and Credit Clause or because of some other constitutional principle such as equal protection or due process. Article V on the constitutional amendment process offers an opportunity to look at recently proposed constitutional amendments, including the Federal Marriage Amendment (FMA). How might textbook authors use same-sex marriage to illustrate these key principles, and what have recent editions of leading American government texts chosen to do in this regard?

### The Full Faith and Credit Clause

Marriage questions have traditionally been reserved to the states. Since the country's founding, the states have adopted varying laws concerning eligibility for entering into and requirements for dissolving marriages. There is a long history of interstate conflict over these issues, with some states refusing to recognize certain marriages or divorces allowed by others.[6] Most notorious, perhaps, was the division between states that allowed interracial marriages and those that did not. One case, *Loving v. Virginia*, provided an opportunity for the United States Supreme Court to rule on whether the Full Faith and Credit Clause requires states to recognize such marriages; however, the Court passed on this opportunity and chose to invalidate the prohibition of interracial marriages on Fourteenth Amendment grounds of equal protection.

It appears that the issue of interstate recognition of same-sex marriages is likely to confront the Court with this Article IV issue once again. The national concern over this issue began in 1993, when state courts in Hawaii first ruled that the state's constitution did not allow it to deny marriage licenses to same-sex couples—although the state constitution was amended to protect the right to discriminate in marriage before the court decisions became final.[7] In 2000, the Vermont state courts almost established a right to marry for same-sex couples, but provided the state legislature a way out of compliance by allowing them to create a substitute form of relationship that has come to be known as civil union. In 2004, however, the state of Massachusetts became the first state to allow same-sex couples access to the same form and rights of marriage previously afforded only to opposite-sex couples and the concern about interstate recognition became a reality. Constitutional issues of same-sex marriage arise through the application of the Full Faith and Credit Clause (Article IV, Section 1) as well as the amendment process.

### The Supremacy Clause

Shortly after the initial court decision in Hawaii and despite its traditional deference to state governments on marriage issues, Congress passed the Defense of Marriage Act (DOMA) in 1996. The DOMA allows states to consider null and void the acts of other states regarding same-sex marriage. In addition, the DOMA denied such federal benefits as Social Security, Medicaid, and Medicare to spouses in same-sex unions. DOMA also created federal definitions of *marriage* and *spouse* for the first time in American history. Among the criticisms that can be leveled against this act is one that argues that marriage laws are not the province of the national government but a power reserved to the states. The Supremacy Clause of the Constitution states that laws "made in pursuance" of powers granted in the Constitution "shall be the supreme Law of the Land." Was DOMA made "in pursuance" of legitimate constitutional powers?

### The Amendment Process

In more than two hundred years of American history, the United States Constitution has been amended only seventeen times since the Bill of Rights was ratified. Explaining both the amendment process and remarking on the relatively few times that the document has been amended are standard fare for government texts, as is noting the fact that amendments tend either to adjust the procedural rules of the political system or expand the federal government's protection of individual rights. The notable exceptions to these two types of amendments are those that adopted and repealed Prohibition.

Because of concerns that DOMA may not be constitutional, conservative activists have been pushing since 2003 for a Federal Marriage Amendment, a constitutional amendment that would define marriage as a legal union only between a man and a woman. The proposed amendment illustrates two fundamental issues associated with Article V. On the one hand, this amendment would be the only one that singles out one class of Americans to deny them a right enjoyed by other Americans. On the other hand, this amendment may be seen as an effort to constitutionalize a social policy in a manner similar to the Eighteenth Amendment's goal of stopping alcohol consumption. And if the latter comparison is made, it could engender a discussion about why the only time the method of ratification made use of state conventions rather than state legislatures was the Twenty-first Amendment.

Is there something about "social policy" amendments that lend themselves to this alternative method?

## DEMOGRAPHIC ISSUES

Most textbooks include a chapter or a section within one that discusses the diversity of the American population. These sections typically focus on the ethnic, racial, religious, economic, and ideological diversity among citizens. Gender differences are often discussed as well. The opportunity thus presents itself to include a discussion of sexual orientation and gender identity issues. Interestingly, given the focus of this essay on same-sex marriage, one should note that the idea of marriage itself as a demographic variable of political interest is rarely introduced. Likewise, the effect of parenthood is rarely included at this point either.

When textbook authors discuss ideological differences for their readers, often distinguishing liberals from conservatives, they might add a discussion of attitudes or beliefs about homosexuality and individual rights as factors underlying one's personal ideology. As with other fundamental beliefs, the issue here is not so much a person's opinion on a particular contemporary political issue but the fundamental beliefs about homosexuality that are likely to shape those specific opinions.

## FEDERALISM

The movement to open civil marriage to same-sex couples has been fought primarily at the state level. The issue offers opportunities to illustrate several of the key elements of textbook discussions of federalism. One, already noted, concerns the applicability of the Full Faith and Credit Clause to recognition of marriages across state lines. But even further, the variation in state reactions to the issue of same-sex marriage illustrates the continuing importance of state sovereignty in American politics. In recent years, states have fallen into one of two camps—and some states have swung back and forth—states in which the rights of same-sex couples to public recognition and access to marital privileges have advanced and states that have taken action to foreclose any official recognition of same-sex couples. Since the latter activity has primarily taken the form of amendments to state constitutions, textbook writers have an opportunity to talk about the importance, nature, and "amendability" of state constitutions in comparison to the federal constitution. Likewise, because many states use initiatives or referenda (or both) as methods of lawmaking and constitution amending, and because both methods have been used to prohibit same-sex marriages, these variations in state political processes can be illustrated by using same-sex marriage as an example.

## CIVIL RIGHTS AND LIBERTIES

Fundamentally, the issue of same-sex marriage is an issue of civil rights and civil liberties, the distinction between rights and liberties being important although not always clear. Traditionally, *civil liberties* are seen as fundamental rights that are "inalienable" (such as "life, liberty, and the pursuit of happiness"), while *civil rights* refer to specific political privileges granted by the government, such as the right to vote. If rights are "fundamental," then the government should not be allowed to take any action that would impair an individual's ability to exercise those rights. If they are "only" civil, then the rights must be made available on an equal basis to all citizens. The Fourteenth Amendment, along with the rights enumerated in the Bill of Rights, is critical to understanding the debate over civil rights and liberties. It leads to the question as to whether the Fourteenth Amendment's equal protection clause should be applied to an individual's right to select his or her own marriage partner regardless of that person's sex.

The question for political debate turns on whether civil marriage is a privilege granted by the government or if, as supporters of same-sex marriage will argue, it is a fundamental right. If marriage is a fundamental right, then the government must justify in some way its decision to deny the right to marry to same-sex couples. A discussion of the levels of review in civil rights cases, such as strict scrutiny and rational basis, could be introduced as well. Failure to allow such marriages can be seen as a denial of a right to which all citizens are entitled.

But even if marriage is seen only as a civil right, gay and lesbian couples in life-long relationships that presently lack legal status as marriages can be understood as being denied equal protection under the law. Same-sex couples pay costs from which married couples are exempt, such as estate taxes when a partner dies and significant tax penalties when inheriting a 401(k) retirement plan from their partner. In addition, same-sex couples are denied government benefits given to married couples, including Social Security survivor benefits upon the death of a partner and family leave under the Family and Medical Leave Act.[8] Even where states have chosen to recognize same-sex relationships in some form under state laws, and even when state taxes and social program benefits are applied to such couples as if they were married, federal tax laws and benefit programs exclude them under the provisions of the Defense of Marriage Act (DOMA).

A response to the preceding arguments is that while there may be a fundamental right to marriage, that right is a fundamental right only with respect to opposite-sex marriage. Likewise, every gay man or lesbian in the country is entitled to marry someone of the opposite sex and become entitled to all the benefits of marriage that heterosexual married citizens receive. These arguments are similar to those raised in defense of prohibitions on interracial marriages, which were struck down by the U.S. Supreme Court in *Loving v. Virginia*, however. Can the reasoning in that case be extended to same-sex marriages, or are the cases different, and if so, how?

## INTEREST GROUPS

Chapters on interest groups focus attention on the role such groups play in the political process, including the ways in which they form, the resources they bring to their efforts, and the techniques they use to influence politicians and government officials. The battle over same-sex marriage is a classic example of the role that ideological, as opposed to economic, interest groups play in the American political system.

Interest groups on both sides of the same-sex marriage issue have been most active since 1993, when the Hawaii court's decision put the issue firmly on the political agenda. There is a "Coalition for Marriage" opposed to same-sex marriage that is comprised of fifteen national groups. The coalition includes such major players as Focus on the Family, the Family Research Council, Concerned Women for America, and the Traditional Values Coalition. Together these organizations have more than one hundred and twenty million dollars in annual income to support their causes. This coalition compares with the list of organizations seeking to gain marriage equality rights for same-sex couples: the Human Rights Campaign, the National Gay and Lesbian Task Force, and the Freedom to Marry Foundation—which together have less than twenty million dollars of annual income at their disposal.[9]

Groups on both sides of the issue have used all of the lobbying techniques described in textbooks—meeting with elected legislators and their staffs; contributing funds to political candidates; purchasing broadcast time (radio and television) and space (newspapers and magazines) for advertisements designed to pressure officials on specific issues like the Federal Marriage Amendment; lobbying officials in the executive branch regarding regulations or policies that would seem to favor or disfavor recognition of same-sex couples; activating letter-writing campaigns among their supporters, and instituting class action suits and test cases in the courts.

And the groups can be compared with one another in terms of the resources that they bring to bear in support of their positions. Frequently, comparisons are made between the large number of members and great financial resources of the groups opposed to same-sex marriage and the numbers and resources of groups favoring it. On the other hand, some of the groups in favor of same-sex marriage have become major players in making campaign contributions and producing effective leaders.

## THE MEDIA AND PUBLIC OPINION

Discussions of the media in American government texts frequently cover the historical development of the press; regulations affecting the media; the corporate structure of the major media outlets; the relatively unstructured nature of the Internet; the role of the mass media in a democratic society; and factors related to potential media bias and its expressions. Same-sex marriage can be used to illustrate the last two topics particularly well.

One of the key functions of the media with respect to politics is their ability to set the agenda of issues that politicians must address. One could argue that extensive media coverage of same-sex marriage has propelled it to the forefront of domestic political issues in the early 2000s. After all, the earliest lawsuits seeking the right for same-sex couples to marry date from the 1970s; with relatively little media coverage, however, these cases retained only local interest where they occurred and interest for activists on either side of the question. But beginning in the 1990s, particularly with the decision in Hawaii, major media coverage has kept the story on or near the front pages of major newspapers each year. Some specific events, such as the decision of Gavin Newsom, the mayor of San Francisco, to defy state law in 2004 and perform marriages at City Hall, as well as the first legal same-sex marriages in Massachusetts that same year, receive intense international coverage and discussion on almost every political talk show on television and radio.

Further, different media outlets can be compared with respect to their coverage of this issue. How does the concept of balance in coverage play out in this case? To what extent are image selections reflective of media bias? Can the media influence public attitudes on issues like same-sex marriage?

In addition to describing the role of the media in shaping and reflecting public opinion, most texts in American government devote a significant amount of space to reporting data that demonstrate the various opinions Americans have on a number of critical or current policy issues. Such opinions are often analyzed in terms of partisanship, race, age, geographic region, or gender. Obviously, same-sex marriage is an issue that one would expect to see included in any analysis of current issues on which Americans are divided.

Textbook chapters on public opinion also usually discuss political socialization—that is, how persons come to hold the values, beliefs, attitudes, and opinions that they have. The impact of family, school, religion, peers, and socioeconomic class are often identified as critical factors in shaping opinions. Another commonly included factor influencing opinions is specific events that one lives through or experiences one has. Experiences can range from living through the great depression of the 1930s to having been the victim of a crime or winner of the lottery. With respect to same-sex marriage, this latter criterion would seem to be of particular interest in two ways. On the one hand, the experience gay people and those close to them have when a person "comes out" may have an important impact on their opinion of same-sex marriage. Some survey data have suggested that knowing someone who is gay or lesbian increases tolerance of gay people and support for issues like nondiscrimination laws regarding sexual orientation. How does such an experience affect attitudes toward same-sex marriage?

## POLITICAL PARTIES, CAMPAIGNS, AND ELECTIONS

Political parties, as distinct from interest groups, are concerned with electing their candidates to public office. Textbook chapters generally describe the historical development of the American two-party system; the role political parties play in a democracy; the structure of party organizations; the different philosophies of each party; and the ways in which voters identify with parties. Although discussions of political campaigns and the electoral system are sometimes found in separate chapters, campaigns and elections are also often discussed in the context of political parties. Since the two major parties in the American political system offer decidedly different positions on the issue of same-sex marriage, the issue lends itself to inclusion at this point as well.

The two major parties are quite far apart on the issue of same-sex marriage. The Republican Party platform supports the traditional definition of marriage as the union of a man and a woman. Furthermore, the party believes that federal judges should not force states to recognize other living arrangements as constituting marriage. Republicans regard same-sex marriage as preferential treatment, namely "special legal protection or standing in the law."[10]

The Democratic Party platform does not specifically address marriage of any type but opposes discrimination based on sexual orientation and supports the appointment of "justices to the Supreme Court who have a demonstrated concern for and commitment to the individual rights protected by our Constitution, including the right to privacy."[11]

Voter identification with each major political party is often described in terms of the percentage of various demographic groups that supported the party in the last election. As noted earlier, most texts do not include sexual orientation or marital status in their sections describing the diversity of the population, so it would be surprising if they discussed the gay and lesbian vote at this stage. In a number of recent postelection polls, however, gay and lesbian voters have been identified and their party affiliation noted—about 75 percent supported the Democratic Party candidate in the last three presidential elections. And while being gay or lesbian does not automatically translate into support for same-sex marriage, sexual orientation is a reasonable proxy for such support in the absence of more specific survey data.

A final related issue concerns the role that same-sex marriage played in the 2004 presidential election. The initial explanations for George W. Bush's victory tended to credit the large turnout by "values voters," a code phrase that was meant to identify voters opposed to same-sex marriage. Subsequent research, however, has raised questions as to whether the issue of same-sex marriage was as critical as some pundits maintained.[12] Regardless of which interpretation is ultimately proven correct, however, the role that a single issue might play in electoral contests can be illustrated by same-sex marriage.

## CONGRESS

Like other chapters on the institutions of American government—the presidency, the judiciary, and the federal bureaucracy—much of the space in textbooks is devoted to the history, the basic structure, and the most prominent procedures of the legislative branch. Chapters on Congress, however, often include two topics related to the issue of same-sex marriage.

A portion of these chapters is usually devoted to the demographic characteristics of both houses of Congress. While the focus of such chapters is primarily race, ethnicity, and gender, the occupational backgrounds and income levels of Senators and Representatives are also often included here. Occasionally reference is made to the fact that in recent years, two or three members of the House have openly identified themselves as gay or lesbian. What these sections typically do not include, however, is information on the marital status of elected representatives. But with same-sex marriage and the defense of traditional marriage on the political agenda, such information may be relevant. Certainly, when Congress was considering DOMA in 1996, a number of opponents criticized the chief sponsor of the bill, Representative Bob Barr (R-GA), for having been married three times. They asked him which of his marriages he intended to "defend."

The second area in which same-sex marriage might reasonably be introduced is a discussion of the ways in which elected legislators approach their responsibilities as representatives of the people. Some approach the role as "delegates" who vote in a manner consistent with the wishes of a majority of their constituents, while others see themselves as "trustees" who vote in accordance with their personal beliefs about what is best for the polity. These contrasting perspectives offer an opportunity to ask students how they think representatives *should* view their roles. Unlike many issues that Congress has to deal with that have low salience among the general public, same-sex marriage has both high levels of salience and intensity of views—that is, almost everyone has a strong opinion on this issue.

## THE PRESIDENCY AND THE BUREAUCRACY OF THE EXECUTIVE BRANCH

Textbook chapters on the presidency focus on the structure and personnel of executive offices and the nature and sources of the formal and informal powers of the position. Discussions of presidential power offer several opportunities for the introduction of issues related to same-sex marriage.

Chapters in government textbooks typically emphasize the various considerations a president takes into account when making various types of appointments—ranging from basic qualifications to political loyalty to ensuring representation of various groups. Could a president appoint someone to a high-level position who is a partner in a same-sex marriage? Is a person's position on same-sex marriage relevant to a decision to appoint them?

Richard Neustadt concluded that the principal power of the president is the power to persuade.[13] The "bully pulpit" of the presidency can be used for many purposes. One of the best examples in recent years has been the decision by President George W. Bush to speak out in favor of the Family Marriage Amendment. There is an interesting history behind his initial reluctance to speak out on this issue, but in his 2004 State of the Union address, he called on Congress to pass a constitutional amendment defining marriage. Did he decide to speak out to get the policy adopted? Was he concerned to reassure a core constituency? Did he want to divert attention from more problematic political policies? Why and when presidents choose to use their power to promote certain issues and not others is an important subject.

Often separate from the chapter on the presidency is a chapter on the bureaucracy attached to the executive branch. One of the key parts of the discussion here concerns the power of the bureaucracy and its ability to make policy decisions regarding the implementation of laws. While this topic may seem far removed from the issue of same-sex marriage, the subject has, in fact, come into play in some recent cases of bureaucratic decision making—including compensation to the survivors of the victims of the 9/11 attacks on the World Trade Center and the Pentagon. Another example is the decision of the U.S. Department of Housing and Urban Development to negotiate certain domestic partnership benefits with its unionized employees.

## THE JUDICIARY

In addition to describing the dualistic structure of the American judicial system (federal and state), chapters on the judiciary devote much space to the selection of judges, factors that influence judicial decision making, the varying jurisdictions and roles of different types of courts, and the power of judicial review as a check on the other branches of government. Given that the recent history of the same-sex marriage issue has largely been carried out in the courts, there are many opportunities to introduce the topic of same-sex marriage here.

The personal characteristics of judges are thought by some observers to influence both the manner in which they decide cases and, in the case of high court judges, their choice of cases to accept for consideration. Again, race, ethnicity, gender, and religion are usually identified as important factors; region and political party membership often come into play as well. Sexual orientation and marital status have not been identified as important factors so far, but if background does influence decision making, one would expect that these characteristics should be relevant, especially with regard to legal challenges in the area of same-sex marriage.

Similarly, the subject of ideology often arises in discussions of the confirmation process for federal judges, and a position on same-sex marriage may soon become one of the so-called litmus tests for nomination or confirmation.

Same-sex marriage also offers an opportunity to discuss the different jurisdictions of different types of courts—both differences between state and federal courts and differences in subject matter, such as military, bankruptcy, tax, or domestic relations courts. Most of the same-sex marriage cases have been tried in state courts; those cases argued by legal interest groups have often been very careful to structure their case in terms of state law in order to prevent the case being appealed to the U.S. Supreme Court for failure to raise a federal question. Why would someone *not* want the U.S. Supreme Court to decide a question? What does this tell us about jurisdiction? And in a number of cases in specialized state courts, judges have begun to treat same-sex couples who are not legally married as if they were married; that is, in finding that domestic partners can inherit rent-controlled apartments in New York City in the same manner as a spouse. Can a couple be considered married for some purposes and not for others? And most recently in Ohio, following the adoption of a state constitutional amendment that prohibits the government (including the courts) from giving "legal status" to any relationship not sanctioned by the state as a marriage, the courts have started denying claims of domestic violence from partners who are not legally married to their alleged abusers. Students are often surprised by the ways in which the law itself can define the jurisdiction of a court.

Finally, the same-sex marriage issue presents a classic case for the argument over "judicial activism" versus "judicial restraint" and "strict construction." In the last few years, the use by politicians of the phrase *activist judges* has come to refer almost exclusively to judges who have made rulings that were favorable to supporters of same-sex marriage. What does the term mean in this context? It could be argued, for example, that in Massachusetts, the justices were strict constructionists of the state constitution in that they could find nothing in the text that said same-sex marriages were prohibited; but they did find language saying that every citizen of the state should have equal access to the benefits provided by government, which in their view included marriage. Or was the fact that they reached a decision that had never been reached by any court before enough to make them "judicial activists?" It would be important to note that the advocates of the Federal Marriage Amendment are correct in saying that a constitutional amendment is the only sure way to prevent the possibility of judges ruling that one or another of the provisions of either the federal or state constitutions requires the finding that same-sex marriages be allowed on the grounds of equal protection, due process, privacy, or some other basis.

## METHODOLOGY

American government textbooks present a somewhat confusing universe from which to draw a sample. There is no single source listing all texts that are currently used in American colleges and universities. Furthermore, there are often multiple editions of the same text—not just chronological editions coming out every few years, but multiple contemporaneous editions of the same text designed for different audiences, teaching preferences, or school calendars. Hence one often finds the same title and authors listed with some combination of a brief edition, an alternative edition, a paperback edition, a national edition, a state or local edition, and, presumably, a regular edition. For this study, the authors simply tried to obtain copies of as many different American government textbooks with publication copyright dates of 2005 or 2006 as possible. When more than one version of the same book by the same authors met this requirement, the authors selected the version that appeared to be either the standard edition or the most comprehensive. While it is possible that information on the same-sex marriage issue that was included in the edition we reviewed would not be present in a brief or alternative edition, it is at least as likely that if it were included, it would be discussed in approximately the same format and language as in the edition we reviewed. This approach provided us with twenty different textbooks representing eighteen different authors or author teams.[14] Since the purpose of this chapter is not to provide a review of specific texts but rather to note trends in coverage of the issue, we will not discuss specific characteristics of individual texts.

Following a common approach in textbook studies,[15] we used the index and tables of contents to search for information on the same-sex marriage issue. We searched such terms as *marriage, gay, lesbian, homosexual, civil rights*, and *same-sex*. We also searched tables of contents and lists of figures, tables, maps, boxes, and photos for items that might be relevant. We then examined each entry, table, or photograph for relevance to the study. Relevant passages, sections, tables, boxed items, and photos were then analyzed by both authors and assessed in terms of the extent of coverage; placement of the discussion or photo in the text; language used; factual accuracy; and bias. Of these twenty books, all but one included an index reference to same-sex marriage at some point—not necessarily a primary listing under that term, but often as a subcategory under "gays and lesbians" or "marriage." The one text that did not include an index reference did make mention of the term at least once, as we accidentally discovered in simply scanning some relevant sections of the text.

## FINDINGS

As noted above, all but one of the texts had an index entry for same-sex or gay marriage. Four texts mentioned the issue of same-sex marriage in only one chapter; six texts raised it in two chapters; two texts found three subject areas in which to discuss it; three texts placed it under four different headings; four texts used the issue to illustrate five different topics; and one book raised the issue in six different chapters.

While there was some variety in the topics that authors chose for discussing the issue of same-sex marriage, they overwhelmingly saw it as a civil rights issue (sixteen of twenty). Two additional texts discussed it as a civil liberties issue, meaning that eighteen textbooks saw the issue as one having implications for a discussion of individual rights and liberties. The next most frequent chapter in which the topic was discussed was federalism, where it was raised as an illustration of the Full Faith and Credit Clause of the Constitution (nine of twenty). Introductory chapters, chapters on the Constitution, and chapters on public opinion included discussions of same-sex marriage in four textbooks, while three placed it in chapters on parties, elections, the judiciary, and state and local government. Two texts had chapters on public policy that mentioned same-sex marriage. The subject appeared in chapters on demographics, Congress, and the presidency chapters in only one textbook each. This count does not mean, for example, that a text that did not place the discussion in the chapter on federalism did not raise the issue of full faith and credit, or that public opinion about the issue was not raised in a chapter on elections, but it does provide some guidance in understanding how the textbook authors conceived the issue within the context of the American political system.

Some critics[16] have argued that placing a topic in a separate box suggests that the issue is marginal and may lead students to discount it. On the other hand, it is possible to see boxed items as drawing students' attention to the importance or currency of an issue in a way that might not be accomplished by merely incorporating the topic in the text. Sixteen of these texts placed some aspect of the same-sex marriage issue in a separate box outside the normal flow of the text. Some presented a general discussion of the issue while others focused specifically on the Federal Marriage Amendment, and one addressed the process of amending state constitutions. In addition, two texts—including one with a boxed discussion—selected the issue of same-sex marriage to open their chapter with a vignette illustrating some of the basic principles of federalism. This primacy of place can be seen as enhancing the importance of the issue.

Fourteen of the texts included at least one photograph to illustrate the same-sex marriage issue, for a total of twenty-three photos. Photographs can be interpreted in different ways, obviously, by different viewers. There is a long history of debate within the gay and lesbian community, for example, about the impact of print and broadcast images of gay pride parades that focus on certain types of participants (for example, drag queens, leathermen, or bare-breasted women) rather than more "normal-looking" folks.[17] Of the texts examined, four included photographs of couples being married or just married. All of these were lesbian couples—two women of color in San Francisco, one of Rosie O'Donnell and her partner, and two sets of photos of the Goodridges, who were the first-named plaintiffs in the Massachusetts court case. Three of the texts showed public officials supposedly addressing the same-sex marriage issue—one of President Bush announcing support for the Federal Marriage Amendment, one of Gavin Newsom, the mayor of San Francisco, and one of Georgia State Assembly member Nan Orrock at a rally opposed to the anti–same-sex marriage constitutional amendment on the state ballot. Eleven texts showed photos of demonstrations or rallies over the issue; two texts showed only anti–same-sex marriage demonstrators; six showed only pro–same-sex marriage demonstrators. In all but one of the photos, which pictured four bare-chested men at a gay pride rally with a caption raising questions about same-sex marriage, the individuals shown getting married or protesting in favor of same-sex marriage were "normal-looking" people.

The issue of language is important here; the terms used to describe the issue convey meaning in and of themselves. Supporters of same-sex marriage currently frame the issue using the emotionally laden terms *freedom* (as in "freedom to marry") and *equality* (as in "marriage equality"). These terms are especially important in an introductory class in American government, often stating a theme that is carried throughout the course. While none of the authors used these terms to characterize the issue in their discussions, photographs that included same-sex marriage supporters sometimes showed placards with these mottos. On the other hand, same-sex marriage opponents are disinclined to even use the word *marriage* to describe this issue. Some sources, such as the *Washington Times*, put the word *marriage* in quotation marks whenever they use it in connection with the same-sex marriage issue.[18] None of the textbook authors used this method of discussing the issue. *Gay marriage* is seen as somewhat misleading and pejorative because it implies that this union is something other than a real marriage; for many, *gay* is a term that refers only to male homosexuals, thus leaving lesbians out of the discussion.[19] *Same-sex marriage* is seen by many advocates as the more neutral way to describe the issue, since the principal difference in their eyes is only that unlike traditional opposite-sex marriage, the two partners belong to the same sex. There are some, however, like the National Lesbian and Gay Journalists Association, who argue against using either *gay marriage* or *same-sex marriage*, since either version implies that the issue is something other than marriage equality.[20] Of the texts we reviewed, five were consistent in using only the term *same-sex marriage* whenever the issue was raised; three used only *gay marriage*. The remaining twelve texts used both terms, while one also used the term *homosexual marriage*. It is possible that this variation in usage within a text is due to the fact that some of them were written by multiple authors or that the authors simply employed what they viewed as harmless stylistic variations. It should be noted, though, that one author consistently used the terms *same-sex marriage* and *opposite-sex marriage* whenever discussing the issue.

## CONCLUSION

Textbooks in American government have always made an effort to engage student interest by including material on current topics. The same-sex marriage issue has proven to be a popular topic for these authors, given that all of the texts raise the issue at least once. It is also significant that eighteen texts included their discussion of the issue under the heading of civil rights or civil liberties. This is a characterization consistent with the way most advocates of same-sex marriage regard the issue. Opponents of same-sex marriage are much more likely to see the issue as one of either federalism (involving states' rights) or the judiciary (as an example of judicial activism that they dislike). Additionally, half the texts examined explicitly raise the issue of same-sex marriage in at least three of the traditional text chapters. This finding suggests that they are willing to see the issue in a broad context rather than as one that can be isolated as a mere curiosity or as an issue of limited impact. Nearly three-fourths of the texts included a photograph to illustrate their discussions; the photos for the most part simply presented the issue and participants on both sides of the debate as ordinary people exercising their political rights in one form or another. The language used was respectful for the most part of both supporters and opponents of same-sex marriage. Eleven of the texts identified the issue for special consideration by making it a boxed item, often asking students to carefully consider both sides of the debate.

When one actually examines the text describing the issue, most of the books do a reasonably good job. Not every book covers every aspect of the same-sex marriage issue nor do they cover each aspect equally well within a single text. Several of the texts have sections of surprisingly different quality, presumably due to being written by different coauthors. But overall, students reading these texts will have a fairly accurate picture of the issue. A few texts left the impression that Hawaii and Vermont had actually legalized same-sex marriages; some texts confused the year of the Massachusetts court decision with the year that same-sex couples first got married. But on the whole, the students reading most of these texts will learn about the court decision in Hawaii, civil unions in Vermont, and the Massachusetts Supreme Judicial Court decision. Most texts make clear that the 1996 Defense of Marriage Act has not yet been tested in the U.S. Supreme Court, so it isn't clear whether the Constitution's Full Faith and Credit Clause will apply to the case of same-sex marriages. Students will know that opponents of same-sex marriage have introduced a constitutional amendment defining marriage in the U.S. Congress, that it didn't pass when it was voted on the first time, and that several states have recently passed state constitutional amendments designed to prevent such marriages. Several of the texts mentioned that same-sex marriage was an issue that contributed to motivating some conservative voters in the 2004 election, but none of these blamed Kerry's loss on the issue. A number of texts tracked public opinion on the same-sex marriage issue and used the information to explain differences among different demographic groups. Overwhelmingly, the students reading these books are between the ages of eighteen and twenty-five, so perhaps most importantly, the public opinion data in various charts show that young people are far more supportive of same-sex marriage than their elders.

Most of the texts make clear that the debate over same-sex marriage is simply another political issue that this nation happens to be confronting in the early 2000s. Although the specific facts and questions are different from those in other political debates, same-sex marriage is not a freakish or unique issue. Most textbooks provide students with the basic facts of the legal and constitutional issues at stake and a reasonable presentation of the arguments used by both sides in the current debate. Most suggest that public opinion is changing in a positive direction. There is always room for improvement—a lot of room for improvement in a few cases—but it would be unfair to conclude that textbooks in American government are inadequate in presenting students with fair and balanced information about same-sex marriage.

NOTES

1. David G. Adler, "The Law: Textbooks and the President's Constitutional Powers," *Presidential Studies Quarterly* 35 (2005): 376–88.

2. See for example J. M. Sanchez, "Awaiting Rehabilitation: The Carter Presidency in Political Science Textbooks," *Presidential Studies Quarterly* 27 (1997): 284–96.

3. See for example Denise Robson, "Women and Minorities in Economics Textbooks: Are They Being Adequately Represented?" *Journal of Economics Education* 32 (2001): 186–91; Tamar Mayer, "Consensus and Invisibility: The Representation of Women in Human Geography Textbooks," *Professional Geographer* 41 (1989): 397–409; Jason Low and Peter Sherrard, "Portrayal of Women in Sexuality and Marriage and Family Textbooks: A Content Analysis of Photographs from the 1970s, 1980s, and 1990s," *Sex Roles* 40 (1999): 309–18; K. Zittleman and D. Sadker, "Teacher Education Textbooks: The Unfinished Gender Revolution," *Educational Leadership* 60, no. 4 (2002/2003): 59–63; and Jeffrey S. Ashley and Karen Jarrat-Ziemski, "Superficiality and Bias: The (Mis)Treatment of Native Americans in U.S. Government Textbooks," *American Indian Quarterly* 23, no. 3 (1999): 49–62.

4. Vicki L. Eaklor, "How Queer-Friendly Are U.S. History Textbooks?" *History News Network*, January 26, 2004, http://hnn.us/articles/3200.html (accessed January 3, 2006).

5. See for example Bruce Rind, "Biased Use of Cross-Cultural and Historical Perspectives on Male Homosexuality in Human Sexuality Textbooks," *Journal of Sex Research* 35 (1998): 397–407; Hendrika Van de Kemp, "Religion in College Textbooks: Allport's Historic 1948 Report," *International Journal for the Psychology of Religion* 5 (1995): 199–211; and Tracey Hurd and Mary Brabeck, "Presentation of Women and Gilligan's Ethic of Care in College Textbooks, 1970–1990: An Examination of Bias," *Teaching of Psychology* 24, no. 3 (1997): 159–67.

6. Brian H. Bix, "State Interests in Marriage, Interstate Recognition, and Choice of Law," *Creighton Law Review* 38 (2005): 337–51.

7. There are a number of sources describing the recent legal cases concerning same-sex marriage, including Robert Baird and Stuart E. Rosenbaum, eds., *Same-Sex Marriage: The Legal and Moral Debate* (Amherst, NY: Prometheus Books, 1997); Sean Cahill, *Same-Sex Marriage in the United States* (Lanham, MD: Lexington Books, 2004); Martin Dupuis, *Same-Sex Marriage, Legal Mobilization, and the Politics of Rights* (New York: Peter Lang, 2002); and Daniel R. Pinello, *America's Struggle for Same-Sex Marriage* (New York: Cambridge University Press, 2006).

8. Human Rights Campaign, "Top 10 Reasons for Marriage Equality," http://www.hrc.org/Template.cfm?Section=Center&CONTENTID=14392&TEMPLATE =/ContentManagemen/ContentDisplay.cfm (accessed November 14, 2005).

9. Sean Cahill, "Anti-Gay Groups Active in Massachusetts: A Closer Look," National Gay and Lesbian Task Force, http://www.thetaskforce.org/downloads/AntiGayMA.pdf (accessed November 14, 2005).

10. National Gay and Lesbian Task Force, "The 2000 Republican Party Platform Includes Numerous Statements that Attack Lesbian, Gay, Bisexual, and Transgender Citizens and Families," July 2, 2003, http://www.thetaskforce.org/downloads/Rep2000Platform.pdf (accessed November 18, 2005).

11. National Gay and Lesbian Task Force, "The 2000 Democratic Party Platform Includes Numerous Statements that Support Lesbian, Gay, Bisexual, and Transgender Citizens and Families," July 2, 2003, http://www.thetaskforce.org/downloads/Dem2000 Platform.pdf (accessed November 18, 2005).

12. Kenneth Sherrill and Patrick Egan, "Lesbians, Gays, Bisexuals, and the Electorate," *APSA News Room*, 2005, http://www.apsanet.org/content_5215.cfm (accessed January 3, 2006).

13. Richard E. Neustadt, *Presidential Power and the Modern Presidents* (New York: Free Press, 1991).

14. Larry Berman and Bruce Allen Murphy, *Approaching Democracy*, 4th ed. (Upper Saddle River, NJ: Prentice Hall, 2005); Jon R. Bond, Kevin B. Smith, and Richard A. Watson, *The Promise and Performance of American Democracy*, 7th ed. (Belmont, CA: Thomson Wadsworth, 2006); Milton C. Cummings Jr. and David Wise, *Democracy Under Pressure*, 10th ed., alternate version (Belmont, CA: Thomson Wadsworth, 2005); Thomas R. Dye and Harmon Zeigler, *The Irony of Democracy: An Uncommon Introduction to American Politics*, 13th ed. (Belmont, CA: Thomson Wadsworth, 2006); Thomas R. Dye, *Politics in America*, 6th ed., basic version (Upper Saddle River, NJ: Pearson Prentice Hall, 2005); George C. Edwards III, Martin P. Wattenberg, and Robert L. Lineberry, *Government in America: People, Politics, and Policy*, 12th ed. (New York: Pearson Longman, 2006); Morris P. Fiorina, Paul E. Peterson, Bertram Johnson, and D. Stephen Voss, *The New American Democracy*, 4th ed. (New York: Pearson Longman, 2005); Morris P. Fiorina, Paul E. Peterson, D. Stephen Voss, and Bertram Johnson, *America's New Democracy*, 3rd ed. (New York: Pearson Longman, 2006); Benjamin Ginsberg, Theodore J. Lowi, and Margaret Weir, *We the People: An Introduction to American Politics*, shorter 5th ed. (New York: W. W. Norton & Company, 2005); Edward S. Greenberg and Benjamin I. Page, *America's Democratic Republic* (New York: Pearson Longman, 2005); Matthew R. Kerbel, *American Government* (Cincinnati, OH: Atomic Dog, 2006); Kenneth Janda, Jeffrey M. Berry, and Jerry Goldman, *The Challenge of Democracy: Government in America*, 8th ed. (Boston: Houghton Mifflin Company, 2005); Karen O'Connor, Karen and Larry J. Sabato, *American Government: Continuity and Change*, alternate 2006 ed. (New York: Pearson Longman, 2006); David B. Magleby, David M. O'Brien, Paul C. Light, James MacGregor Burns, J. W. Peltason, and Thomas E. Cronin, *Government by the People*, 21st ed. (Upper Saddle River, NJ: Prentice Hall, 2006); Thomas E. Patterson, *The American Democracy*, 7th ed. (Boston: McGraw-Hill, 2005); Thomas E. Patterson, *We the People: A Concise Introduction to American Politics*, 6th ed. (Boston: McGraw-Hill, 2006); Steffen W. Schmidt, Mack C. Shelley, and Barbara A. Bardes, *American Government and Politics Today*, 2005-2006 alternate ed. (Belmont, CA: Thomson Wadsworth, 2005); Edward Sidlow and Beth Henschen, *America At Odds*, 5th alternate ed. (Belmont, CA: Thomson Wadsworth, 2007); Walter E. Volkomer, *American Government*, 10th ed. (Upper Saddle River, NJ: Pearson Prentice Hall, 2005); James Q. Wilson and John J. DiIulio, Jr., *American Government*, 10th ed. (Boston: Houghton Mifflin Company, 2006).

15. See note 5.

16. Zittleman and Sadker, "Teacher Education Textbooks," 62 (see note 3).

17. See Edward Alwood, *Straight News: Gays, Lesbians, and the News Media* (New York: Columbia University Press, 1996); Larry Gross, *Up from Invisibility: Lesbians, Gay Men, and the Media in America* (New York: Columbia University Press, 2001).

18. S. A. Miller, "State Legislatures Will Open to New Faces, Partisan Battles," *Washington Times*, January 11, 2006, http://www.washingtontimes.com/metro/20060110 -103844-2179r.htm (accessed January 11, 2006).

19. Gay and Lesbian Alliance Against Defamation, "Marriage Equality for Same-Sex Couples," May 14, 2004, http://www.glaad.org/media/resource_kit_detail.php?id=3457 #terminology (accessed January 11, 2006).

20. National Lesbian and Gay Journalists Association, "Open Letter from the National Lesbian and Gay Journalists Association to the News Industry on Accurate Reporting About Marriage for Gays and Lesbians," February 10, 2004, http://www.nlgja.org/news/news 10feb04.html (accessed January 11, 2006).

# Part III

## CULTURAL PERSPECTIVES

# 10

# "AR'N'T WE A COUPLE?": A HISTORICAL COMPARISON OF SLAVE MARRIAGES AND SAME-SEX MARRIAGES

*Randolph W. Baxter*

In her 1985 book from which this chapter derives its title, *Ar'n't I A Woman*, Deborah Gray White, like many historians of slavery, reviews the legal denial of civil marriage rights to slaves in the antebellum United States.[1] Slaves did enjoy private marriage ceremonies, some even officiated by their white owners on the plantation, but only within the distorted constructions of the slave system. There was no guarantee that slaves would not be separated from their chosen partner by sale or removal unless they proved themselves to be loyal workers—and, for women, a childbearing asset to the slave owner. Since Western marriage customs have historically involved some form of economic, family, and property rights, slaves were ineligible as they themselves were considered property. Nonetheless, informal marriage ceremonies for slaves were never *prohibited* in American law and were even unofficially sanctioned by whites who either projected their eighteenth- or nineteenth-century moral values onto slaves and/or pragmatically hoped to help redeem slaves from their apparent prenuptial sexual liberality. Slave owners developed loose criteria for allowing slave marriage ceremonies to occur; they would either preside themselves at ceremonies or encourage slave preachers to do so. Each case provided a sense of moral legitimacy or social stability.

Despite these concessions, slaves' romantic attachments and emotional, social, or moral commitments were ultimately subordinated to—and could be functionally invalidated by—the hegemonic demands of a culture focused on a social status defined in racial terms and on economic productivity. Slaves' standards for marriage were more practical and less orthodox than the prevailing mores of the day. Ceremonies often followed the birth of the couple's first child by a few months or even years. Slaves prudently waited to ensure they could remain together before making public commitments to each other. Becoming parents may have proven the female's fertility but failed as a form of marriage legitimization, since childbearing merely raised the possibility that the slave woman had been raped by her white owner. Slave-slave relationships were constantly under threat of outside violence which delegitimated the slaves' pledges to each other. The union of two slaves was not necessarily consummated by sexual intercourse between two virgins on the wedding night, per the traditional norms of the dominant Western or Judeo-Christian culture. Indeed, some white observers—including those seeking to justify their racial and class domination—dismissed the seriousness of slave relationships altogether, since slaves sometimes "tried each other out" before marrying and seemed to dispense with the concept of the immorality of premarital sex. Only during and after the Civil War could former slaves have their marriages formally recognized. They did so by the tens of thousands, using institutions like the Freedmen's Bureau to institutionally legitimize what the individuals involved had privately declared to be valid years before.

Lesbian and gay couples in the century following the abolition of slavery in the United States faced a similar set of restrictions on their ability to have their commitments recognized by the hegemonic power structures of the day.[2] While bounded more by religious, moral and social condemnations of homosexuality in general and of nonheterosexual marriage in particular, including occasionally violent repression by homophobic fanatics, today's homosexual Americans seeking to legally wed suffer on a more emotional level than did slaves, though also in an economic sense. Taxation, insurance, and inheritance matters, legal protections, housing and employment issues, and jurisdiction over children (among a great many topics) are affected by social conservatives' rejection of the legitimacy of lesbian and gay marriages. Informal lesbian and gay marriage ceremonies, like slave marriages before the Civil War and other modern blessings of such items as houses and pets, have never been prohibited by law but have been denied cultural and legal validation. Like slave marriages, homosexual unions have enjoyed individual sanction by various heterosexual friends, family members, and even by liberal-minded clergy. Unlike the attitude of some whites toward slaves, heterosexuals have—so far—not promoted lesbian or gay marriage as a means of "saving" homosexuals from the moral evils of sexual promiscuity. Indeed, such a move would imply the recognition that culturally and legally institutionalized homophobia, not homosexuals' own moral failure, has largely and unfairly constructed gay and lesbian people as perverts and deviants.

Like former slaves, nonheterosexual people in the United States have rarely if ever based their unions on the traditional foundation of premarital virginity. Formal relationships have been autonomously validated in the form of private and personal commitments. These ceremonies often occur years after the relationship was established emotionally and sexually. Starting in the 1970s, lesbian and gay members of religious organizations began seeking ecclesiastical recognition of their unions. Since the 1990s, individuals and organizations in several states have championed governmental recognition of marriage rights for all consenting adults regardless of sexual orientation; in at least one state, Massachusetts, gay marriages were legalized in 2004, and more limited civil unions or domestic partnerships have been established in a few other states. Indeed, analysts of the 1970s homosexual rights movement may find it ironic that a community which—in the name of self-exploration, individuality, and sexual variety—had officially rejected "old-fashioned" heterosexist ideas like monogamous relationships (much less lifelong commit-ments), had within three decades shifted its focus and collective voice. Same-sex marriage and the associated right to adopt children have become two of the most hotly contested civil rights issues of the twenty-first century.

What we may call "slave culture" and "gay culture," therefore, each involved the promotion of marriage ceremonies despite contemporary legal prohibition of such acts. Both groups pragmatically adapted the concept of marriage to societies which, in the name of morality and tradition, refused to allow such acts despite their own potentially immoral promotion of institutionalized slavery and homophobia. Deborah White's illustration of slaves' inability to control their own marital destinies raises several questions. What constituted a marriage to slaves and slave owners, and what constitutes marriage today to lesbian and gay Americans? Why did slaves then, and why do same-sex couples now, choose to make public commitments in the face of pointed denial by their larger cultures to sanction legal marriages for their respec-tive groups? Did members of each group merely "try each other out" for a while, like a new pair of shoes, before making a marriage-like commitment to symbolize their intent for a permanent or monogamous relationship? Did slaves then, and do lesbian and gay people today, show admirable realism in waiting to legally marry until the consent of the master/government can be ascertained?

This essay seeks to answer some of these questions, specifically those relating to the meaning of marriage to restricted communities or heterodox groups. Other historians must take up the task of examining more fully the creation and historical development of white slave owners' and heterosexuals' construction of the "other" in regard to slaves and homosexuals—images that allow the former both to con-demn that "other" while celebrating themselves as the normative or orthodox group. The author seeks here to compare the phenomena of self-initiated slave and lesbian or gay marriages from the viewpoint of the participants. Evidence here is admittedly weighted toward the slave experience—a perspective more distant from current memory and no longer available for personal elaboration and direct comparison. While each instance of such legitimization of marriage after sexual contact or alter-native marriage symbolism is specific to its time and situation, parallels can be drawn between them. One hopes that contemporary analysts of same-sex unions can appreciate a past example of one culture's independent investment of meaning in rit-uals. Similar social, legal, and economic circumstances coincided in the experience of slaves and today's homosexual communities to the point at which a significant portion of the oppressed heterodox group disregarded their era's prohibitions and consciously constructed ways to validate their marriages autonomously.

## SLAVE MARRIAGES IN THE SOUTH

Despite the fact that most slaves were illiterate, a wealth of material survives to allow historical analysis. One may grant that ascertaining the symbolism of marriage and other customs from a vanished culture based on oral history is not easy. Slave narra-tives from the 1840s and 1850s and the narratives of former slaves recorded in the 1930s provide views of marriage from the slave perspective and clues to how these events were legitimated in the slaves' minds—though these stories must be carefully separated from contemporary biases. Most antebellum narratives of escaped slaves, for example, were published with an eye to highlighting the moral evil of slavery; if they mentioned marriage at all, they usually made only disparaging comments about the slave owners' interference with slaves' wishes. Many comments on slave behavior survive in the writings of slave owners themselves, but these must be carefully strained to surmount the Victorian moralism that prevailed among nineteenth-century whites. Records from the Freedmen's Bureau, civil registers, and the U.S. Army reveal the actions and motives of those who desired formal validation of existing marriages by having them recorded after the former slaves were able to obtain legal marriage licenses. Twentieth-century recollections of former slaves also suffer from heavy emphasis on the negative experiences of slavery, subsequent segregation, and ongoing racism. Stories about such rare happy events in life as marriage do emerge in the oral histories taken by Depression-era historians as less affected by the former slaves' more horrific memories.

Slaves in every era have faced unavoidable restrictions, given their enforced lack of freedom and access to basic rights. Roman law formed the legal basis of most Western societies, the majority of which were slaveholding at one point or another. Slave marriages were not legally recognized, although "Christianity did lead to a significant improvement in the marital and familial condition of slaves," thus "encourage[ing] masters to respect the integrity of slave marriages and families"[3] through such core texts as St. Paul's Epistle to Philemon. Christian pressure contributed to the abolition of slavery in the Roman Empire, but not until centuries had passed. Laws forbidding slaves to marry were revived in the British Empire, including the North American colonies that broke away to form the United States. The United States Constitution left slave law in the hands of the states; as late as 1857, the North Carolina State Supreme Court declared, "A slave cannot make a contract. Therefore, he cannot marry legally. Marriage is based upon contract. Consequently, the relation of 'man and wife' cannot exist among slaves."[4]

Class-based economics and religion had complicated the status of marriage and sexual relations over the intervening eighteen hundred years. The papacy had originally "accepted the Roman legal maxim of mutual consent as the judicial form of marriage" wherein "sexual intercourse was considered a testament of the vow, the presumption being that full consent had been exercised." When the Roman Catholic Church raised marriage to the status of a sacrament in the thirteenth century, however, it declared that nonforced unions were legitimate only if the partners' consent was certified by a priest. The Council of Trent even declared the superiority of celibacy and lifelong virginity in its 1563 marriage canons. Subsequent political battles between Rome and the Spanish Crown led the latter to prohibit the legitimization of "unequal unions" between persons from different social classes in 1776, since they were deemed "detrimental to the economic prosperity of honorable families and to their social exclusivity" and since they "undermined the hierarchy and integrity of the state." Egalitarian unions based on romantic love threatened status, inheritance, and kinship structures in Europe's feudal systems, which were replicated in the New World in such socioeconomic institutions as the *rancherias* of colonial Latin America and the plantations of the Anglo American South.[5]

Anglo Americans struggled with the moral implications of slavery. Marriage, like religious conversion, humanized slaves. The Puritan minister Cotton Mather upset many Massachusetts slaveholders when he urged whites to treat Negroes "not as Bruits but as Men, those rational creatures whom God has made your Servants…he is thy Brother, too," having "equal Right with other Men, to the Exercises and Privileges of Religion." Many slave owners chose to see conversion to Christianity and marriage as a threat to the security of the slave-master hierarchy and definitions of property. Free status was denied to any slave born in the colonies, starting with Virginia's Act of 1705. This change from an earlier custom, which had granted freedom to American-born slaves who reached the age of twenty-one, at once exempted slaves from laws pertaining to fornication (premarital sex), adultery, and bigamy; and abolished the imposition of punishment (for both free and enslaved people) for the rape of slaves. After the direct import of new slaves decreased in the early 1800s, the informal acceptance of both white men's rape of slave women and of the slaves' reproduction through their own promiscuity or marriages gained an economic motive, if not an imperative. The nineteenth-century antebellum South is the "best-known case" where slaves' "natural reproduction" became "both profitable and necessary. For these reasons stable unions and households were encouraged, sometimes even required, by the master class." Slave owners debated the merits of exogamous marriages, whereby one slave would marry another from a different farm or plantation; most owners had too few slaves to limit marriages to their own holdings. Some masters thought that such "broad" (that is, abroad) marriages "kept things in balance," while others bragged about having never separated a husband and wife by sale.[6]

How did the enslaved themselves view the concept of marriage? Slaves and former slaves alike recognized that their unions did not confer the same legal rights and privileges as those of whites, yet still attached their own symbolic importance to marriage. To most slaves, as historian Deborah White explains, "Marriage sanctioned motherhood, not sexual intercourse. Prenuptial intercourse was not considered evil, nor was it, as too many Southern whites mistakenly assumed, evidence of promiscuity. Slaves rejected guilt-laden white sexual attitudes." Since the rape of slaves by white men—always a possibility for slave women—was sanctioned by slave owners eager to increase the value of their "property" and thus dismissed as a moral construct, slaves in response could pragmatically dispense with the moral concern over the lack of "chaste" (virginal) women as suitable marriage partners. Eugene Genovese, the eminent analyst of slave culture, adds that "Virginity at marriage carried only small prestige…a 'good girl,' therefore, was one who could be expected to be a loving and faithful wife, not one who could claim to have been untouched by human hands. That particular pretension, staunchly adhered to by the whites, although much less in their guilt-producing practice than in their hotly maintained theory, the slaves found slightly ridiculous." The moral concept of "illegitimate" children also lost its potency for slaves. Indeed, bearing children was "a way to anchor oneself to a given plantation for an extended period of time, and thus maintain enduring relationships with family and friends." It was "not surprising to find," White noted, the common event of "slave women marrying the father of [her] first child after its birth." The historian Herbert Gutman concurs, reflecting, "It hardly mattered whether the child was born prior to or after a slave marriage" since couples "realized that if they had children early, their owners would have both economic and ethical reasons to allow them to remain together."[7]

White observers reported that the majority of slaves engaged in premarital sex among themselves, yet did "not consider this intercourse an evil thing." An 1853 North Carolina court case noted that slaves generally "respect[ed] the exclusive rights of fellow-slaves who are married." One Northerner in 1863 reminded his readers that "Negro marriages are not the less enduring from their lack of form. They usually last for life...regardless of the *ceremony* of marriage, it did not take away" from "the idea of fidelity between man and wife." The concept of "trial marriage" troubled many whites, though. A Mississippi slave owner unwittingly recognized the new relational ethics when he remarked that his slaves rarely married "for good...without trying each other out, as they say, for two or three weeks, to see how they are going to like each other." Eighty years later, a former slave recalled that such behavior was labeled a "make-out." Harriet Beecher Stowe learned of a Florida slave who had agreed to what appears to have been a trial marriage, and who explained, "we lib along two year—he watchin' my ways and I watchin' his ways."[8]

Slave marriage symbolism grew in part out of the need to redress the lack of legal sanction. Slaves developed broad definitions of "legitimate" marriages, autonomously validating what white society denied them. Once they did decide to marry, slaves often had simple ceremonies with symbolism that whites may have found quaint or odd, yet inoffensive. "In the defiant spirit of love, black folk created ways to celebrate and bless their chosen unions," one modern human-rights group recalls. "Many chose to continue the traditional African marriage custom of jumping the broom—a ritual symbolizing new life and commitment."[9] Since most slave couples had already had sexual intercourse, the emotional and physical climax of the wedding day was diminished. The former slave May Satterfield recalled that "niggers didn't git marr'ed lack white folks. Didn't have no cer'mony [with] papers an' a preacher...de master say sumpin' f'om a book; den you would jump ovah de broomstick an' you was marr'd to go back to de cabin what de gal come f'om and raise chillun." Slaves invested the practice with symbolic authority. "When yer married, yer had to jump over a broom three times. Dat wuz de license," former slave Georgianna Gibbs recalled in the 1930s. Some couples held hands while jumping; some jumped over and then back again. Less common rituals included carrying a lamp or pail of water over the head. Other couples merely declared their ties "by the blanket." "We comes together in the same cabin," one former slave from Georgia recalled, "and she brings her blanket and lay it down beside mine; and we gets married that a-way." Escaped slaves wrote in their 1850s narratives that they "tried to make it [marriage] as lawful as they can." More than any, the broomstick was included so that "they felt more married." This ritual carried "as binding force with negroes, as if they had been joined by a clergyman; the difference being the one was not so high-toned as the other," as one white observer noted, adding, "Yet, it must be admitted that the blacks always preferred being married by a clergyman."[10]

Other aspects of slave marriage ceremonies illustrate the ways in which African Americans had appropriated Victorian customs and altered them to exclude references to virginity. Having "de bride dresse[d] all up in white with a pretty vail," for instance, was a common practice, though the brides often had already borne children. After the Civil War, more formal and public weddings of former slaves featured "white bridal veils, orange-blossom bouquets, and the children and even the grandchildren of some of the newlyweds." White dresses symbolized the solemnity of the occasion and the respect given the bride by fellow slaves, therefore, and not sexual "purity." Music, dancing and feasting after the ceremony also provided a rare occasion when slaves could "have one good time, jus' de same es us wuz white folks."[11]

Slaves recognized the economic expedience, threat of violence, and lack of romance surrounding their possible unions. Owners were under no obligation to keep slave couples together, and would often sell one or both after the woman had borne a child and had thus proven her added value. "A woman who bore children fast, they would sell her for as much as a man," one former slave recalled, but "[a] woman who was barren, they wouldn't sell her for so much." The abolitionist Alexander Crummell, who had escaped from slavery, recalled in 1883 how his sister had been "mated as the stock of the plantation were mated, not to be the companion of a loved and chosen husband, but to be the breeder of human cattle for the field or the auction block." One Charleston slave had been jailed after she attacked her "damn, white, pale-faced bastard" owner for having sold the woman's daughter "who jus' married las' night." Former slaves noted how "Massa" would never include phrases such as "What God done jined, cain't no man pull asunder" in the marriage ceremony, but would merely "jus' say, 'Now you married.'" Referring to the Gullah (Carolina Sea Islander) term for whites, a black minister used the phrase, "Till death or buckra part you" in his ceremonies. "You see, it's dis way," former slave Minnie Logan summarized. "God made marriage, but de white man made de law."[12]

God was clearly on the side of the slaves, in their eyes. Religion provided a spiritual and communal legitimacy to rites that had no standing in white law. Occasionally, "de leadin' colored man dat had learned to read an' write" would read from the Bible. One female slave matriarch forced a prospective couple to postpone their nuptials so they could "think 'bout it hard fo' two days, 'cause marryin' was sacred in de eyes of Jesus." Another female slave elder prayed at a wedding "fo' de union dat God was gonna make" and invited the couple to "in de eyes of Jesus step into Holy land of mat-de-money."[13]

Whites had mixed opinions of the validity of slave marriages. Revealing their feelings of cultural superiority, many whites encouraged slaves' jumping the broomstick "as the form appropriate to slaves," while other whites preferred the practice "to avoid the embarrassment of having to perform a Christian ceremony that had no legal status in law and could not include the usual words 'Till death do you part.'" Who performed the marriage was complicated in places like Louisiana after the Jefferson purchase in 1803, since the Roman Catholic Church prohibited the separation of couples and families. Most Catholic plantation owners therefore refused to let a priest officiate at slave marriage ceremonies, although evidence survives of deathbed marriages of slaves by priests. Otherwise, the slaves knew that only the "massa's word" made their marriages as official as they could be.[14]

While slaves accepted a slave preacher or their white "marstuh" to provide a sense of formality to marriage ceremonies (some of which were held in "the Big House" as a bonus to good slaves), most knew that "the Man" speaking solely on his own authority held little real value. One runaway slave, William Craft, was a rarity in that he deferred marriage until he and his fiancée Ellen could be free. "I did not, at first, press the marriage, but agreed to assist her in trying to devise some plan by which we might escape from our unhappy condition, and then be married." Plantation owners also knew that their authority was merely symbolic, and some were known to have thwarted the efforts of those who offered legal marriages to former slaves during the Civil War. Ellen Betts, born in slavery in Louisiana, recalled when "One time de river boat come bearin' de license for niggers to git marry with. Marse [Master] chase 'em off and say, 'Don't you come truckin' no no-count papers roun' my niggers. When I marry 'em, dey marry as good as if de Lawd God hisself marry 'em and it don't take no paper to bind de tie.'"[15]

Two new opportunities for slaves seeking to marry legally arose even before the end of the Civil War and the constitutional abolition of slavery in 1865. Those slaves who found themselves in territory occupied by the Union Army benefited from the Emancipation Proclamation, issued on January 1, 1863, which declared free status to all within federal jurisdiction, and in 1864 Congress established the Bureau of Freedmen and Abandoned Lands for a period of five years. The tasks of the Freedmen's Bureau included "uniting in Holy Matrimony Negro men and women who were living together without benefit of clergy." Now, thousands of former slaves flocked to registration centers to have "a real sho' nuff weddin' wid a preacher." Bongy Jackson recalled the privilege of attending her parents' nuptials. "During slavery, us niggers just jumped the broom wit' the master's consent. After the Cibil War, soon's they got a little piece of money they got a preacher and had a real weddin'."[16]

Efforts by the newly freed who sought to legalize their existing marriages speak for and occasionally against the validity of slave-era marriages. Newly married couples testified to the length of their pre-emancipation union, yet still "had profound respect" for their prized certificates. Northern observers noted the pride in former slaves who arrived for their ceremonies with the woman following the man, but left in a more egalitarian fashion, "walking away side by side, for the first time with the honorable title of husband and wife." Union Army officers were surprised by the number of blacks who came forward to have a "real" ceremony. Fortunately for historians, officials "gathered some unusual social and demographic data" while registering the marriages of former slaves, including the number of children born, previous (slave) marriages, the duration of these previous unions, and the reasons for their ending. In Union-occupied Mississippi, of 4,627 couples married in 1864 and 1865, one in six registrants was at least fifty years of age, the oldest being 101; one-third reported a previous marriage broken by forced sale. Seven in ten in the District of Columbia "had lived together for at least a decade," and one in eight had lived together thirty or more years. Many registries listed the number of applicants who had *not* had conventional Christian ceremonies when they were married as slaves—over 40 percent, in a few areas. The fact that many former slaves legalized their relationships, however, should be distinguished from their having viewed earlier ceremonies as anything but legitimate unions. Non-Christian rituals like "jumping the broom" still certified "legitimate unions, telling neighbors and kin that the status of a man and woman had changed, and impressing new duties and obligations upon husband and wife."

Problems could arise when a slave had been sold away and had remarried—should one return to one's first spouse or stay with the current one? A few slaves had had several partners over the years, and a small number dispensed with them all and started over in freedom with a brand-new spouse. "Sometimes two men claimed the same woman, whilst she coquetted not a little, evidently disposed to take the one that bid the highest," one Northern observer noted. "But this rarely if ever happened where there were children." The same narrator recalled how a Virginia slave who had remarried after having been sold away from her first husband came across him a few years later in 1863; he had also remarried. The distraught woman bemoaned, "Twas like a stroke of death to me...White folks got a heap to answer for the way they've done to colored folks!"[17]

In addition to such emotional challenges, the transition from informal unions to marriages with full legal status put pressure on African Americans to bring their marriage symbolism and meanings into closer alignment with those of white culture. If slaves had suffered from whites' moralistic criticism of their premarital sexual activity and presumed "experimentation" before marriage as "evidence of the absence of sexual standards" and even an indication of the "'savage' or 'natural' behavior" of Africans, former slaves now suffered Victorian condemnation of the same as proof of blacks' inferiority. Black women who were "known to have given birth to a child out of wedlock" were "'ruined,' 'fallen,' or 'gone astray.'" Despite these pressures, the rate of premarital intercourse and bridal pregnancy followed by marriage among Southern blacks did not decrease for at least a half-century after the Civil War; motherhood for black women remained an important rite of passage to the extent that it outweighed white culture's condemnation of illegitimacy. Basing the start of one's marriage on a legal document, in a sense, now delegitimized the previous relationship. But while "jumping the broomstick" decreased in practice and ultimately faded away as a common ritual, the phrase still remained as shorthand for marriage.[18]

## SAME-SEX MARRIAGE

To some, the thought of comparing the experience of homosexuals—most of whom have the opportunity to hide their sexual identity by remaining "in the closet"—to that of African Americans, whose skin color undeniably identifies them, may insult the history of the African Diaspora and its children's conditions under slavery and segregation. The levels of oppression may have been more extreme and blatant for slaves and former slaves, but for homosexuals in America, first-class status has long been available only at the figurative cost of one's soul. Countless individuals over the generations have made the Faustian bargain of enjoying the economic and social benefits of legal marriage, yet only within the strict confines of a deceptively professed heterosexuality. The need for camouflage has driven many homosexuals to despair of true love, leading them into depression, alcohol and drug abuse, or even suicide. Whatever moral issues today's African Americans may have with gays' and lesbians' sexual activity, therefore, the honest analyst cannot deny the two groups' shared experience of general oppression and official denial of legitimate relationships. The similar histories of legal, religious, and sociocultural assault at the hands of a racist and homophobic white-majority hegemonic society should allow great empathy between today's black and lesbian or gay Americans.

Strictures against homosexual acts have been pillars of European and American culture for centuries. Recent studies have revealed, however, that the Christian Church was not always as antihomosexual as later legal and ecclesiastical condemnations of homosexuality might imply. The historian John Boswell showed how same-gender couples were blessed in some form by the early Church in the fourth century, well before the formal sanctioning of religious rites for heterosexual marriages in the sixth century. These marriages had been previously governed chiefly by economic, familial, or tribal considerations. Only in the thirteenth century did the Western Christian (Roman Catholic) Church declare procreation to be the only legitimate basis for human sexual activity, require celibacy for priests, expunge lesbian and gay saints from the canons, and elevate marriage to the status of a sacrament. Heteronormative and procreative marriage has thus been the only norm in canon law for less than half of Christian history (eight hundred years), undermining conservatives' claim today of the historical status of "traditional" marriage. Nonetheless, sodomy was criminalized in England starting in 1533, and in almost every American state well into the mid-twentieth century. Starting in the late 1800s, a social construction of sexuality based on Freudian psychoanalysis bolstered traditionalists' condemnation of homosexuals as "abnormal" and delayed for another half-century the development of positive concepts of gay or lesbian identity and communities. Such demonizing was strengthened by the classification of homosexuality as a mental disorder by the American Psychiatric Association (APA) from 1951 to 1973. The U.S. Supreme Court at first upheld sodomy laws in the 1986 *Bowers v. Hardwick* case but reversed itself in *Lawrence v. Texas* in June 2003. On the basis that "moral disapproval of a group does not justify discrimination," the Court invalidated statutes then still remaining on the law books in fourteen states.[19]

Before and after such legal changes, cultural and religious condemnation of homosexual relationships has remained. Few homophobic heterosexuals, as did slave owners, see any advantage to promoting same-sex marriage in the name of social stability or economic gain, although strong arguments might be made to those ends. In condemning homosexuality in its entirety, the heteronormative culture has not, in general, differentiated between types of lesbian and gay relationships. Like "promiscuous" slaves, gays and lesbians have been judged to be "perverted" through some innate or chosen lewdness that precludes any "legitimate" relationships. Both one-night stands and committed marriages of several years' length were conflated as equally invalid, solely on account of their homosexual component. Either in defense of the traditional man-and-woman union or to protect the procreative nature of marriage and gender roles within the family, many churches and "ex-gay" ministries have condemned the idea of same-sex marriage since the issue was first raised nationally in the early 1990s.[20] In an ironic twist of history, many African American church groups have recently allied politically with their traditional opponents on civil rights issues—conservative white fundamentalists—to oppose legal marriage for lesbian or gay couples. One organization, however, the National Black Justice Coalition (NBJC), has led efforts to promote "same-gender" marriage rights. "Dedicated to fostering equality by fighting racism and homophobia," the NBJC challenges Americans to consider the historically similar forms of opposition to slave, mixed-race and lesbian or gay marriages.[21]

What parallels can be found between the two disenfranchised groups' conceptions of committed relationships? Since slave women were often forced to engage in sexual intercourse with white men, slaves did not view virginity as a precondition of marriage. Similarly, most homosexuals before and after the gay rights and liberation movement of the 1970s—paralleling the heterosexual sexual revolution, "hippie" movement, and "free love" philosophy of the 1960s—began their relationships with sexual contact, though almost always of a voluntary nature. Any desire to make relationships lasting, exclusive, and public, if at all, would come later. The production of children would hardly be a factor in a choice to seek a marriage-like commitment—a clear point of difference with the antebellum slave community, wherein the birth of the couple's first child served as one means of legitimizing the parents' relationship.

Historians' observations about slave marriages, wherein virginity carried little prestige, and in which pregnancy or the birth of children did little to dictate the timing of the ceremony, fit most homosexual relationships of the modern era. Moral sanctions against premarital sex have been set aside, and the slave-era concept of trial marriages is also accepted. The heteronormative and homophobic culture denigrated any homosexual relationships as "promiscuous," leading to a countercultural philosophy that promoted multiple sexual partners as a matter of right and free expression, and in protest against laws criminalizing homosexual acts. As with many white observers of slave culture, today's heterosexist moralists have been quick to point out the comparative lack of lasting gay and lesbian relationships today. Such comments ignore, however, the remarkable rise in the incidence of heterosexual divorce and marital infidelity since the 1960s. Since that time as well, a generally more sexually liberated generation of Americans—heterosexual and homosexual—has broadened the definition of relationships. Many homosexuals of the 1970s and 1980s rejected monogamy and marriage as "heterosexist," "patriarchal," "sexist," and "restrictive" institutions that reduced love to economic benefits and artificially stigmatized "premarital" sexual relations. The idea of "consummating" a relationship often carried much less emotional, social, or moral value to homosexuals, especially for men, who might seem to engage in an endless series of "trial marriages." Having sex meant simply movement beyond the level of a platonic acquaintance or friendship. Some type of emotional attachment might develop but nothing was guaranteed—to the consternation of those more romantically inclined. Slaves may have entered into a "trial marriage" period out of pragmatism, not knowing if self-interested masters would honor the couples' ties. Gay and lesbian Americans may also have had little to stop them from entering into one-night stands or other short-term relationships, but they have enjoyed less social, religious, or economic support to sustain unions deemed to be exclusive, lasting, and respected by others. Stereotypically, lesbian women showed greater interest in forming relationships than did gay men, although the effect of the 1980s AIDS epidemic forced many of the latter to consider monogamous relationships for reasons other than lasting love. The idea of open relationships—having a primary, usually live-in, partner but allowing "flings" on the side—is still debated in gay male circles. Under these circumstances, those who did seek to commit themselves to lasting relationships with one partner could be commended for inner strength and perseverance against pressures from within and without the homosexual community.

Only after the lesbian and gay rights movement matured, so to speak—largely from enjoying the comfort of decriminalization—did the prevailing concepts of relationships change. Rhetorically, changes in gay men's descriptions of their partners "from 'friend' in the 1960s to 'lover' in the 1970s and 'boyfriend' or 'husband' in the 1980s and 1990s, provide an excellent barometer of the legitimization of gay relationships." By the 1990s, legal marriage as an exclusively heterosexual domain came under increasing fire. By the 2000s, a self-appointed elite of the national lesbian, gay, bisexual and transgender (LGBT) community, which had previously defended a broader scope of self-interest and thus disagreed on the value of monogamous relationships, found itself accommodating a previously silent majority of proponents of lesbian or gay marriage and the right to adopt children.[22]

That many lesbian and gay unions came to be egalitarian in nature and not based on previous constructions of premarital virginity and postmarital childbirth should come as no surprise to students of America following the rise of feminism. "Boston marriages" had been common among lesbian women in New England in the latter half of the nineteenth century, and Bertrand Russell noted the emergence of the ideal of "companionate marriage" as early as 1925.[23] For the lesbian or gay couple, the formalization of a marriage-like ceremony serves to "announce and confirm their relationships before friends, family and co-workers."[24] A lesbian woman united with her partner in Orange County, California, in 1993 explained, "We believe in God, and I wanted to have my lifelong partner marry me because it's more of a commitment, more binding. It's not only a religious but a social bond when you're out there in front of your friends and family...Gay people have the right to be married, too. We're in love."[25] A decade later, an African American from Maryland and her partner declared that what they sought "is no different than any other couple who met and fell in love—the right to marry; raise a healthy, happy family; and take care of one another."[26] One gay rights leader admitted that "despite the oppressive nature of marriage historically, and in spite of the general absence of edifying examples of modern heterosexual marriage...every lesbian and gay man should have the right to marry the same-sex partner of his or her choice."[27] The historian Herbert Gutman's comment about African Americans' self-claimed agency in appropriating marriage as valid applies equally to same-sex couples in a homophobic society: "Life experiences...had not convinced" them "that legal marriage was a privilege belonging only to the owning class and to other whites."[28]

Like slaves, homosexuals have independently validated their commitments despite the opprobrium of a hegemonic culture that denied legal sanction to them. In addition to their own individual and collective authority, slaves were at least afforded the veneer of the "massa's word" and notation in plantation ledgers for unofficial recognition of their marriages. Homosexuals, by contrast, have had until recently only their own assertions that their ties are different from more fleeting relationships. One gay author wrote that he and his partner's formal exchange of vows made them feel "more profoundly committed and secure in the relationship" and "changed how supported we felt in our relationship by our friends and family, who treated us differently after we'd made a public commitment... There could be no doubt in their minds that we were a dedicated couple. He is no longer my boyfriend, a potentially temporary thing; he is my partner."[29] Couples either invent symbols of their pledges or borrow from heterosexual examples. Ceremonies often include songs of love and fidelity. Cakes are topped with hearts, doves, flowers, or a pair of same-gender figurines. Most couples speak a variation of marriage-like vows, though usually without the bride's injunction to "obey," signifying a desire for an egalitarian bond. Many take such steps as listing the partner as one's beneficiary on legal documents or combining their finances. Most also exchange rings—the traditional gold band or custom-designed bands—or another piece of jewelry such as a bracelet or necklace. Matching tattoos and other types of body art have also been used as symbolism. Following the lead of slaves, one modern lesbian couple even "jumped the broom" at their wedding.[30]

Spiritually inclusive "holy union" ceremonies began when the Metropolitan Community Church, which was founded by homosexuals, introduced the blessing of same-sex marriages in Los Angeles in 1969. By the mid-1980s, three mainstream Christian denominations—the United Church of Christ (UCC), the Society of Friends (Quakers) and the Unitarian Universalists—had recognized the validity of lesbian or gay commitments. Other groups fought internal battles to allow individual congregations or ministers the choice to adopt euphemistic near-marriage-like blessings, like a 1993 Episcopal diocesan resolution to permit "celebrating the commitment of gay and lesbian members…in life together."[31] Many national religious organizations still remain heavily split over the issues of same-sex marriage and openly homosexual ministers. Meanwhile, at each of the 1987, 1993, and 2000 marches on Washington, thousands of same-sex couples were united in mass interdenominational ceremonies.[32]

## MARRIAGE AND CIVIL LAW

Legal recognition has lagged beyond the ecclesiastical, despite the U.S. Supreme Court's 1978 declaration that marriage is "of fundamental importance to all individuals" in *Zablocki v. Redhail* (434 U.S. 374). The Supreme Court of Hawaii first applied this standard to homosexuals in 1993, finding that current marriage laws were indeed discriminatory. The decision prompted a nationwide series of legislative battles over whether same-sex couples are entitled to equal application of the law. States had to decide to accept the ruling and allow marriage for all or to change their constitutions (by legislative action or popular referendum) to redefine marriage as solely between a man and a woman, thus nullifying court mandates; the vast majority have chosen the latter option. Similar reaction on the federal level led to the 1996 Defense of Marriage Act (DOMA), which expressly denies government benefits to any type of nonheterosexual marriage, union or civil partnership.[33] The first state to not override a court ruling for near-equality was Vermont. On July 1, 2000, two women became the first same-sex couple in the United States to be legally united via Vermont's civil union law, one that provides over two hundred marriage-like benefits yet no rights to adopt children. In November 2003, the Massachusetts Supreme Court ruled in *Goodridge v. Department of Public Health* that the state constitution's equal protection clause mandated the same exact level of rights to same-sex and opposite-sex couples. The state became the first in the nation to issue full-status marriage certificates to lesbian or gay people on May 17, 2004—a fitting coincidence, since the day marked the fiftieth anniversary of the U.S. Supreme Court's *Brown v. Board of Education* decision overturning six decades of legalized racial segregation in public schools. Over six thousand couples registered by the year's end.[34] In reaction to this move and several nonlegal extensions of marriage licenses by local officials in the spring of 2004, voters in ten states changed their constitutions to ban same-sex marriage. In May 2003, the first bill was introduced in Congress for a Federal Marriage Amendment to restrict marriage to heterosexual couples. In July 2004, the Marriage Protection Act (H.R. 3313) passed in the House, 233 to 194, but was narrowly defeated, 50 to 48, in the Senate. California became the first state to voluntarily adopt a broad domestic partnership law (1999, effective in 2000), with provisions significantly expanded in 2003 (effective January 1, 2005). On September 1, 2005, the same assembly became the first U.S. legislature to pass a same-sex marriage bill—the Marriage License Non-Discrimination Act" (A.B. 849)—without judicial mandate; however, Republican Governor Arnold Schwartzenegger quickly vetoed it.[35]

Outside Massachusetts, same-sex couples must create expensive legal arrangements to ensure a level of legal protection for health care and burial wishes, child custody, inheritance, insurance, and other civil rights taken for granted by heterosexuals. One analyst referred to such convoluted procedures as a type of "post-nuptial agreement."[36] Those who cannot afford them risk economic and social injustices to themselves and their children. The task is daunting; an estimated 1,138 federal benefits (plus an additional three hundred state benefits) automatically accrue to couples upon legal marriage.[37] More so than with former slaves, lesbian or gay couples have sought legal marriage or civil unions to protect their families and gain control over custody of their children. Most state laws are biased in favor of heterosexual parents or even grandparents, judging that a homosexual parent's orientation in and of itself is basis for declaring one unfit for custody. The Virginia Supreme Court upheld such a rationale in 1994, adding that being raised by same-sex parents could subject the child to "social discrimination." In 1998, "a judge in Florida shifted custody from a child's lesbian mother to her ex-husband, who had been previously jailed for the murder of his first wife. The judge declared that the child ought to be raised in a 'non-lesbian' world." In 1997 New Jersey became the first state to deem same-gender partners as qualified to be parents as heterosexuals. California included some custody issues in its 2003 expansion of domestic partnership benefits after proponents of a Gay Family Values Bill had urged passage of such provisions every year for the previous decade. By the early 2000s even the most ardent supporters of "alternative parenting" were agreeing that legal marriage is the most definitive basis of family construction.[38]

The possibility of legal marriage presents a dilemma for modern gay and lesbian couples. Does a piece of paper from the government validate a relationship more than a previous private pledge? If a couple has already had their own ceremony, why go through the formality of having a county official extend the legal blessing of the modern "Massa"? Legal ties also mean that divorce becomes a necessary legal procedure if the relationship fails. California's domestic partnership was updated as of January 1, 2005, to include the need for court action before dissolution is legally effected. Of Vermont's first seventy-five hundred entrants into civil unions, seventy-five had been dissolved by the end of 2004; the state's first couple to apply, Carolyn Conrad and Kathleen Peterson, ended their union in October 2005.[39] Like some former slaves, nonheterosexual couples may feel insulted or inconvenienced in having to "marry" after living together faithfully for years, but registration becomes a vital political statement to demonstrate the existence of these previously hidden or ignored commitments. Unlike former slaves, however, same-sex couples lack a

Freedmen's Bureau cadre of registrars who note how long the applicants had been together before legally recording their unions; only personal witnesses and the narratives of the couples themselves can preserve those historical data.

Examples from the slave and lesbian or gay experiences illustrate couples' intent to publicly demonstrate their commitments and receive the blessing of witnesses and God. These examples also reveal that various conventions of premarital sexual activity, including trial marriage, have existed throughout American history, whether the concept has been formally recognized and labeled as such. The timing of marriages in each group broke with traditional concepts centered on virginity and the legitimacy of children; however, further research is needed to ascertain whether contemporary American heterosexuals' increasing age at first marriage and lowered concern over the moral aspects of premarital sex or cohabitation may include some of the same pragmatic aspects of slave-era and pre-legal gay marriages. Both pre–Civil War African Americans and modern homosexuals stressed the first part of the former slave Minnie Logan's 1930s summation, that "God made marriage" and recognized that "de white man" and heterosexuals have made "de law." But laws can change—sometimes dramatically, as with slaves, sometimes more slowly, for today's lesbian and gay Americans. Such symbolic rituals as "jumping the broom" and exchanges of rings still proclaim a couple's passage into another phase of life markedly different from the previous stage. Referring to both slave marriages and same-sex unions, the National Black Justice Coalition reminds us that legally unrecognized yet committed relationships are "far from a new phenomenon" and have been "built on the same foundation that sustains any solid union: trust, loyalty and love.... By partnering for life, these couples enter a covenant made sacred by their faith in each other."[40]

Is a marriage valid and legitimate if it is not legally recognized? Examination of an earlier group's independent use of marriage rituals provides a valuable basis of comparison to a parallel phenomenon in a more recent group. Members of each group disregarded their era's orthodox prohibitions and consciously constructed ways to autonomously validate their collective integrity and individual identities. The experiences of slaves in the American South before, during, and shortly after the Civil War on the one hand, and lesbian and gay Americans since the mid-twentieth century on the other, show remarkable similarities in the legal, socioreligious, and economic climate each group faced, and in the responses by oppressed heterodoxies that resisted hegemonic denial of legalized marriages. The growth of autonomous validation—as exemplified by such technically extralegal events as marriage ceremonies—vividly illustrate slaves' and lesbian or gay Americans' firm commitment to their basic human rights. The act of appropriating a ritual from the dominant culture and investing it with new meaning not only testifies to the persistence of the oppressed group to break their real or symbolic bonds but warns others how difficult it is to maintain hegemony. Be it slave-slave, man-man or woman-woman, marriage in America has already been changed, whether or not the self-proclaimed guardians of culture and tradition approve.

## NOTES

1. Deborah Gray White, *Ar'n't I A Woman? Female Slaves in the Plantation South* (New York: W. W. Norton, 1985).

2. For the sake of expedience, the author employs the terms homosexual, gay, or lesbian interchangeably to refer to those of a nonheterosexual orientation. No offense is meant to bisexual, transgender, or other people belonging to a sexual minority, whose specific experience is beyond the scope of this essay. Use of the expedient term community in reference to the national collective of lesbian or gay people is not meant to imply a formal organization or communal voice for those who may prefer the label LGBTQ (lesbian, gay, bisexual, transgender, and queer) in the 2000s. Such terms as queer will not be employed, given their pejorative definitions during most if not all of the period under discussion.

3. Orlando Patterson, *Slavery and Social Death: A Comparative Study* (Cambridge, MA: Harvard University Press, 1982), 189.

4. Ibid.; John Hope Franklin, *The Free Negro in North Carolina, 1790–1860* (New York: Russell & Russell, 1969), 155. In addition to Philemon, an epistle in which Paul appealed for the voluntary freeing of a slave who had converted to Christianity, the New Testament writer reinforced the notion of slaves' spiritual equality with free citizens in Galatians 3:28 yet did not condemn slavery as an institution in Ephesians 6:5–9 and 1 Corinthians 7:20–24.

5. Ramon A. Gutierrez, *When Jesus Came, The Corn Mothers Went Away: Marriage, Sexuality, and Power in New Mexico, 1500–1846* (Stanford, CA: Stanford University Press, 1991), 217, 228, 233, 242, 248, 287, and 315.

6. Eugene D. Genovese, *Roll, Jordan, Roll: The World the Slaves Made* (New York: Random House, 1976), 472, 475, 481; Patterson, *Slavery and Social Death*, 187–90 (see note 3). Mather's 1706 "The Negro Christianized" essay is quoted in Albert J. Raboteau, "The Invisible Institution: The Origins and Conditions of Black Religion before Emancipation" (PhD diss., Yale University, 1974), 136. See also Gutierrez, *When Jesus Came, The Corn Mothers Went Away*, 235, 295, and 333 (see note 5); and Charles L. Perdue, Jr., Thomas E. Barden, and Robert K. Phillips., eds., *Weevils in the Wheat: Interviews with Virginia Ex-Slaves* (Charlottesville, VA: University Press of Virginia, 1976), 89, 161.

7. White, *Ar'n't I A Woman?*, 60–67, 78–79, 105–06, 108–09, 114, and 163 (see note 1); Genovese, *Roll, Jordan, Roll*, 465–66 (see note 6); and Herbert G. Gutman, *The Black Family in Slavery and Freedom, 1750–1925* (New York: Pantheon/Vintage Books, 1976), 31–33, 64–67, and 74–77 [quote from 76]. Post-childbirth marriage has not been limited to nineteenth-century American slaves. An 1833 analyst of the English "manufacturing population" observed that "sexual intercourse was almost universally prior to marriage in the agricultural district" but with a "tacit understanding" that "marriage be the result." In 1927, the anthropologist Bronislaw Malinowski described late medieval German peasants' "trial night" courting practices, which "occurred commonly in many premodern cultures and were not 'licentious.'" Both cited in Gutman, *The Black Family in Slavery and Freedom, 1750–1925*, 64. Americans in the 1820s also seem to have viewed premarital sex as "a token of betrothal" which would not bar a woman from "respectable" marriage; see Christine Stansell, *City of Women: Sex and Class in New York, 1789–1860* (Chicago: University of Chicago Press, 1987), 87, 179–80.

8. Gutman, *The Black Family in Slavery and Freedom, 1750–1925*, 62–68, 271 (see note 7). For information on Stowe, *Key to Uncle Tom's Cabin* (Boston: John P. Jewett and Company,1854), 298–301 and Gutman, 64.

9. *Jumping the Broom: A Black Perspective on Same-Gender Marriage* (Silver Spring, MD: Equality Maryland Foundation, Inc.; Washington, DC: National Black Justice Coalition, 2005), 13, http://www.nbjcoalition.org/jump_broom1.pdf (accessed July 20, 2006).

10. Perdue, Barden, and Phillips., eds., *Weevils in the Wheat*, 95, 105, and 245 (see note 6); Raboteau, "The Invisible Institution," 226–27 (see note 6); and Gutman, *The Black Family in Slavery and Freedom, 1750–1925*, 275–76 (see note 7). The latter's comment about pre-

ferring clergy authority may also have been added to calm white readers' concern about non-Christian religious practices among African Americans. Contemporary narratives of escaped slaves dispensed with the literally translated dialect employed by 1930s-era oral historians of former slaves, proffering standard English to gain further legitimacy with their white abolitionist audience. For other descriptions of broomstick jumping, see George P. Rawick, *The American Slave: A Composite Autobiography* (Westport, CT: Greenwood Publishing Company, 1972), vol. 2, pt. 1, 323; ibid., vol. 4, pts. 1, 23, 189, 293; Perdue, Barden, and Phillips., eds., *Weevils in the Wheat*, 122 and 129 (see note 6); and the Writers' Program of the Work Projects Administration in the State of Virginia, *The Negro in Virginia* (1940; repr., New York: Arno Press, 1969), 81–83. On origins, see Gutman, *The Black Family in Slavery and Freedom, 1750–1925*, 276–83; and Writers' Program of the Work Projects Administration in the State of Virginia, *The Negro in Virginia*, 79.

11. Perdue, Barden, and Phillips., eds., *Weevils in the Wheat*, 231 (see note 6); George R. Bentley, *A History of the Freedmen's Bureau* (Philadelphia: University of Pennsylvania Press, 1955), 86; and Gutman, *The Black Family in Slavery and Freedom, 1750–1925*, 284 (see note 7). For a further example of white dresses, see George P. Rawick, *The American Slave: A Composite Autobiography* (Westport, CT: Greenwood Publishing Company, 1972), vol. 4, pts. 2, 236.

12. George P. Rawick, *The American Slave: A Composite Autobiography* (Westport, CT: Greenwood Publishing Company, 1972), vol. 18 (Fisk), 41–42; W. E. B. DuBois and Augustus Granville Dill, eds., *Morals and Manners among Negro Americans. Report of a Social Study made by Atlanta University under the Patronage of the Trustees of the John F. Slater Fund; with the Proceedings of the 18th Annual Conference for the Study of the Negro Problems, held at Atlanta University, on Monday, May 26th, 1913* (Atlanta: Atlanta University Press, 1914), 68–69; George P. Rawick, *The American Slave: A Composite Autobiography* (Westport, CT: Greenwood Publishing Company, 1972), vol. 2, pt. 2, 234–36; and Writers' Program of the Work Projects Administration in the State of Virginia, *The Negro in Virginia*, 86 (see note 10). See also Raboteau, "The Invisible Institution," 226 (see note 6); and Perdue, Barden, and Phillips., eds., *Weevils in the Wheat*, 158 (see note 6). Darlene Hine and Kate Wittenstein, "Female Slave Resistance: The Economics of Sex," in Filomina Steady, ed., *The Black Woman Cross-Culturally* (Cambridge, MA: Schenkman Publishing Company, 1981), 297, cites a case in which "a good, strong buck" was sold for $1,500 while $1,200 fetched "a hardworking, childbearing wench."

13. Perdue, Barden, and Phillips., eds., *Weevils in the Wheat*, 15 and 161 (see note 6); George P. Rawick, *The American Slave: A Composite Autobiography* (Westport, CT: Greenwood Publishing Company, 1972), vol. 4, pt. 2, 246. For similar Christian ceremonies, see Rawick, *The American Slave*, vol. 7, 63 and 151–52.

14. Genovese, *Roll, Jordan, Roll*, 481 (see note 6); George P. Rawick, *The American Slave: A Composite Autobiography* (Westport, CT: Greenwood Publishing Company, 1972), vol. 4, *Texas Narratives*, pt. 2, 226. See also Stafford Poole and Douglas J. Slawson, *Church and Slave in Perry County, Missouri, 1818–1865* (Lewiston, NY: Edwin Mellen Press, 1986), 54 and 74–75.

15. William and Ellen Craft, "Running a Thousand Miles for Freedom," in Arna Bontemps, ed., *Great Slave Narratives* (Boston: Beacon Press, 1969), 285. Betts quoted in George P. Rawick, *The American Slave: A Composite Autobiography* (Westport, CT: Greenwood Publishing Company, 1972), vol. 4, pt. 1, 79–80. On slaves who valued the master's authority at ceremonies, see Perdue, Barden, and Phillips., eds., *Weevils in the Wheat*, 36, 51, 237, and 275 (see note 6); and Rawick, *The American Slave*, vol. 2, pt. 2, 234.

16. Perdue, Barden, and Phillips., eds., *Weevils in the Wheat*, 122 (see note 6); Raboteau, "The Invisible Institution," 227 (see note 6); Bentley, *A History of the Freedmen's Bureau*, 86 (see note 11).

17. Elizabeth H. Botume, *First Days Amongst the Contrabands* (1892; repr., New York: Arno Press, 1968), 157–60 and 167; Bentley, *A History of the Freedmen's Bureau*, 86–87 (see note 11); and Gutman, *The Black Family in Slavery and Freedom, 1750–1925*, especially 11–12, 14–15, 18–21, 51, 149, 271–73, and 319 (see note 7). Blacks registered in large numbers even in Southern states that tried to downplay the legitimacy issue by decreeing that marriages contracted during the slave era would be recognized ex post facto as common-law unions; Virginia and South Carolina, for example, simply declared by legislative action that marriages would be recognized solely by evidence of cohabitation or reputation. A vast number of North Carolina's ex-slaves registered before an 1866 deadline, despite the 25-cent cost. Gutman, *The Black Family*, 14.

18. On white moralizing, see Genovese, *Roll, Jordan, Roll*, 461 (see note 6); Raboteau, "The Invisible Institution," 227 (see note 6); Gutman, *The Black Family in Slavery and Freedom, 1750–1925*, 61–63 (see note 7); and Ruth Reed, *Negro Illegitimacy in New York City* (1926; repr., New York: AMS Press, Inc., 1968), 24. On postwar black motherhood, see Gutman, *The Black Family*, 65, 74–75, 449–50, 501–5; DuBois and Dill, eds., *Morals and Manners among Negro Americans*, 70 (see note 12); White, *Ar'n't I A Woman?*, 164 (see note 1); and Joyce Ladner, *Tomorrow's Tomorrow: The Black Woman* (New York: Doubleday, 1971), 128, 212–33.

19. *Lawrence v. Texas* (July 2003), quoted in Davina Kotulski, *Why You Should Give a Damn about Gay Marriage* (Los Angeles: Advocate Books/Alyson Publications, 2004), 11. On Roman Catholic rejection of homosexual unions, see "Pope Calls Gay Marriage Threat to Family," *New York Times*, February 23, 1994, A5. On the early Christian church's potentially benign approach, see John Boswell, *Same-Sex Unions in Pre-Modern Europe* (New York: Villard Books, 1994), especially 80–83, 91–92, 106–7, 178–98, 267–70, 317–23. See also John Boswell, *Homosexuality, Social Tolerance and Christianity* (Chicago: University of Chicago Press, 1980); Tom Horner, *Jonathan Loved David: Homosexuality in Biblical Times* (Philadelphia: Westminster Press, 1978); and Sylvia Pennington, *Good News For Modern Gays: A Pro-Gay Biblical Approach* (Hawthorne, CA: Lambda Life Publications, 1985). On the nineteenth- and twentieth-century transition from the social construction of sexuality based on gender roles to one centered on sexual orientation, see Michel Foucault, *The History of Sexuality: An Introduction* (New York: Vintage Books, 1990), vol. 1, especially 26, 36–38, 46–47, and 105–8.

Some have tried to claim the APA's decision to remove homosexuality from the third edition of its *Diagnostic and Statistical Manual of Mental Disorders* (DSM-III) was the result of political pressure, but the revision was undertaken based on the APA's standard evaluation criteria, which found that homosexuality was neither socially dysfunctional nor subjectively disabling. See Judd Marmor, "Epilogue: Homosexuality and the Issue of Mental Illness," in Judd Marmor, ed., *Homosexual Behavior: A Modern Reappraisal* (New York: Basic Books, 1980), 391–401; Ronald Bayer, *Homosexuality and American Psychiatry: The Politics of Diagnosis* (1981; repr., New York: Basic Books, 1982); and Roy Cain, "Disclosure and Secrecy among Gay Men in the United States and Canada: A Shift in Views," in John C. Fout and Maura S. Tantillo, eds., *American Sexual Politics: Sex, Gender, and Race since the Civil War* (Chicago: University of Chicago Press, 1993), 293–309. Montana was the last state to criminalize homosexual acts, in 1973. Starting in 1962, Illinois was the first to decriminalize gay sex acts, followed by Connecticut in 1972, with over half the rest following suit over the next fifteen years. Most of the remaining states kept sodomy laws on the books for polit-ical if not moral reasons, though few enforced them.

20. Since the mid-1970s, "ex-gay" Christian ministries have based their claim that homosexuals can change on the works of such long-discredited analyses as those presented in Irving Bieber, *Homosexuality: A Psychoanalytic Study of Male Homosexuals* (New York: Vintage Books, 1962) and Charles Socarides, *The Overt Homosexual* (New York: Grune & Stratton, 1968). The lone proponent of this pseudopsychology is Joseph Nicolosi; see his *Reparative Therapy of Male Homosexuality: A New Clinical Approach* (1991; repr., Northvale, NJ: Jason Aronson, 1997). Religious and sociocultural arguments against homo-sexuals adopting children have been challenged by the American Psychological Association, which has declared "not a single study has found children of lesbian and gay parents to be disadvantaged in any significant respect relative to children of heterosexual parents." Quoted in *Jumping the Broom*, 37 (see note 9). Such groups as the Family Research Council, who claim that same-sex marriage would be a "serious blow" to "the idea of marriage as a sexu-ally exclusive and faithful relationship" have cited as evidence only a single Dutch study on the spread of HIV/AIDS, which found that among "homosexual men in particular, casual sex, rather than committed relationships, is the rule and not the exception." Xiridou, M., et al. (2003), quoted in *AIDS* 17:1029-38, cited in P. Sprigg, (2003); from Alain Dang and Somjen Frazer, *Black Same-Sex Households in the United States: A Report from the 2000 Census* (New York: National Gay and Lesbian Task Force Policy Institute; Washington, DC: National Black Justice Coalition, 2004), http://www.nbjcoalition.org/assets/BCRNational Report.pdf (accessed January 4, 2006).

21. Quoted in *Jumping the Broom*, 1 (see note 9). See also Kasey Reynolds, "Common Sense Says that Anti-Gay Marriage Arguments Are Resurrecting Old Prejudices" (e-newslet-ter of the Common Sense Foundation, Raleigh, NC), http://www.common-sense .org/?fnoc=/common_sense_says/05_february (accessed January 3, 2006). African American men in general have remained more homophobic than their white counterparts, within and outside of churches. In terms of rhetoric, this difference can be seen in blacks' preference for such terms as same-gender and same-gender-loving instead of same-sex and gay; the latter term in particular has come to be seen as meaning white, especially by proponents of Men With Men (MWM) groups who support intimate ties between males but still equate homo-sexuality with effeminacy. See Delroy C. Simms, *The Greatest Taboo: Homosexuality in Black Communities* (Boston: Alyson, 2001). The Reverend Richard Richardson of the Black Ministerial Alliance of Greater Boston, for instance, found it "offensive" when Hilary Shelton, an official of the NAACP, condemned as discriminatory a move to amend the Constitution to exclude gay marriages; from Leonard Pitts, Jr., "A Civil War Between Gays and Blacks," *Detroit Free Press*, March 12, 2004; http://www.hrc.org/Template.cfm?Section =Center&CONTENTID=17806&TEMPLATE=/ContentManagement/ContentDisplay.cfm (accessed Jan. 5, 2006). On potential changes to the Constitution, see below.

State-level bans on miscegenation (interracial marriage, first enacted in Maryland in 1664 and Virginia in 1705), apart from Maryland's (repealed in 1843), were struck down only by court action, starting in California in 1948. The remaining twenty-nine such state laws were rendered moot after the U.S. Supreme Court's 1967 *Loving v. Virginia* decision, though many Southern states kept the invalidated statutes on the books as a slight to blacks. Alabama was the last to formally remove its ban, in 2000. See Peggy Pascoe, "Why the Ugly Rhetoric against Gay Marriage Is Familiar to This Historian of Miscegenation," *History Network News*, April 19, 2005, http://hnn.us/articles/4708.html (accessed January 4, 2006).

22. Daniel Harris, "The Evolution of the Personals and Gay Romance," in Daniel Harris, ed., *The Rise and Fall of Gay Culture* (New York: Hyperion, 1997), 40–63 [quote from

48–49]; see also Paula L. Ettelbrick, "Since When Is Marriage a Path to Liberation?" in Suzanne Sherman, ed., *Lesbian and Gay Marriage: Private Commitments, Public Ceremonies* (Philadelphia: Temple University Press, 1992), 90–91; Bert N. Adams, *The American Family: A Sociological Interpretation* (Chicago: Markham, 1971), 176–202. On lesbians, see the studies from the 1970s and 1980s cited in Richard A. Mackey, Bernard A. O'Brien, and Eileen F. Mackey, *Gay and Lesbian Couples: Voices from Lasting Relationships* (Westport, CT: Praeger, 1997), 8. On gay men, see also Gilbert Herdt, "'Coming Out' as a Rite of Passage," and Martin P. Levine, "The Life and Death of Gay Clones," in Gilbert Herdt, ed., *Gay Culture in America: Essays from the Field* (Boston: Beacon Press, 1992), 29–67, 68–86; and John Loughery, *The Other Side of Silence: Men's Lives and Gay Identities: A Twentieth-Century History* (New York: John Macrae/Henry Holt, 1998), 356–70. On monogamy and nonmonogamy, see Eric Marcus, *Together Forever: Gay and Lesbian Marriage* (New York: Anchor/Doubleday, 1998), 71–88.

23. Lillian Faderman, *Surpassing the Love of Men: Romantic Friendship and Love Between Women from the Renaissance to the Present* (1981; repr., New York: HarperCollins, 1998); Bertrand Russell, "Trial Marriage," in Edwin M. Schur, ed., *The Family and the Sexual Revolution: Selected Readings* (Bloomington, IN: Indiana University Press, 1964), 140–47.

24. Brad Bonhall, "Partners for Life," *Los Angeles Times*, February 13, 1994.

25. Ibid.

26. Khadijah Tribble and Robin Dickerson, quoted in *Jumping the Broom*, 9 (see note 9).

27. Thomas Stoddard, "Why Gay People Should Seek the Right to Marry," in Suzanne Sherman, ed., *Lesbian and Gay Marriage* (Philadelphia: Temple University Press, 1992), 14.

28. Gutman, *The Black Family in Slavery and Freedom, 1750–1925*, 20 (see note 7). See also the couples interviewed in Suzanne Sherman, ed., *Lesbian and Gay Marriage: Private Commitments, Public Ceremonies* (Philadelphia: Temple University Press, 1992), 33–34, 74, 83, 101, 104, and 108. For examples of couples raising children, see Marcus, *Together Forever*, 237–57 (see note 22); and Peggy Gillespie, ed., *Love Makes a Family: Portraits of Lesbian, Gay, Bisexual, and Transgender Parents and Their Families* (Amherst, MA: University of Massachusetts Press, 1999).

29. Marcus, *Together Forever*, 151 (see note 22).

30. From examples cited in ibid., 146–57, 159; one couple had been together for fifty years. Broom-jumping from Sherman, ed., *Lesbian and Gay Marriage*, 80 (see note 28). The couple's ethnic background is not stated. Prime-time television hosted its first same-sex wedding in 1995, when two men tied the knot on *Roseanne*: see http://www.tv.com/roseanne/december-bride/episode/28286/recap.html (accessed Jan. 5, 2006).

31. Kim Byham, "Massachusetts and Rhode Island Call For Commitment Rites," *The Voice of Integrity*, Winter 1994, 13.

32. "Presbyterians Propose Ban on Same-Sex Ceremonies," *Christianity Today*, July 3, 2000, http://www.christianitytoday.com/ct/2000/127/33.0.html (accessed January 4, 2006). The earliest same-sex ceremony in a mainstream denomination was performed in the Starr King Unitarian Universalist Church in Hayward, California, when the Reverend Jonathan Dobrer united two women in 1970. The union was approved after the fact by the church board. Dobrer recalls with humor what had been a serious ongoing conversation between various ministers with whom he was then associated in the days before California decriminalized sodomy in 1974. Those who argued against same-sex unions said the marriages could never be valid because they could not be consummated, and when supporters of the rite replied that same-sex couples could indeed consummate sexual relationships, the opponents would condemn the couples for having committed a felony! Jon Dobrer, in discussion with the author, January 10, 2006.

33. Technically, the first-ever U.S. legal same-sex marriage license was issued in Colorado by a fluke in April 1975, when the county clerk was unable to find a law mandating opposite-sex applicants; see the letter from the founder of the Metropolitan Community Church, the Reverend Troy Perry, February 27, 2004, http://www.mccpittsburgh.com/serv021.htm (accessed July 20, 2006). As of 2005, various courts found same-sex couples to have a constitutional right to marriage in Hawaii, Alaska, Washington, Oregon, California, Vermont, New York, and Massachusetts, while thirty-two states have banned same-sex marriage, including fourteen states whose voters amended state constitutions in November 2004 (Arkansas, Georgia, Kentucky, Michigan, Mississippi, Montana, North Dakota, Ohio, Oklahoma, Oregon, and Utah). Another two states (Kansas and Texas) amended their constitutions in 2005. Nebraska's legislature-enacted ban, however, was struck down in federal court in 2005. Congress passed the Defense of Marriage Act (DOMA) (85 to 14 in the Senate and 342 to 67 in the House) in September 1996. It was signed into law by President Bill Clinton. The reader should note that the Tenth Amendment is generally interpreted to oblige states to recognize one another's laws unless specifically prohibited. While no term has been established to parallel the Jim Crow laws of the segregation era, the most antigay states roughly overlap with those that banned interracial marriage. "Queer Crow" laws, anyone?

34. As of 2006, the District of Columbia, Maine, Hawaii, and New Jersey have instituted limited partnership registrations, while Connecticut followed Vermont in recognizing civil unions in October 2005. Internationally, similar action had already occurred in Denmark in 1989. The Netherlands became the first nation to grant full marital status to same-sex couples in 2001, followed by Canada and Spain in 2005, and South Africa expected in 2006. Belgium allowed same-sex marriages in 2003 but without provisions for the adoption of children, while Great Britain legalized "civil partnerships" in December 2005. Several other nations have followed Denmark's example of authorizing limited rights through various types of civil contracts, including Norway (1993); Iceland (2000); Portugal (2001); Finland (2002); Croatia and Sweden (2003); France, Germany, Israel, and Slovenia (2004); and New Zealand and Switzerland (2005). See Alan Cowell, "Gay Britons Signing Up as Unions Become Legal," *New York Times*, December 6, 2005, A14.

35. Over four thousand couples took advantage of the maverick offer of San Francisco's (heterosexual) mayor to issue marriage licenses to lesbian and gay couples in February 2004. Court action stopped the practice in March 2004, but the state's prohibition is now under judicial review in the same manner it had been in Massachusetts, as a violation of the equal protection mandate in the state's constitution. A similar action in Multnomah County, Oregon, led to three thousand couples receiving licenses before the court's prohibition, but state voters enacted a constitutional change to invalidate potential "judicial activism" in November 2004. On this and the Federal Marriage Act, see http://www.hrc.org and http://www.marriageequality.org (accessed July 20, 2006).

In a further historical parallel, Georgia Congressman Seaborn Roddenberry introduced a bill for a constitutional ban on interracial marriage in Congress in 1911 following revelations that the first Negro heavyweight boxing champion, Jack Johnson, had bragged about wanting to marry his white girlfriend. Roddenberry claimed that interracial marriage was "repulsive and averse to every sentiment of pure American spirit. It is abhorrent and repugnant. It is subversive to social peace. It is destructive of moral supremacy." Cited in *Jumping the Broom*, 24 (see note 9).

36. Quoted in Sherman, ed., *Lesbian and Gay Marriage*, 75 (see note 28).

37. General Accounting Office report (Washington, DC: General Accounting Office, 2004), http://www.gao.gov/new.items/d043534r.pdf (accessed July 20, 2006). The GAO's previous (1997) report, completed after the 1996 passage of DOMA, had found 1,049 benefits—hence the smaller figure still touted by many gay-rights groups. Narratives of partners

denied rights based on lack of legal standing can be found in Marcus, *Together Forever*, 157–59 (see note 22); and "To Have and to Hold? Maybe Not. True Stories from Same-Sex Couples Denied the Protection of Marriage in Life and Death," report of the Human Rights Coalition Foundation (Washington, DC: Human Rights Coalition Foundation, May 17, 2005), http://www.hrc.org/Template.cfm?Section=About_HRC&Template=/ContentManagement/C ontentDisplay.cfm&ContentID=26888 (accessed January 5, 2006).

38. Sherman, ed., *Lesbian and Gay Marriage*, 80–81 (see note 28); Bonhall, "Partners for Life," (see note 24); Bob Dallmeyer, "Gay Parents…" *The Blade*, February 1994, 43–44; April Urban, "Two Moms and a Baby," *The Blade*, February 1994, 46; Doug Sadownick, "We Are Family: 2 Dads Are Better Than 1," *Genre* 12 (June/July 1993), 36; Gillespie, ed., *Love Makes A Family*, xi–xii (see note 28). An estimated three million lesbian and gay people were raising over ten million children as of 1994.

39. Vermont statistics from http://www.breitbart.com/news/2005/12/15/D8EGT8A80 .html (accessed January 4, 2006).

40. *Jumping the Broom*, 46 (see note 9).

# 11

## AFRICAN AMERICAN RESPONSES TO SAME-SEX MARRIAGE

*Samiya Bashir, H. Alexander Robinson, and Lisa Powell*

In this chapter, three leading activists in the fight for both racial equality and for gay and lesbian rights discuss the distinctive ways in which marriage discrimination affects African American same-sex couples.

### WE ARE FAMILY: DEFEATING THE SHAME GAME IN THE FIGHT FOR THE FREEDOM TO MARRY

by Samiya Bashir, Communications Director, Freedom to Marry

African American lesbian, gay, bisexual, and transgender (LGBT) people have long fought to stake their claim to the American promise, enshrined in the Declaration of Independence, of equal rights to "life, liberty and the pursuit of happiness." They have done it for the most part while acquiescing to the black community's demands to not live too loud, to not act so free, and to avoid flaunting any happiness they come by or decrying the violence and discrimination they suffer too broadly in public. Oftentimes, playing into the assumption that who they are is something of which to be ashamed, they are told that it is their responsibility to keep quiet, go away, or fade into the background while continuing to fight undaunted for the equal rights of the rest of African America.

Most black gays and lesbians did not grow up as the only black person in their families, although that is a claim that is becoming more difficult to make as the structure of families in America continues to change. A great many black lesbian, gay, bisexual, and transgendered people did grow up, however, believing that they were the only ones in their families, peer groups, and communities who were "different"—whether it was true or not. They were raised to believe that there was something shameful about who they were, and in an atmosphere in which their families were already under attack, in which their collective humanity seemed always in need of protection, many of them grew up with the idea that remaining silent about their difference was the only way to guarantee their safety and that of their families and communities.

At a time of escalating division and destruction of black communities across region, class, and gender as well as sexual orientation, it is frustrating that the latest assault is being joined not only by those who might benefit from division within the black community but also by those who stand to lose so much: black LGBT individuals, their families, and their friends. This situation is exemplified in one of the most divisive weapons hurled against black LGBT individuals, couples, and families in the current fight against equal marriage rights. Those who oppose black gays and lesbians, while claiming to love them, maintain that they must be denied equality in order to preserve and sustain the struggling black family. In truth, gays and lesbians too are members of the black family, and their struggle is compounded by continued exclusion from the rights, responsibilities, and protections marriage provides.

### Supporting Black Families

History has shown that when it is time to speak out against injustices leveled at African American communities, black gays and lesbians are there, often on the front lines. Yet where is the black community when it is time to support black gay people and their families? Those in the black LGBT community engaged in the struggle for equality are told from the pulpit, the dinner table, and the halls of Congress that it is time to put down "moral relativism" and stand up in support of narrowly defined black families.

It is long past time to stop pretending that lesbians and gay men have not always been an integral part of the black family. Black lesbian couples, for instance, have rates of parenthood similar to those of married black opposite-sex couples (61 percent to 69 percent). By contrast, black lesbian households report annual incomes 21 percent lower than those of married black opposite-sex households.[1] The issue goes far beyond tolerance when, without the security that marriage affords, gay and lesbian families face the real prospect of losing their homes in the tragic event of one parent's death. Are their children less deserving of health insurance? It is not right that committed, hard-working lesbian and gay couples struggle with increased difficulty putting food on the table or saving for their children's education when so much of their often lower combined wages must go to pay higher taxes and legal fees to contract for the few—but not all—basic rights that they can have, when those rights would automatically be afforded by marriage. It is this self-serving brand of "moral relativism" that stands in the way of stabilizing all black families. The black family must be inclusive if it is to be preserved.

*Washington Post* columnist Colbert I. King wrote, "I do believe that [lesbian and gay couples] are subject to prejudice and that they are forbidden the same rights and safeguards that heterosexuals enjoy, including the right to marry. That, in my book, is wrong. There is justice to their cause that should be ours, too. Leaving the security of the majority to stand up and say so ought not be so hard in 2005.

Sadly, for many Americans, it is."[2] We are heartened by the support of many prominent black leaders, such as Coretta Scott King; Carol Moseley-Braun, former
ambassador and U.S. Senator; Julian Bond, the chair of the National Association for
the Advancement of Colored People (NAACP); John Lewis, U.S. Representative
(D-GA); the Reverend John L. Selders, Jr., bishop in the Church of God; the Reverend Peter Gomes; Henry Louis Gates, Jr., W.E.B. DuBois Professor of the Human-
ities at Harvard University; and Dr. M. Jocelyn Elders, the former surgeon general.
U.S. Representative Tommie Brown (D-TN) had it right when she said, "I do want
the record to show on this day of our Lord that this seventy-and-a-half-year-old
African American woman cannot bring herself to vote for bad public policy simply
because the masses are [in favor]. You see, I am from a time and generation when
the masses said that I was not even a person."[3]

These leaders understand that any argument purporting that fairness for gay- or
lesbian-headed black families is a threat to those headed by nongay couples is nothing but a bright red herring. The fight against marriage equality actually destabilizes
black families and does nothing to improve the lives of nongay African Americans
struggling to keep their own marriages together.

*Brothers and Sisters!*

Black lesbians and gay men are also not immune to the need to stand up for their
own safety and security. We have to ask ourselves: Whose movement is this? The
right wing has been allowed to successfully frame the struggle for LGBT liberation
as solely about the rights of wealthy white gay men. But this civil rights struggle
belongs to people of color as much as it does to anyone else. And it belongs to
LGBT and non-LGBT folks alike, as does any movement to end oppression and
ensure civil rights for all. Once we and our antiracist allies, both within and outside
the movement, embrace this reality, we will be able to lay the groundwork for heal-
ing and unification. My own organization, for instance, which is a founding partner of both the National Black Justice Coalition and the National Latino Coalition
for Justice in Marriage, is composed almost entirely of fiercely committed people
of color.

Black LGBT communities can no longer afford to play Monday-morning quar-
terbacks when their lives remain at stake. According to the 2000 census, African
Americans represent 14 percent of the cohabiting lesbian and gay couples in the
United States—a full percentage point higher than our representation in the general
population. They are also more likely than white couples to be raising children,
more likely to hold jobs in the public sector—those with a higher availability of the
domestic partner benefits, currently threatened by antigay, antifamily ballot
measures—and less likely to own the homes they share. Discrimination in marriage
affects them disproportionately and leaves their families weaker and less able to
thrive. It is essential that we stand up taller, increase our visibility, and demand our
civil rights, but we need the help of the entire black family to succeed.

In 2004, eleven states passed constitutional amendments banning lesbian and
gay couples from marrying. In most cases the African American community did not
show up to support safety, security, and fairness for LGBT families. In Detroit, for
example, 58 percent of voters supported a constitutional amendment to exclude

lesbian and gay couples from marriage, many with the idea that in doing so they were voting to support black families. In some areas black support for discrimination in marriage was even higher. These numbers are not as high as the Right would like, but our community has had enough experience with discrimination and exclusion that to support it at levels even as high as these is a shameful act.

In 2005, Kansas joined the growing list of states to write discrimination against LGBT families into their constitutions. In November 2006, Texas voters will have the chance to decide the question of equality in their state. "[T]his is the politics of divisiveness at its worst," said Texas State Representative Senfronia Thompson in a bold speech to her fellow state representatives. "I know something about hate and fear and discrimination. When I was a small girl, white folks used to talk about 'protecting the institution of marriage' as well.... Fifty years ago, white folks thought inter-racial marriages were a 'threat to the institution of marriage'.... Members, I'm a Christian and a proud Christian," she continued. "I read the good book, and do my best to live by it. I have never read the verse where it says, 'gay people can't marry.' I have never read the verse where it says, 'thou shalt discriminate against those not like me.' I have never read the verse where it says, 'let's base our public policy on hate and fear and discrimination.'"[4]

In 2006, Alabama, Indiana, Wisconsin, South Carolina, Colorado, California, Arizona, Florida, Tennessee, South Dakota, and Virginia will also face antigay and antifamily ballot measures. The LGBT community may not be able to beat them all back, but it needs the help of its black family, friends, and community to win where it can and raise awareness about the harm this does to *all* families where a full win is not possible. In his much-acclaimed speech at the Democratic National Convention in 2004, Senator Barack Obama (D-IL) asked his audience this question: "Do we participate in a politics of cynicism or do we participate in a politics of hope?"[5] The answer to this question is crucial as we roll up our sleeves and move forward in the continuing fight for equal rights and equal protection. As we look at how we engage in this work, it is important to keep the focus on the future we wish to create, not on the opposition fighting to tear us down. Yet the fact remains that it is time to turn this shame game on its head. Loving, committed couples and their children, people who work hard and pay taxes just like their parents did, are not the ones who should be ashamed of their lives or their families. Those who stand in opposition to fairness for our families are the ones who should be ashamed.

*Lying with Dogs*

When I was a child, my grandmother taught me that it is important to be mindful of the company we keep. The slow-burn infiltration of African American churches by the Religious Right is effecting a shift from the Black Church tradition of liberation theology to one based on discrimination and exclusion. Recently, at the Reverend T.D. Jakes's wildly popular MegaFest, over one hundred thousand participants were welcomed with gifts and a long-armed embrace by the Reverend James Dobson's virulently right-wing Focus on the Family. "James Dobson's entrepreneurial spirit and personal political agenda," said Kerry Lobel, the former chair of the National Gay and Lesbian Task Force, "has turned racism, sexism, and homophobia into a profitable business."[6] Joining hands with such deceptively named organizations, whose leadership has only recently severed outward ties with racist, segregationist, and bigoted platforms, is bad enough. The Reverend Gregory Daniels, senior pastor of Chicago's Greater Shiloh Missionary Baptist Church and president of the right-wing group that recently popped up called United Voters for Truth and Change, embraced the trend head-on when he boldly declared, "If the [Ku Klux Klan] was opposing same-sex marriage, Reverend Daniels would ride with them."[7]

Has our collective memory become so shortsighted that members of the black community are no longer ashamed to stand with those who, except when it is polit-ically inconvenient for them, hasten and boldly cheer our destruction? Have we lost the ability to see how the discriminatory and divisive tactics we are being recruited to support so directly lead to an agenda that will eventually be our own undoing? By signing onto the right-wing talking points that claim that "civil rights" belong only to African Americans, we are rapturously signing away our own political power. Once civil rights, as supported by our Constitution's Bill of Rights, belong not to all Americans but only to one group, then our entire community has lost the civil rights battle for good. What lurks further inside the snake hole of the right-wing agenda—which a simple look at the current fight to keep alive both affirma-tive action and the voting rights act will illuminate—is the desire to reframe *all* civil rights as "special rights." Today it's lesbian and gay couples and their families; tomorrow it's all families who are pinned with the label of asking not for equal rights but so-called special rights.

Let us not be fooled. Our opposition is fierce, cutthroat, and commands more resources by a margin of at least 4:1. But a mere look at our history should be enough to help us remain undaunted, especially with stakes as high as these. Over eleven hundred rights and responsibilities come from equal marriage protection for our families. Our community hinges on a win, and right now, despite the odds, we are winning. A recent national poll released by the Pew Research Center, reports that a majority of Americans (53 percent) are in favor of legal recognition for les-bian and gay couples that would offer many of the same rights and responsibilities as nongay married couples. In a shift from some postelection declines, 35 percent of Americans said they support a complete end to discrimination in marriage, while an encouraging *L.A. Times* poll shows that fully 44 percent of Californians support marriage equality for lesbian and gay couples.[8]

The poet Claude McKay put words to the continuing fight of minorities against those who, strong and determined, wish us to remain oppressed. "Though far out-numbered," he said, "let us show us brave."[9] When we look at the millions of dol-lars, the long head start in infrastructure, and the fork-tongued claim to moral authority asserted by our opposition, we know that we must "show us brave," for while we are the minority in terms of numbers, our case is strong and our cause is just. But few will understand this point unless we believe it ourselves and assert it with the passion of conviction. It is up to us to give those who may not understand the importance of the issue but who believe in fairness the information that they need to understand why this equal rights fight is central to the American promise we are purporting to defend both at home and abroad.

Opponents of equal marriage rights are targeting black churches because they assume that these bodies—in a roundabout, self-fulfilling prophesy of an argument—are more conservative than their white counterparts. Black churches, the argument goes, are the last places one would expect to find LGBT people. The truth is that lesbian and gay Christians have assumed leadership positions within the church for as long as the church has existed. At least 85 percent of African American LGBT people report some sort of religious affiliation. Unfortunately, just as in the military, where we are also disproportionately represented, we often serve in silence.

*Coming Home*

Lesbian and gay African Americans and our nongay friends and families no longer have time to hide in the fringes of society and remain silent about the importance of our lives. This is about more than pride; this is about justice. Every Friday or Sunday that one of us goes to the mosque or the church and worships or serves in silence is a gift that we give our opposition. Every week that we allow our families, our schools, or our neighbors to deny the humanity of our lives, our partners, and our children is a step backward; an ink stain blotting out our right to equal protection under the law.

When I speak to groups about the importance of marriage equality I am often asked why I care so much when I am single and have no children of my own. That very question denies me both my community and my responsibility to it. I wonder whether they would similarly question the well-off African Americans who lent their cars to activists in the Montgomery bus boycott. I think about being raised in a family that did not eat grapes for years in support of farm workers we would never meet, or of the millions of women and men who have long supported a woman's right to choose even though they may never have to make that difficult decision for themselves. "In the end," said Dr. Martin Luther King, Jr., "we will remember not the words of our enemies, but the silence of our friends."[10] Opposing marriage equality does nothing but *hurt* black families, especially the most vulnerable, from those headed by two women (who earn even less than their male counterparts), to those headed by single mothers who need such protections as those offered by domestic violence laws that many of the current antigay amendments actually take away.

Winning the freedom to marry is a crucial goal in the battle to stabilize and protect *all* our families, and it requires the support of all of us, LGBT and non-LGBT, to stand up for the equal rights of the entire black community. I remember the year that my mother called me, elated, on Martin Luther King, Jr. Day with the news that she had joined the support group Parents, Families, and Friends of Lesbians and Gays (PFLAG) in honor of Dr. King. Although both my sister and I had been sending her articles and information for years as dutiful lesbian daughters, it was the first time she stepped out on her own in public to meet others who were seeking support for themselves and their families and demanding equality for their LGBT loved ones. Of course I was thrilled and proud. I felt honored that my mother had taken that step for me, for my lesbian sister, and for our entire family. I know that every time she speaks out, whether it is in her church, in her sorority meetings, in the grocery store, or out with friends, it carries the weight of the majority that I simply do not have when it comes to speaking about equal rights for lesbian, gay, bisexual, and transgendered persons.

Certainly, if I have children, I hope that I can offer them all the benefits and protections that they need to grow up healthy, smart, and strong. I hope that my children grow up never expecting or accepting less than equal access, equal rights, and equal protection under the law and in society. But the need of black gays and lesbians to engage in the movement for marriage equality is about more than their own families. It is about protecting, uplifting, and empowering the black community as a whole, and creating a society that treats its minorities as full citizens and exempts no one from the promise of "life, liberty and the pursuit of happiness."

## AFRICAN AMERICANS AND SAME-SEX MARRIAGE

by H. Alexander Robinson, Executive Director, National Black Justice Coalition

### A History of Discrimination

Equality and freedom from discrimination are core American values and of utmost political consequences for all minorities, especially African Americans. So it should concern everyone that some opponents of gay equality insist that by claiming the legacy of our nation's civil rights struggle, gay civil rights advocates are misappropriating African Americans' fight for justice. The right not to suffer discrimination is an American birthright that we all expect to enjoy under our laws and our Constitution. If America is to be a truly fair and open country, then the quest for civil rights must be universal. The fight to end discrimination against gay and lesbian couples and our nation's history of racial discrimination in marriage share many characteristics. For instance, the justifications for both anti–gay and anti–interracial marriage laws have been couched in religious, moral, cultural, or legal terms. These justifications share the same stench of greed, jealousy, bigotry, ignorance, and judgment and the same politics of majoritarian oppression.

America's prohibitions of interracial marriages were deeply rooted in our history and tradition. Laws prohibiting interracial marriage were enforced in American colonies and states for more than three centuries. Similar to today's bans on marriage between same-sex partners, the so-called antimiscegenation laws were the majority's attempt to determine who was—or was not—an appropriate spouse. Likewise, anti–gay marriage laws are deeply rooted in our nation's history of prejudice against homosexuals. Based on the majority's moral judgments, religious beliefs, or cultural values, they seek to define who should and should not be allowed to marry.

Like the current bans on same-sex marriage, antimiscegenation laws started in a few communities and quickly spread throughout the nation. By 1860, twenty-three of the thirty-three states banned interracial marriage. By the time of the Civil War, laws prohibiting interracial marriage covered most of the states in the South and many in the Midwest, and they were beginning to appear in the West as well. A few southern states repealed their antimiscegenation laws during the Reconstruction era, but societal pressure to spurn interracial relationships remained intact. Today, in state after state we have witnessed the passage of laws and state constitutional amendments that seek to define marriage in such a way as to exclude gay couples.

Uncertain that state bans on marriage will advance their discriminatory objectives, proponents of state "one man-one woman" constitutional amendments seek to amend the United States Constitution in a similar fashion. This movement is history repeating itself. Despite the proliferation of antimiscegenation laws, opponents of interracial marriage feared that state laws were insufficient to protect the "sanctity of marriage," and in 1912 they started a campaign to amend the Constitution to outlaw marriage between Negroes or persons of color and Caucasians. The campaign eventually failed.

If readers are not convinced that our current struggle is analogous to that of our forebears who fought to end racial discrimination in marriage, they need look no further than public opinion. Bans on interracial marriage reflected contemporary public sentiment. In 1958, a Gallup poll indicated that 96 percent of all Americans opposed interracial marriage. So too, today's opposition to marriage equality is supported by a majority of Americans. Even many so-called supporters of gay rights want to keep marriage as the sole preserve of heterosexual couples.

Just as we did not allow the ignorance and prejudice of the past to dictate our beliefs about racial equality, we must not allow prejudice to be the guidepost of our view of the constitutional promise of equality.

*Inalienable Rights*

Opponents of gay equality are quick to point out that race and skin color are not choices, that race is often difficult if not impossible to hide, and that race is a benign human difference. They argue that people of color carry the insignia of who they are on their faces and that sexual orientation—in practice if not in fact—is a choice. This argument is most often employed to dismiss the assertion that what gay Americans seek is civil rights or that the Fourteenth Amendment's guarantee of equal protection under the law should be applied to gay Americans. While the validity of this argument is dismissed by some gay rights advocates, several polls have shown that if sexual orientation is an inborn trait like race, eye color, or sex, an overwhelming majority of Americans accept it and support equal rights for gay people. It may well be that the debate about gay rights will turn on this one simple question.

Julian Bond, the chair of the National Association for the Advancement of Colored People (NAACP), often uses the premise of sexual orientation as an immutable characteristic when he speaks of reasons for citing the Constitution in support of marriage equality. "Sexual disposition parallels race—I was born black and had no choice," he said during a recent speech. "Like race, our sexuality isn't a preference—it is immutable, unchangeable, and the Constitution protects us all against prejudices and discrimination based on immutable differences."[11] By using this formulation, Bond seems to realize that sexual orientation is not in any meaningful way a choice and that its immutability is a prerequisite to winning the constitutional debate.

Science has not uncovered a gay gene; however, much of the research suggests that sexual orientation, like handedness, is not a choice. This debate is likely to continue for many years. Yet the application of America's founding principle of equality and justice would recommend that citizens have a duty to err on the side of fairness when making judgments about access to American institutions, and in particular, to an institution as significant as marriage. When in doubt, one should opt for inclusiveness.

Again we must look to history to learn some important lessons. It was not so long ago in our nation's history that pseudoscientific evidence was used to support the notion of black inferiority, and misguided biblical scholarship was often the basis for statutory and constitutional discrimination against African Americans. People would do well to learn from these grievous errors, which continue even today to cause divisions. While we might not be able to point to the existence of a gay gene, it is an undeniable fact that gay Americans fall in love and want to protect and take responsibility for their partners. Their love is real and natural and should be inviolate.

*Marriage and Religion*

Of particular significance when addressing marriage in black communities are the arguments advanced by some gay rights opponents based on biblical passages that they assert condemn homosexuality and homosexuals. These gay rights opponents are quick to raise two primary concerns: first, they say that the Bible says that homosexuality is an abomination; and second, that their churches will be forced to perform marriages of same-sex couples in violation of their religious or moral beliefs. What the Bible says about homosexuality is a topic of much debate, as is the appropriate role of religion in civil society. What is not at all unclear, however, is that gay Americans are seeking the right to civil marriage and that the exercise of that right would not impede the free exercise of any religious beliefs.

The similarity between these arguments and the justifications for opposition to interracial marriage and integration are overwhelming. Some churches feared that they would be forced to integrate; others found Biblical passages that they insisted forbade the mixing of the races, and that interracial marriages were so unnatural that God and nature seemed to forbid them. And of course there was the concern about the children. Interracial offspring were said to be impure and "generally sickly and effeminate."[12] Today's false claims of fear of the government's intrusion in religious or negative affects on children ring just as hollow as the racist claims of yesteryear and should not be allowed to distract us from our march toward equality.

Gay Americans' demand for the right to marry is not about the rite of marriage. While it is true that many gay people are working within their own faith traditions to challenge the exclusion of same-sex couples from the rites of marriage, the public and legal campaign to end discrimination in marriage is not a movement to further blur the lines drawn in the Constitution that separate church and state. No one has proposed that churches or religious institutions be forced to perform same-sex marriages. To the contrary, gay people seek the right to obtain a marriage license from city hall like their heterosexual neighbors. Likewise, all the evidence suggests that the children of gay families, like their heterosexual counterparts, are healthy and loved.

*Where Do We Go from Here?*

Opponents of gay equality have fastened on African Americans' understandable suspicions of any efforts that might undermine the principle of equal treatment under the law. The Far Right has used marriage equality and the centrality of the Black Church in the experience of black Americans to disingenuously raise the specter of government inference in church practices and antigay religious beliefs. Together these suspicions and preexisting religious and cultural objections to homosexuality have combined to create a wedge in an otherwise cohesive army fighting to ensure equality for all Americans.

It is in this context that the National Black Justice Coalition (NBJC) was founded in 2003. Prompted by the antigay ballot initiatives and support from anti-gay right extremists, a small but vocal minority of black clergy took to the streets and the airwaves to support banning marriage for gay couples and to condemn gay Americans. The NBJC was founded to provide some balance to this discussion. There is a paucity of black voices standing up against these antigay forces. African Americans' feelings about sexuality vary greatly; however, most opinion polls sug-gest that African Americans reject discrimination of all types, including discrimina-tory policies and practices directed against gay people. Marriage, however, remains a challenge since marriage is still viewed primarily as a religious institution.

In turn, the history of discrimination in America has created many community pathologies that are often characterized by a rejection of those who are different or fail to conform. Gay-identified black people often express feelings of personal con-flict between their black identity and feelings of support for the African American community, and their gay identity and love for their same-sex partners. Torn between the two, many black homosexual people often choose to be silent about their sexuality in exchange for the seemingly comfortable embrace of the black com-munity. This dangerous mix of self-delusion, public and private dishonesty, and communal denial has had devastating adverse consequences. Denial keeps the truth from being spoken in our homes, workplaces, and places of worship. In turn it has left our community ill equipped to deal with such challenges as HIV and AIDS, antigay violence, and discrimination against gay families.

NBJC's challenge is to raise the voices of black gay, lesbian, bisexual, and transgendered people, along with those of our families, friends, and allies. Its strat-egy is to engage openly LGBT and same-gender-loving people in a proactive cam-paign to speak openly about their lives, hopes, dreams, and challenges. Its goal is to end the fear and ignorance that leads to prejudice and discrimination.

## BLACK LESBIANS AND SAME-SEX MARRIAGE

by Lisa Powell, Executive Director, United Lesbians of African Heritage

Imagine if the government of the United States were to enact a policy that gave one particular right to everyone in the country—except Baptists, who are defined as inel-igible to receive this right. Imagine further that this right automatically conveyed hun-dreds of financial benefits that either could not be otherwise obtained or could be obtained only at great expense. We can readily agree that such a policy is simply unfair and likely amounts to illegal discrimination. After all, why should Baptists be treated differently from anyone else in this country? In a nutshell, precisely this type of invidi-ous discrimination is at work when gays and lesbians are denied the right to marry.

For black lesbian couplhomees in particular, many of whom are already experi-encing the triple jeopardy of discrimination or stigma based on race, sex, and sexual orientation or gender expression, denial of the right to marry inflicts a disproportion-ate economic and social penalty. The 2004 report from the U.S. General Accounting

Office reported that there are at least 1,138 federal benefits, rights, and responsibilities that flow from marriage to couples and their children. This vast and complicated system of interwoven policies, rules, and regulations covers virtually every area of life, including death, debts, divorce, family leave, definitions of next of kin, health care, housing, immigration, inheritance, insurance, parenting and child support, property ownership, retirement, and taxation. According to the 2000 Census, black lesbian couples have a lower household income than either black opposite-sex couples or white lesbians, and 68 percent of black lesbian households are raising children. Interestingly, black lesbian couples are just about as likely to be raising children as are black opposite-sex couples. Black lesbian couples, however, are less likely to own their own homes.[13]

Since black lesbian couples have a lower median income, are less likely to own homes (one of the major sources of financial wealth and security), and 68 percent are raising children, any benefits that are not afforded to them will have a disproportionate impact. Add to this the fact that it is usually a woman in the black family—regardless of sexual orientation—who steps up to care for ailing parents or grandparents, needy grandchildren, and nieces or nephews. So when black lesbian couples are denied, for example, Social Security benefits should one partner die, the right to receive Medicare and Medicaid spousal benefits, or the right to file joint tax returns—all rights afforded only to married couples—economic hardships are magnified.

Given the fact that black lesbians as a group have so much at stake and stand to gain so much from equal access to marriage, it would naturally follow that black lesbians should be a large and vocal presence in the fight for marriage equality. In fact, while many black lesbian leaders have been working on this issue for years, only a sliver of the forty-five thousand black lesbian couples in the United States and a tiny fraction of the thousands and thousands of black lesbians who hope to be in a loving couple are making their voices heard on marriage equality. One of the frequent explanations black lesbians give for their low visibility in this fight is that blacks as a community have other, higher, and more pressing priorities. Often we hear that marriage equality is a luxury issue that would provide few tangible benefits to black lesbians. Ironically, many of the most severe economic hardships faced by black lesbian couples and their children would immediately be addressed by the safety net that marriage provides. The fewer resources a couple has, the more that access to marriage makes a real difference.

While it appears that black lesbians may be underestimating the extent to which access to marriage would improve their socioeconomic status, black lesbians may also be underestimating the effects of marriage equality on the ways in which their extended biological family, friends, coworkers, and the community see and understand their relationships. Consider how often black lesbian relationships are trivialized and marginalized. For example, long-term couples are referred to as "roommates." Or consider the black community's classic reference to a lesbian's long-term partner as "her *friend*." Married couples do not share this experience. It's *wife* and *husband* or even *fiancée* and *fiancé*. Even more importantly, no matter what a couple is called, same-sex couples are reduced to second-class status when they are denied the same rights bestowed on opposite-sex couples. So extending the right to marry to same-sex couples would be a powerful societal acknowledgment that everyone deserves to be treated equally.

Additionally, marriage provides clarity. It provides a known and familiar template for understanding the nature of the relationship between two people who love each other and have made a commitment to each other. Instead of black lesbians being called "that way"—that is, "other," which of course by extension is "less than"—couples would be a part of the larger community's understanding of commitment, responsibility, and shared futures. Part of the reason why antigay stigma and prejudice are so intractable is that these pernicious attitudes largely operate at the conceptual level of "they" or "those people." Invisible gays and lesbians can be demonized much more easily than the ones who are living openly in the community, fixing cars, teaching children, and directing choirs.

Unfortunately, the best explanation of the reluctance of black lesbians to mobilizing *en masse* to fight for marriage equality is that in order to fight, one must be willing to share the fact that one is a lesbian. And to be a vocal advocate one must be fully "out of the closet." It was very interesting to try to spot a black lesbian couple in the long line of same-sex couples waiting to get married in San Francisco in early 2004. Although the story was covered extensively by many stations for weeks, black lesbian couples were virtually nonexistent. The reality is that many black lesbians simply do not feel that it is safe to "come out of the closet," let alone be seen on CNN standing in line to be married to another woman. Without protections against job discrimination and loss of livelihood, along with the assurance that one's family, friends, neighbors, coworkers, and church will be supportive and accepting, many black lesbians choose to keep their same-sex relationships private or limited to a social network of those "in the know." As discussed earlier, many black lesbian couples are already burdened by family responsibilities, and the specter of losing critical support is deemed too great a risk.

Moreover, it is fairly well established that most black lesbians and gays perceive that they are not fully accepted by a large segment of the nongay black community. At least on the issue of marriage equality, among a representative sample of registered voters in California, 68 percent of blacks/African Americans opposed same-sex marriage, and 50 percent of blacks/African Americans favored an amendment to the U.S. Constitution to define marriage as a union between a man and a woman. These findings revealed that black opposition to gay marriage is much stronger than that of the whites, Latinos, and Asians who were surveyed.[14] Black lesbians have long experienced the harm caused by these attitudes, which are largely based on certain religious beliefs prevalent in the black community. Of course, it will have to be black lesbians who insist that our black community embrace equality without regard to a particular religious doctrine. We must be the ones who remind our community of the ways in which the Bible can be used by the majority to oppress the minority. And yes, black lesbians, who stand so much to gain from marriage equality, will ultimately need to stand up and help our entire black family to learn to value us and our relationships fully.

## NOTES

1. See the National Gay and Lesbian Task Force (NGLTF) Policy Institute and the National Black Justice Coalition (NBJC), "Black Same-Sex Households in the United States: A Report from the 2000 Census" (Washington, DC: NGLTF 2004).

2. Colbert I. King, "Marriage in the March of Time," *Washington Post*, February 12, 2005.

3. Skip Cauthorn, "Finance Panel Passes Gay Marriage Ban," *Nashville City Paper*, March 2, 2005.

4. Senfronia Thompson, (speech, Texas House of Representatives, Austin, TX, April 25, 2005), full text available at http://www.freedomtomarry.org/document.asp?doc_id=2646 (accessed August 2, 2006).

5. Barack Obama, "The Audacity of Hope" (2004 Democratic National Convention Keynote Address, Boston, MA, July 27, 2004) http://www.americanrhetoric.com/speeches/ convention2004/barackobama2004dnc.htm (accessed August 2, 2006).

6. "Founder of right wing group apologizes for organization's bigotry" (press release); National Gay and Lesbian Task Force, quote by Kerry Lobel (then executive director), http://www.qrd.org/qrd/religion/anti/FOF/founder.apologizes.for.bigotry-08.14.97 (accessed August 2, 2006).

7. Frank Phillips and Raphael Lewis, "A Hunt for Middle Ground: Travaglini Voices Confidence on a Marriage Accord Today," *Boston Globe*, March 11, 2004, http://www.boston .com/news/local/articles/2004/03/11/a_hunt_for_middle_ground (accessed August 2, 2006).

8. PollingReport.com, "Law and Civil Rights," http://www.pollingreport.com/civil.htm (accessed August 2, 2006).

9. *Complete Poems: Claude McKay*, ed. William J. Maxwell (Urbana: University of Illinois Press, 2004).

10. John Blaydes, *The Educator's Book of Quotes* (Thousand Oaks, CA: Corwin Press, 2003).

11. Julian Bond, untitled speech at the Human Rights Campaign National Dinner, Washington, DC, October 1, 2005, http://www.hrc.org/dinner/speech_jbond.htm (accessed August 2, 2006).

12. *Scott v. Georgia*, 39 Ga. 321, 323, 327 (1869).

13. See note 1.

14. Field Research Corporation, *The Field Poll*, release #2109, February 26, 2004, tables 2, 3, http://www.field.com/fieldpollonline/subscribers/RLS2109.pdf (accessed August 2, 2006).

# 12

## SPEAK NOW OR FOREVER HOLD YOUR PEACE: SAME-SEX MARRIAGES IN NATIVE AMERICAN CULTURE

*Mark Vezzola*

When same-sex marriage came to the foreground of a worldwide debate in 2004, few people considered its impact on Native America. Until May of that year, sovereign Indian nations might have thought themselves insulated from the larger debate over the morality and legality of same-sex marriage, but in a short time that would change forever. On May 18, 2004, two female members of the Cherokee Nation of Oklahoma were united in matrimony and issued a Cherokee marriage license by mistake, making history in the field of gay rights and stirring up controversy in Native America.

The story of same-sex marriage in Indian country began long before Dawn McKinley and Kathy Reynolds attempted to file their marriage license with the tribe. European explorers observed what they considered to be immoral and deviant relationships between men as early as the sixteenth century. Some tribes traced the world's creation back to spirit figures who embodied masculine and feminine attributes but transcended male or female labels. These observations and creation myths provide us with a picture of tolerance among Native communities toward individuals who did not conform to strict boundaries for sexuality or gender.

### NOMENCLATURE

At the outset, the terminology used to refer to Native peoples of alternative genders and sexualities will be traced from the beginning of European colonization of indigenous North America. This approach is important for several reasons. First, studying the names and labels applied to these individuals will give readers a sense of the way in which the Native peoples were perceived by the European colonizers, which explains why overt same-sex relations seemed to disappear in Native America. Second, the terms applied to Native peoples who engaged in homosexual activity were usually inaccurate and often culturally offensive. And third, tribes differed in their cultural beliefs and social norms, making it difficult to apply broad terms to all tribes.

Historically, Native peoples who engaged in homosexual relations were called *berdaches*, a flawed term that never had an agreed-upon meaning. *Berdache* is a French term derived from an Arabic word for "male prostitute" or "slave." The French applied it to Native men observed wearing women's clothing.[1] Likewise, people who had sexual contact with or ultimately married a person of the same sex were also labeled berdaches, since sexuality and gender were virtually indistinguishable to the colonizers of the Western world. The most widely accepted meaning of the term is that it refers to a person who was born a member of one sex but assumed the social status of the other, including cross-dressing and engaging in household duties typically associated with the opposite gender.

In addition to degrading a person, *berdache* has been incorrectly used as a synonym for *homosexual, hermaphrodite*, and *transvestite* since it came into use more than three hundred years ago. One early-twentieth-century anthropologist referred to a Zuni *lhamana* as a "man-woman," "berdache," and "hermaphrodite" interchangeably within the same article and used the term *transvestite* as a synonym a quarter of a century later.[2] A scholar conducting research in Alaska erroneously reported a high percentage of berdaches among the Kaska culture because so many young girls wore caribou parkas commonly used by boys while hunting game. His application was baseless, however, for he failed to consider that large Kaska families with few or no sons had little choice but to send their daughters out into harsh conditions to provide sustenance for the family.[3] Such reckless use of language did a tremendous disservice to subsequent generations of scholars seeking the right word to encapsulate the sexual and social behavior of two-spirits.

In *Men as Women, Women as Men*, Sabine Lang distinguished several categories of people labeled as berdaches by generations of explorers and scholars: (1) individuals who had sex with members of their own sex without changing gender roles; (2) individuals who wore the clothing of the opposite sex without carrying out a change in gender role or engaging in sexual relations with people of the same sex; (3) feminine men and masculine women who retained their gender status in a sexual and social sense, such as a masculine woman married to a man and living as his wife; (4) "warrior women" and other persons who crossed gender role boundaries without exchanging their gender status for an ambivalent one by so doing; and (5) men who were forced to wear women's clothing in disgrace and occasionally take on a woman's role because they had failed in the warrior role. These men wished to be considered masculine again and occasionally reclaimed their status by undertaking a daredevil act of war.[4] While Lang's list is not exhaustive, it does help illustrate the range of identities that were mistakenly categorized as berdaches.[5]

Besides confusing generations of students interested in Native American or gender studies, this careless use of inaccurate labels perpetuated colonization through language appropriation, often obscuring Native understandings of and reverence for two-spirited individuals. Explorers and researchers ascribed a degraded station in life to men who did work traditionally done by women. The artist George

Catlin, who chronicled Native American life in North America in his sketches and oil paintings during the 1830s, described the Sauk "Dance to the Berdache," a ritual that the famous painter regarded as disgraceful to a person of honor.[6] Such statements highlight the necessity to heed the French writer Jean-Guy Goulet's admonition to "always question whether our terminology and categories correspond to [Native] constructions of personhood and gender identities in specific cultural traditions and social contexts."[7]

Despite these variations in definition, *berdache* held its place as the most common term for a homosexual Indian and continued to be applied even though its application was almost always overly broad and usually inconsistent.[8] Anthropologists used *berdache* to describe people born male but regarded as female by society, although within a decade the definition was expanded to include biological females and was focused on the "adoption of the role and status of the opposite sex by a person of non-ambiguous sex." [9] Only in the last quarter-century did scholars caution against grouping people into a "socially acceptable form of perverted sexual activity" while overlooking his or her social and sexual role in a cultural context.[10] By the 1980s scholars agreed that a berdache's choice of sexual partner is less significant in his or her social role than the person's occupations, dress, or demeanor, making homosexual acts an inconclusive basis on which to define someone as a berdache or two-spirited person.[11]

Names and labels are important to our larger discussion of same-sex but heterogender relationships in Indian country for several reasons. First, knowing a culture's word for something or someone may offer a glimpse into the ways in which that culture perceived the thing or person referred to by the name. Second, in Native American studies it is important to recognize the individual identity of each tribe and cultural group even when it may be convenient to lump them together with groups having similar social, religious, or linguistic traits. And third, applying tribal names to people of alternative genders is the more culturally sensitive and historically accurate way to truly capture the meaning assigned to such people by their communities.

Naturally, no word or phrase gained uniform use among the hundreds of different indigenous cultures that inhabited North America; rather, each community used a term with a unique meaning reflecting that society's understanding of a two-spirited person. Of the 250 Native languages still spoken today in North America, at least 168 have been identified as having words for individuals who are neither male nor female but another gender.[12] When used, these words will be italicized. In Navajo, persons with two spirits are referred to as *nadlé*, which literally means "changing one" or "one who is transformed," but includes hermaphrodites as well as those who only appear to be *nadlé* by taking on a social role distinct from those of men or women.[13] Among the Lakota, persons with two spirits were known as *winkté*, a word that generally refers to biological males and can be translated as "would-be woman," but may be a derivative of the Lakota word for sodomy.[14] Some Native cultures have several words for different variations of gender and/or sex, making it impossible for a single English word to encapsulate all the concepts described above.

In reference to Native peoples of alternative genders and sexualities in general, the term *two-spirit* will be used to describe individuals who embody qualities of both the male and female genders and constitute a third unique gender. A translation of a Chippewa word, *two-spirit* was adopted by a group of Gay American Indians (GAIs) who met in Canada in 1988 to agree on a name that captured the spiritual significance of people of alternative genders without the value judgments inherent in Western terms. *Two-spirit*, like *berdache*, does not necessarily define the sexual preferences of the person being referred to—some people identify themselves as two-spirit but not gay while others feel just the opposite.[15] A future generation of scholars starting from a cultural rather than a psychological focus may perhaps formulate an even more fitting term some day, but as of the early 2000s, *two-spirit* is the most accurate and culturally sensitive term to apply to members of Native communities across the board.

## CULTURE

Before discussing the reaction to and potential implications of same-sex marriage in contemporary Native communities, it is necessary to understand Native attitudes toward sexuality, gender, and spirituality. Much of the information we have on the various aspects of two-spirit life comes from foreigners who infiltrated Native communities and applied their own biases and predispositions to two-spirits. These records and observations should not be permitted to distort our view of the significant roles two-spirits played in tribal contexts. For this reason, this section on culture surveys various Native attitudes toward gender and sexuality and provides examples recorded throughout history, with a eye to those who recorded them and their personal biases.

Homosexuality, transvestitism, bisexuality, and same-sex marriage were all known to Native America long before there were courts to rule on the legality of such practices. Of course they took different forms among various tribes and received an array of receptions ranging from tolerance to indifference and perhaps even moral objection. But the purpose of this section is to put into context the history and traditions concerning sexuality and alternative genders in Native communities, with emphasis placed on homosexual relationships and same-sex marriage.

Essential to this survey of the sexual habits and gender roles in various Native societies is a general understanding of how Native Americans viewed the world. Terms like *queer* or *homosexual* oversimplify a person's sense of identity as well as his role in the community. Although I try to avoid generalizing in this paper, I will break my own rule to make the following point. For Native Americans, a person's sexuality was of little concern to members of the community and provided only a minimal amount of gossip. Of more importance was a person's gender, which would determine his role in society, guide the behaviors of others around him, and dictate to some extent how parents would raise their child.

A person's sex might be readily discernible at birth, but his or her gender would take time to be shaped by environment and spiritual influence, sometimes as early as the age of five or six. Nor would a person be limited to one of the two common genders, male or female. Several Native American cultures, including the Navajo, recognized multiple genders, the five most common being: male, female, people born with both male and female sex organs (hermaphrodites), biological males who

assumed predominantly female undertakings, and biological females who functioned socially as men. Because of this potential complexity, a person's choice of
sexual partner said little about that person's own gender.

With this complexity in mind, sexual relationships in the Native world must be
considered in terms of gender rather than sexuality. Modern society considers a
male who takes another male as a lover a homosexual, because both parties are biologically male, and in Western thought, members of the same gender. In Native
American cultures, however, a male who finds a lover among one of the other three
(or in some cases, four) genders is *not* a homosexual, because each party to the relationship represents a different gender despite their similar anatomy. Very few scholars have ever touched upon this key distinction between gender and sexuality,
leading them haphazardly to associate cross-dressing, gender transference, female
masculinity, and male femininity with homosexuality.

The gender status of a two-spirit was ambivalent because it might be masculine,
feminine, a hybrid of the two, or even a new gender. A biological male could opt for
the social status of a female but retain some or none of the habits characteristic of
men in his culture, such as hunting or going into battle. Since Native traditions
emphasize transformation and change, individuals are expected to change throughout their lives, including their gender.[16] Among the Crow tribe lived a *boté* (two-
spirit) named Osh-Tish ("Finds-Them-and-Kills-Them"), who wore female clothing
and socialized with women, yet participated in the Battle of Rosebud as a scout for
General Crook only a week before the Sioux and Cheyenne defeated Custer at the
Little Big Horn in 1876.[17] Two-spirits like Osh-Tish sometimes took other males as
sexual partners and even husbands, but were known to marry women for the purpose
of procreation or helping the family of a young widow or an abandoned wife. Similar
variations existed among female two-spirits, but the sources are less specific.

Just as most two-spirits enjoyed unrestricted access to multiple genders, some
cultures permitted people of male or female gender to enjoy sex with members of
the same gender without being considered two-spirits. Sexual relationships between
two masculine men, neither of whom was a two-spirit, were common, especially
when wives or lovers were unavailable for sex or indisposed because of pregnancy
or ill temper. Oftentimes a male companion could supply the same sexual gratification found in a female, depending on the type of sexual act preferred.[18] Although such
relationships might not be discussed openly, neither were they condemned or considered taboo by members of the community. The Western world would be quick to label
such a relationship as homosexual, but Native American cultures considered it an
alternative form of physical pleasure that did not stigmatize the participants.

Such beliefs were unfathomable to the generations of European explorers, missionaries, soldiers, and scholars who studied Native cultures. For them, cross-dressing and copulation with a person of the same sex signified one thing—homosexuality,
a mortal sin in the eyes of the Christian conquerors. As early as the sixteenth century, when Europeans had little interest in Native cultures aside from their rich land
base and potential strength as allies, explorers noticed alternative sexual and gender roles among the peoples of the New World. During an expedition through
Florida in 1564, for example, the French adventurer Jacques Le Moyne observed
"hermaphrodites" retrieving the bodies of fallen Timicua warriors in the aftermath
of battle.[19] Unfortunately, Le Moyne recorded no basis for using this descriptive

term, explaining only that these "'hermaphrodites' partake of the nature of each sex."[20] Yet the mere fact that he made such an observation is remarkable, considering that his encounter with the Timicua was most likely brief and took place during battle, offering little time to survey the physical traits of their warriors.

Prior to colonization, two-spirits often enjoyed the respect of their communities for their unique connection to the spirit world. Because many tribes believed that a boy who dressed as a girl (or vice versa) represented the will of a greater being rather than a personal choice, such individuals found acceptance among their kinsmen. In the Papago culture, two-spirits were fairly common. Their identity was determined at a young age by an elaborate test. If a small boy seemed more drawn to female pursuits, his family would gauge his preference by building a small brush enclosure with a man's bow and a woman's basket placed inside. After he entered the enclosure, it would be set on fire while the family watched to see which tool the boy took with him as he fled. If the boy took the basket, his parents reconciled themselves to having a two-spirited child and raised him with little complaint.[21]

Sometimes the Creator or another spirit would visit the young person in a dream or vision and ordain him or her a two-spirit with ceremonial responsibilities. The Yuma of Arizona associate two-spiritedness with intense dreaming, which reflects a person's ability to transform his or her mind. This connection was especially strong among Plains tribes like the Lakota, who believe a dream about the "Double Woman" gave the dreamer the power to seduce men. In such a dream, Double Woman would present the dreamer with female tools, which the dreamer could accept or refuse, allowing a choice over one's destiny.

As keepers of special ceremonial knowledge, two-spirits played key roles in many sacred rites of passage in Native American life, especially with respect to marriage and childbirth. A family interested in marrying off their son or daughter could hire a two-spirit as an intermediary to arrange a marriage to a child of another similarly situated family. Among the Plains tribes, two-spirits were responsible for bestowing special names on newborn children—names that held spiritual significance rather than everyday titles. The Lakota believed a name conferred by a *winkté* provided the child with spiritual protection and insured a long and healthy life.[22] Such names would never be revealed to other people because of their sacred esoteric power, although it is known that eminent Lakota leaders like Sitting Bull and Crazy Horse were given special names as infants.

During times of crisis two-spirited individuals could be relied on to assume the responsibilities of a deceased person, whether male or female. If a married woman died while her children were still young, a two-spirit person might become a maternal figure in the deceased woman's household, tending to the farming and rearing the motherless children. A two-spirit might go hunting in order to provide food and clothing for the widow and children of a slain warrior until they were capable of fending for themselves. In a typical scenario, the Zapotec people recall how a widowed man married a *muxe* who cooked, laundered the family's clothes, and encouraged each child to attend school, much to the admiration of the tribe.[23] Such duties might be uncharacteristically masculine for a male two-spirit but would be undertaken without complaint for the sake of the family.

Even when two-spirits were not acting for the benefit of another, they were still highly regarded for their industry and skill in weaving, farming, cooking, and other chores. Because male two-spirits possessed the physical strength of men, they often produced more goods and performed more chores than their female counterparts. The Zuni considered the *lhamanas* the finest potters and weavers in the pueblo, more talented when it came to women's tasks than the women themselves. A strong two-spirit might be adept at hunting and weaving and still manage to hunt for herself and bring home enough game to feed several poor families. Yet despite their physical strength, other reasons existed for the incredible productivity of male two-spirits. Stated simply, their duties were not delayed or made more difficult by menstruation, pregnancy, or nursing, allowing male two-spirits to devote all their energy to chores.[24]

The decision to marry is highly individual. Several considerations, however, made marriage to a two-spirit an attractive option for a masculine "normal" Native American man. First, as discussed above, a union between a man and a two-spirit was typically twice as productive as a marriage between a man and a woman in terms of game, clothing, and crops. In addition, any marriage, including one to a two-spirit, usually doubled the size of the other spouse's family, thereby increasing his economic security. The fact that two-spirits could not produce children did not matter much because they were often second or third wives, marrying men who already had a wife or possibly children from a previous marriage. Second, marriage to a two-spirit often brought more stability than a conventional union, making the former more appealing. This was the case among the Mojave tribe, whose women could accept or reject lovers whimsically, while *alyhas* preferred long-term commitments. Besides the practical aspects of marriage to a two-spirit, men could usually often find the same kind of sexual pleasure with two-spirits as they did with women without the possibility of pregnancy or long-term nursing.[25]

Although the marriage of a man to a woman was more common, no threat of social stigma attached to a man who married a two-spirit before or after his marriage to a woman. Occasionally, the men in these relationships were the subject of jokes, but not because they married a two-spirit. Because of their strength and industry, a two-spirit wife might make her husband look lazy, since his wife could both hunt and cook for him, minimizing his own responsibilities and self-importance. If the man in the relationship decided to leave his two-spirit wife, he could do so without fear of judgment from the families of potential female wives. Marriage to a two-spirit did not make men homosexual or less masculine in any way, as Native Americans recognized sexual preference and gender identity as separate variables.[26]

Up to this point the discussion has consisted mostly of the sexual habits and social habits of male two-spirits; that is, individuals born biological males who assumed female identities. Early accounts of female two-spirits are scarce and largely based on their masculine demeanor or appearance rather than their preference for female partners or wives. Two women earned such acclaim during the largely male-dominated eighteenth century. Slave Woman, a Chippewa leader, was called a berdache because of her role in negotiating peace between her people and their ancestral enemies, the Cree, in order to facilitate trade between both tribes and the Hudson Bay Company. Her contemporary, Madame Houle, a *métis*,[27] wore buckskins and carried a knife in her belt to exude an air of authority over the workmen she employed on the Liard River near her home in northwestern Canada.[28]

At this point a disclaimer may be in order. Although no one can know the true sexual habits and preferences of either woman mentioned above, both were thought of as two-spirits simply because they appeared more male than female. Using the word *berdache* to refer to Slave Woman and Madame Houle was presumptuous and unfounded, based on little or no inquiry into their sexual preferences or gender roles within tribal contexts. In both cases, external factors required them to set aside typical gender roles in order to help their people endure changes in the world—changes they were powerless to stop. Readers who encounter the word *berdache* should always be suspicious of its application and bear in mind its repeated misuse.

Documented marriages between two women are scarce yet curiously include several well-known accounts of extraordinary women who enjoyed wealth and acclaim rather than discrimination and scorn. A nineteenth-century Kootenai woman who called herself *Kaúxuma Núpika* or "Gone to the Spirits," eschewed women's dress from an early age in favor of men's leggings and took many wives during her extraordinary life as a war leader and diplomat.[29] At least one storyteller, however, discounts the possibility of true matrimony between this woman and her wives, explaining that marriage to another female was the only option for one who lacked sex appeal.

Generations of Crow people heard stories about Woman Chief, a war leader among the tribe known more for her assumption of a male role than her multiple marriages to women. Her biographer, Edwin Denig, described Woman Chief as an anomaly because she always dressed in female garb but earned a place in the coveted Crow council of warriors through her exploits during hunting and raiding expeditions against their tribe's ancestral enemies, the Blackfeet. Denig noted that Woman Chief elevated her social standing among men, both Indian and white, by taking several wives who increased her wealth by preparing her many hunting trophies for trade.[30] Whether these marriages symbolized love or economic opportunity is anybody's guess, but the fact that they took place is beyond dispute and suggests a tolerance of same-sex unions among the Crow.

Not all Native women who chose to marry women achieved the notoriety of *Kaúxuma Núpika* or Woman Chief, but many others married women and spoke of themselves as men. The relative scarcity of prominent women who took wives suggests that only the female-female relationships of flamboyant or successful women were noticed by visitors and academics. It is likely that many more cases of marriage between women, or at least uncommonly close physical and emotional bonds, existed throughout Indian country. A photograph exists of two Brulé women, one sitting in front of the tipi they shared together while the other watches her pose. According to the photographer, both subjects were over ninety years old at the time and had lived together throughout their adult lives.[31] Of course, the extent of their relationship may never be known, but it does suggest that relationships between women were more common than just the well-known examples cited above.

Besides being meager in quantity, much of the information left to us by generations of social scientists and casual observers of Native American cultures casts lesbianism in a negative light. In his 1909 essay *The Assiniboine*, the anthropologist Robert Henry Lowie recounted a myth about a woman eloping with her husband's sister and impregnating her. When the husband discovered what had happened, Lowie reported, he "killed his wicked wife" and the child born to her marriage to her sister-in-law.[32] Although it is not clear whether the original story-teller or Lowie himself added the value judgments expressed about this relation-ship, at some point during transmission of the story a social stigma became attached to lesbian relationships.

It would be a mistake to assume that the rhetoric of discussion of *berdache* in academic works indicates a uniform acceptance of alternative genders across Indian country. Tribes varied in their spiritual beliefs and social norms. To apply a social rule to the hundreds of tribes and bands that populated the United States in precon-tact times would be to ignore their individual identities. Most authors recorded scanty evidence of third and fourth genders, while few others described their lifestyles and social and religious roles in great depth. None of the authors who wrote extensively on Native American cultures totally denied the existence of these people, however. The strongest evidence that people of alternative genders were anomalies or unknown to Native Americans comes from sources lacking references, which read more like casual observers' impressions of communities with which they were barely acquainted. Indeed, one writer claimed he had never heard of a homosexual or lesbian Indian, except for a distasteful joke told to him by an Indian acquaintance.[33] A trained researcher would have followed this thread and explored the spirituality, sexuality, and beliefs about gender that pervaded Native cultures.

The absence of third- and fourth-gender reports in ethnographies and anthropo-logical studies should not be accepted as fact without further investigation. There are many reasons why scholars did not mention alternative genders in the works left to academia. A narrow focus of study may have precluded a discussion of alterna-tive genders for the sake of saving space. Scholars who observed men and women assuming the roles of the opposite genders may have omitted these observations about sexuality in an effort to avoid stretching the limits of propriety. Other researchers were regarded as outsiders seeking to appropriate culture by tribal com-munities and therefore were not privy to matters as intimate as sex and marriage.

But the foibles and strategies of scholars alone cannot bear the blame for the scant written record of alternative genders or homosexual activity. Native Americans had very legitimate reasons for withholding information or denying what they did know to be true. Realizing that outsiders considered two-spirits sexual perverts or just plain "queer" was reason enough to make many traditional Native people reluc-tant to talk about their views on gender and sexuality. Talking about a person's homo-sexual habits was also thought to expose two-spirits to what would today be termed hate crimes at the hands of bigoted white people—or worse, bigoted fellow tribal members. A more serious reason for Native silence on this subject was connected to Native spirituality: the ceremonial role played by two-spirits in many Plains societies surpassed that of distinguished tribal leaders in importance; thus talking about a two-spirit's power might cost him his spiritual connections.[34]

Only after the reservation era began in the 1880s did studies of Native American oral traditions reveal the presence of these alternative genders in Native Ameri-can societies. A Comanche story describes how eight handsome young men on a war party temporarily turned into women one by one every four days for thirty-two days without ever speaking of the changes they experienced. None of the eight wanted to return to their tribe as half-women and half-men, so they continued their expedition. The Pawnee talked of a man who was told by Spider Woman that he would become a woman because he bathed in a spring after sexual intercourse that left him unclean. The immense embarrassment and disgrace the man felt at the prospect of changing gender led him to commit suicide rather than live as a "half woman and half man."[35]

Although the characters in these stories feel shame at the prospect of being physically transformed into women, the stories do not necessarily reflect condemnation of gender transformation among these tribes. First, the stories were recorded by two anthropologists, George Dorsey and Alfred Kroeber, and narrated by tribal informants, automatically calling into question the accuracy of the translation. Given the distinction made between biological sex and gender, a second explanation is also possible: the men in these tales changed into biological females but maintained their gender, leaving them males by gender trapped in physically female bodies. In most cases, individuals assumed another gender because they felt more comfortable with that identity or sought to comply with a message from the Creator received during a dream or vision quest.

The third and most plausible argument is that the researchers transcribed the stories in the early twentieth century, after the reservation period had come to an end and Christian beliefs had permeated Native communities. In other words, the shame these characters associate with changing from male to female (or vice versa) might be the result of efforts to assimilate Native American thought to Western ideas of religion and propriety, which condemned sodomy and other homosexual activities. A Lakota medicine man clearly but regretfully recounted the social changes affecting two-spirits in his culture as a consequence of assimilation:

> When the people began to be influenced by the missions and the boarding schools, a lot of them forgot the traditional ways and the traditional medicine. Then they began to look down on the *winkté* and lose respect. The missionaries and the government agents said *winktés* were no good, and tried to get them to change their ways. Some did, and put on men's clothing. But others, rather than change, went out and hanged themselves. I remember the sad stories told about this.[36]

A similar change took place among the Crow in Montana after Baptist preachers moved to the reservation and established mission schools for children. Although the Crow sought out the missionaries, they wanted an education for their children more than they wanted salvation, though they undoubtedly heard sermons calling for the rejection of the *boté* in Crow culture. Baptist ideas in particular became so engrained in younger Crow generations that the *boté* role seemed to die out or at least go underground with the death of Osh-Tish in 1929.[37] There can be little doubt that many indigenous customs and belief systems were casualties of the assimilation movement in Native America, but a less clear and perhaps more pertinent question is whether the Cherokee acceptance of two-spirits was among them.

Despite the traditional acceptance of homosexuality and gender transference practiced among many tribes, Native American cultures fell victim to homophobia and discrimination, the remnants of which still linger today. Western attitudes toward sexuality, particularly the Christian view, permeated Native America and often supplanted the general attitude of acceptance and appreciation for individuality that once existed in many Native communities. Whether or not those communities adopted such ideas varies from one community to another; in some cases, Christian morality simply coexisted with traditional Native attitudes, perhaps silencing those attitudes without totally obliterating them. In other cases, the Christian mission of converting Native peoples succeeded and claimed a victory in replacing Native ideas with Christian ones, especially on moral issues.

Homophobia in its ugliest form began to surface not long after the European conquest of the Americas began in the fifteenth century. The Spanish attempted to eradicate the "hateful sin" of sodomy in a variety of ways, first coaxing it out of Native converts through the sacrament of penance and then administering punishment, which in one extreme case included throwing forty guilty parties to a pack of dogs.[38] The earliest laws of colonial settlements, whether Spanish or English, criminalized sodomy along with other nonviolent but no less immoral crimes as heresy, blasphemy, and treason, and punished them with whippings and in some cases execution.[39] Interestingly enough, one scholar pondered in his writings whether colonial European men persecuted for homosexuality in North American settlements ever sought refuge among their more tolerant Indian neighbors. No evidence for this proposition was found in researching this thesis, but it does raise an interesting question for another time.

Centuries later, the sentiment of Europeans living among Native communities continued to be one of condemnation of homosexuality, although often for less pious purposes than enforcing Christian morality as encoded in law. Indian agents and missionaries, as well as politicians and local white settlers, found claims of immorality effective tools in challenging any Native rights or practices that disadvantaged their own goals. In an effort to force the enrollment of Zuni children in government schools, the acting Indian agent requested a military force to help enforce his policies to end ceremonial dances he considered "demoralizing and likely to debauch the old and corrupt the young.[40]

The most damaging comments and criticism of same-sex relations came from Native Americans who eschewed traditional attitudes and ceremonies after embracing Christianity. Christianity taught its Native converts to believe they were tainted by their traditions, which made them immoral and evil. This attitude soon led to the erosion of the converts' cultural and ceremonial roles in society. Christianity's underpinning of male superiority required adherents to reject any males who did not fulfill their dominant social roles, which were not applicable to two-spirits.[41] The Native mythology that showcased prominent roles for people of third and fourth genders was rejected and replaced by the Judeo-Christian Scriptures, which addressed male-to-male relations briefly but forcefully in declaring that men "shall not lie with man as with a woman. It is an abomination."[42]

Antigay attitudes persist today in some Native cultures. Although this paper does not seek to trace their origins, a number of possible sources spring to mind, namely Christian missionaries and colonizers who conquered in the name of religion and monarchical rule. The Communist witch hunt of the 1950s initiated a new wave of antigay sentiment that still continues in the jocular use of words like *faggot* or *fairy*. Still, the author Walter Williams concluded that Indians are "more accepting of peoples' differences than are white people"[43] and sought to return some traditional knowledge that generations of non-Native teachers, missionaries, government officials and explorers worked hard to obscure or eliminate completely.

It is not clear to what extent two-spirits live openly in modern Native communities; they may be shielded by their communities from academics out of fear of being treated like museum exhibits or oddities.[44] They might also feel shame about their lifestyle and gender roles, since Western values and religious beliefs condemning homosexuality have permeated the boundaries of many reservations and Native enclaves. The pride and importance that two-spirits once symbolized may no longer exist in some communities, making openness unlikely and even dangerous.

Some authors claim that two-spirits went underground after European colonization, while others subtly imply that two-spirits became extinct long ago along with their cultures. Both claims may contain a kernel of truth. In his 1986 book *The Spirit and the Flesh*, the gender studies scholar Walter Williams drew on many interviews with contemporary two-spirits from various tribes who still serve important social and ceremonial functions in their tribal communities. Other scholars maintain that the two-spirits evolved into people known today as Gay American Indians (GAIs), defined as Native people who identify more closely with Western ideas of homosexuality than with Native notions of gender. In search of their sexual identity, many GAIs leave their Native communities for urban centers with large gay populations.[45]

In spite of the potential for gay bashing and discrimination in any community, including Native ones, some Native people have attempted to bridge their cultural traditions with the modern world. The efforts of these people brought about the general acceptance of the term *two-spirit* as a more accurate label for gay and transgendered Native Americans. Finding its root in the Anishinabe (Chippewa) language, *two-spirit* was adopted by a group of GAIs at the Third International Native Gay and Lesbian Gathering at Winnipeg, Canada, in 1988. The term acknowledges the relationship between the spirit world and people who cross gender lines.[46]

## TRIBAL CASES

Traditional attitudes toward same-sex marriage became the subject of much dispute in 2004 when the two largest Native nations in the United States faced the decision about legalizing the institution. The Cherokee Nation of Oklahoma amended their tribal marriage code in June 2004, after a lesbian couple received a marriage license from the tribe and attempted to file it. For the next year, the Cherokee appellate court system heard arguments in the case of *In re: The Marriage License of Dawn L. McKinley and Kathy E. Reynolds* in order to decide whether Dawn McKinley and Kathy Reynolds's marriage was valid. One year later, on the Navajo reservation in Arizona, the tribal legislature voted in favor of banning same-sex marriage.

### Cherokee

Dawn McKinley and Kathy Reynolds did not intend their marriage to force the Cherokee Nation of Oklahoma into recognizing same-sex marriages. The couple made the decision after Reynolds suffered a medical emergency and the treating hospital denied McKinley access to her partner's bedside because she was technically neither a relative nor a spouse. The Cherokee Nation had no choice but to address the issue when the couple attempted to file their tribal marriage license, issued by mistake, with the tribe after they exchanged vows in Tulsa, Oklahoma, on May 18, 2004.

One day after the marriage license was issued to Dawn McKinley and Kathy Reynolds, the Cherokee Judicial Appeals Tribunal ordered a thirty-day moratorium on all applications for marriage licenses at the request of a tribal member, Todd Hembree. As the moratorium was about to expire in June, Hembree, who happened to be the Cherokee Tribal Council's attorney, filed an objection to the issuance of a marriage license to a lesbian couple. Hembree based his objection to the issuance of the marriage license on the ground that a same-sex couple did not qualify under the Cherokee Nation Tribal Code Annotated Title 43(ct) seq.[47] His objection was meant to stall for time to allow the Tribal Council to pass a ban on same-sex marriages.

In addition to asking the Cherokee District Court for an injunction preventing the couple from registering their marriage license with the tribe, Hembree asked the Court to hold that same-sex marriages are not permissible under Cherokee law and contravene Title 43 of the Cherokee Nation Code.[48] Hembree argued that the plain language of the marriage statute, which defined "husband" as "a married man who has a lawful wife" and "wife" as "a woman united in marriage to a man," clearly prohibits marriage between two people of the same sex. More debatable was his request that the court rule same-sex marriage unlawful on the grounds that it is "not part of Cherokee history or tradition," nor was it envisioned by Cherokee society in 1892 when the constitution that inspired the Cherokee Nation Code was drafted.[49]

McKinley and Reynolds relied on the same sources as Hembree to argue that any members of the Cherokee Nation could contract marriage provided they did not fall into one of the classes specifically barred from marrying: first cousins, the insane, and those already married to another person.[50] Since the list does not specifically include couples of the same sex, McKinley and Reynolds interpreted the Code to allow same-sex marriage. They also argued that denying same-sex couples the right to marry constitutes an equal protection violation under the Cherokee Constitution, which adopted the Indian Civil Rights Act of 1968.[51] The Act requires the Cherokee Nation and all other adopting tribal nations to apply all their laws equally among tribal citizens. Moreover, McKinley and Reynolds pointed out that even two months after obtaining their marriage license, the District Court had not heard evidence on whether same-sex marriage existed in the tribe's history or whether the Cherokee language offers any clues as to the roles of husband and wife being gender-specific in Cherokee tradition.[52]

The final argument drew distinctions between the Oklahoma Constitution, amended in 1976 to restrict marriage to one man and one woman, and the Cherokee Marriage Act of 1993, which left out references to gender even though it otherwise copied the language of the Oklahoma Constitution.[53] They argued that this difference in wording allows Cherokee officials to uphold their oath of office, which requires them to "protect, defend, and promote the heritage, language, and culture of The People." The couple also refuted Hembree's claim that he had standing to bring the suit in order to have a general question of law answered for the entire Cherokee community, since he failed to demonstrate any specific harm he suffered as a result of their marriage.[54]

The Cherokee Nation Council echoed Hembree's outspoken views on same-sex marriage when it voted unanimously to amend Title 43 of the Cherokee Nation

Code to restrict marriage to one man and one woman, tying up the loophole Dawn McKinley and Kathy Reynolds had used as legal justification for marriage between two people of the same sex. Tribal officials candidly articulated their opposition to same-sex marriage following the vote. Chief Chad Smith claimed to speak for the Cherokee Nation when he said "the definition of marriage is *only* between a man and woman" (emphasis added).[55]

Opponents of same-sex marriage supported the amendment of the Marriage Code, which also includes language prohibiting bigamy and adultery in addition to same-sex marriage. This action alone is indicative of the fervent opposition to same-sex marriage; the amendment likens same-sex marriage to two acts that are generally considered immoral and, in some cases, criminal. The sting of the vote was sharper because many of the council members who voted in favor of the amendment had not received a copy of the proposed legislation until the meeting had already begun.[56] The amendment's sponsor feared that a different outcome would have been a "black eye on the Cherokee Nation."[57]

Following the amendment of the Cherokee Nation Marriage Code, Todd Hembree asked the Tribal Council to deny Dawn McKinley and Kathy Reynolds recognition of their marriage, citing concern for the irreparable harm that same-sex marriage would cause the Cherokee Nation. McKinley and Reynolds took the position that same-sex unions were common among the Cherokee and other tribes prior to colonization. They pointed out that the Cherokee marriage ceremony did not use gender-specific terms like "husband" and "wife." Gender-neutral terms that can be translated as "provider" and "cooker" were the norm.[58] Unfortunately, the couple, who represented themselves during the first half of their year-long legal battle, lacked any other documentary evidence showing that same-sex marriage was a social norm or at least tolerated within Cherokee society. This weakness was not carelessness on the part of the couple, however; even the most thorough scholars have yet to find sufficient evidence to support or refute the presence of alternative gender or same-sex marriages in Cherokee culture.

The first same-sex marriage case in a tribal court escalated all the way to the Cherokee Supreme Court, but the court's holding failed to provide a resolution to the same-sex marriage debate. The Court dismissed Todd Hembree's petition to deny recognition of Dawn McKinley and Kathy Reynolds's marriage, holding that an individual lacked standing to challenge another couple's marriage.[59] To date, McKinley and Reynolds hold the distinction of being the only same-sex couple married under a tribal marriage license. Because of the amendment to the Cherokee Code in June 2004, they will likely hold that distinction for some time to come. But this outcome left the issue of whether same-sex marriage existed at one time in Cherokee culture unresolved.

In contrast to the copious amount of information on Navajo attitudes about and treatment of alternative genders and same-sex marriage, references to those subjects in Cherokee society are rare. In *The Spirit and the Flesh*, Walter Williams refers to the Cherokee only three times while discussing alternative genders and sexuality in Native societies. Two of his references merely mention Cherokee accounts of women going to war, which are not conclusive indicators of homosexuality or even gender transference; while the third, based on an obscure document written in 1825, the source of which was never identified, suggests that two-spirits were known among the Cherokee prior to that date. Williams concedes that more research is needed.

Will Roscoe, in his *Tribal Index of Alternative Gender Roles and Sexuality*, notes that an alternative gender status existed among the male Cherokee population.[60] Unfortunately, the basis for Roscoe's suggestion is none other than Walter Williams; it therefore sheds no additional light on Cherokee attitudes regarding gender. Another author also noted "berdachism" among the Cherokee, based on one anonymous account of Cherokee cross-dressers. He added that because sodomy and cross-dressing were observed among the Choctaw, Chickasaw, and Creek, cultures similar to the Cherokee, it is probable that similar behavior existed among the latter.[61] While similarities did exist among these southeastern tribes, imputing the social and sexual habits of one group to a different but related group risks false assumptions about a culture.

Had such deviations from the social norm existed within Cherokee culture, it is likely they would have been met with one of two possible reactions: joking or fear. If a man carried water, which was associated with fertility and therefore associated with females, he would be disgraced and most likely scorned by other men.[62] Women were not ridiculed but revered because of their biological power, which included spilling blood during menstruation—an act that men could accomplish only in battle. A woman who waged war, however, was phenomenally powerful, since she had two available indices of power.[63] Men who functioned as women by choosing the hoe over the hatchet, however, lacked both opportunities to accumulate power through spilling blood, and thus possessed little power.

Cherokee society also viewed the duties of men and women differently and associated specific tasks with a single gender. For example, Cherokee men were expected to go into battle and hunt, occasionally helping women with horticulture during the planting and harvest seasons. But in general, farming was done by women.[64] As part of the Cherokee marriage ceremony, the two parties walked toward each other, the groom presenting his bride with venison as a promise to provide their family with meat, the bride offering the groom corn, symbolizing her promise to keep the home stocked with vegetables.[65]

Perhaps two-spirits disappeared among the Cherokee prior to the nineteenth century, when the Cherokee began to look more and more Western in their self-governance and economy. By 1800, the Cherokee and other southeastern tribes had adopted European fashions in dress, began to raise cattle, and on a small scale converted to Christianity, including some sects notorious for condemning homosexuality. This cultural shift resulted in part from intermarriage between European traders and Cherokee women, which produced a generation of children educated in Western schools and taught Christian morality, who understood the need for social change.[66] These children introduced their Cherokee families to Western styles of government and Christian values in order to maintain Cherokee unity by adapting to Western cultural and social norms.[67]

After the Western-style Cherokee government was established, the tribal courts embarked on a journey to integrate traditional tribal norms and values into a legal system previously unknown to the Cherokee and their neighboring tribes in the southeast. Marriage under Cherokee law forbade certain types of marriage and certain people from marrying. Cherokee law in its earliest written form prohibited polygamy and marriage between members of the same clan, which was considered incestuous. Few restrictions on sexual activity existed, however; one Cherokee scholar noted that sex was "considered [of] little threat"[68] to Cherokee society and therefore went virtually unmentioned in the nation's historical record. But if the Cherokee had had moral or social objections to homosexuality or alternative genders in the early years, surely they would have been codified in writing.

*Navajo*

In the summer months of 2004, sentiment against same-sex unions began to surface on an official level among the Navajo. A member of the Navajo Tribal Council from Fort Defiance, Arizona, proposed an amendment to the tribe's code banning same-sex marriage, arguing that "in Navajo way [sic], you don't have same-sex marriages," implying that the institution was previously unknown in Navajo culture.[69] The bill's sponsor sought support for it as a vehicle for promoting "strong families and strong family values."[70]

Prior to 2005, the Navajo had regulated marriage in several ways but never formally addressed the issue of same-sex marriage. Section 4(E) of the Navajo Nation Code forbids marrying family members within the third degree of affinity or closer, while a separate provision prohibits members of the same maternal clan from marrying one another—indicating a strong presence of tradition in this modern legal system.[71] While the Navajo codified traditional standards for marriage, the absence of language related to same-sex marriage left the tribe's position on the issue ambiguous, or at least it did until the Diné Marriage Act.

The Diné Marriage Act of 2005 amended the Navajo Code to "recognize marriages validated outside of the Navajo Nation," except those between blood relatives, polygamous marriages, and same-sex unions.[72] With a vote of With a vote of sixty-seven to zero, the legislation passed but dissent grew among the people. Within months of the proposal, opponents of the legislation banded together to form the Diné Coalition for Cultural Preservation, a grassroots organization designed to combat what it considers to be a discriminatory and oppressive agenda in Navajo government. In addressing the Tribal Council, the group urged representatives to recall "the oppression that has been dealt with on all Native Peoples for hundreds of years and to not pick up the tools of the oppressors."[73]

That May, the president of the Navajo Nation, Joe Shirley, Jr., vetoed the ban on gay marriage, explaining that the act was discriminatory and antithetical to the Navajo way of avoiding harm to others.[74] President Shirley openly doubted the benefit of the act, since it failed to address "rampant domestic problems" on the reservation, including domestic abuse, sexual assault, and gang violence.[75] Stopping short of supporting same-sex marriage, he suggested that any decision on the subject be left to Navajo voters rather than the legislature.[76]

Unfortunately the people did not get a vote. The Navajo legislature overrode President Shirley's veto of the Act and instituted the ban on same-sex marriage. Of the fifty-nine votes in the eighty-eight-member Navajo Council needed to override a presidential veto, the bill passed into law by just three votes, without any debate on the Council floor.[77] Before the law changed, however, the Navajo people made their voice heard, most in support for marriage equality and a return to traditional attitudes.

Reaction on both sides of the controversy was quite strong, with critics and supporters on both sides. The Office of the President reportedly received an "unprecedented number of calls" in support of Shirley's veto, but not a single call or e-mail in support of the original ban on same-sex marriage.[78] One letter to the editor of the *Navajo Times*, the Nation's newspaper, framed homosexuality as a third gender and marriage as being open to all people but lamented that the *Diné*[79] have been "corrupted by Western beliefs and Christianity, causing many Natives to view gays as perverts or sodomites."[80] While the roots of such antigay sentiment remain open to question, at no time in history has homosexual behavior faced such fearful hostility.

Wesley Thomas, a professor of anthropology at Indiana University and member of the Navajo Nation who has written extensively on sexuality and gender in Native America, has described homosexual relationships as a normal part of Navajo life. Thomas traced modern disapproval of same-sex marriages among the Navajo to Christian ideals thrust upon the people centuries ago, which led him to predict the passage of the ban against same-sex marriage before the vote took place.[81] Other tribal members agreed with Thomas; one of them described the proposed ban as a "step backwards" and uncharacteristic of a people he called "accepting and loving."[82]

Gender among the Navajo was more complicated than in many other Native societies, partly as the result of the existence of five unique genders acknowledged by the people.[83] In matrilineal societies like the Navajo, heterosexual women constituted the first gender while heterosexual men made up the second. The third gender consisted of people born with both male and female genitals but often functioning as women. People born with male sex organs who adopted the attributes of a woman referred to themselves as female and made up the fourth gender. The fifth gender was just the opposite, biological females who considered themselves socially male.

In Navajo, the word *nadlé* means "changing one" or "one who is transformed," and describes people who do not conform to the gender roles typical of their biological sex but assume the gender role of the opposite sex or integrate aspects of both genders to form an alternative third gender. Pronouns used to refer to a person of this status varied between "he" and "she," even when the *nadlé* was referring to himself or herself. Like the language, the *nadlé's* wardrobe also oscillated between male and female attire according to the tastes and functions of the wearer. It sometimes included male attire and sometimes female, or a combination of the two.

Among the roles filled by the *nadlé* were those of healers, chanters, and midwives—essentially living, breathing good-luck charms during important and often dangerous passages of life, as reported by Walter Williams in *The Spirit and the Flesh*.[84] Because of the ability of the *nadlé* to see both sides of the world—feminine and masculine—they also served as go-betweens for young opposite-sex couples during courtship, and as mediators for couples mired in a marital spat.[85] Trusting such important matters to the *nadlés* not only highlights the tremendous respect these people enjoyed from the tribe, but also deemphasizes their sexual habits.

The earliest appearance of the *nadlé* in Navajo cultural history is in the tribe's creation story, when two changing ones, Turquoise Boy and White Shells Girl, the first a *nadlé*, made important contributions to the people in the third of five worlds recognized in Navajo oral history.[86] Turquoise Boy shaped the first pottery bowl out of clay while White Shell Girl used reeds to weave the first basket, illustrating the *nadlés'* ingenuity and continued presence throughout Navajo history. Turquoise Boy also taught the women how to grind corn and eventually rescued the Navajo from a great flood by bringing the people a large reed that they used to escape to the fourth and current world.[87]

Despite the appearance of two-spirits in the Navajo creation story, the *Diné* traced two-spiritedness to the "personal inclinations of the individual" rather than to divine origin.[88] Parents and other members of the Navajo community would nurture the desire to become a *nadlé* only after a child indicated his preference to become one; the role was not forced upon a young person.[89] In this sense, the experience of a Navajo two-spirit was more akin to that of a modern homosexual who must accept himself before finding acceptance from his family and community.

Although it is convenient to think of the *nadlé* in terms of simply adopting the social role of the opposite gender without totally abandoning their biological gender, this explanation is not entirely accurate. The Navajo thought two-spirited people to be continually fluctuating between genders, assuming the cultural or familial role of the gender that a given situation called for.[90] This gender transference could be understood by the example of a Navajo two-spirit who was biologically male but identified as a female. He reverted to traditional male tasks for the sake of a family without a husband and father. Marriage to a person of another gender did not limit a *nadlé* to the opposite-gender role but allowed him or her to combine elements from both genders, thereby maximizing productivity.

Early scholars of Navajo customs reported marriages between men and *nadlé* as early as the 1930s.[91] Unions between two people of the same biological sex were almost indistinguishable from heterosexual relationships, as they were composed of masculine and feminine roles and characteristics. Often these unions produced great wealth since the male would go to war and hunt game while his two-spirited counterpart would engage in primarily female activities, including sheep herding, farming, gathering, weaving, knitting, basketry, and pottery.[92] Because male two-spirits possessed the physical strength of a man along with a predisposition to perform female chores, their productivity often surpassed that of female wives and made them valued life partners.

These same-sex but heterogender marriages were also subject to the same restrictions and social taboos as heterosexual marriages, including a ban on marriage between people whose parents belonged to the same clan. Violation of the same-clan taboo was tantamount to incest in modern society.

For the *nadlé*, Navajo society did not remain openly nurturing and tolerant of their lifestyle. Even a society as hospitable to multiple and alternating genders as the *Diné* could not withstand external pressures from the rapidly growing non-Indian world around them. In the 1930s an anthropologist recorded a tribal member's comments on the respect formerly paid people of alternative genders "giving way to [an attitude of] ridicule."[93] The impact of this indoctrination was noticeable from the outset; most two-spirits at that time were middle-aged and stopped wearing women's clothing to avoid unwanted and potentially dangerous attention.[94]

Although the responses of both the Cherokee Nation of Oklahoma and the Navajo Nation paint a dismal picture of the state of same-sex marriage in Native America, much progress has been made. Sovereign Native Nations are now engaged in a dialogue over same-sex marriage that did not end with a court ruling or the passage of a bill. Same-sex marriage is currently a part of contemporary Native America;

hundreds of Native Nations will have to navigate the waters charted by the Cherokee and Navajo Nations. With time, attitudes may change and research will continue to be gathered, perhaps renewing traditional tolerance and breaking away from Western models of governance.

## NOTES

This chapter is dedicated to the memory of my partner, Ting Chou Yu, 1974–2006.

1. F. Thomas Edwards, "Native American Sexuality: Two-Spirit in Two Worlds," *Village Voice* 41, July 2, 1996.

2. Will Roscoe, *The Zuni Man-Woman* (Albuquerque: University of New Mexico Press, 1991), 124. In the early twentieth century, a German sexologist defined *transvestite* as a person who harbors a psychological need to dress in the clothing of the opposite sex, "often for erotic pleasure." The term became a common synonym for *berdache* even though many people labeled as berdaches did not exhibit the requisite "erotic pleasure" associated with cross-dressing.

3. Jean-Guy Goulet, "The Berdache/Two Spirit: A Comparison of Anthropological and Native Constructions of Gendered Identities among the Northern Athapaskans," *Journal of the Royal Anthropological Institute* 2, no. 4 (December 1996): 683.

4. Sabine Lang, *Men as Women, Women as Men: Changing Gender in Native American Cultures*, trans. John L. Vantine (Austin: University of Texas Press, 1998), 24.

5. Ibid., 10.

6. Jonathan Katz, *Gay American History: Lesbians and Gay Men in the U.S.A.: A Documentary* (New York: Thomas Y. Crowell, 1976), 454–55.

7. Ibid.

8. Ibid.

9. Walter L. Williams, *The Spirit and the Flesh: Sexual Diversity in American Indian Culture* (Boston: Beacon Press, 1986), 234. Following this understanding, Williams, a widely cited authority on alternative genders in Native America, suggests using the term *Amazon* to describe female berdaches because their gender-crossing was often characterized by fighting alongside the men of the village in battle. This term, however, fails to include Native women who wore male clothing and performed some male activities like hunting but avoided others like warfare.

10. James Thayer, "The Berdache of the Northern Plains: A Socio-Religious Perspective," *Journal of Anthropological Research* 36 (1980): 288–89.

11. Lang, *Men as Women, Women as Men*, 37 (see note 4). See also Charles Callender and Lee Kochems, "The North American Berdache," *Current Anthropology* 24 (1983): 443–70; and Harriet Whitehead, "The Bow and the Burden Strap: A New Look at Institutionalized Homosexuality in Native America," in *Sexual Meanings: The Cultural Construction of Gender and Sexuality*, ed. Sherry Ortner and Harriet Whitehead (New York: Cambridge University Press, 1981).

12. Beverly Greene, ed., *Ethnic and Cultural Diversity among Lesbians and Gay Men: Psychological Perspectives on Lesbian and Gay Issues* (Thousand Oaks, CA: Sage Publications, 1997), 4.

13. Williams, *The Spirit and the Flesh*, 19 (see note 9).

14. Will Roscoe, *Changing Ones: Third and Fourth Genders in Native North America* (New York: St. Martin's Press, 1998), 216.

15. Edwards, "Native American Sexuality" *Village Voice* (see note 1).

16. Greene, ed., *Ethnic and Cultural Diversity among Lesbians and Gay Men*, 5 (see note 12).

17. The Battle of Rosebud on June 17, 1876, marked the defeat of General George Crook and part of the Seventh Calvary at the hands of the Sioux; the Indian victory foreshadowed the Battle of the Little Big Horn on June 25. During the Sioux campaign, the United States Army relied heavily on Crow and Shoshone scouts, who were traditional enemies of the Sioux.

18. This is the same principle that exists among heterosexual males in prison. Very often male inmates engage in sex acts with other men, either consensually or through the use of force, simply because they do not have contact with women. When asked about their sexual orientation, most of them would vehemently deny being homosexuals and assert their heterosexuality.

19. Katz, *Gay American History*, 430–31 (see note 6).

20. Ibid. According to *Merriam-Webster's Collegiate Dictionary*, 11th ed. (2003), the modern definition dates back to the fourteenth century and refers to an animal or plant having both male and female reproductive organs.

21. Williams, *The Spirit and the Flesh*, 24 (see note 9).

22. Ibid., 37. Not every Lakota child was entitled to a secret name given by a *winkté*. Walter Williams reports that the *winkté* agreed to name the child only after the child's father flirted with the *winkté* in a sexual way, provided that he favored the father.

23. Williams, *The Spirit and the Flesh*, 120 (see note 9).

24. Ibid., 58–59.

25. Ibid., 113–15. Among the Mojave tribe of California, men particularly enjoyed anal sex and fellatio, which could be supplied by two-spirits as well as women. For this reason, sexual gratification could be obtained just as easily from a two-spirit, or *alyha*, with male genitalia as from a woman. Western culture, however, generally refuses to distinguish between sexuality and gender and automatically labels someone who indulges in such recreation as homosexual.

26. Ibid., 115.

27. *Métis* refers to people born of mixed Native North American and French heritage, historically the products of intermarriage between French fur trappers and the women of Native tribes with whom they traded.

28. Goulet, "The Berdache/Two Spirit," 683 (see note 3).

29. Katz, *Gay American History*, 451–60 (see note 6).

30. Ibid., 464–69.

31. Paul Dyck, *Brulé: The Sioux People of the Rosebud* (Flagstaff, AZ: Northland Press, 1971), 107.

32. Katz, *Gay American History*, 482 (see note 6).

33. Jack Glover, *The Sex Life of the American Indian* (Sunset, TX: Cow Puddle Press, 1973), 28–29. This source was loaned to me by a colleague, who discovered it on a public auction Web site. While it is very helpful to compare society's attitudes toward Native Americans, the book is not a scholarly work and has no references other than anonymous third parties. More striking is the book's offensive language and condescending tone. In the foreword, the author states that "the Indian had an animal-like nature," and notes that sexuality among Indians was "hilarious to the white man." Ibid., 1.

34. Williams, *The Spirit and the Flesh*, 32 (see note 9).

35. Jim Elledge, *Gay, Lesbian, Bisexual and Transgender Myths from the Arapaho to the Zuni* (New York: Peter Lang Publishing, 2002), 99–102.

36. Williams, *The Spirit and the Flesh*, 182–83 (see note 9).

37. Roscoe, *Changing Ones*, 36 (see note 14).

38. Roscoe, *The Zuni Man-Woman*, 172–73 (see note 2); see also Williams, *Spirit and the Flesh* (see note 9). See generally Francisco Guerra, *The Pre-Columbian Mind* (London: Seminar Press, 1971) and Dennis Werner, "A Cross-Cultural Perspective on Theory and Research on Male Homosexuality," *Journal of Homosexuality* 4 (Summer 1979): 358–59. Both Roscoe and Williams allude to several possible reasons why the Spanish treated homosexuality among Native cultures with particular severity. The reasons include the Spanish need to feel culturally superior to their technologically advanced Islamic enemies, the Moors; the greedy desire to accumulate wealth in the name of the Catholic Church by confiscating the property of condemned individuals; and even promoting population growth in order to strengthen Spain, which lost many people to warfare and plague during the centuries immediately prior to North American contact.

39. Williams, *The Spirit and the Flesh*, 162–63 (see note 9).

40. Roscoe, *The Zuni Man-Woman*, 114–15 (see note 2).

41. Williams, *The Spirit and the Flesh*, 189 (see note 9).

42. The Holy Bible, English Standard Version, Leviticus 18:22 (Good News Publishers, 2001).

43. Williams, *The Spirit and the Flesh*, 234 (see note 9).

44. Ibid., 8–9. Williams highlights a problem many historians faced when pursuing research on berdachism, namely, the "inhibitions of informants." Even if berdaches found acceptance within their community, outsiders especially shied away from taking about them, perhaps out of respect for the person or just to avoid the ugliness of the word's original definition, "male prostitute." The author quotes a standard reply historians encountered when they inquired about a particular berdache: "Yes, I know quite a bit about her—but I can't tell you."

45. Wesley Thomas, "Multiple Genders in Historical and Contemporary Native American Communities," in *The Native North American Almanac*, ed. Cynthia Rose and Duane Champagne, 2nd ed., (Detroit: UXL, 1997), 747–54.

46. Elton Naswood, "Workshop for Service Providers on HIV/AIDS among Native Americans and Alaska Natives" (oral presentation, AIDS Project Los Angeles, Los Angeles, CA, 2004).

47. See *In re: The Marriage License of Dawn L. McKinley and Kathy E. Reynolds*, Case No.: CV-04-36, filed June 11, 2004.

48. Petition for Declaratory Judgment, *In re: The Marriage License of Dawn L. McKinley and Kathy E. Reynolds*, Case No.: CV-04-36, filed June 16, 2004.

49. Ibid.

50. Response and Motion to Quash, *In re: The Marriage License of Dawn L. McKinley and Kathy E. Reynolds*, Case No.: CV-04-36, filed July 12, 2004.

51. Indian Civil Rights Act of 1968, 25 U.S.C. 1302 (8) ("No Indian tribe in exercising powers of self government shall…deny to any person within its jurisdiction the equal protection of its laws or deprive any of liberty or property without due process of law"). Congress passed this act during a pan-Indian movement throughout the United States that demanded individual rights and protections for people on Indian land akin to those afforded to American citizens by the Bill of Rights. Not all the rights enumerated in the Bill of Rights, however, are included in the Indian Civil Rights Act, creating a disparity between federal law and Indian law that still exists in the early 2000s.

52. Response and Motion to Quash, *In re: The Marriage License of Dawn L. McKinley and Kathy E. Reynolds* (see note 50). The motion went on to suggest that neither the couple nor Hembree, who petitioned the court for declaratory judgment outlawing same-sex marriage, were qualified to speak on traditional marriage in Cherokee society or the social climate of the Cherokee Nation in 1892, when the Cherokee Constitution was ratified. They also

called into question Hembree's claim that the Cherokee concept of marriage was the same as the European American concept.

53. Oklahoma Constitution, art. 2, sec 35(a) "Marriage in this state shall consist only of the union of one man and one woman." See also sec. 35(b), "A marriage between persons of the same gender performed in another state shall not be valid or binding in this state as of the date of marriage," which was adopted by voter referendum in November 2004.

54. See Response and Motion to Quash, *In re: The Marriage License of Dawn L. McKinley and Kathy E. Reynolds*, Case No.: CV-04-36. See also Cherokee Nation Code, title 43, section 4.

55. "Cherokee Nation Seeking to Ban Same Sex Marriage," www.indianz.com, May 17, 2004, http://www.indianz.com/News/archive/002244.asp (accessed July 30, 2006).

56. Travis Snell, "Tribal Judge Extends Marriage Moratorium," *Cherokee Phoenix*, July 2004, 5.

57. Will Chavez, "Council Bans Same-Sex Marriages," *Cherokee Phoenix*, July 2004, 6.

58. Joyce Rock, "Baptists Taught Cherokee Bigotry," October 1, 2004, http://www.southernvoice.com/2004/10-1/view/columns/babtists.cfm (accessed July 30, 2006).

59. Response to Petitioner's Response to Motion to Dismiss, *In re: The Marriage License of Dawn L. McKinley and Kathy E. Reynolds*, 3. The couple alleged that Hembree brought a personal suit against the two because of his disapproval of their choice of spouse, based on his "hateful and bigoted ideologies," and that allowing him standing would lead to further challenges to any marriages sanctioned by the Cherokee Nation, not just same-sex unions. In the end, the couple's argument succeeded but provided little hope to other Native same-sex couples seeking tribal recognition of their unions.

60. Roscoe, *Changing Ones*, 226. The Tribal Index is an elaborate table listing more than 150 North American Indian tribes, Pueblos, and Alaskan Native groups documented as having alternative gender status, some kind of alternative gender behavior, or homosexuality within their society. The Index provides the citations for each example and includes Williams as the only source claiming that an alternative gender status exists among the Cherokee. Under the Navajo, the list of sources is quite lengthy, however. About 90 percent of tribal groups have documented an alternative gender status for the male role, referring to men who assumed the dress and performed the duties of women.

61. Theda Perdue, *Cherokee Women: Gender and Culture Change 1700–1835* (Lincoln: University of Nebraska Press, 1998), 37.

62. Ibid., 23.

63. Ibid., 39. The anomaly of bodily fluid leaving the human body was considered very powerful, especially the blood that left women during menstruation. One Cherokee myth relates the story of Stone Man, a cannibal who threatened the Cherokee people long ago. When the village was alerted to Stone Man's presence, seven menstruating women were sent to meet him before he endangered anyone. Stone Man grew weaker and weaker as he passed each woman; by the time he reached the seventh, he had lost all his power. The belief that a menstruating woman held power was so pervasive that women having their periods were forbidden to participate in ceremonies, perform their daily chores, or even come into contact with the sick.

64. Perdue, *Cherokee Women*, 19 (see note 61).

65. Ibid., 24–25.

66. Duane Champagne, "Native Directed Social Change in Canada and the United States," *American Behavioral Scientist*, forthcoming.

67. Duane Champagne, "A Multidimensional Theory of Colonialism: The Native North American Experience," *Journal of American Studies of Turkey* 3 (1996): 3–4.

68. Rennard Strickland, *Fire and the Spirits: Cherokee Law from Clan to Court* (Norman: University of Oklahoma Press, 1975), 100.

69. Pamela Dempsey, "Navajos Take Steps to Ban Gay Marriage," *Gallup Independent*, July 14, 2004, http://www.gallupindependent.com/2004/07july04/071404gaymarriage.html (accessed October 23, 2006).

70. Ibid.

71. The Navajo have a matrilineal society composed of various clans that have spiritual significance and connections to the animal world. An individual inherits the clan of his or her mother in such a society. Intermarriage within one's clan continues to be viewed as incestuous by the Navajo. As of the early 2000s, the Navajo Marriage Code prohibits marriage to members of a person's maternal or paternal clan.

72. Dempsey, "Navajos Take Steps to Ban Gay Marriage" (see note 69).

73. Pamela Dempsey, "Marriage Act Opponents Speak Out: Claim Navajo Nation Government Is Trying to Legalize Discrimination," *Gallup Independent*, Web Edition, June 2, 2005, http://www.gallupindependent.com/2005/june/060205act.html.

74. Brenda Norrell, "Navajo President Vetoes Gay Marriage Ban," *Indian Country Today*, May 3, 2005.

75. Ibid.

76. Adam Tanner, "On the Reservation, U.S. Indians Debate Gay Unions," *Reuters*, March 21, 2005, http://groups.msn.com/BayAreaIndianCalendar/activismissues.msnw ?action=get_message&mview=0&ID_Message=3455 (accessed October 23, 2006).

77. Ryan Hall, "Navajo Council Overrides Marriage Veto," *Farmington Daily Times*, June 4, 2005.

78. Ryan Hall, "Same Sex Marriage Do or Don't?" *Farmington Daily Times*, May 17, 2005.

79. The Navajo people refer to themselves by the word *Diné*, which literally means "The People."

80. Ryan Hall, "Letter to the Editor," *The Navajo Times*, May 3, 2005.

81. "Gay Marriage Debate Comes to Navajo Nation," *The Advocate*, January 19, 2005, http://www.advocate.com/news_detail_ektid02974.asp (accessed October 23, 2006).

82. Dempsey, "Navajos Take Steps to Ban Gay Marriage," (see note 69).

83. Thomas, "Multiple Genders in Historical and Contemporary Native American Communities," 752–53 (see note 45).

84. Williams, *The Spirit and the Flesh*, 35 (see note 9).

85. Thomas, "Multiple Genders in Historical and Contemporary Native American Communities," 753 (see note 45).

86. The importance of origin myths to Native peoples cannot be overstated. The term *myth* should not be construed as a tall tale or invented yarn; as Wesley Thomas notes, these stories are not myth but true stories to tribal peoples who retell them for the benefit of each successive generation. These myths, Thomas continues, are "a catalyst on which [Native people] base their lives, both morally and ethically." Thomas, "Multiple Genders in Historical and Contemporary Native American Communities," 753 (see note 45).

87. Williams, *The Spirit and the Flesh*, 19–20 (see note 9).

88. Lang, *Men as Women, Women as Men*, 239 (see note 4).

89. Williams, *The Spirit and the Flesh*, 49 (see note 9).

90. Thomas, "Multiple Genders in Historical and Contemporary Native American Communities," 752 (see note 45).

91. Ibid., 200.

92. Ibid., 41.

93. Williams, *The Spirit and the Flesh*, 183 (see note 9).

94. Ibid.

# 13

## HISPANIC AND LATINO SAME-SEX COUPLE HOUSEHOLDS IN THE UNITED STATES: A REPORT FROM THE 2000 CENSUS

*Jason Cianciotto*

An amendment of this type is divisive, discriminatory and seeks to treat one group of citizens differently than everyone else. As a community that knows discrimination all too well, we oppose any constitutional amendment that is intended to deny rights to anyone.

—National Hispanic Leadership Agenda
Statement against the proposed Federal Marriage Amendment, March 5, 2004[1]

Latinos must be cautious about accepting any form of legal discrimination. If it becomes acceptable to write discrimination into our Constitution, who will be the next group selected out for unequal treatment—immigrants? Latinos? We cannot be bystanders in this debate. We must protect those in the minority; by doing so, we are protecting ourselves.

—Mexican American Legal Defense and Education Fund
Statement against the proposed Federal Marriage Amendment, May 12, 2004[2]

## INTRODUCTION

As the debate over same-sex marriage became a central political issue during the 2004 election, Mel Martinez, a Florida senatorial candidate who would become the first Cuban American elected to the U.S. Senate, aired a radio advertisement in support of the Federal Marriage Amendment. In the advertisement, Martinez stated that he immigrated to the United States "to escape a totalitarian dictator who had no respect for the traditional values of family and faith."[3] By linking the issue of same-sex marriage to the dictatorship of Fidel Castro, Martinez's advertisement depicted marriage equality for lesbian, gay, bisexual, and transgender (LGBT) people not only as antidemocratic but also, more subtly, as anti-Hispanic.

Other anti-LGBT politicians and religious leaders have similarly attempted to cash in on traditional Hispanic social conservatism by pitting Hispanics against LGBT people. The Religious Right, for example, frequently attempts to portray civil rights as a limited resource; it claims that equal rights for LGBT people threaten the civil rights of people of color.[4] This false claim ignores the fact that civil rights are neither limited nor are they something that only people of color have. The claim also ignores the millions of LGBT people of color who are harmed by anti-LGBT laws. This claim is just one of the reasons why documenting the experiences of Hispanic same-sex couples is vital to informing the debate over equal rights for LGBT people.

Many Hispanic leaders have recognized that the entire Hispanic community, including its LGBT members and their children, stands to lose from anti-LGBT policies and legislation. At the 1987 March for Lesbian and Gay Rights in Washington, D.C., the Mexican American labor organizer Cesar Chavez said, "Our movement has been supporting lesbian and gay rights for over 20 years. We supported lesbian and gay rights when it was just a crowd of 10 people."[5]

Just as Chavez did in the 1970s and 1980s, contemporary Hispanic leaders recognize that civil rights for people of color and for gay people are part of a larger struggle against all forms of discrimination. In 2004, when President George W. Bush announced his support for a federal constitutional amendment banning same-sex marriage, Hispanic leaders issued strong statements against it. For example, in March 2004, the National Hispanic Leadership Agenda (NHLA), a nonpartisan organization that includes forty major Hispanic national organizations and distinguished Hispanic leaders, said:

> The Constitution and its subsequent amendments were designed to protect and expand individual liberties. If an amendment such as the currently proposed [Federal Marriage Amendment], or another like it, makes it through the process necessary to amend the Constitution, this would be the first time in history that the Constitution was amended *to restrict the rights of a whole class of people, in conflict with its guiding principle of equal protection.*[6] (original emphasis)

Other prominent Hispanic leaders and organizations opposing the Federal Marriage Amendment include Representatives Charles A. Gonzalez (D-TX), Xavier Becerra (D-CA), and Raúl Grijalva (D-AZ), as well as the National Council of La Raza, the Mexican American Legal Defense and Educational Fund (MALDEF), the League of United Latin American Citizens, and the Labor Council for Latin American Advancement. Most Hispanics agree on this issue: a September 2004 study of eight hundred Latino registered voters nationwide found that a majority (55 percent) oppose a federal constitutional amendment banning same-sex marriage.[7]

Although many Hispanic leaders support full equality for LGBT people, and most Hispanics oppose a federal constitutional amendment banning same-sex marriage, the Hispanic population at large tends to be more socially conservative than the general population.[8] This is one of the reasons why documenting the experiences of Hispanic same-sex couples is vital to informing the debate over same-sex marriage, particularly now that anti–same-sex marriage amendments to state constitutions are expected to be on the ballot in states with large Hispanic populations, including Arizona, California, and Florida. Although Hispanic same-sex couples represent an important constituency across the nation, little research has been conducted on their experiences.

## METHODOLOGY

How do anti-LGBT family policies, including current and proposed state constitutional amendments against same-sex marriage, specifically affect Hispanic same-sex couples and their families? To answer this question, we conducted an analysis of data from the 2000 Census on Hispanic same-sex couple households in the continental United States, Alaska, and Hawaii. This study sheds light on the basic demographics of Hispanic same-sex couple households, including immigration and citizenship status, residence patterns, parenting, use of public assistance, educational attainment, employment status, income, housing, and military service. The public affairs research firm Lopez & Cheung, Inc. (Seattle, WA) provided the data for our analysis, which were derived from a custom tabulation of the U.S. Census 5 percent Public Use Microdata Sample (PUMS).

The census gathers data on same-sex couple households through a series of questions that allow a householder to identify those who live in the house and his or her relationship to them (see Table 13.1 for definitions of key terms used by the 2000 Census). Householders may select "husband/wife" or "unmarried partner" to describe another adult of the same sex living in the same household.[9] Although the census does not ask respondents to report their sexual orientation or gender identity, it is assumed that these unmarried same-sex partners are in amorous relationships of mutual caring and support. Most of the men and women in same-sex couples are likely to identify as lesbian, gay, bisexual, or some other synonym for *homosexual*.[10] Bisexuals and transgender people are found in both opposite-sex and same-sex couples.[11]

While the census does allow individuals in same-sex couples who are living together in the same home to self-identify, it does not capture identifiable information on single LGBT people; individuals in same-sex relationships who are not living together; LGBT youth living with their parents; LGBT seniors living with their children and/or grandchildren who do not have a partner or do not live

**TABLE 13.1: KEY TERMS USED BY THE 2000 CENSUS**

**Household**: A household includes all the people who occupy a housing unit as their usual place of residence.

**Householder**: The person who filled out the Census form on behalf of him or herself and the other people who live in the household. The Census Bureau prefers that the householder be the person, or one of the people, in whose name the home is owned, being bought, or rented.

**Same-sex couple household**: Household in which the householder identifies his or her "husband/wife" as someone of the same sex or in which the householder indicates that he or she lives with an "unmarried partner" of the same sex to whom he or she is not legally married.

**TABLE 13.2: HOUSEHOLD DEFINITIONS**

**Hispanic same-sex couple household**: Either the householder or the unmarried partner is Hispanic and they are the same sex

**Same-sex couple household in which both partners are Hispanic**: A subset of Hispanic same-sex couple households, where both the householder and unmarried partner are Hispanic

**Hispanic "interethnic" same-sex couple household**: A subset of Hispanic same-sex couple households, where one partner is Hispanic and the other is not

**White non-Hispanic same-sex couple household**: The householder and the unmarried partner are white and not of Hispanic ethnicity

**Hispanic married opposite-sex couple household**: Either the householder or the husband/wife is Hispanic and they are defined as living with a husband or a wife of the opposite sex

**Hispanic cohabiting opposite-sex couple household**: Either the householder or the opposite-sex partner is Hispanic and they are defined as living with an unmarried partner of the opposite sex

with their partner; LGBT homeless people; LGBT undocumented immigrants, and, of course, those not comfortable "outing" themselves to a government agency as being in a same-sex relationship. Due to these significant limitations, the census does not reflect the actual number or the full diversity of lesbian, gay, bisexual, and transgender people in the United States.[12] Some researchers estimate that the true number of same-sex couples in the United States is 10 to 50 percent higher than what is reported by the census.[13] Despite these limitations, the 2000 Census amassed the largest representative national data set available for same-sex couple households.

To better understand how anti–LGBT family policies specifically affect Hispanic same-sex couples and their children, we compared information about Hispanic same-sex couple households from the 2000 Census to data from the same census on white non-Hispanic same-sex couple households, as well as Hispanic married oppo-site-sex couple households and Hispanic cohabiting opposite-sex couple house-holds. Of the Hispanic same-sex couple households in this study, 61 percent include couples in which both partners identify as Hispanic. The remaining 39 percent are interethnic couples in which one partner is Hispanic and the other is not (see Table 13.2 for household definitions). In this study we sometimes make comparisons between households using these two subgroups.

After reporting the findings from our analysis of 2000 Census data, we also dis-cuss their public policy implications where applicable. For example, information from the 2000 Census on income and parenting is important to informing the debate over the impact of anti–same-sex marriage constitutional amendments on Hispanic same-sex couples and their children. Before presenting our findings and their pol-icy implications, we first review research on the demographics and experience of Hispanic Americans, gay and straight.

## HISPANIC AND LATINO SAME-SEX COUPLE
## HOUSEHOLDS IN CONTEXT

According to the U.S. Census Bureau, as of July 1, 2004, the nation's Hispanic pop-ulation reached 41.3 million.[14] Among this population, approximately 67 percent are of Mexican origin, 14 percent are Central and South American, 9 percent are Puerto Rican, 4 percent are Cuban, and the remaining 7 percent are of other Hispanic origins.[15] With a growth rate that is over three times that of the general population (3.6 percent versus 1 percent), Hispanics of any race accounted for approximately one half of the nation's population growth of 2.9 million between July 2003 and July 2004.[16] The U.S. Census Bureau estimates that the Hispanic population will grow to almost 48 million by 2010, comprising nearly 16 percent of the total U.S. population. In comparison, the Census Bureau estimates that by 2010 African Americans will comprise just over 13 percent of the U.S. population.[17]

On average, Hispanics are more likely than white non-Hispanics to live in large cities and metropolitan areas, to be under age eighteen, and to live in larger households. In 2002, 40 percent of the Hispanic population of the United States was foreign-born, with over half (52 percent) of that group having entered the country within the preceding twelve years.[18] Given these facts, it is not surprising that Hispanic voters are less likely than other Americans to support restrictions on immigration.[19]

The Census Bureau does not specifically define the demographic characteristics of the Hispanic undocumented migrant population that may have been counted in the 2000 Census. The Pew Hispanic Center estimated, however, that the total undocumented migrant population reached nearly 11 million as of March 2005. Approximately 57 percent of those undocumented migrants—more than 6 million—come from Mexico. According to the Center, 1.7 million or 17 percent of undocumented migrants are children under the age of eighteen.[20]

*Education, Employment, and Income Disparities*

According to the U.S. Census, Hispanic Americans, regardless of their sexual orientation or gender identity/expression, are significantly disadvantaged in terms of education, wealth and income, and other measures. Hispanics are far less likely than white non-Hispanics to obtain higher levels of education. Eighty-nine percent of white non-Hispanics have a high school diploma compared to 71 percent of Cubans, 67 percent of Puerto Ricans, and only 51 percent of Mexicans. Only 11 percent of all Hispanics have obtained a college degree, compared to 29 percent of white non-Hispanics.[21]

Hispanics are much more likely than white non-Hispanics to be unemployed. Some 8 percent of Mexicans, 10 percent of Puerto Ricans, 7 percent of Central and South Americans, and 9 percent of Cubans in the civilian labor force age sixteen or over are unemployed, compared to 5 percent of the white non-Hispanic population. Those Hispanics who are employed tend to work at lower-paying jobs in less skilled sectors (such as service occupations) than white non-Hispanics. Over half (54 percent) of white non-Hispanics earn over $35,000 per year, compared to just 26 percent of Hispanics.[22]

According to the Census Bureau, the median annual household income in 2003 for white non-Hispanics was $48,000, compared to just $33,000 for Hispanics.[23] Only 48 percent of Hispanic householders own their homes, compared to 75 percent of white non-Hispanic householders.[24] The 2000 Census also found that the median net worth for Hispanic householders is $9,750 as opposed to $79,400 for white non-Hispanic householders—a difference of almost $70,000.[25] Given these facts, it is not surprising that Hispanics are nearly three times as likely as white non-Hispanics to live in poverty.[26]

*Religion and Political Participation*

According to the Pew Hispanic Center, even though Hispanics accounted for half of the population growth in the United States between the 2000 and 2004 presidential elections, they comprised only one-tenth of the increase in total votes cast. Pew suggests that this is primarily due to the fact that a high percentage of Hispanics are either too young to vote or are ineligible because they are not citizens. In fact, only 39 percent of the Hispanic population was eligible to vote in the 2004 election, compared to 76 percent of white non-Hispanics and 65 percent of African Americans.[27] The political participation of the Hispanic population in the United States that is eligible to vote is influenced by a variety of factors. Specifically, National Exit Poll (NEP) data show that understanding religious faith in Hispanic communities is vital to understanding their political participation and position on anti–same-sex marriage amendments and other anti–LGBT legislation.

According to the Pew Hispanic Center's analysis of NEP data, George W. Bush's share of the Hispanic vote grew from 34 percent in 2000 to 40 percent in 2004.[28] This increase is partially attributed to evangelical Protestant Hispanic voters, who comprised 25 percent of the Hispanic vote in 2000 but increased to 32 percent in 2004. The evangelical Protestant segment of the Hispanic electorate voted even more heavily in favor of President Bush in 2004; 56 percent supported Bush in 2004 compared to 44 percent in 2000. In comparison, President Bush's share of the Hispanic Roman Catholic vote remained the same in both elections at 33 percent. Given these findings, just how important is religious faith in the Hispanic electorate in determining which party they vote for and their position on contentious social issues, including same-sex marriage?

According to a report released by the Gallup Organization in July 2005, approximately 90 percent of Hispanics identify with the Christian religion, which is slightly higher than the 84 percent of Americans in general. Sixty-three percent of Hispanics identify themselves as Roman Catholic, 16 percent as Protestant, 10 percent identify with other forms of Christianity, and only 6 percent report no religious affiliation at all. According to Gallup, the fact that such a large majority of Hispanics identify with Christianity does not mean that they are also likely to identify as Republicans. A plurality (48 percent) of Hispanics identify as independent voters. Thirty-five percent identify as Democrats and 18 percent identify as Republicans.[29] With the exception of Cuban Americans, Hispanic voters have historically cast more ballots for Democratic candidates than for Republicans since the 1930s.

Though the majority of Hispanic Americans still identify as Democrats or independents, their religious beliefs often translate into social conservatism. In 2003 the Institute for Latino Studies at the University of Notre Dame released a report that found over half of all Latinos believe that religious leaders should try to influence public affairs. The report also stated that strong majorities of Latinos support policies like faith-based initiatives, prayer in public schools, and teaching creationism in public schools.[30] In comparison, a March 2005 Gallup poll found that less than a third of all Americans (30 percent) actively want creationism rather than evolution taught in public schools.[31]

Hispanics may also be more likely to hold conservative social views on homosexuality than other Americans. A comprehensive national survey of U.S. Latinos by the Pew Hispanic Center and the Kaiser Family Foundation in 2002 found that 72 percent of Latinos believe that homosexual intercourse between adults is "unacceptable," compared to 59 percent of white non-Hispanic Americans.[32] Poll data also indicate, however, that Hispanics may be less likely to support constitutional amendments banning same-sex marriage. The 2004 national survey of over two thousand Latinos found that less than a majority (45 percent) favors "a constitutional amendment that would define marriage as a union between one man and one woman thereby prohibiting legally sanctioned marriages for same-sex couples."[33] In comparison, a 2005 Gallup poll found that 53 percent of all Americans favor such an amendment.[34]

If Hispanic Americans are socially more conservative, why do they not vote for conservative candidates? This finding may be due in part to the fact that Hispanic voters weigh other concerns more heavily than homosexuality and other contentious social issues. Hispanic voters consistently rate education and the economy as their central policy issues. They rate moral values issues like same-sex marriage as one of the least likely to decide their vote.[35] Even Hispanics who identify as born again or evangelical Christians prioritize the economy and jobs over "moral values": only 13 percent of Hispanic evangelicals in a 2004 national poll said that moral values came first among their domestic concerns, compared to 37 percent of white non-Hispanic evangelicals.[36]

Conservative political and religious leaders have stated their intent to help Hispanics bridge the gap between their traditional social conservatism and actually voting for conservative candidates. In a speech before Roman Catholic and Hispanic leaders in Miami, Florida, Ken Mehlman, the chairman of the Republican National Committee (RNC) said, "I will continue to make it clear that the GOP offers Latino and Catholic Americans the best choice—with our compassionate conservative policies that uphold the sanctity of life, marriage and social justice."[37] The RNC hopes to build upon the gains made with the Hispanic electorate in 2004 by attracting more Hispanic voters using conservative wedge issues like same-sex marriage.[38]

*Intersecting Identities: Hispanic and Latino Lesbian,*
*Gay, Bisexual, and Transgender People*

According to the 2000 Census, 9 percent of all households in the United States are Hispanic households.[39] Similarly, 12 percent of all *same-sex* couple households in the United States are Hispanic same-sex couple households.[40] Hispanic LGBT people in the United States constitute a large but under-researched population that often faces additional disadvantages as a result of their combined status as racial, sexual, and socioeconomic minorities.

A 2001 study of roughly twelve hundred Hispanic gay and bisexual men found that 64 percent of respondents experienced verbal harassment during their childhood for being gay or effeminate, and 20 percent were harassed by policy because

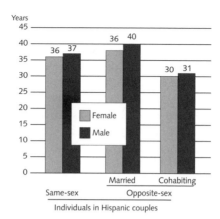

**Figure 13.1: Median age of individuals in Hispanic couples.**

of being gay.[41] Respondents also reported powerful messages—both explicit and covert—in their communities telling them that their homosexuality made them "not normal" or "not truly men;" that they would grow up alone without children or families; and that ultimately their homosexuality is dirty, sinful, and shameful to their families and loved ones. Many opted for exile and migration in order to live their lives openly and honestly away from their loved ones. Hispanic gay and bisexual men also reported experiencing racism not only from society at large but also from the LGBT community, whether in the form of exclusion from social venues or of sexual objectification by white non-Hispanic same-sex partners or lovers.[42]

## DEMOGRAPHICS

According to our analysis of 2000 Census data, some 105,025 households in the United States identify as Hispanic same-sex couple households. In comparison, the 2000 Census counted nearly four hundred and sixty thousand white non-Hispanic same-sex couple households, over 6 million Hispanic married opposite-sex couple households, and over seven hundred and seventy thousand Hispanic cohabiting opposite-sex couple households.[43]

### Age

Because the couples in the households we analyzed are of different ages on average, some of the findings in this study may be the result of the differences in life stage that people experience as they age. For example, income often increases with age until late in life, as does the likelihood of home ownership. The median age differences between the partnered men and women in the households we analyzed, however, are not that large. This factor decreases the likelihood that our findings are affected by differences in age. Where appropriate, we also considered age when we reported differences between households to ensure that those differences were statistically significant.

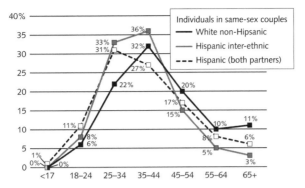

**Figure 13.2: Percentage of individuals in Hispanic couples by age.**

Figure 13.1 illustrates the median age by sex of individuals in the various types of Hispanic couples we considered in this analysis. On average, the individuals in Hispanic married opposite-sex couples are slightly older than those in Hispanic same-sex couples, who are in turn older than those in Hispanic cohabiting opposite-sex couples. Married women report the highest median age of all females in the study (thirty-six), followed by women in same-sex couple households (thirty-six), and women in cohabiting opposite-sex couples (thirty). Married Hispanic men report the highest median age (forty), followed by Hispanic men in same-sex couples (thirty-seven) and Hispanic men in cohabiting opposite-sex couples (thirty-one).

As illustrated in Figure 13.2, the majority of individuals in Hispanic same-sex couples are between the ages of twenty-five and forty-four years: 58 percent of individuals in same-sex couples in which both partners are Hispanic are between the ages of twenty-five and forty-four, compared to 54 percent of individuals in white non-Hispanic same-sex couples and 69 percent of individuals in Hispanic interethnic same-sex couples. Individuals in white non-Hispanic same-sex couples are more likely to be age fifty-five or older (21 percent) than individuals in same-sex couples in which both partners are Hispanic (14 percent). Likewise, individuals in same-sex couples in which both partners are Hispanic are more likely to be age fifty-five or older than individuals in Hispanic interethnic same-sex couples (8 percent).

### Policy Implications: Lesbian, Gay, Bisexual, and Transgender Elders

While all LGBT people are harmed by anti-LGBT laws, including anti–same-sex marriage laws and constitutional amendments, LGBT elders are among the most vulnerable. For example, same-sex couples are ineligible for Social Security survivor benefits, which provide support to the surviving spouse of an opposite-sex married couple based on the deceased spouse's income history. Everyone who pays Social Security taxes, including single individuals and unmarried couples, contributes toward this benefit. Same-sex couples, however, are not eligible to receive it regardless of how long they have been together.[44]

Same-sex couples are also ineligible for Medicaid spend-down protections. Following the death of a spouse in a nursing home or assisted care facility, Medicaid regulations allow the surviving widow or widower of a married opposite-sex couple

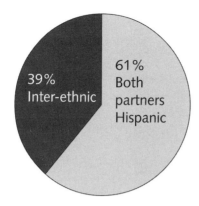
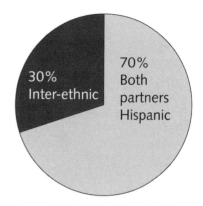

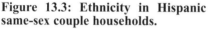

**Figure 13.3: Ethnicity in Hispanic same-sex couple households.**     **Figure 13.4: Ethnicity in Hispanic opposite-sex couple households.**

to remain in the couple's home for the rest of his or her life without jeopardizing the right to Medicaid coverage. Upon the survivor's death, the state may then take the home to recoup the costs of terminal care. Because same-sex couples cannot marry, they are not eligible for this protection, and they may be forced to choose between their home and life's savings or medical coverage.[45]

Additionally, same-sex couples are not eligible to participate in the Family and Medical Leave Act, a federal law passed in 1993 that provides job-loss protection and the right to take up to 12 weeks of unpaid leave for a variety of reasons, including after the birth or adoption of a child; to facilitate recovery from a "serious health condition"; or to care for an immediate family member who is extremely sick. "Family" in the law is defined specifically as being headed by opposite-sex married couples[46] or single parents, and excludes those headed by same-sex couples. This definition prevents same-sex partners from taking care of their families on equal terms with families headed by opposite-sex married couples, and it exposes them to additional vulnerabilities in the workplace. Unlike married opposite-sex couples, same-sex couples must spend thousands of dollars to draw up legal contracts that protect their relationships in sickness and death.[47]

*Ethnicity and Race*

According to the U.S. Census Bureau, "Race and Hispanic origin (also known as ethnicity) are considered distinct concepts and therefore require separate questions in censuses and surveys. Hispanics or Latinos may be any race."[48]

Of the Hispanic same-sex couple households analyzed in this study, 61 percent include couples in which both partners identify as Hispanic, while 39 percent are interethnic couples in which one partner identifies as Hispanic and the other does not (see Figure 13.3). Hispanic same-sex couples are approximately one-third more likely to be interethnic than Hispanic married opposite-sex couples (see Figure 13.4).

Figure 13.5 illustrates the racial breakdown of individuals in same-sex couples in which both partners are Hispanic. These individuals are about as likely to report "some other race" (49 percent) as they are to report that they are white (47 percent).

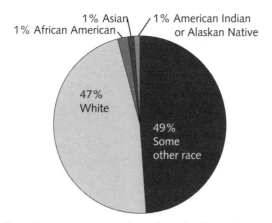

**Figure 13.5: Race in same-sex couples where both partners are Hispanic.**

Two percent report that they are African American, 1 percent is American Indian or Alaska Native, and 1 percent is Asian.

Some 97 percent of all those who checked "some other race" on the 2000 Census also report that they are Hispanic—a fact that, according to Hispanic advocates, indicates the population's desire to have *Hispanic* included as a racial category rather than a matter of ethnic origin.[49] Responding to considerable pressure from Hispanic advocacy organizations, the Census Bureau abandoned a plan to drop the "some other race" category from the 2010 Census. The Bureau claims that dropping the category will improve the accuracy of the Census's racial data, but many Hispanic advocates are concerned that eliminating the category will exclude Hispanics who do not identify themselves according to standard racial classifications.

These disputes reflect the Census Bureau's decades-long difficulty with ethnic and racial categories for Hispanic people, which began in 1930 with the introduction of *Mexican* as a racial category in an attempt to address the growing Mexican population in the southwestern United States. Since census data are used to monitor voting rights and civil rights enforcement, and are often cited by researchers and politicians, the question of Hispanic race and ethnicity is a major concern to Hispanic advocates and policymakers.

*Country or Region of Origin*

Persons in Hispanic same-sex couples report similar countries or regions of origin to those in Hispanic married opposite-sex couples.[50] As shown in Figure 13.6, individuals in Hispanic same-sex and Hispanic married opposite-sex couples are equally likely to report South America (approximately 4 percent), Central America (approximately 5 percent), and Cuba (approximately 4 percent) as their country or region of origin. They also report similar rates of "other Latino" places of origin, including Spain (approximately 12 percent).

Reported rates of Mexican and Puerto Rican heritage varied slightly between individuals in Hispanic same-sex couples and those in Hispanic married opposite-sex couples, with individuals in Hispanic same-sex couples reporting slightly lower

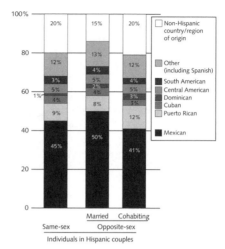

**Figure 13.6: Region of origin of individuals in Hispanic couples.**

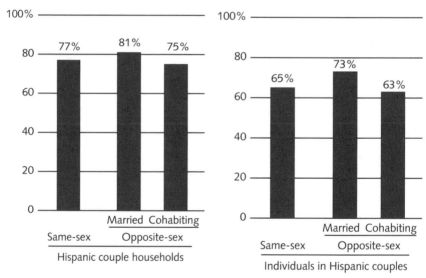

**Figure 13.7: Percentage of Hispanic couples that report Spanish as their primary household language.**

**Figure 13.8: Percentage of individuals in Hispanic couples that report Spanish as their primary personal language.**

rates of Mexican descent and slightly higher rates of Puerto Rican descent than those in Hispanic married opposite-sex couples. Individuals in Hispanic interethnic same-sex couples are less likely to report Mexican heritage but are slightly more likely than those in the other couple types to report Puerto Rican heritage.

*Language*

The 2000 Census allowed the householder to report whether Spanish is the primary "household language" (language primarily spoken in the home). The householder

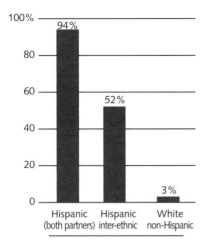

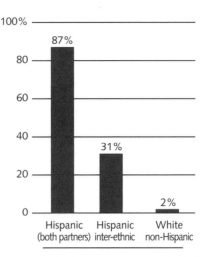

**Figure 13.9: Percentage of Hispanic same-sex couples who report Spanish as their primary household language.**

**Figure 13.10: Percentage of individuals in Hispanic same-sex couples who report Spanish as their primary per-**

could also report whether Spanish is the primary "personal language" (language primarily spoken by the individual) of the householder as well as of anyone else who lived in the home, including a spouse or same-sex partner.

As Figure 13.7 illustrates, Hispanic same-sex couple households are nearly as likely (77 percent) to report Spanish as their primary household language as Hispanic married opposite-sex couple households (81 percent) and Hispanic cohabiting opposite-sex couple households (75 percent). Figure 13.8 illustrates, however, that individuals in Hispanic married opposite-sex couples are more likely to report Spanish as their primary *personal* language (73 percent) than those in Hispanic same-sex couples (65 percent) and those in Hispanic cohabiting opposite-sex couples (63 percent). There is little difference between the Hispanic couple household types we analyzed in household and personal language use by sex.

Differences in reported language use were greater when we analyzed same-sex couple households in more detail (see Figure 13.9). Same-sex couple households in which both partners are Hispanic are far more likely than Hispanic interethnic same-sex couple households to report Spanish as their primary household language (94 percent in contrast to 52 percent). Spanish is the primary household language in only 3 percent of white non-Hispanic same-sex couple households.

As Figure 13.10 illustrates, Spanish is the primary personal language of 87 percent of individuals in same-sex couples in which both partners are Hispanic. Individuals in Hispanic interethnic same-sex couples are far less likely to report Spanish as their primary personal language (31 percent). Only 2 percent of individuals in white non-Hispanic same-sex couples report speaking Spanish as their primary personal language. There is little difference in household and personal language use between individuals in Hispanic female same-sex couples and those in Hispanic male same-sex couples.

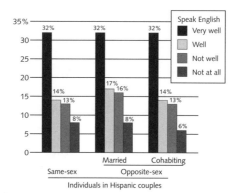

**Figure 13.11: Levels of English fluency among Hispanic couples.**

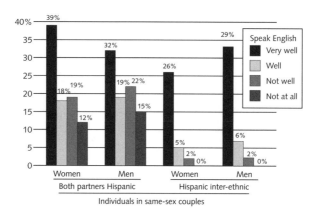

**Figure 13.12: Levels of English fluency among Hispanic same-sex couples.**

When asked to rate their fluency in English on a four-point scale—ranging from "very well" to "not at all"—nonnative English-speaking individuals in the Hispanic couples we analyzed report similar responses. Some 32 percent of the individuals in Hispanic couples say that they speak English "very well" (see Figure 13.11). Analysis by sex revealed few differences in ability to speak English.

More nuanced trends in English-language speaking ability were revealed when we compared individuals in same-sex couples in which both partners are Hispanic to individuals in Hispanic interethnic same-sex couples (see Figure 13.12). In same-sex couples in which both partners are Hispanic, 32 percent of nonnative English-speaking men and 39 percent of nonnative English-speaking women report that they speak English "very well."

Nonnative English-speaking men in same-sex couples in which both partners are Hispanic are most likely to report that they do not speak English at all (15 percent). Individuals in Hispanic interethnic same-sex couples are the least likely to report that they are nonnative English speakers and also are the least likely to report that they speak English "not well" or "not at all."

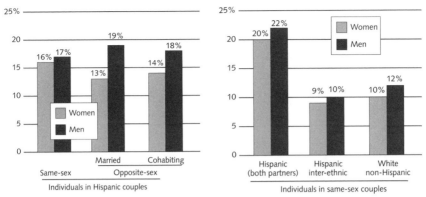

**Figure 13.13: Percentage of men and women in Hispanic couples reporting a disability.**

**Figure 13.14: Percentage of men and women in Hispanic same-sex couples reporting a disability.**

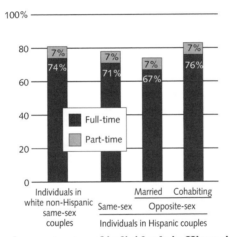

**Figure 13.15: Employment rates of individuals in Hispanic couples.**

*Disability Status*

Figure 13.13 illustrates the percentage of men and women in Hispanic couples reporting a disability, which is similar for partnered men and women across all household types. Individuals in same-sex couples in which both partners are Hispanic are about twice as likely to report a disability as individuals in Hispanic interethnic and white non-Hispanic same-sex couples (see Figure 13.14). Further research is needed to explore why individuals in same-sex couples in which both partners are Hispanic are so much more likely to report having a disability.

EMPLOYMENT

As illustrated in Figure 13.15, individuals in same-sex couples report rates of full-time and part-time employment in the previous year (1999) similar to those in the

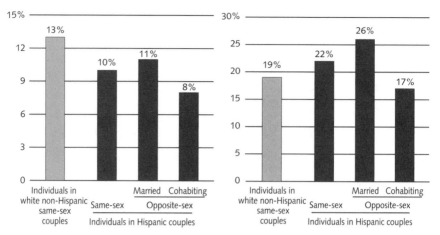

**Figure 13.16: Percentage of individuals in Hispanic couples working in the public sector.**

**Figure 13.17: Unemployment rates of individuals in Hispanic couples.**

other couples we analyzed. Seventy-one percent of individuals in Hispanic same-sex couples report that they are employed full time compared to 74 percent of individuals in white non-Hispanic same-sex couples and 67 percent of individuals in Hispanic married opposite-sex couples. Of individuals in Hispanic cohabiting opposite-sex couples, 76 percent report working full time in 1999.

As illustrated in Figure 13.16, individuals in Hispanic same-sex couples (10 percent) report working in the public sector at rates comparable to those in Hispanic married opposite-sex (11 percent) and Hispanic cohabiting opposite-sex couples (8 percent). Individuals in Hispanic same-sex couples are slightly less likely to work in the public sector than those in white non-Hispanic same-sex couples (10 percent in contrast to 13 percent).

Individuals in Hispanic same-sex couples report rates of not working similar to those reported by individuals in Hispanic married opposite-sex and white non-Hispanic same-sex couples (see Figure 13.17). The census does not track unemployment rates in the same way as the Department of Labor. Individuals who report working zero hours in the previous year are categorized as "not working." Of individuals in same-sex couples, 22 percent report that they did not work in 1999, as do 26 percent of individuals in Hispanic married opposite-sex couples and 19 percent of individuals in white non-Hispanic same-sex couples. Of individuals in cohabiting opposite-sex couples, 17 percent report not working in 1999.

*Policy Implications: Nondiscrimination Ordinances and the Impact of Anti–same-sex Marriage Amendments on Domestic Partner Benefits for Public Sector Employees*

Census data on public sector employment have important policy implications. First, executive orders or laws banning discrimination on the basis of sexual orientation and gender identity in public sector employment, such as those enacted in 2003 by the governors of Pennsylvania and Kentucky, offer protection for individuals in same-sex couples who work in the public sector. As of July 2005, sixteen states and Washington, D.C., have laws that prohibit discrimination in the workplace on the basis of sexual orientation.[51]

Second, domestic partner policies that cover municipal or state employees could provide health and other benefits to the partners of many individuals in same-sex couples who work in the public sector. The anti–same-sex marriage amendments to state constitutions that were recently enacted in several states could overturn these policies, causing many same-sex partners and their children to lose their health care and other benefits. For example, in late 2004, Jennifer Granholm, the governor of Michigan, stripped state employees of domestic partner health insurance, claiming that she was forced to do so because Michigan voters approved the state's broad anti–same-sex marriage amendment in November 2004.[52] In April 2005, the attorney general of Michigan, Mike Cox, ruled that the domestic partner benefits offered by the city of Kalamazoo to municipal employees also violated the amendment. City leaders planned to end those benefits at the end of 2005.[53] The attorney general's ruling likely means the end of domestic partner benefits for public sector employees in Ann Arbor, Washtenaw County, and other localities throughout Michigan. In total, approximately half a million individuals in families led by same-sex or cohabiting opposite-sex couples are now ineligible for domestic partner benefits in Michigan.

## EDUCATIONAL ATTAINMENT

Individuals in same-sex couples in which both partners are Hispanic report significantly lower levels of educational attainment than those in white non-Hispanic same-sex couples and those in Hispanic interethnic same-sex couples (see Figure 13.18).[54] Only 23 percent of individuals in same-sex couples in which both partners are Hispanic report completing some level of post-secondary (beyond high school) education. In comparison, 66 percent of individuals in white non-Hispanic same-sex couples and 72 percent of individuals in Hispanic interethnic same-sex couples report that they completed any education beyond high school.

Figure 13.19 illustrates that individuals in Hispanic same-sex couples are more likely to obtain postsecondary education (43 percent) than individuals in Hispanic married opposite-sex couples (36 percent). Individuals in Hispanic cohabiting opposite-sex couples are least likely to obtain any education beyond high school.

The fact that individuals in same-sex couples in which both partners are Hispanic report significantly lower levels of educational attainment than those in white non-Hispanic same-sex couples warrants further research as to its effects on the employment options and life experiences of Hispanic same-sex couples.

## INCOME

As illustrated in Figure 13.20, Hispanic female same-sex couple households report a median household income ($43,000) comparable to that of Hispanic married

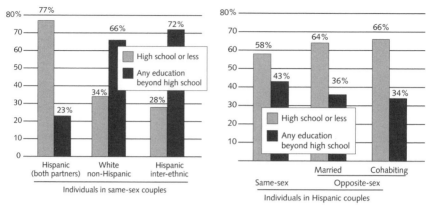

**Figure 13.18: Level of education attained by individuals in Hispanic same-sex couples.**

**Figure 13.19: Level of education attained by individuals in Hispanic couples.**

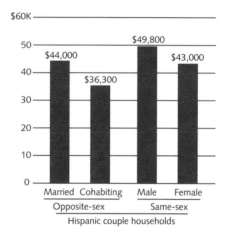

**Figure 13.20: Median annual income of Hispanic couple households.**

opposite-sex couple households ($44,000). Hispanic male same-sex couple households report the highest median household income ($49,800) relative to the other Hispanic couple households we analyzed.[55] Further analysis revealed an interesting story about these income differences, particularly between male same-sex couple households in which both partners are Hispanic and male same-sex couple households in which one partner is Hispanic and the other is not.

As Figure 13.21 illustrates, Hispanic interethnic male same-sex couple households report a median annual household income that is higher than any of the other households we analyzed. In fact, male interethnic same-sex couple households report a median annual household income that is over $31,000 higher than the median annual household income of male same-sex couple households in which both partners are Hispanic. This difference may be attributable to a variety of factors. For example, men in Hispanic interethnic same-sex couples report obtaining

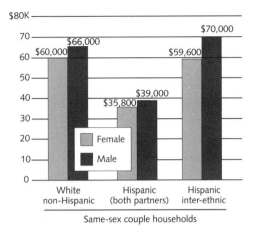

**Figure 13.21: Median annual income of Hispanic same-sex couple households.**

some form of postsecondary education (that is, college and graduate school) at a much higher rate than any of the other households we analyzed.[56] They are also the least likely type of family to report that they are raising children. Consequently, men in Hispanic interethnic same-sex couples may have not only dual incomes but also access to higher-paying jobs because they have higher levels of postsecondary education. They are also more likely to be working full time, possibly because they are not burdened by the responsibility of raising children.

This fact may also help to explain the income differences between Hispanic interethnic male and female same-sex couple households, because Hispanic interethnic female same-sex couples are three times more likely to be raising children than Hispanic interethnic male same-sex couples (see parenting section for more details). This finding warrants further research that could focus on additional reasons for this disparity, including the gender gap in pay.

When we separated out the significantly higher income of Hispanic interethnic male same-sex couple households, a far more realistic picture of the income disparity between Hispanic and white non-Hispanic same-sex couple households was revealed. Male same-sex couple households in which both partners are Hispanic earn more than female same-sex couple households in which both partners are Hispanic but far less than white non-Hispanic male same-sex couple households (see Figure 13.21). Female same-sex couple households in which both partners are Hispanic earn over $24,000 less than white non-Hispanic female same-sex couple households[57] and over $30,000 less than white non-Hispanic male same-sex couple households.

Male same-sex couple households in which both partners are Hispanic also earn significantly less, with a difference of $27,000 between them and white non-Hispanic male same-sex couple households[58] and a difference of $21,000 between them and white non-Hispanic female same-sex couple households.

Differences in income between Hispanic same-sex couple households and white non-Hispanic same-sex couple households mirror trends in the general population. Hispanic Americans are three times as likely as white non-Hispanic

Americans to live in poverty.[59] In 2003 Hispanic families reported a 3 percent decline in real income—from $33,600 in 2002 to $33,000 in 2003—which was still only 69 percent of the median income of white non-Hispanic families.[60] The 2000 Census found that the median net worth for all Hispanic householders is $9,750 as opposed to $79,400 for white non-Hispanic householders, a difference of almost $70,000.[61]

*Policy Implications: The Financial Impact of Discrimination*

Anti-LGBT leaders often argue that gay and lesbian people do not need protection from discrimination because they are wealthier than heterosexuals. For example, a pamphlet titled "What's wrong with 'gay rights'? You be the judge!" distributed by Colorado for Family Values, claims that "gays"

> have an average household income of more than $55,400—nearly $23,000 more than average American households, and a whopping $43,000 more than African Americans with 1–3 years of high school education. Gays are three times more likely to be college graduates. Three times more likely to hold professional managerial jobs. Four times more likely to be overseas travelers. Almost four times more likely to earn over $100,000 annually.[62]

To the contrary, an analysis of General Social Survey data and 1990 Census data found that same-sex couples actually earn about the same or less than opposite-sex married couples. The economist Lee Badgett reviewed several studies of income differences between gay, lesbian, and bisexual people and heterosexuals based on the 1990 Census' same-sex household sample, as well as data from other national surveys. Gay and bisexual men earned from 13 percent to 32 percent less than heterosexual men after controlling for factors like education and age. Lesbian and bisexual women earned the same or slightly more than heterosexual women, but because of the gender gap in pay, lesbian couples earned less on average than married heterosexual couples.[63] 2000 Census data on same-sex couples also refute the stereotype that gay and lesbian people are wealthier and more privileged than heterosexuals, particularly for Hispanic same-sex couple households.

The extent of same-sex couples' economic disadvantage is actually understated because the census collects pretax data on income. Since same-sex couples often pay more in state and federal taxes than their heterosexual peers because they cannot file jointly,[64] the true income differences between same-sex couples and opposite-sex married couples are not recorded by the census. For example, same-sex couples must report domestic partner health insurance as income and pay taxes on it, while married opposite-sex couples are not taxed on spousal health insurance. Furthermore, same-sex partners do not have access to their partners' pensions or Social Security survivor benefits when one of them dies, and they must pay taxes on assets they inherit even if those assets include a house in which both partners lived and owned jointly for many years. There are 1,138 federal benefits and protections available to married couples that same-sex couples cannot obtain.[65] States, municipalities, and private entities also offer many benefits contingent upon marital status.

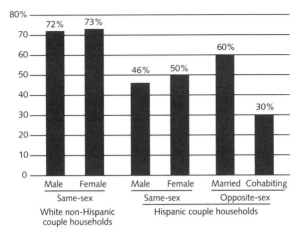

**Figure 13.22: Percentage of home ownership in Hispanic couple households.**

HOME OWNERSHIP

The United States government measures wealth and poverty in terms of income. While there is a significant racial and ethnic gap in income, the gap is even greater when assets are considered. Key among these assets is home ownership. Anti-LGBT political and religious leaders often claim that same-sex relationships are unstable and short term, and are therefore unworthy of the benefits and protections of marriage. For example, in written testimony submitted to the Wisconsin Legislature in support of the state's anti–same-sex marriage ballot measure, the Family Research Council claimed that "the vast majority of homosexual relationships are short-lived and transitory."[66] To the contrary, Census data on home ownership and the residential patterns of same-sex couples provide evidence of stability and commitment.

As Figure 13.22 illustrates, male and female Hispanic same-sex couple households (46 percent and 50 percent respectively) are more likely to report owning their homes than Hispanic cohabiting (unmarried) opposite-sex couple households (30 percent). Hispanic female same-sex couple households report home ownership rates (50 percent) that are lower than the rate reported by white non-Hispanic female same-sex couple households (73 percent) and Hispanic married opposite-sex couple households (60 percent). White non-Hispanic same-sex couple households report the highest home ownership rates: 73 percent for female same-sex couple households and 72 percent for male same-sex couple households.

Even when one accounts for differences in age, Hispanic same-sex couple households are like Hispanic married opposite-sex couple households in that they are significantly more likely to own their homes than Hispanic cohabiting opposite-sex couple households.[67]

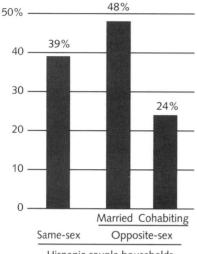

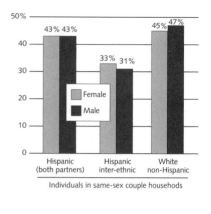

**Figure 13.23: Percentage of individuals in Hispanic couple households who report living in the same residence as five years earlier.**

**Figure 13.24: Percentage of individuals in Hispanic same-sex couple households who report living in the same residence as five years earlier.**

## RESIDENTIAL PATTERNS

The Census asks a number of questions that can be used to analyze the residential patterns of Hispanic couple households, including the length of time couples have lived in their current home. Overall, the residence patterns of individuals in Hispanic same-sex couples are more like those of Hispanic married opposite-sex couples than those of Hispanic cohabiting (unmarried) opposite-sex couples.

Figure 13.23 illustrates that individuals in Hispanic same-sex couples are significantly more likely than those in Hispanic cohabiting opposite-sex couples to report living in the same residence as five years earlier (39 percent versus 24 percent). Individuals in Hispanic same-sex couples report living in the same residence as five years earlier at a lower rate than those in Hispanic married opposite-sex couples (39 percent versus 48 percent).

The fact that individuals in Hispanic same-sex couples are nearly two-thirds more likely than individuals in Hispanic cohabiting opposite-sex couples to report living in the same home as five years earlier is an indicator that their relationships may be more stable and long term. Even when age is taken into account, this difference is statistically significant.[68]

Individuals in same-sex couples in which both partners are Hispanic are nearly as likely as those in white non-Hispanic same-sex couples to report living in the same residence as five years earlier, with little difference by sex. As shown in Figure 13.24, 43 percent of men and women in same-sex couples in which both partners are Hispanic report living in the same residence as five years earlier. Thirty-three percent of women and 31 percent of men in interethnic same-sex couples report living in the same residence as five years earlier, compared to 47 percent of men and 45 percent of women in white non-Hispanic same-sex couples.

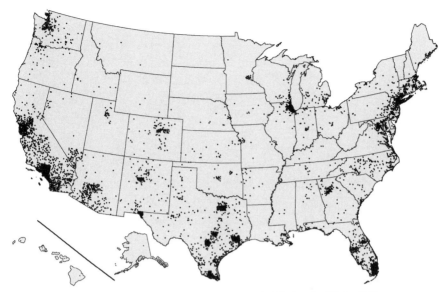

**Figure 13.25 Hispanic same-sex couple households in the United States.**

Key: 1 dot = 10 Hispanic same-sex couple households

Map by Lopez & Cheung, Inc.    Data: 2000 U.S. Census, Summary File 4

## GEOGRAPHIC DISTRIBUTION

The 2000 Census documents Hispanic same-sex couple households in virtually every state, with the highest concentrations in Arizona, California, Florida, Texas, and the New York City metropolitan area (see Figure 13.25). This pattern mirrors that of the Hispanic population overall; according to the 2000 Census, over half of the Hispanic population lives in two states, California and Texas, and over three-fourths live in seven states: California, Texas, New York, Florida, Illinois, Arizona, and New Jersey. Hispanic same-sex couples live where most Hispanic couples live and are part of their respective communities, sending their children to local schools and dealing with the same issues other Hispanic households face.

The top ten metropolitan areas with the highest number of Hispanic same-sex couple households are Los Angeles-Riverside-Orange County, CA; New York-Northern New Jersey-Long Island, NY-NJ-CT-PA;[69] Miami-Fort Lauderdale, FL; San Francisco-Oakland-San José, CA; Chicago-Gary-Kenosha, IL-IN-WI; Houston-Galveston-Brazoria, TX; Dallas-Fort Worth, TX; Phoenix-Mesa, AZ; San Diego, CA; and San Antonio, TX (see Figure 13.26).

The top ten metropolitan areas with the highest proportion of Hispanic same-sex couple households among all same-sex couple households are concentrated in the Southwestern states, California, and the state of Washington. In fact, six of the ten are located in Texas, a finding that has important policy implications. In November 2005, Texans will vote on a ballot measure prohibiting same-sex marriage. Texas already passed a law in 2003 that not only prohibits same-sex marriage but may also

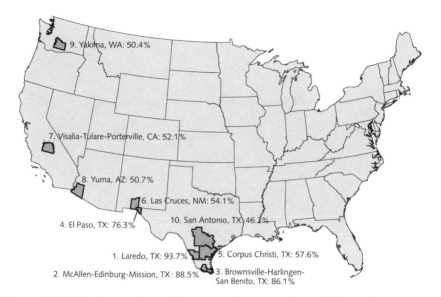

**Figure 13.26 Top ten metropolitan areas by proportion of Hispanic same-sex couple households among all same-sex couple households in the United States.**

Key: Metropolitan area name: Proportion of Hispanic same-sex couple households among all same-sex couple households

Map by Lopez & Cheung, Inc.        Data: 2000 U.S. Census, Summary File 4

prohibit other forms of partner recognition, including civil unions and domestic partnerships.[70]

The metropolitan areas outside Texas with the highest proportion of Hispanic same-sex couple households among all same-sex couple households include Las Cruces, NM; Yuma, AZ; Visalia-Tulare-Porterville, CA; and Yakima, WA.

## IMMIGRATION AND CITIZENSHIP STATUS

Immigration policy is consistently cited as a primary concern for Hispanic communities nationwide.[71] Our analysis of 2000 Census data indicates that immigration issues are also a significant factor in the lives of Hispanic same-sex couples and their children.

As Figure 13.27 illustrates, individuals in Hispanic same-sex couples are ten times as likely as individuals in white non-Hispanic same-sex couples to report that they were born outside the United States (51 percent versus 5 percent). Fifty-seven percent of individuals in Hispanic married opposite-sex couples and 45 percent of individuals in Hispanic cohabiting opposite-sex couples also report that they are foreign born.

As illustrated in Figure 13.28, individuals in Hispanic same-sex couples are fifteen times as likely as individuals in white non-Hispanic same-sex couples to report

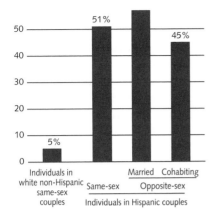

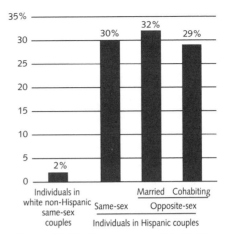

**Figure 13.27: Percentage of individuals in Hispanic couple households who report being born outside the United States.**

**Figure 13.28: Percentage of individuals in Hispanic couple households who report that they are not United States citizens.**

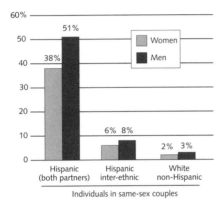

**Figure 13.29: Percentage of individuals in Hispanic same-sex couple households who report that they are not United States citizens.**

not being citizens of the United States (30 percent versus 2 percent). Individuals in Hispanic married opposite-sex couples (32 percent) and individuals in Hispanic cohabiting opposite-sex couples (29 percent) report similar rates of not being United States citizens.

Figure 13.29 further illustrates how immigration issues disproportionately affect same-sex couples in which both partners are Hispanic, compared to Hispanic interethnic same-sex couples and white non-Hispanic same-sex couples. These data are also broken down by sex. Men and women in same-sex couples in which both partners are Hispanic are far more likely to report not being United States citizens than men and women in white non-Hispanic same-sex couples. In fact, men in same-sex couples in which both partners are Hispanic are about seventeen times more likely than men in white non-Hispanic same-sex couples and over six times more likely than men in Hispanic interethnic same-sex couples to report not being citizens. More than half (51 percent) of men in same-sex couples in which both partners are Hispanic report not being citizens of the United States, compared to only 3 percent of men in white non-Hispanic same-sex couples and 8 percent of men in Hispanic interethnic same-sex couples.

Although women in same-sex couples in which both partners are Hispanic report not being citizens at a lower rate than men in same-sex couples in which both partners are Hispanic (38 percent versus 51 percent), the rate is still significantly higher than the rate reported by the partnered men and women in the other same-sex couple households we analyzed.

*Policy Implications: Treating Same-Sex Partners the Same as Opposite-Sex Married Spouses for the Purposes of Immigration Rights and Benefits*

As illustrated by data from the 2000 Census, Hispanic couples, gay and straight, are affected by citizenship status and resulting immigration issues. Unlike Hispanic opposite-sex couples who legally are able to marry, however, existing anti–same-sex marriage laws and the federal Defense of Marriage Act (DOMA) prevent same-sex couples in which only one partner is a citizen from sponsoring their noncitizen partner for immigration purposes.

Fifteen countries, including Canada, Denmark, Israel, South Africa, France, and the United Kingdom, recognize same-sex couples for purposes of immigration. Even though U.S. immigration policy is largely based on the principle of family unification, which allows citizens and legal permanent residents of the United States to sponsor their spouses and other immediate family members for immigration purposes, same-sex partners of citizens and permanent residents of the United States are not considered spouses, and cannot be sponsored by their partners for family-based immigration.[72] This places many binational same-sex couples in limbo, forcing them to find ways to stay together illegally and live in fear of deportation. Many same-sex couples are forced to move to Canada or else-where to stay together.[73]

In the summer of 2005, the Uniting American Families Act (S. 1278), formerly known as the Permanent Partners Immigration Act, was introduced in Congress by Senator Patrick Leahy (D-VT). The bill would add the words "permanent partner" to the federal Immigration and Nationality Act, enabling same-sex domestic partners to be treated the same as opposite-sex married spouses for purposes of immigration rights and benefits. The bill defines a permanent partner as a person who is eighteen years or older, unmarried, and in a financially interdependent, committed, lifelong intimate relationship with another individual eighteen years or older.[74]

Access to the institution of marriage recognized by both the federal and state governments would also allow immigration rights for binational same-sex couples, as well as thousands of other benefits and protections. Proposed federal and state anti–same-sex marriage constitutional amendments further enshrine this discrimination in immigration and many other family policies.

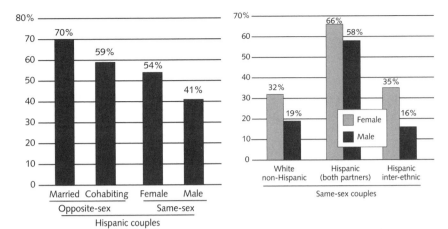

**Figure 13.30: Percentage of Hispanic couple households raising children.**

**Figure 13.31: Percentage of Hispanic same-sex couple households raising children.**

## PARENTHOOD

According to the 2000 Census, many Hispanic same-sex couples are raising children under the age of eighteen, including biological and nonbiological children. The census defines biological children as children who are the "natural born" offspring of the householder in the same-sex unmarried partner household. It defines nonbiological children as a) blood relatives of the householder, such as a niece, nephew, or grandchild, or b) foster children or adopted children who are not blood relatives of the householder.

As illustrated in Figure 13.30, more than half (54 percent) of Hispanic female same-sex couples report raising at least one child under the age of eighteen compared to 70 percent of Hispanic married and 59 percent of Hispanic cohabiting opposite-sex couples. Hispanic male same-sex couples (41 percent) are least likely to report that they are raising children.[75]

A more accurate picture of parenting in Hispanic same-sex couples is revealed when Hispanic interethnic same-sex couples are compared to same-sex couples in which both partners are Hispanic. Figure 13.31 illustrates that male same-sex couples in which both partners are Hispanic (58 percent) are raising children at almost three times the rate reported by white non-Hispanic male same-sex couples (19 percent).[76] Hispanic interethnic male same-sex couples report the lowest rates of raising children (16 percent). Female same-sex couples in which both partners are Hispanic are raising children at the highest rate (66 percent), followed by Hispanic interethnic female same-sex couples (35 percent) and white non-Hispanic female same-sex couples (32 percent).

Figure 13.32 illustrates parenting rates by type of child, biological or nonbiological. We see similarities by sex, with female same-sex couples parenting at generally higher rates than male same-sex couples. Female same-sex couples in which

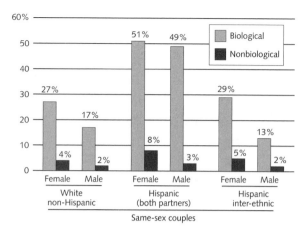

**Figure 13.32: Percentage of Hispanic same-sex couple households raising biological versus nonbiological children.**

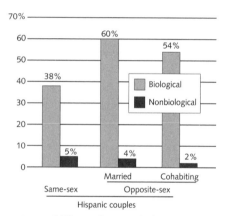

**Figure 13.33: Percentage of Hispanic couple households raising biological versus nonbiological children.**

both partners are Hispanic are most likely to be raising biological children (51 percent), followed by male same-sex couples in which both partners are Hispanic (49 percent), and interethnic Hispanic female same-sex couples (29 percent). Male same-sex couples in which both partners are Hispanic (49 percent) are almost three times more likely than white non-Hispanic male same-sex couples (17 percent) and almost four times more likely than Hispanic interethnic male same-sex couples (13 percent) to report raising a biological child.

As illustrated in Figure 13.33, Hispanic same-sex couples report raising nonbiological children at similar rates to Hispanic married opposite-sex couples. Nonbiological children can include adopted children, foster children, grandchildren, nephews, and nieces (who are biologically related to the householder who is their grandparent, aunt, or uncle but are not technically biological children of the householder).

*Policy Implications: Antigay Parenting and Adoption Laws in the United States*

Political and religious leaders who oppose same-sex marriage often argue against allowing gay and lesbian people to adopt children. For example, in January 2003, Focus on the Family ran a full-page advertisement in the *Boston Globe* warning that gay and lesbian parenting is "a massive, untested social experiment with coming generations of children."[77] The Family Research Council argues that "the homosexual lifestyle is inconsistent with the proper raising of children,"[78] and that only a "small minority of homosexual couples choose to raise children."[79] At the 2004 Republican National Convention, Mitt Romney, the governor of Massachusetts, said, "Because every child deserves a mother and a father...marriage should be between a man and a woman."[80]

Six states now prohibit or restrict foster or adoptive parenting by gay and lesbian people or same-sex couples,[81] and courts around the country also take sexual orientation and gender identity into consideration in awarding child custody. Utah prohibits adoption by cohabiting unmarried couples, which applies to same-sex couples in Utah and 48 other states. Mississippi bans same-sex couples from adopting. While Arkansas does not explicitly prohibit gay men, lesbians, and bisexuals from adopting, its Child Welfare Agency Review Board has banned them from foster parenting since 1999. Adoption law in North Dakota allows agencies that receive state contracts and licenses to refuse to place children with prospective parents to whom they object on religious grounds, including those who are gay, lesbian, or bisexual. Oklahoma passed an antigay adoption law banning the recognition of an adoption by more than one individual of the same sex from any other state or foreign jurisdiction in May 2004.[82]

Due in part to Anita Bryant's "Save Our Children" campaign, which overthrew an inclusive nondiscrimination law in Dade County, Florida, in 1977, adoption by "homosexuals" has been explicitly banned in Florida since 1977. Given that the Miami-Fort Lauderdale metropolitan area ranks third among metropolitan areas with the largest number of Hispanic same-sex couple households, the policy implications of census data on parenting are extremely important.

Following the success of thirteen anti–same-sex marriage state constitutional amendment ballot measures in 2004, anti-LGBT political and religious leaders have signaled their intent to pursue antigay parenting and adoption laws, which could threaten the integrity of hundreds of thousands of same-sex couple families with children, including those that are Hispanic. In 2005 anti–gay parenting legislation was proposed but either died in committee or was defeated in one chamber of the legislatures in six states—Arkansas,[83] Alabama,[84] Indiana,[85] Oregon,[86] Tennessee[87] and Texas.[88] The bill proposed in Texas is one of a few that also explicitly banned adoption by bisexuals. Legislation was also proposed in Virginia[89] that would have required courts to inquire whether a prospective adoptive parent is gay or lesbian. The bill passed in the state House of Representatives but died in a state Senate committee.

Adoptions that codify the parental relationship of both parents are essential to ensuring the rights and security of the children of same-sex couples. When a child is not biologically related to either parent, a joint adoption allows both parents to simultaneously adopt a child. Joint adoption is currently allowed in the District of Columbia, California, Connecticut, Massachusetts, New Jersey, New York, and

Vermont, and it has also been granted at the trial court level in a number of jurisdictions.[90] Adoption by a second parent allows the biological or adoptive parent to retain his or her parental rights while consenting to the adoption of the child by his or her partner. Although courts in twenty states have permitted second-parent adoptions by same-sex partners, and laws in three states explicitly permit them, the children of same-sex couples in most states are still faced with the emotional and economic insecurity of not having their relationship to their second father or mother legally recognized. In fact, courts in four states have ruled that the state's law does not permit second-parent or stepparent adoptions by same-sex partners.[91]

Equitable adoption and parenting laws are important to same-sex couples because if parents have no legal relationship to their children, they cannot, for example, include them in their health insurance coverage or make decisions about their care should one parent die or the couple separate. Additionally, if the child of a same-sex couple becomes sick, the legal parent's partner may be unable to authorize medical treatment or could even be denied hospital visitation rights.

Laws that restrict gay men, lesbians, bisexuals, same-sex couples, or cohabiting opposite-sex couples from adopting or foster parenting also harm children in need of a good home. According to the U.S. Department of Health and Human Services, there are over one hundred thousand children waiting to be adopted nationwide, and over ten thousand of them are Hispanic.[92] Approximately five hundred and twenty-three thousand children are currently in foster care.[93] Seventeen percent of children in foster care are Hispanic, equaling their proportion of all children in the United States.[94] Sadly, many children mature into adulthood while in foster care and are more likely to exhibit emotional problems, delinquency, substance abuse, and academic difficulties. This is not surprising given that some children in foster care live in twenty or more homes by the time they are eighteen years old.[95]

The vast majority of medical and mental health professional organizations, including the American Academy of Pediatrics,[96] the National Association of Social Workers,[97] and the American Psychological Association (APA),[98] recognize that there is no inherent difference in the social functioning and emotional health of children raised by same-sex couples, gay men, or lesbians. According to the APA, "not a single study has found children of gay or lesbian parents to be disadvantaged in any significant respect relative to children of heterosexual parents."[99] Other peer-reviewed research in the social sciences has also found that children being raised by lesbian and gay parents are not disadvantaged relative to children being raised by heterosexual parents.[100] Currently, six states restrict parenting by gay men and lesbians, same-sex couples, and unmarried cohabiting couples. There is no justification for these laws.

Despite attempts by anti-LGBT political and religious leaders to portray the terms *gay* and *family* as mutually exclusive, our analysis of data from the 2000 Census shows that Hispanic same-sex couples are forming stable families and that 47 percent of them are raising children under the age of eighteen. Simply documenting the existence of Hispanic same-sex couples with children is important in and of itself, particularly given the threat of existing and proposed laws that could threaten the security and stability of same-sex couple families.

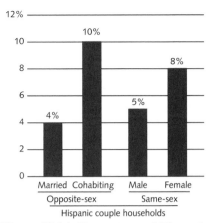

Figure 13.34: Percentage of Hispanic couple households who report receiving public assistance.

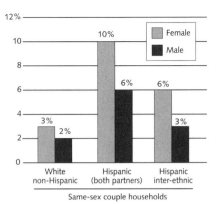

Figure 13.35: Percentage of Hispanic same-sex couple households who report receiving public assistance.

## PUBLIC ASSISTANCE

"Public assistance," as measured in the 2000 Census, includes the use of general assistance and Temporary Assistance for Needy Families (TANF) in 1999, commonly referred to as welfare. It does not include Supplemental Security Income (SSI) or separate payments received for hospital or other medical care. As illustrated in Figure 13.34, Hispanic female same-sex couple households (8 percent) and Hispanic cohabiting opposite-sex couple households (10 percent) are more likely to report that they receive public assistance than Hispanic male same-sex couple households (5 percent) or Hispanic married opposite-sex couple households (4 percent).

Among same-sex couple household types, female same-sex couple households in which both partners are Hispanic receive public assistance at a much higher rate (10 percent) than white non-Hispanic female same-sex couple households (3 percent) or Hispanic interethnic female same-sex couple households (6 percent) (see Figure 13.35). The census data do not explain why female same-sex couple households in which both partners are Hispanic report receiving public assistance at a higher rate. This finding may be due to the fact that they also report the lowest median annual household income and are also more likely to be parenting children than other same-sex couple households.[101] Given that a low income and the presence of children are main TANF eligibility requirements, female same-sex couple households in which both partners are Hispanic are more likely to be eligible for such assistance.

*Policy Implications: Heterosexual Marriage Promotion, Fatherhood Promotion, and Faith-Based Initiatives*

The Bush-Cheney administration has promoted heterosexual marriage, fatherhood, and an increased role of faith-based service providers as key components of welfare reform and solutions to long-term poverty. These policies pose a particular threat to low-income same-sex couples raising children and especially to those receiving public assistance.

Heterosexual marriage and fatherhood promotion programs, on which the Bush administration has tried to spend at least $1.6 billion over five years,[102] assume that all low-income single parents are heterosexual or desire to marry a person of the opposite sex. Of course, this assumption leaves out lesbians, gay men, and many bisexuals. Some key welfare policymakers appointed by President George W. Bush, such as Wade Horn and Andrew Bush of the U.S. Department of Health and Human Services, have recently advocated policies that privilege married opposite-sex couples and penalize other kinds of families.[103]

Heterosexual marriage promotion policies devote limited funds toward activities of questionable value that fail to acknowledge the existence of people on welfare who are unable to marry because of discriminatory public laws. In many states, cash bonuses are available to married low-income couples.[104] Lesbians and gay men on welfare are not eligible. Fatherhood initiatives, which argue that children who are not raised by a married mother and father are disadvantaged in comparison to their peers, stigmatize lesbian and gay families, especially lesbian-headed families. Some proposals—such as a ban on donor insemination of unmarried women—may make it harder to form same-sex couple families in the first place. Compulsory paternity establishment and child support cooperation could force a lesbian or bisexual woman on welfare to allow her child's biological father to co-parent in order to be eligible for benefits. Women who do not or cannot establish paternity risk a cut of 25 percent in benefits and even termination of all assistance. And this policy involves a basic double standard: there is no requirement that a single father—gay or straight—establish "maternity" or any other parental obligation on penalty of having his Temporary Assistance for Needy Families (TANF) benefits decreased or terminated.

Other proposals—such as the promotion of adoption as the first option for children born out of wedlock[105]—could threaten families headed by LGBT people. While programs intended to help low-income families achieve and maintain stable family arrangements are appropriate and laudable, these proposals should be reconceptualized to promote stable families and responsible parenthood by supporting the involvement of two loving parents regardless of gender and providing women the skills and education necessary to provide for their children as single parents. Millions of families with children headed by single mothers or lesbian couples exist in the United States and deserve fair treatment under the social safety net. They are not intrinsically pathological, as those promoting heterosexual marriage and fatherhood as solutions to poverty often claim, either explicitly or implicitly.

Faith-based initiatives involve the shifting of public funds for social services formerly provided by a government agency or a secular nonprofit group to sectarian religious organizations. Under the 1996 welfare reform law, religious organizations are explicitly permitted to discriminate on the basis of religion, even with TANF funds. Unfortunately, experience demonstrates that religion-based discrimination can be a proxy for discrimination based on sexual orientation. In Kentucky and Georgia, lesbian employees have lost human service jobs under faith-based

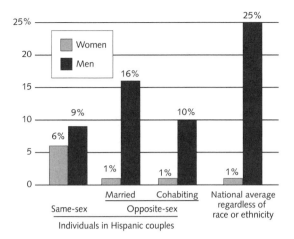

**Figure 13.36: Percentage of individuals in Hispanic couple households who report military service.**

initiatives.[106] Low-income same-sex couple families could also experience discrimination as well as evangelization when they try to obtain services.

The faith-based initiative proposals supported by the Bush administration threaten to make such discrimination against LGBT people by religious-based providers explicitly legal. An internal Salvation Army document, exposed in 2001, stated that the White House had made a "firm commitment" to the Salvation Army to issue a regulation protecting such charities from state and city laws banning sexual orientation discrimination.[107] Although the White House denied knowledge of the Salvation Army proposal, President Bush explicitly called on Congress in 2003 to allow religious entities to discriminate on the basis of sexual orientation in hiring and to ignore local nondiscrimination laws, arguing that Title VII of the Civil Rights Act of 1964 allows religious entities to discriminate in hiring on the basis of sexual orientation, even if they are receiving federal funds.[108] The Bush-Cheney administration characterized this antigay discrimination with tax dollars as religious freedom.

## MILITARY SERVICE

According to the U.S Department of Defense, 9.9 percent of all active-duty enlisted personnel and 4.7 percent of active-duty officers are Hispanic. Additionally, Hispanics make up 9.1 percent of enlisted personnel and 4.3 percent of officers in the reserves.[109] Hispanic same-sex couples also include many individuals who report military service, and they are among the many lesbians, gay men, and bisexuals in the military who risk their lives to fight for a country in which they do not have equal rights and protections.

As illustrated in Figure 13.36, Hispanic women in same-sex couples serve at six times the rate of Hispanic women living with a husband or cohabiting with a male partner.[110] Hispanic men in same-sex couples serve at about half the rate of Hispanic men married to a woman (9 percent versus 16 percent) and at about the same rate of Hispanic men cohabiting with a woman (10 percent). Overall, according to the

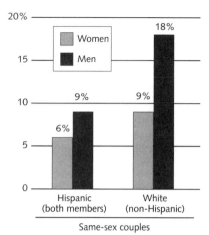

**Figure 13.37: Percentage of individuals in Hispanic same-sex couple households who report military service.**

2000 Census, approximately 1 percent of women and 25 percent of men nationwide are veterans.[111]

Of women in Hispanic same-sex couples, 6 percent report military service, a higher rate than married Hispanic women. Figure 13.37, however, shows that they serve at a lower rate than white non-Hispanic women in same-sex couples (9 percent). Hispanic men in same-sex couples are also less likely to report military service than white non-Hispanic men in same-sex couples (9 percent versus 18 percent).

*Policy Implications: "Don't Ask, Don't Tell"*

Since Hispanic women in same-sex couples serve in the military at disproportionately higher rates than most other women, discriminatory military policies also affect the Hispanic community at a disproportionate rate. For example, "Don't Ask, Don't Tell"—a policy that bans openly lesbian, gay, and bisexual people from serving—has been used to discharge Hispanic women from the military at a higher rate than other groups. In fact, Hispanic women are discharged under "Don't Ask, Don't Tell" at two times the rate that they serve in the military. Although Hispanic women make up just 0.31 percent of service personnel, they comprise 0.60 percent of those discharged under the policy.[112]

Lesbian, gay, and bisexual military personnel and veterans suffer from discriminatory military policies, especially when military discharges lead to loss of employment, pay, and benefits. During the first ten years of "Don't Ask, Don't Tell," more than ten thousand service members have been discharged, at an estimated cost of $1.2 billion in taxpayer dollars.[113] Even when lesbian, gay, and bisexual members of the military are able to hide their sexual orientation and avoid discharge, discriminatory military policy still prevents their same-sex partners from obtaining a myriad of veterans' benefits because they are not legally married. Discrimination against these veterans continues throughout their lives.

A growing majority of Americans supports allowing gays and lesbians to serve openly in the armed forces. According to a poll conducted in July 2005 by the Pew Forum on Religion and Public Life and the Pew Research Center, 58 percent of

Americans support lifting the ban—an increase from 52 percent in 1994. The poll also found that those who strongly oppose gays and lesbians serving openly fell from 26 percent in 1994 to just 15 percent in 2005.[114] Support for lifting the ban is even high regardless of religious affiliation. The poll found that along with a solid majority of secular Americans (72 percent), 72 percent of white Catholics and 63 percent of white mainline Protestants believe that gays and lesbians should be allowed to serve openly in the military.[115]

In the face of documented widespread anti-LGBT harassment and violence, as well as the challenges presented by the "Don't Ask, Don't Tell" policy, data from the 2000 Census indicate that Hispanic same-sex partners, particularly women, have chosen to serve their country in the military at high rates. Revoking "Don't Ask, Don't Tell" would allow them and their families to enjoy the benefits they deserve as service members and veterans. They would no longer have to serve in fear of being exposed and losing their careers and incomes.

## CONCLUSION

As of January 2006, eighteen states have passed constitutional amendments banning same-sex marriage. At least four more states, including California and Florida, which are among the states with the highest populations of Hispanic same-sex couple households, are expected to vote on similar amendments before the end of 2006. During a local television news broadcast in Austin, Texas, a lobbyist named David Contreras claimed to be an advocate of the state's anti–same-sex ballot measure on behalf of Hispanics, stating, "It's very important to us as Hispanics, Latinos, when issues pertain to the family, we are for traditional family values."[116] Contreras' statement ignores the existence of Hispanic lesbian, gay, or bisexual people who are harmed by the amendment, and it implies that "family values" somehow exclude the protection of thousands of families headed by same-sex couples and their children who live in communities throughout Texas. This is just one example of why it is important to document the demographics of Hispanic same-sex couple families.

Data from the 2000 Census refute common stereotypes of lesbian and gay people as predominantly white, wealthy, childless, and unable to maintain stable long-term relationships.[117] In fact, there are over one hundred thousand Hispanic same-sex couple households in the United States, and one of the most important findings of this study is that nearly half of them are raising children, which has many implications for the debate over the legal recognition of same-sex couple families.

Data from the 2000 Census show that Hispanic same-sex couple households are in many respects similar to other Hispanic households. For example, they are raising adopted or foster children at similar rates. The adults work in the public sector at similar rates and report similar rates of living in the same home for the previous five years, which is an indicator of relationship and family stability. Hispanic same-sex couples live in areas where most Hispanic couples live, and they are part of their respective communities, sending their children to local schools and dealing with the same issues other Hispanic couples face.

This report also documents that Hispanic same-sex couple households are disadvantaged compared to white non-Hispanic same-sex couple households in terms of education, income, home ownership, and disability. Men and women in Hispanic same-sex couples are also significantly more likely than men and women in white non-Hispanic same-sex couples to not be U.S. citizens. As a result of these differences, Hispanic same-sex couples are disproportionately affected by anti-LGBT laws and policies, including those that prevent them from obtaining the benefits and protections of marriage. Allowing all same-sex couples to legally formalize their relationships and commitments to care for each other and their children will allow them greater economic security, legal protection, and peace of mind. This is especially important as people grow older or face such crises as a partner's illness or death.

For many reasons, including higher rates of parenting, lower relative income, lower home ownership rates, and greater prevalence of having partners who are not United States citizens, Hispanic same-sex households are disproportionately impacted by anti–LGBT family legislation and will be further harmed if proposed anti–same-sex marriage state and federal constitutional amendments become law.

## NOTES

1. National Hispanic Leadership Agenda, "National Hispanic Leadership Agenda Opposition to a Constitutional Amendment," *NHLA*, http://www.aclu.org/getequal/ffm/section2/2d2nhla.pdf (accessed 5 October 2006).

2. Marisa Demeo, "MALDEF Condemns Proposal to Amend the Constitution to Discriminate Against Gay Men and Lesbians," *MALDEF*, May 12, 2004, http://www.maldef.org/news/press.cfm?ID=220 (accessed August 17, 2005).

3. Phil LaPadula, "Martinez Likens Gay Marriage Advocates to Castro," *Express Gay News*, July 23, 2004, http://www.expressgaynews.com/advertising/etearsheets/pdf/07-23-2004/007.pdf (accessed August 17, 2005). Coincidentally, during the same week, two of Martinez's top campaign advisors, including one who liaised with conservative Christian groups, were exposed as being gay. Mubarak Dahir, "Anti-Gay Martinez Has Two Gay Advisors," *Express Gay News*, http://www.expressgaynews.com/advertising/etearsheets/pdf/07-23-2004/001.pdf (accessed August 17, 2005).

4. For example, in a 1992 video called *Gay Rights, Special Rights*, the Traditional Values Coalition claimed that granting rights to homosexuals diminishes the rights of people of color. See Jean Hardisty, *Mobilizing Resentment: Conservative Resurgence from the John Birch Society to the Promise Keepers* (Boston: Beacon Press, 1999).

5. LLEGÓ, "The Federal Marriage Amendment: Why Latinos and Hispanics Do Not Support FMA H.J. Res 56–S.J. Res 30," http://www.llego.org/PDF/Why%20Latinos%20do%20not%20support%20the%20FMA%20FINAL.pdf (accessed 22 February 2005).

6. LLEGÓ, "National Hispanic Leadership Agenda Opposition to a Constitutional Amendment to Define Marriage," March 5, 2004, http://www.llego.org/PDF/NHLAfinal statement%20Letterhead.pdf (accessed February 22, 2005).

7. Sergio Bendixen, "Latino Poll Findings on Gay Issues in 2004 Elections," Bendixen and Associates, memo to Human Rights Campaign, September 22, 2004, http://www.hrc.org/pollingmemo (accessed August 17, 2005).

8. See the section on religion and political participation below.

9. For more information, see U.S. Census Bureau, "Technical Note on Same-sex Unmarried Partner Data from the 1990 and 200 Censuses," U.S. Census Bureau, Population Division, Fertility & Family Statistics Branch, July 31, 2002, http://www.census.gov/population/www/cen2000/samesex.html (accessed August 26, 2005). See also Tavia Simmons and Martin O'Connell, "Married-Couple and Unmarried-Partner Households:

2000," Census 2000 Special Reports, February 2003, http://www.census.gov/prod/2003pubs/censr-5.pdf.

10. Dan Black, Gary J. Gates, Seth G. Sanders, and Lowell Taylor, "Demographics of the Gay and Lesbian Population in the United States: Evidence from Available Systematic Data Sources," *Demography*37, no. 2 (2000): 139–54.

11. Transgender people are those whose identity or behavior falls outside stereotypical gender expectations. Transsexuals, crossdressers, and other gender nonconforming people are included in this "umbrella" category. For more on definitions of transgender people, see Lisa Mottet and John M. Ohle. "Transitioning Our Shelters: A Guide to Making Homeless Shelters Safe for Transgender People," 2003,National Gay and Lesbian Task Force Policy Institute, http://www.thetaskforce.org/downloads/TransHomeless.pdf (accessed October 12, 2006).

12. M. V. Lee Badgett and Marc A. Rogers. *Left Out of the Count: Missing Same-Sex Couples in Census 2000*(Amherst, MA: Institute for Gay and Lesbian Strategic Studies, 2003).

13. Gary J. Gates and Jason Ost, *The Gay and Lesbian Atlas*(Washington, DC : Urban Institute Press, 2004).

14. Robert Bernstein, "Hispanic Population Passes 40 Million," U.S. Census Bureau press release, June 9, 2005, http://www.census.gov/PressRelease/www/releases/archives/population/005164.html (accessed 5 October 2006).

15. Roberto R. Ramirez and G. Patricia de la Cruz, "Hispanic Population in the United States," June 2003, http://www.newsdesk.umd.edu/pdf/HispanicCensus2002.pdf (accessed October 5, 2006). These numbers add up to more than 100 percent due to rounding.

16. Robert Bernstein, "Hispanic Population Passes 40 Million," (see note 14)U.S. Census Bureau press release, June 9, 2005, http://www.census.gov/PressRelease/www/releases/archives/population/005164.html (accessed 5 October 2006).

17. U.S. Census Bureau, "U.S. Interim Projections by Age, Sex, Race, and Hispanic Origin," March 18, 2004, http://www.census.gov/ipc/www/usinterimproj/natprojtab01a.pdf (accessed August 29, 2005).

18. Roberto R. Ramirez and G. Patricia de la Cruz, "Hispanic Population in the United States," June 2003, http://www.newsdesk.umd.edu/pdf/HispanicCensus2002.pdf (accessed October 5, 2006)(see note 15).

19. National Annenberg Election Survey, "Bush 2004 Gains among Hispanics Strongest with Men, and In South and Northeast, Annenberg Data Show," December 21, 2004, http://www.annenbergpublicpolicycenter.org/naes/2004_03_hispanic data-12_21_pr.pdf (accessed August 17, 2005).

20.This estimate is based on analysis of the Census Bureau's Current Population Survey (CPS) from March 2004. See Jeffrey S. Passel, "The Size and Characteristics of the Unauthorized Migrant Population in the U.S.," PewHispanic Center, March 21, 2005, http://pewhispanic.org/files/reports/61.pdf (accessed August 29, 2005).

21. Ramirez and Cruz, "Hispanic Population in the United States" (see note 15). Ramirez and Cruz, "Hispanic Population."

22. Ibid.

23. Carmen DeNavas-Walt, Bernadette D. Proctor, and Robert J. Mills, "Income, Poverty, and Health Insurance Coverage in the United States: 2003," U.S. Census Bureau Current Population Reports, 2003, http://www.census.gov/prod/2004pubs/p60-226.pdf (accessed October 5, 2006).

24. U.S. Census Bureau, "Table 7: Homeownership Rates by Citizenship Status and Race and Ethnicity of Householder: 1994 to 2002 and Ethnicity of Householder: 1994 to 2002," http://www.census.gov/hhes/www/housing/hvs/movingtoamerica2002/tab7.html (accessed September 8, 2005).

25. Shawna Orzechowski and Peter Sepielli, "Net Worth and Asset Ownership of Households: 1998 and 2000," U.S. Census Bureau Current Population Reports, May 2003, http://www.census.gov/prod/2003pubs/p70-88.pdf (accessed October 5, 2006).

26. Ibid.

27. Roberto Suro, Richard Fry, and Jeffrey Passel, "Hispanics and the 2004 Election: Population, Electorate and Voters," Pew Hispanic Center, June 27, 2005, http://pewhispanic.org/reports/report.php?ReportID=48 (accessed 5 October 2006).

28. Ibid. The National Exit Poll (NEP) showed that President George W. Bush received 44 percent of the Hispanic vote. A number of researchers and polling experts, however, believe that this percentage is too high, based in part on overrepresentation of Cuban respondents in Miami-Dade County, who are historically the most pro-Republican segment of the Hispanic electorate. Subsequent analysis of NEP data based on aggregating exit polls in fifty states and the District of Columbia revealed that Bush's actual share of the Hispanic vote was 40 percent. See also David L. Leal, Matt A. Barreto, Jongho Lee, and Rodolfo O. de la Garza, "The Latino Vote in the 2004 Election," *PS: Political Science & Politics*38, no. 1 (January 2005), http://www.apsanet.org/imgtest/CJ312-Leal%5B41-49%5D.pdf, 41–49 (accessed October 5, 2006).

29. Linda Lyons, "Where do Hispanic-Americans Stand on Religion, Politics? Nearly Two-Thirds Identify as Catholic," Gallup Organization, July 19, 2005, http://www.gallup.com/poll/content/default.aspx?ci=17404 (accessed August 26, 2005).

30. Espinosa, Elizondo, and Miranda, "Latino Churches in American Public Life: Summary of Findings," Institute for Latino Studies, University of Notre Dame, March 2003, http://www.nd.edu/~latino/research/pubs/HispChurchesEnglishWEB.pdf (accessed August 17, 2005).

31. D. K. Carlson, "Americans Weigh In on Evolution vs. Creationism in Schools: Responses Vary by Religiosity, Education, Ideology," Gallup Organization, May 24, 2005, http://www.gallup.com/poll/content/?ci=16462&pg=1 (accessed August 26, 2005).

32. Pew Hispanic Center/Kaiser Family Foundation, "2002 National Survey of Latinos: Summary of Findings,"December 2002, http://pewhispanic.org/files/reports/15.pdf (accessed August 17, 2005).

33. Pew Hispanic Center/Kaiser Family Foundation, "2004 National Survey of Latinos: Politics and Civic Participation," July 2004, http://pewhispanic.org/files/reports/33.pdf (accessed August 29, 2005).

34. L. Saad, "Gay Rights Attitudes: Broad Support for Equal Rights, But Not for Gay Marriage," Gallup Poll News Service, May 20, 2005, http://www.gallup.com/poll/content/print.aspx?ci=16402 (accessed August 29, 2005).

35. Pew Hispanic Center/Kaiser Family Foundation, "2004 National Survey of Latinos," July 2004(see note 33).See also M. Barreto R. O. de la Garza, J. Lee, J. Ryu, and H. P. Pachon, "Latino Voter Mobilization in 2000: A Glimpse into Latino Policy and Voting Preferences," Tomás Rivera Policy Institute, http://www.hrc.org/pollingmemo (accessed August 17, 2005).

36. *Religion and Ethics Newsweekly*, "Poll: America's Evangelicals More and More Mainstream But Insecure: Diversity, Differences Mark Their Views on Society, Culture, and Politics," April 2004, http://www.pbs.org/wnet/religionandethics/week733/release.html (accessed August 17, 2005).

37. Republican National Committee, "RNC Chairman Ken Mehlman Takes 'Conversations with the Community'to Catholic and Hispanic Leaders in Miami," April 19, 2005, http://www.gop.com/News/Read.aspx?ID=5366 (accessed August 29, 2005).

38. See Joan Vennochi, "Can GOP 'Unplay'the Race Card?" *The Boston Globe*, July 19, 2005, http://www.boston.com/news/globe/editorial_opinion/oped/articles/2005/07/19/can_gop_unplay_the_race_card (accessed August 26, 2005). See also C. J. Karamargin,

"Bush Owes 'Gracias'to Latino Voters," *Arizona Daily Star*, November 8, 2004 http://www.dailystar.com/dailystar/relatedarticles/47072.php (accessed August 29, 2005).

39. Lopez & Cheung, Inc., analysis of 2000 Census Summary File 4 (SF4) data. The universe of Hispanic same-sex couple households in SF4 data is more limited than the universe of Hispanic same-sex couple households in the PUMS 5 percent sample because SF4 data are based solely on the race or ethnicity of the householder. This criterion excludes households in which the householder is non-Hispanic but the partner is Hispanic.

40. Ibid.

41. Rafael M. Diaz and George Ayala, "Social Discrimination and Health: The Case of Latino Gay Men and HIV Risk,"National Gay and Lesbian Task Force Policy Institute, http://www.thetaskforce.org/downloads/DiazEng.pdf (accessed August 17, 2005).

42. Ibid.

43. See note 39.

44. See Terence Dougherty. "Economic Benefits of Marriage Under Federal and Connecticut Law,"National Gay and Lesbian Task Force Policy Institute, March 23, 2005, http://www.thetaskforce.org/downloads/CTMarriageStudy.pdf (accessed August 30, 2005).

45. See Laura Dean, et al., "Lesbian, Gay, Bisexual, and Transgender Health: Findings and Concerns,"*Journal of the Gay and Lesbian Medical Association*4, no. 3 (2000), 102–51, http://www.glma.org:16080/pub/jglma/vol4/3/j43text.pdf (accessed August 30, 2005).

46. As well as opposite-sex couples who have a common-law marriage; see Sean Cahill, Mitra Ellen, and Sarah Tobias, "Family Policy: Issues Affecting Gay, Lesbian, Bisexual and Transgender Families," National Gay and Lesbian Task Force Policy Institute, January 22, 2003, http://www.thetaskforce.org/downloads/familypolicy/familypolicy-fullversion.pdf (accessed October 12, 2006).

47. For more information about the particular experience of lesbian, gay, bisexual, and transgender elders, see Sean Cahill, Ken South, and Jane Spade, "Outing Age: Public Policy Issues Affecting Gay, Lesbian, Bisexual and Transgender Elders," 2000, National Gay and Lesbian Task Force Policy Institute, http://www.thetaskforce.org/downloads/outingage.pdf (accessed August 17, 2005).

48. U.S. Census Bureau, "Why Ask Race and Hispanic Origin Questions?" http://ask.census.gov/cgi-bin/askcensus.cfg/php/enduser/std_adp.php?p_sid=LXjqs Lyh&p_lva=315&p_faqid=307&p_created=1078244592&p_sp=cF9zcmNoPTEmcF9ncm-lkc29ydD0mcF9yb3dfY250PTQ5JnBfc2VhcmNoX3RleHQ9cmFjZSBjYXRlZ29yeSZwX3 BhZ2U9MQ**&p_li= (accessed August 17, 2005).

49. Ian Haney Lopez, "The Birth of a 'Latino'Race," *Los Angeles Times*, December 29, 2004.

50.The countries included in the South American region are: Argentina, Bolivia, Chile, Colombia, Ecuador, Paraguay, Peru, Uruguay and Venezuela. The countries included in the Central American region are Costa Rica, Guatemala, Honduras, Nicaragua, Panama, and El Salvador.

51. These states include California, Connecticut, Hawaii, Illinois, Maine, Maryland, Massachusetts, Minnesota, Nevada, New Hampshire, New Jersey, New Mexico, New York, Rhode Island, Vermont, and Wisconsin. California, Hawaii, Illinois, Maine, Minnesota, New Mexico, and Rhode Island also forbid discrimination based on gender identity. National Gay and Lesbian Task Force, "State Nondiscrimination Laws." See also S. Cahill, "The Glass Nearly Half Full: 47 Percent of U.S. Population Lives in Jurisdiction with Sexual Orientation Nondiscrimination Law," January 25, 2005, National Gay and Lesbian Task Force Policy Institute, http://www.thetaskforce.org/downloads/GlassHalfFull.pdf (accessed August 17, 2005). Hawaii's gender identity or expression-inclusive nondiscrimination law covers housing, not workplace discrimination. Hawaii's nondiscrimination law, however, does protect against discrimination based on sexual orientation in employment and housing.

52. Jen Christensen, "Michigan Moves to Revoke Partner Benefits," December 2, 2004, *PlanetOut Network*, http://www.gay.com/news/election/article.html?2004/12/02/2 (accessed August 17, 2005). See also Associated Press, "Michigan Governor Pulls Same-Sex Benefits," *The Bakersfield Californian,*December 1, 2004.

53. 365gay.com, "Fallout Expands over Michigan Gay Marriage Ban, " April 19, 2005, http://www.365gay.com/newscon05/04/041905michBens.htm (accessed September 8, 2005).

54. Educational attainment was averaged for both partners in same-sex couples regardless of their race. 2000 Census data do not indicate which individual in the same-sex interethnic couple is Hispanic and which is not.

55. Income data are collected in exact figures before taxes on the long form of the census. Median household income was calculated using the household income variable provided by the census. A weighted median was computed for each of the households we analyzed using the person weight provided by the census for each householder.

56. The reader is referred to the education section for more detail.

57. This difference is statistically significant at the 0.01 level.

58. This difference is statistically significant at the 0.01 level.

59. Ramirez and de la Cruz, "Hispanic Population."

60. DeNavas-Walt, Proctor, and Mills, "Income, Poverty, and Health Insurance Coverage." (see note 23).

61. Orzechowski and Sepielli, "Net Worth and Asset Ownership." (see note 25).

62. Colorado for Family Values Campaign, "What's Wrong with 'Gay Rights'? You Be the Judge!" 1992, leaflet in favor of Amendment Two, reprinted in Jean Hardisty, "Constructing Homophobia: How the Right Wing Defines Lesbians, Gay Men and Bisexuals as a Threat to Civilization," *The Public Eye*, March 1993. For an analysis of the myth of gay affluence, see M. V. Lee Badgett, *Money, Myths, and Change: The Economic Lives of Lesbians and Gay Men*(Chicago: University of Chicago Press, 2001).

63. Badgett, *Money, Myths, and Change.*

64. See Terence Dougherty, "Economic Benefits of Marriage Under Federal and Oregon Law," National Gay and Lesbian Task Force Policy Institute, 2004, http://www.thetaskforce.org/downloads/OregonTaxStudy.pdf (accessed August 17, 2005)(see note 44).

65. General Accounting Office, "Report to Senate Majority Leader William Frist," GAO-04-353R, January 23, 2004. This figure represents an increase since 1997, when the GAO issued its first report that listed 1,049 federal laws and benefits that only married couples can obtain.

66. Timothy J. Dailey, "Testimony in Support of Wisconsin Constitutional Amendment," Family Research Council, February 16, 2004, http://www.frc.org/get.cfm?i=TS04B01 (accessed September 1, 2005).

67.This was determined by estimating a logistic regression predicting home ownership from age and type of Hispanic couple household with Hispanic cohabiting opposite-sex couple households as the reference category. Indicator variables were created for Hispanic same-sex couple and married opposite-sex couple households. Hispanic male and female same-sex couple and married opposite-sex couple households'*t*-values were greater than 1.96, significant for a two-tailed test at the 0.05 level. The fact that these coefficients are positive and statistically significant means that Hispanic same-sex couple households are statistically more likely than Hispanic cohabiting opposite-sex couple households to report that they own their own homes.

68. This was determined by estimating a logistic regression predicting residence from age and type of Hispanic couple with cohabiting Hispanic couples as the reference category. Indicator variables were created for Hispanic same-sex and married opposite-sex couples. The same independent variables were used as for homeownership. Hispanic same-sexand

married opposite-sex couples'*t*-values were greater than 1.96, significant for a two-tailed test at the 0.05 level. The fact that these coefficients are positive and statistically significant means that individuals in Hispanic same-sex couples are statistically more likely than individuals in Hispanic cohabiting opposite-sex couples to report living in the same residence as five years earlier.

69. The Consolidated Metropolitan Statistical Area (CMSA) for New York, NY, an area defined by the Office of Management and Budget as a federal statistical standard, also includes Long Island and parts of northern New Jersey, northern Connecticut, and northern Pennsylvania. The New York, NY, CMSA does not include Philadelphia.

70. See "Anti-Gay Marriage Measures in the U.S." National Gay and Lesbian Task Force, August 31, 2005, http://www.thetaskforce.org/downloads/marriagemap.pdf (accessed September 1, 2005).

71. Pew Hispanic Center/Kaiser Family Foundation, "2002 National Survey of Latinos." (see note 32).

72. Immigration Equality, "Uniting American Families Act," http://www.lgirtf .org/uploadedfiles/UAFA-fact%20sheet.pdf (accessed August 17, 2005).

73. For more on this issue, see Cahill, Ellen, and Tobias, "Family Policy," 54–57. (see note 46).

74. Paul Olsen, "Leahy Reintroduces Gay Partners Immigration Act," Out in the Mountains, August 12, 2005, http://www.mountainpridemedia.org/oitm/issues/2005/ 08aug2005/news06_leahy.htm (accessed September 8, 2005).

75. Gates and Ost describe a measurement error in 2000 Census data resulting from opposite-sex married couples inadvertently checking the incorrect sex of one of the partners in the household. Although this error is small, it could affect some of the characteristics of same-sex couple households. For example, estimates of parenting could be overstated as a result of this measurement error because opposite-sex couples, in general, are more likely to have children. Gates and Ost suggest that the magnitude of the error is not easy to ascertain, but provide an example of its potential impact on parenting rates. While unadjusted national figures show that 28.2 percent of same-sex couples are raising children, a more accurate estimate that accounts for this measurement error is 27.5 percent, a slight difference of less than 1 percent. The estimates of parenting in this study do not adjust for this form of error and may somewhat overstate this characteristic. See Gates and Ost, *The Gay and Lesbian Atlas*, 13–15 (see note 13).

76. This difference is statistically significant at the 0.01 level.

77. See Sean Cahill, *Same-Sex Marriage in the United States: Focus on the Facts* (New York: Lexington Books, 2004), 31–32.

78. Timothy J. Dailey, "Homosexual Parenting: Placing Children at Risk," *Insight* 238 (October 30, 2001), http://www.frc.org/get.cfm?i=IS01J3 (accessed September 1, 2005).

79. Dailey, "Testimony in Support of Wisconsin Constitutional Amendment." (see note 66).

80. FDCH E-Media, Inc., "Remarks by Mass. Gov. Romney to the Republican National Convention," *Washington Post*, September 1, 2004, http://www.washingtonpost.com/ wp-dyn/articles/A54468-2004Sep1.html (accessed September 22, 2005).

81. Florida, Mississippi, Arkansas, Utah, North Dakota, and Oklahoma. Source: National Gay and Lesbian Task Force, "Anti-Gay Parenting Laws in the US," June 2004, http://www.thetaskforce.org/downloads/adoptionmap.pdf (accessed August 17, 2005).

82. Cahill, Ellen, and Tobias, "Family Policy," 73–77. (see note 46).

83. HB 1119 (2005) would have banned adoption by individuals who are "cohabiting," including same-sex partners. The bill passed in the state House of Representatives 78–13, but died in a state Senate committee.

84. SB 57 (2005) would have amended state adoption law so that "no adult person may adopt a minor if the adult person is a homosexual." The bill died in a state Senate committee.

85. SB 580 (2005) would have mandated that "only a married couple that consists of individuals of the opposite sex are eligible to adopt." SB 585 (2005) would have banned adoption and foster parenting by "homosexuals." Both bills died in a state Senate committee.

86. HB 2401 (2005) would have amended adoption law, mandating preference for placing children in married-couple households over unmarried or same-sex couple households. The bill died in committee.

87. SB 829/HB 543, SB 161/HB 775, and SB 193/ HB 2234 (2005) all would have banned adoption by "homosexuals." SB 1924/ HB 2230 would have banned foster care placement with "homosexuals" or in homes with homosexuals in them. All of these bills died in committee.

88. Am. 60 to SB 6 would havebanned "homosexuals" and "bisexuals" from being foster parents. The bill died in committee.

89. HB 2921 passed in the state House of Representatives 71–24 but died in a state Senate committee.

90. See National Gay and Lesbian Task Force, "Second-parent Adoption in the US," January 2005, http://www.thetaskforce.org/downloads/secondparentadoptionmap.pdf (accessed August 25, 2005)

91. Ibid. See also Cahill, *Same-Sex Marriage*, 45–55. (see note 77).

92. U.S. Department of Health and Human Services, "Fact sheet: How Many Children Are Waiting to Be Adopted?" 1999, http://www.acf.hhs.gov/programs/cb/publications/afcars/rpt0199/ar0199e.htm (accessed Retrieved August 17, 2005).

93. Child Welfare League of America, "Facts and Figures," http://www.cwla.org/programs/fostercare/factsheet.htm (accessed August 17, 2005).

94. National Clearinghouse on Child Abuse and Neglect Information (HHS), "Foster Care National Statistics," 2003, http://nccanch.acf.hhs.gov/pubs/factsheets/foster.cfm (accessed February 16, 2005); T. Lugaila and J. Overturf, "Children and the Households They Live In: 2000," 2004, U.S. Census Bureau, http://www.census.gov/prod/2004pubs/censr-14.pdf (accessed August 17, 2005).

95. R. Eagle, "Separation Experience of Children in Long-Term Care: Theory, Resources, and Implications for Practice," *The American Journal of Orthopsychiatry* 64: 421–34.

96. Ellen C. Perrin and The Committee on Psychosocial Aspects of Child and Family Health, "Technical Report: Co-Parent or Second-Parent Adoption by Same-Sex Parents," *Pediatrics*109, no. 2 (2002): 341–44.

97. E. Ferrero, J. Freker, and T. Foster, "Too High a Price: The Case Against Restricting Gay Parenting," 2002, ACLU Lesbian and Gay Rights Project, http://www.aclu.org/Files/getFile.cfm?id=17244 (accessed August 17, 2005).

98. Charlotte J. Patterson, "Lesbian and Gay Parenting: A Resource for Psychologists," American Psychological Association, 1995, http://www.apa.org/pi/parent.html (accessed August 17, 2005).

99. Ibid. These conclusions are likely to be true of bisexual parents as well. Although there is a lack of research focusing specifically on bisexual parents, clearly there are bisexuals in the same-sex couples included in the samples of many of these studies as well as in many opposite-sex couples. Since many of these studies do not ask people to self-identify by sexual orientation, there are no conclusive findings on bisexual parents.

100. J. Stacey and T. Biblarz, "(How) Does the Sexual Orientation of the Parent Matter?" *American Sociological Review* 66, no. 2 (2001): 159–83.

101. The reader is referred to the sections on income and parenthood for more details.

102. Theodora Ooms, Stacey Bouchet, and Mary Parke, "Beyond Marriage Licenses: Efforts in States to Strengthen Marriage and Two-Parent Families," Center for Law and Social Policy, April 2004, http://www.clasp.org/publications/beyond_marr.pdf (accessed October 12, 2006).

103. Sean Cahill and Kenneth T. Jones, "Leaving Our Children Behind: Welfare Reform and the Gay, Lesbian, Bisexual and Transgender Community," 2001, National Gay and Lesbian Task Force Policy Institute, http://www.thetaskforce.org/downloads/WelfRef.pdf (accessed October 12, 2006). Horn has since distanced himself from some of these proposals.

104. Ooms, Bouchet, and Parke, "Beyond Marriage Licenses,"23–65. (see note 102).

105. Wade F. Horn and Andrew Bush, *Fathers, Marriage, and Welfare Reform* (Washington, DC: Hudson Institute, 1997).

106. Elayl Press, "Faith-based Discrimination: The Case of Alicia Pedriera," *New York Times Sunday Magazine*, April 1, 2001. See also Liptak, "A Right to Bias Is Put to the Test," *New York Times*, October 11, 2002.

107. Dana Milbank, "Charity Cites Bush Help in Fight Against Hiring Gays: Salvation Army Wants Exemption from Laws," *The Washington Post*, July 10, 2001.

108. Jim Towey, "Protecting the Civil Rights and Religious Liberty of Faith-Based Organizations: Why Religious Hiring Rights Must Be Preserved," White House Faith-Based and Community Initiatives, 2003, http://www.whitehouse.gov/government/fbci/booklet.pdf (accessed September 9, 2005).

109. Donna Miles, "DoD Aims to Attract More Hispanics to Its Work Force," *American Forces Press Service*, October 12, 2004, http://www.defenselink.mil/cgi-bin/dlprint .cgi?http://www.defenselink.mil/news/Oct2004/n10122004_2004101208.html (accessed August 17, 2005).

110. Six percent of Hispanic women in same-sex couples report military service compared to just 1 percent of Hispanic married women. This difference is statistically significant at the 0.01 level.

111. The 2000 Census counted approximately 281.4 million Americans; approximately 108. 2 million are women age eighteen and over. See U.S. Census Bureau, "Female Population by Age, Race and Hispanic or Latino Origin for the United States: 2000," October 3, 2001, http://www.census.gov/population/cen2000/phc-t9/tab03.pdf (accessed September 28, 2005). Another 101 million are men age eighteen and over. See U.S. Census Bureau, "Male Population by Age, Race and Hispanic or Latino Origin," October 3, 2001, http://www.census.gov/population/cen2000/phc-t9/tab02.pdf (accessed September 28, 2005). Of the 108.2 million women age eighteen and over, 1.6 million or approximately 1 percent are veterans. Of the 101 million men age eighteen and over, 24.8 million or approximately 25 percent are veterans. See C. Richardson and J. Waldrop, "Veterans: 2000," U.S. Census Bureau, May 2003, http://www.census.gov/prod/2003pubs/c2kbr-22.pdf (accessed September 26, 2005).

112. Service Members Legal Defense Network, "Conduct Unbecoming: The Ninth Annual Report on 'Don't Ask, Don't Tell, Don't Pursue, Don't Harass,'" March 25, 2003, http://www.sldn.org/binary-data/SLDN_ARTICLES/pdf_file/837.pdf (accessed August 17, 2005). Discharge data are for fiscal year 2001. People can be discharged under "Don't Ask, Don't Tell" even if they are not gay or lesbian. This report suggests that women are disproportionately affected by the policybecause men accuse women who refuse unwanted sexual advances of being lesbians, or because the women are successful and some men do not want to serveunder them.

113. Service Members Legal Defense Fund, "Ten years of 'Don't Ask, Don't Tell': A Disservice to the Nation," 2004, http://www.sldn.org/binary-data/SLDN_ARTICLES/ pdf_file/1452.pdf (accessed August 17, 2005).

114. Laurie Goodsten, "Teaching of Creationism is Endorsed in New Survey," *New York Times*, August 31, 2005, http://www.nytimes.com/2005/08/31/national/31religion.html? adxnnl=1&adxnnlx=1125684165-hilRoTGdZY5pclY47/VGFA (accessed September 2, 2005).

115. Associated Press, "Poll: Support for Gay and Lesbian Soldiers Rising," *The Advocate*, September 1, 2005 http://www.advocate.com/news_detail_ektid20257.asp (accessed September 2, 2005). Pew's survey divided white Protestants into two subcategories: "white evangelical" and "white mainline."

116. Hermelinda Vargas, "Campaigns Gear Up in Fight Over Gay Marriage Ban," *News 8 Austin*, August 22, 2005, http://www.news8austin.com/shared/print/default.asp?ArID=143848 (accessed August 26, 2005).

117. For example, see Colorado for Family Values Campaign, "What's Wrong with 'Gay Rights?'" For an analysis of the myth of gay affluence, see Badgett, *Money, Myths, and Change.* (see note 62).This statement ignores the fact that white, wealthy, and privileged people can still experience discrimination based on their real or perceived sexual orientation or gender identity.

# SELECTED RESOURCES

———————— • ————————

## STATE COURTS

*Keddie v. Rutgers, the State University*, 148 N.J. 36 (N.J. 1997)
*Lewis v. Harris* 378 N.J. Super. 168, 875 A.2d 259 (N.J. 2005)
*Hennefeld v. Township of Montclair*, 22 N.J. Tax 166 (N.J. 2005)

## SECONDARY LITERATURE

American Anthropological Association. *Statement on Marriage and the Family from the American Anthropological Association*. Arlington: American Anthropological Association, 2004. http://www.aaanet.org/press/ma_stmt_marriage.htm (accessed June 20, 2006).
American Psychiatric Association. *Support of Legal Recognition of Same-Sex Civil Marriage*. Washington, DC: American Psychiatric Association, 2005. http://www.psych.org/edu/other_res/lib_archives/archives/200502.pdf (accessed June 20, 2006).
American Psychological Association. *Sexual Orientation and Marriage*. Washington, DC: American Psychological Association, 2004. http://www.apa.org/pi/lgbc/policy/marriage.html (accessed June 20, 2006).
Apple, Michael W., and Linda K. Christian-Smith, eds. *The Politics of the Textbook*. New York: Routledge, 1991.
Badgett, M. V. Lee. *Money, Myths, and Change: The Economic Lives of Lesbians and Gay Men, Worlds of Desire*. Chicago: University of Chicago Press, 2001.
Badgett, M. V. Lee, and Marc A. Rogers. *Left Out of the Count: Missing Same-Sex Couples in Census 2000*. Washington, DC: Institute for Gay and Lesbian Strategic Studies, 2003. http://www.iglss.org/media/files/c2k_leftout.pdf (accessed June 25, 2006).

Britton, Bruce K., Arthur Woodward, and Marilyn Binkley, eds. *Learning from Textbooks: Theory and Practice.* Hillsdale, NJ: Lawrence Erlbaum Associates, 1993.

D'Emilio, John. *Lost Prophet: The Life and Times of Bayard Rustin.* Chicago: University of Chicago Press, 2004.

DuBois, W. E. B., and Augustus Granville Dill, eds. *Morals and Manners among Negro Americans. Report of a Social Study made by Atlanta University under the Patronage of the Trustees of the John F. Slater Fund; with the Proceedings of the 18th Annual Conference for the Study of the Negro Problems, held at Atlanta University, on Monday, May 26th, 1913.* Atlanta: The Atlanta University Press, 1914. http://docsouth.unc.edu/church/morals/menu.html (accessed October 24, 2006).

Dubler, Ariela R. *From* McLaughlin v. Florida *to* Lawrence v. Texas*: Sexual Freedom and the Road to Marriage.* New York: Columbia Law School, 2006. http://www.columbia lawreview.org/pdf/Dubler.pdf (accessed June 25, 2006).

Elledge, James. *Gay, Lesbian, Bisexual and Transgender Myths from the Arapaho to the Zuni.* New York: Peter Lang, 2002.

Elliot, David L., and Arthur Woodward, eds. *Textbooks and Schooling in the United States*, pt. 1. Chicago: University of Chicago Press, 1990.

Equality Federation. *Equality Federation.* San Francisco: Equality Federation, 2006. http://www.equalityfederation.org/ (accessed June 21, 2006).

Equality Maryland Foundation, Inc., and National Black Justice Coalition. *Jumping the Broom: A Black Perspective on Same-Gender Marriage.* Silver Spring, MD: Equality Maryland Foundation, Inc.; Washington, DC: National Black Justice Coalition, 2005. http://www.nbjcoalition.org/jump_broom1.pdf (accessed July 20, 2006).

Eskeridge, William N., Jr. "Equality Practice: Liberal Reflections on the Jurisprudence of Civil Unions." *Albany Law Review* 64, no. 3 (2001) :853.

Freedom to Marry. *Freedom to Marry.* New York: Freedom to Marry, 2006. http://www.freedomtomarry.org/about.asp (accessed June 21, 2006).

Genovese, Eugene D. *Roll, Jordan, Roll: The World the Slaves Made.* New York: Pantheon Books, 1974.

Gutman, Herbert George. *The Black Family in Slavery and Freedom, 1750–1925.* New York: Pantheon Books, 1976.

Herman, Andrew. *The World Wide Web and Contemporary Cultural Theory: Magic, Metaphor, Power.* Oxford: Routledge, 2000.

Hick, Steven, and John G. McNutt, eds. *Advocacy, Activism, and the Internet: Community Organization and Social Policy.* Chicago: Lyceum Books, 2002.

Hollingdale, Linda. *Creating Civil Union: Opening Hearts and Minds.* Hinesburg, VT: Common Humanity Press, 2002.

Holmes, David, ed. *Virtual Politics: Identity and Community in Cyberspace*, Politics and Culture. Thousand Oaks, CA: Sage Publications Limited, 1998.

Kindregan, Charles P., Jr. *Same-Sex Marriage: The Cultural Wars and the Lessons of Legal History.* Boston: Suffolk University Law School, 2004. http://lsr.nellco.org/suffolk/fp/papers/25 (accessed June 25, 2006).

King, Martin Luther, Jr. *Why We Can't Wait.* New York: Harper and Row, 1964.

Lang, Sabine. *Men as Women, Women as Men: Changing Gender in Native American Cultures.* Translated by J. L. Vantine. Austin: University of Texas Press, 1998.

Marriage Equality USA. *Marriage Equality USA.* Oakland, CA: Marriage Equality USA, 2006. http://www.marriageequality.org/main_home.php (accessed 5 October 2006).

National Gay and Lesbian Task Force. *Policy Institute of the National Gay and Lesbian Task Force.* Washington, DC: National Gay and Lesbian Task Force, 2006. http://www.thetaskforce.org/ourprojects/pi/index.cfm (accessed June 25, 2006).

National Organization for Women. *Equal Marriage NOW*. Washington, DC: National Organization for Women, 2006. http://www.now.org/issues/marriage/index.html (accessed June 21, 2006).

Nietz, John Alfred. *The Evolution of American Secondary School Textbooks: Rhetoric & Literature, Algebra, Geometry, Natural History (Zoology), Botany, Natural Philosophy (Physics), Chemistry, Latin and Greek, French, German & World History as Taught in American Latin Grammar School Academies and Early High Schools before 1900*. Rutland, VT: C. E. Tuttle, 1966.

Patterson, Orlando. *Slavery and Social Death: A Comparative Study*. Cambridge: Harvard University Press, 1982.

Roscoe, Will. *The Zuni Man-Woman*. Albuquerque: University of New Mexico Press, 1991.

Ross, Josephine. "The Sexualization of Difference: A Comparison of Mixed-Race and Same-Gender Marriage." Harvard Civil Rights-Civil Liberties Law Review 37 (February 2004): 255–88. http://www.law.harvard.edu/students/orgs/crcl/vol37_2/ross.pdf (accessed June 25, 2006).

Suro, Roberto, Richard Fry, and Jeffrey Passel. *Hispanics and the 2004 Election: Population, Electorate, and Voters*. Washington, DC: Pew Hispanic Center, 2005. http://pew hispanic.org/reports/report.php?ReportID=48 (accessed June 25, 2006).

White, Deborah G. *Ar'n't I a Woman?: Female Slaves in the Plantation South*. New York: W. W. Norton, 1985.

Williams, Walter. *The Spirit and the Flesh: Sexual Diversity in American Indian Culture*. Boston: Beacon Press, 1986.

Wolfson, Evan E. *Why Marriage Matters: America, Equality, and Gay People's Right to Marry*. New York: Simon and Schuster, 2004.

## ORGANIZATIONS

Vermont Freedom to Marry Action Committee, Inc.
P. O. Box 1038
Middlebury, VT 05753
(802) 388-6356
info@vtmarriageaction.org
URL: http://www.vtmarriageaction.org/

Vermont Freedom to Marry Task Force
P.O. Box 481
South Hero, VT 05486
(802) 388-2633
info@vtfreetomarry.org
URL: http://www.vtfreetomarry.org/index.php

# CUMULATIVE INDEX

—————————— • ——————————

**Boldface** numbers refer to volume numbers.

**1**. "Separate but Equal" No More
**2**. Our Family Values
**3**. The Freedom-to-Marry Movement

# ABOUT THE EDITORS
# AND THE CONTRIBUTORS

——————————— • ———————————

**Martin Dupuis** is the assistant dean of the Burnett Honors College and associate professor of political science at the University of Central Florida. He earned a JD from American University and a PhD from the University of Southern California. His research on same-sex marriage and gay and lesbian politics has been published in a number of books and journals.

**William A. Thompson** is a librarian with the rank of assistant professor at Western Illinois University. He has been, is now, and ever shall be, an activist for gay and lesbian concerns.

**Samiya Bashir** is communications director for Freedom to Marry. She has worked in communications and editorial consulting with a wide variety of community, health care, cultural, and academic clients. She served as an editor for a number of publications, including *Ms. Magazine*, *Black Issues Book Review*, and *Curve*, and her articles, stories, and poetry have appeared in books, magazines, and journals internationally. Her most recent book, *Where the Apple Falls*, a collection of poetry, was recently published by RedBone Press.

**Randolph W. Baxter** received his PhD in history in 1999 from the University of California, Irvine, after having received a master's degree in international affairs from Columbia University in 1990 and a bachelor's degree in European history from the University of California, Berkeley, in 1986. He has published numerous articles and won the 2004 James L. Sellers Memorial Award from the Nebraska State Historical Society for "'Homo-Hunting' in the Early Cold War: Senator Kenneth Wherry and the Homophobic Side of McCarthyism," *Nebraska History* 84

(Fall 2003): 118–32. Since 2001, he has lectured in history and American studies at the California State University, Fullerton.

**Elizabeth Bergman** is currently adjunct professor of political science at California State Polytechnic University, Pomona. Dr. Bergman also serves on the advisory board of the Pollworker Institute (PI), a nonprofit organization in Washington, D.C., focused on issues related to election administration in the United States. Bergman has been active in local and statewide politics for more than ten years, serving on campaigns and as a lobbyist in Sacramento. In 1992, Bergman cofounded a Los Angeles political nonprofit 501(c)(3) dedicated to supporting women running in local elections. Her research interests include political behavior, elections, and legislative processes; her work has appeared in *Legislative Studies Quarterly*, among other publications.

**Paul R. Brewer** is associate professor of journalism and mass communication at the University of Wisconsin, Milwaukee. His research on public opinion and political communication has appeared in such journals as the *American Journal of Political Science*, the *Journal of Broadcasting & Electronic Media*, the *Journal of Politics*, *Political Communication*, and *Public Opinion Quarterly*. The National Science Foundation and the Russell Sage Foundation have funded his research.

**Anthony M. Brown** graduated from Brooklyn Law School, where he served as research assistant to Nan Hunter, the founder of the Gay and Lesbian Project at the ACLU. While in Brooklyn, he worked as a law guardian at the Children's Law Center, representing the legal needs of children in Brooklyn Family Court. Anthony also served as a legal intern in the summer of 2002 at Lambda Legal, the nation's foremost LGBT litigation organization. While at Lambda, he assisted in the briefing for what has become one of the most important civil rights cases of our time. In the landmark case of *Lawrence v. Texas*, Anthony's research was quoted specifically in Justice Sandra Day O'Connor's concurring opinion. Anthony currently heads the Nontraditional Family and Estates Law Division of McKenna, Siracusano & Chianese. Anthony also sits on the board of directors of The Wedding Party, a nonprofit educational organization committed to the power of marriage awareness. He is admitted in both New York and New Jersey and belongs to the American Bar Association, the New York State Bar Association, the New York County Lawyers' Association, and LeGaL, the Lesbian and Gay Law Association of Greater New York.

**Jason Cianciotto** is the research director of the National Gay and Lesbian Task Force Policy Institute, a think tank that conducts research, policy analysis, and strategy development to advance greater understanding and equality for lesbian, gay, bisexual, and transgendered people. Jason earned a BA in political science and an MA in public administration from the University of Arizona.

**Seth Goldman** is a PhD student in the Annenberg School for Communication at the University of Pennsylvania. He received his BA in political communication from the George Washington University, where he was an Enosinian Scholar and George Gamow Undergraduate Research Fellow. He has conducted research on coverage of antigay hate crimes and gay marriage in news media and the effects of such coverage on public opinion. During the 2004 presidential election campaign, he was a research coordinator at Annenberg Political Fact Check (factcheck.org); after the election, he was a news researcher at *Congressional Quarterly*.

**Charles W. Gossett** is a professor of political science and chair of the Department of Political Science at California State Polytechnic University, Pomona. He conducts research in the areas of LGBT politics at the local and state levels and on civil service reform.

**Susan M. Murray** graduated from Smith College and New York University School of Law. She is a partner with the Vermont law firm of Langrock, Sperry & Wool, LLP. She has been involved in a number of leading cases concerning gay and lesbian family issues, including the first gay second-parent adoption case in Vermont and the Vermont same-sex marriage case, *Baker v. State*. She is a founder of the Vermont Freedom to Marry Task Force, a nonprofit organization that works to educate Vermonters about the importance of allowing gay and lesbian couples to marry.

**Markie Oliver**, MA, OEF, is an instructor in religious studies at Ball State University in Muncie, Indiana. She holds master's degrees in religious education and in historical studies from Ashland Theological Seminary and is actively engaged in LGBT advocacy.

**Laura E. Pople**, PhD, is a social psychologist by training and an editor by vocation. Laura jumped into LGBTI activism fifteen years ago and has assumed many leadership roles with statewide organizations. She also serves as editor-in-chief of Jersey Pride's critically acclaimed pride magazine, *The Jersey Gaze*.

**Lisa Powell** is the cofounder and executive director of United Lesbians of African Heritage. She is a 1984 graduate of the UCLA School of Law. She has a long history of activism in the Los Angeles LGBT community, where she cofounded SISTAHfest and West Hollywood's Lesbian Visibility Week.

**Beth Robinson** graduated from Dartmouth College and the University of Chicago Law School. She is a partner with the Vermont law firm of Langrock, Sperry & Wool, LLP. In 1995, along with her law partner, Susan Murray, she cofounded the Vermont Freedom to Marry Task Force. In 1997 the two joined with Mary Bonauto of Gay & Lesbian Advocates & Defenders in representing the plaintiffs in Vermont's first same-sex marriage case, *Baker v. State*. Following the Vermont Supreme Court's mixed decision in *Baker*, Robinson and Murray led the lobbying effort in the Vermont legislature in support of legal marriage equality for gay and lesbian couples. They then founded a political action committee to support legislators who had voted in favor of the compromise civil union law that resulted from that process.

**H. Alexander Robinson** is the executive director of the National Black Justice Coalition, an organization whose primary mission is to work for equality on behalf of LGBT African Americans. He is the former president of the National Task Force on AIDS and a former member of the Presidential AIDS Advisory Council.

**Eric Rofes** passed away in June 2006 as the result of a heart attack at the age of fifty-one. He was associate professor of education at Humboldt State University in Arcata, California. A graduate of Harvard College, he earned his MA and PhD in social and cultural studies from the University of California, Berkeley. He was a long-time activist for gay and lesbian issues and HIV/AIDS concerns, and he was the author of twelve books.

**Renée Rotkopf** is an award-winning advertising creative who is presently an associate creative director at OgilvyInteractive, a global advertising agency. Born and raised in Brooklyn, New York, Renée graduated with a BFA from Brooklyn College in 1988. That same year she also married her college sweetheart. At the age of twenty-eight she divorced him, leaving her nine-year relationship after falling in love with a woman. Seeing life from both sides of the marriage fence, Renée knows first hand the imbalance and inequality that same-sex couples face. Fueled by a desire to help transform people's lives, she drew upon her skills as a creative and strategic thinker and formed The Wedding Party, an organization dedicated to celebrating commitment in the LGBT community and generating awareness of the need for same-sex marriage rights. Her goal is for everyone to have the freedom to marry legally, strengthening our families and empowering ourselves.

**Michael R. Stevenson**, PhD, is assistant to the president for institutional diversity and associate provost of Miami University in Oxford, Ohio. He served as science advisor to Senator Paul Simon in 1995 and 1996, and as president of the Society for the Psychological Study of Lesbian, Gay, and Bisexual Issues, a division of the American Psychological Association, in 2005. His fourth book, *Everyday Activism: A Handbook for Lesbian, Gay, and Bisexual People and Their Allies*, was published in 2003.

**Andy Thayer** is national action coordinator of DontAmend.com, an all-volunteer organization. He also served in that role for the successful StopDrLaura campaign against Dr. Laura Schlessinger. A cofounder of the Gay Liberation Network in Chicago, a multi-issue LGBT organization, he has been very active in that city's movement against the war in Iraq and against police brutality.

**Robin Tyler** is the executive director of the Equality Campaign for DontAmend.com and cofounder of StopDrLaura.com. The first "out" lesbian or gay comic in the United States and Canada, she initiated the calls for the 1979 and 2000 LGBT marches on Washington and produced the main stages for the 1979, 1987, and 1993 marches. In February 2004, Tyler and her partner, Diane Olson, were the first same-sex couple in California to sue for equal marriage rights in *Tyler et al. v. the County of Los Angeles*.

**Mark Vezzola** graduated from the University of Massachusetts, Amherst with a BA in history and a minor in anthropology. He later earned his law degree and MA in

American Indian studies from UCLA in 2006 as part of a joint degree program. As a law student, he assisted in editing the third edition of Felix Cohen's *Handbook of Federal Indian Law*; clerked for the Hopi Appellate Court in Keams Canyon, Arizona; and interned at the Department of Justice for the Office of Tribal Justice, the liaison between the department and federally recognized tribes. Most recently, Mark was appointed adjunct professor of American Indian studies at Palomar College in San Marcos, California, where he teaches federal Indian law and government. He has written on treaties between tribes and the federal government and the constitutional rights of incarcerated Native Americans to practice their religion.

**Evan Wolfson** is executive director of Freedom to Marry, the gay and nongay partnership working to win marriage equality nationwide. Before founding Freedom to Marry, Evan served as the marriage project director for the *Lambda Legal Defense and Education Fund*, was co-counsel in the historic Hawaii marriage case, and participated in numerous gay rights and HIV/AIDS cases. His first book, *Why Marriage Matters: America, Equality, and Gay People's Right to Marry*, was published by Simon & Schuster in July 2004 and was reissued in paperback with a new foreword in June 2005